Criminology and Moral Philosophy

The book examines some of the most important forms of normativity and the relation between facts and values in the context of criminological investigation. In recent decades numerous criminologists have argued that criminology needs to be more explicitly concerned with normative considerations and with morality and this book explains the plausibility of that view and of empirically rigorous non-positivist study of moral values. Hume is often regarded as a key figure in separating facts from values and he was a formidable opponent of moral rationalism. Yet, in his own moral philosophy he sought to explicate the genuineness and authority of moral considerations without endorsing some implausible positivist interpretations of a putative fact/value distinction. The significance of Hume's view and its implications for the empirical study of morality are explored.

The book discusses several layers of normativity explored by criminological investigation including:

- The relation between law and morality
- the concept of the Rule of Law
- the normativity of the notion of criminality
- the justification of sanction
- the presence and significance of moral considerations

This book will be of interest to students taking upper-level courses on criminal justice ethics, punishment, political theory, jurisprudence, and social philosophy.

Jonathan Jacobs is Professor of Philosophy and Director of the Institute of Criminal Justice Ethics at John Jay College, CUNY, USA.

Criminology and Moral Philosophy

Empirical Methods and the Study of Values

Jonathan Jacobs

Routledge
Taylor & Francis Group
LONDON AND NEW YORK

Cover image: © Shutterstock

First published 2022
by Routledge
4 Park Square, Milton Park, Abingdon, Oxon OX14 4RN

and by Routledge
605 Third Avenue, New York, NY 10158

Routledge is an imprint of the Taylor & Francis Group, an informa business

British Library Cataloguing-in-Publication Data
A catalogue record for this book is available from the British Library

Library of Congress Cataloging-in-Publication Data

Names: Jacobs, Jonathan A., author.
Title: Criminology and moral philosophy: empirical methods and the study of values / Jonathan Jacobs.
Description: New York, NY: Routledge, 2022. | Includes bibliographical references and index.
Identifiers: LCCN 2021041229 | ISBN 9780367479329 (paperback) | ISBN 9780367479312 (hardback) | ISBN 9781003037323 (ebook)
Subjects: LCSH: Criminal justice, Administration of—Moral and ethical aspects.
Classification: LCC HV7419 .J328 2022 | DDC 353.4--dc23
LC record available at https://lccn.loc.gov/2021041229

ISBN: 9780367479312 (hbk)
ISBN: 9780367479329 (pbk)
ISBN: 9781003037323 (ebk)

DOI: 10.4324/9781003037323

Typeset in Adobe Garamond
by Deanta Global Publishing Services, Chennai, India

Contents

Preface

This book addresses some topics that first interested me almost fifty years ago as an undergraduate taking courses on the philosophy of social science and social scientific explanation. I have returned to those interests recently. Much of my work on topics in criminal justice in recent years has concerned the aims and justification of punishment, especially in a liberal democracy. Reading more widely in the criminological literature as well as the philosophical literature on those issues reignited my interest in social scientific explanation, especially in regard to morality and the role of moral considerations in understanding human action. As was the case many years ago, the question of the relation between facts and values continues to strike me as a central, very significant question.

To a large extent this book is a study of whether and how moral considerations are properly involved in criminological investigations. To a large extent the book is a critique of views of value in positivist social science. It develops a view through exploring the ways that norms and values figure in a great many departments of human activity generally and in specific ways in several "layers" of normativity concerning criminal justice.

There is something very tempting about the positivist notion that facts and values are utterly distinct and that while we can study people's beliefs about values and what people say about them, moral values are not part of the factual reality, and moral understanding does not have a role in social scientific explanation. There is something tempting in the view but it is, I believe, mistaken. In the book I explain what is lost by adhering to that part of positivist doctrine and what can be gained by recognizing the empirically accessible ethical significance of facts. Hume has a central role in the account and I argue that while he clearly is a key source of the alleged fact/value distinction, his own approach to moral value showed that his epistemological commitments did not weaken or dilute his own view of the authority or genuineness of moral considerations. Recognizing the naturalistic features of his view and appreciating how they shaped his own very significant contribution to moral theory can help us reconsider his role regarding the status and the study of moral judgments.

The book was written during the (continuing) COVID-19 pandemic but contemporary technology made it possible to continue conversations with others, even at a great distance. In particular, Alison Liebling and Tony Bottoms at Cambridge have continued to be enormously helpful in regard to the issues. Their interest in the philosophical issues has had an important role in broadening and deepening my interest in criminological investigations. Getting to know them and their work in recent years has been enormously beneficial, especially because of how they approach the empirical study of morality. They are of course, not responsible for any errors, confusion, or other defects of the book. (They have read and commented upon some of my work on related topics but they have not seen this book.) I hope I have made good use of how they have helpfully focused my attention, broadened my perspective, and asked very hard questions concerning the interaction of criminology and philosophy. That would be at least a start in repaying their generosity.

I have been working on issues at the intersection of Ethics, Politics, and Criminal Justice in recent years and I have tried to do a good deal of "homework," reading criminological literature as well as philosophical literature. I first became interested in issues concerning the aims and justification of punishment more than twenty years ago and getting to know Antony Duff's work, and getting to know Antony, had a considerable impact on the shape and direction of my interest. His work is discussed at several places in this book and in numerous other works of mine. His views and the care with which he develops and defends them have been important to my education in the issues. His work has been a very instructive example of how to formulate and address the normative aspects of issues of criminal justice. Antony is free of any responsibility for errors or other flaws in this book.

I am very grateful to The American Philosophical Society which awarded me a grant that helped support much of the research that is reflected in this book. The Hayek Fund for Scholars at the Institute for Humane Studies also awarded me a grant that supported my work on this book. I am very grateful to both institutions, and I hope that the book that I have written confirms their judgment in awarding support to me.

Faculty and students at institutions where I have presented my work have made very helpful observations, criticisms, objections, and suggestions. I would like to thank the University of York Faculty of Law and Department of Philosophy and audiences at the University of Edinburgh, the Chinese University of Hong Kong, The Hebrew University of Jerusalem, Denison University, Howard League Conferences, the Political Theory Research Unit at the University of Cardiff, the Law School at the University of Silesia, and the Institute of Criminology at Cambridge.

Christopher Trogan is owed thanks for doing a swift and thorough job preparing the Index.

Finally, Tom Sutton, Publisher, Criminology and Criminal Justice at Routledge, is owed thanks for encouraging me to pursue this project. I had begun working on a different book-length undertaking but Tom's urging and patience led me to make this book my priority and I am very glad that he nudged me in this direction.

Introduction

This book examines some connections between philosophy and criminology, focusing chiefly on the explication of forms of normativity and the relation between facts and values. I argue that positivist commitments regarding facts and values have been an impediment to important aspects of the empirical study of morality and that criminology and moral philosophy can be mutually illuminating in some significant ways. Core commitments of positivism block that illumination and misrepresent the phenomena. This is not a blanket indictment of positivism in the social sciences; it has had a constructive influence in various respects and a significant role in debates about the scientific character of the social sciences. But I believe that positivist claims regarding normativity and the relation between facts and values are mistaken and have been unhelpful. Criminology's credentials as empirical science do not depend on a commitment to positivism, and non-positivist criminologists are explicating relations between facts and normative considerations in illuminating ways. I will argue that there are multiple layers of normativity in the criminal justice context and positivist commitments get in the way of understanding them and the relations between them.

There is a great deal of non-positivist empirical study of criminal justice and there is a rich history of theorizing regarding the social sciences. I do not wish to suggest that criminology has been in the dreadful grip of positivism and that criminologists are only just now seeing some other ways forward. In some respects the debate about positivism in the social sciences might seem like an already well-worked terrain and those who wish to move on in other ways have already found ways forward. Still, there is a point in highlighting certain features of positivism and the implications they have for the understanding of values, norms, and the notion of moral requirements. Positivism remains an important epistemic/methodological position and placing it relative to other positions concerning the way we understand normativity and moral considerations is never an irrelevant task. It is the rare philosophical position that gets conclusively, once-for-all, irretrievably "disproved." In the view of many philosophers it might seem that logical positivism has indeed succumbed to that fate. However, a philosophical view can remain important

DOI: 10.4324/9781003037323-1

on account of how it illuminates significant issues and helps us to formulate what is at stake even if we are not convinced that it is a correct view. There is generally not some fact or discovery that invalidates a philosophical theory in a straightforward way. Usually a more complex moment of insight, reflective criticism, and intellectual imagination—a different way of seeing things, to put it informally—is involved. Maybe positivism (in philosophy and in the social sciences) is no longer in the ascendance but there remains a point in taking it seriously, if not also endorsing it. The criticism of it offered here is an attempt to take positivism seriously especially in regard to criminological investigation.

This is not a work in criminal justice ethics. There are many very good books of the latter type. They generally include coverage of a number of ethical issues arising in the context of criminal justice such as the relation between law and morality, criminalization, the roles of prosecutors, courts, and judges, and practices of law enforcement. Many such works also address issues concerning race and wealth in the administration of justice, the aims and justification of punishment, alternatives to incarceration, the reintegration of former prisoners, and numerous other topics. They examine various positions taken on those issues and the ways that different moral theories might approach them. This book's focus is different. The main concern is with philosophical issues concerning normativity and with the relation between facts and values, how those issues impact criminological studies. I also consider the implications for both disciplines. Books in criminal justice ethics often discuss philosophical conceptions of ethical theory but here the project is to give a philosophical explication of some of the chief aspects of normativity to be found in criminal justice, including moral normativity. That is a basis for suggesting how criminology can contribute to the philosophical understanding of various moral issues through its grasp of normativity. Perhaps the issues examined here and the analysis of them can provide an overall conceptual framework for many of the topics of criminal justice ethics.

While I do not elaborate a metaethical view in detail I do try to show that some familiar positivist commitments in the social sciences lead to or reflect implausible views regarding morality and moral considerations.[1] Hume has a prominent place in the discussion. Though Hume is widely and correctly regarded as a key figure in the history of positivist views I argue that along with what Hume said about the mysterious aspects of deriving prescriptive conclusions from descriptive premises he presented an important conception of morality and the empirical character of the study of it. He certainly did not regard his view about the fact/value relation as a hindrance to the empirical study of morality. Various positivist-inspired views of the fact/value distinction have become distracting preoccupations, and they often involve a misinterpretation of his view.

Right here at the start is not too soon for some qualifying remarks. A history of positivism, even a history of it limited to the twentieth century, would be a very complicated project. For one thing, it would need to include the account of logical positivism as a significant movement in the history of philosophy, and an account of positivism as an epistemological/methodological approach in the social sciences. The logical positivism on which many philosophers focused and the positivism of social scientists are not exactly the same and it is quite conceivable that there has been only modest explicit interaction between philosophers focusing on semantic and epistemological issues on the one hand, and social scientists focused on methodological issues on the other. Even though there is mutual relevance it would be a mistake to regard positivism as just one thing, with exactly the same significance for all who claim to be adherents of it, whether philosophers or social scientists. However, the scientific character of positivist method and results, and the notion that there are no objective values or moral facts for the sciences to study were (and are) shared by positivist philosophers and by many social scientists for whom positivism is the mark of scientific rigor and authenticity. Certainly the view that there is a crucial distinction between facts and values, and that only the former are the proper object of scientific investigation, is shared by positivist philosophers and positivist social scientists even if beyond that general characterization they do not share a great deal in terms of actual details of their views.

Moreover, positivism as a methodological commitment is often combined with theorizing that might seem to involve commitments that exceed what an austere positivism, one committed to logical positivist semantics and (anti-) metaphysics would countenance. A commitment to positivism does not automatically rule morality out of consideration. Durkheim's thought is an example of this. As David Garland remarks of Durkheim, "His sociology is, above all, concerned with those distinctive moral bonds which for him constitute the truly social aspects of human life. His fundamental object of analysis is the relationship between social moralities and their conditions of existence."[2] The commitment to positivism in regard to method and explanation in the social sciences might not (and often does not) include the full range of positivist commitments as they are understood by philosophers. Exploring different social scientific theories with a view to explicating that would be a worthwhile and interesting undertaking. My chief concern here with positivism in the social sciences has to do with the way the relation between facts and values is understood. That does not require that every other aspect of a given social scientific theory is also faithful to positivism.

In addition "the social sciences" refers to many disciplines and within each of those there are significant debates regarding theory and methodology. During the last one hundred and fifty years there have been striking developments regarding the social sciences and those developments include numerous non-positivist insights, claims, and conceptions. The way positivism is treated in the present work has one basic focus and there is a huge amount of intellectual history and a great many epistemological and methodological debates that are not even surveyed here. Despite that, it seems clear that there are important positivist claims regarding the relation between facts and values as understood in several social sciences. The issue of whether there is an empirical though non-positivist way to understand normativity and morality seems to me sufficiently important to warrant its being the chief focus of this work.

The discussion here does not examine in depth the debates regarding the study of morality within particular social sciences. It is not as though criminal justice is studied by just one of the social sciences. Many criminologists have been trained as sociologists but of course many other disciplines are represented in criminology and there are scholars who are at home in more than one discipline and in interdisciplinary investigation. But this is not a history and it is not a survey. The broadly positivist claims that values are not among the factual items in the world, that there are no objective values, and that the study of value judgments is largely a study of attitudes, sensibility, and responses rather than a study of judgments with cognitive content and descriptive meaning have had a powerful influence on and presence in the social sciences.

Of course, it is not as though the basic positivist view of the relation between facts and values is (or was) uniformly accepted across the social sciences. There have been many critiques of it and alternatives to it among the many disputes regarding theory and method in the social sciences. There is a considerable diversity of non-positivist social science and even when positivism was especially prominent other approaches were being endorsed and pursued. Nonetheless, it has had a powerful influence and it has proved to be remarkably resilient. As George Steinmetz notes:

> The continuing hold of the positivist imagination can be felt in an emphasis on general, and usually empirical, laws; in doctrines of falsification of pre-diction; in a spontaneous preference for "parsimonious" explanations…or for mathematical and statistical models; and in adherence to a caricatured view of the natural sciences as a role model.[3]

He added that

> reinvigorated modes of positivism remain powerful in a wide swath of the social sciences. Indeed, positivism seems to be gaining strength in some sites. Political science, sociology, economics, psychology, and psychoanalysis all remain deeply enmeshed in a world that many in anthropology, history, and philosophy would locate firmly in their historical past. This explains how an era in which positivism is widely disparaged and barely recognizable might nonetheless give rise to a renewed *Positivismusstreit*.[4]

There is still plenty of positivist social science being done, and even in philosophy there are able defenders of positivist views of epistemology and philosophy of science. It remains important to respond to its view of the relation between facts and values. However, I am fully aware that I am not proposing a strikingly original claim and that criminologists are increasingly recognizing important relations between criminological inquiry and normative concerns. Numerous criminologists have done important work that reflects and confirms the hypothesis that moral value can be studied as a substantive matter in which people's beliefs and commitments can be rationally assessed. Works by Alison Liebling, Anthony Bottoms, Richard Sparks, Nicola Lacey, Ian Loader, Antony Duff, John Braithwaite, and others are especially effective examples of that recognition. In addition there are many scholars whose work is aimed directly at reform of institutions, policies, and practices, such as the reentry into free society of former prisoners. They are doing vitally important work at the intersection of theory and practice. Their projects often involve treatment of some of the main issues of the present work but their focus is often somewhat different.

Criminological topics are apt as a focus for considering relations between facts and values, and work by the authors mentioned (and others) is responsive to normative and moral matters in explicit and carefully elaborated ways. There is no question whether normative issues have a place in the context of criminal justice; the issue is how to understand that place and what are the implications for policy, practices, and institutions as well as for study of such things. Specific topics such as punishment, desistance, criminalization, the rights of offenders, prison conditions, and so forth are morally significant and so are large-scale, framing issues such as the relation between law and morality, the character of the rule of law, and the relation between criminal justice and other aspects of justice.

Also, many philosophers are showing an increasing interest in empirical disciplines and there is much more willingness to include empirical considerations in the analysis of various philosophical issues. That has almost surely been helped by the diminished influence of positivism in philosophy. Philosophers committed to the positivist project saw no role for philosophy in any contexts of substantive issues. Its work was entirely a matter of conceptual analysis and explication of semantic considerations. But at the same time that anthropologists and criminologists are developing approaches to the study of morality philosophers are looking to empirical investigations to help with the explication and elaboration of issues of moral philosophy. (In philosophy more broadly there is increased interest in empirical investigations.)

While I believe there are distinctively philosophical issues that need to be addressed by distinctively philosophical methods I also believe that several important issues concerning criminal justice and the empirical study of it can be better understood through the interaction of philosophical and empirical approaches.

The discussion focuses on Anglophone countries, chiefly the U.S. and U.K. but not only those two.[5] The Anglophone countries share a great deal of political and jurisprudential culture despite some differences in their approaches to numerous issues of criminal justice. Those countries and those differences supply a rich source of empirical considerations and examples while also sharing numerous important normative commitments and concerns. The shared features enable us to attain a perspective much broader than looking at just one nation while the differences suggest that there is much to work with regarding different approaches to the issues.

The fact that logical positivism is no longer in the ascendance in Anglophone philosophy is relevant, and to a large extent this book is a critique of the ways that positivism has shaped much of the social scientific treatment of normativity and values. Positivism has been subject to extensive critique within philosophy during the last several decades. The critique has come from several directions. I will be focusing on only some of the critical concerns. I am not trying to include a mini-history of twentieth century Anglo-American philosophy though much of what I discuss would be addressed by such a project. I refer to *non*-positivist philosophy rather than *post*-positivist because it would be wrong to suggest that there is no longer any significant positivist philosophy. Positivism has a much diminished presence and authority but it is rare that a philosophical view is entirely "over" and safe to simply ignore. However, non-positivist Anglo-American philosophy shows the influences of many different approaches and traditions, including some from Continental philosophy. Current English-language philosophy is much more open, pluralistic, and alert to diverse approaches than it was seventy-five years ago or even forty years ago.

A doctrine of cognitive meaningfulness, or a fixed, universal, and univocal semantic criterion of what counts as factual discourse no longer figures in the way it did in the first half of the twentieth century. Nor does non-positivist philosophy deny that there is any substantive task for philosophy and assert that its role is entirely within the sphere of conceptual analysis or explication of semantic criteria for meaningful discourse. At present there are probably more connections between philosophy and areas of empirical inquiry than have been for a very long time, and this is true whether we are talking about philosophy of mind, philosophy of biology, philosophy of law, philosophy of language, political philosophy, aesthetics or any of a number of other philosophical fields and sub-fields.

Rigor, precision, clarity, and attention to matters of epistemology and philosophy of language continue to be vitally important. I certainly do not wish to suggest that philosophy has become so open-ended and accommodative that *anything goes*. But non-positivist Anglophone philosophy has been much more willing than positivism to pursue philosophical issues in ways that show philosophy having a richer, more substantive agenda than just auditing the language of science or engaging in conceptual analysis—understood in a very specific way. There are important roles for philosophical insight, observation, theorizing, and articulation, and many philosophical topics and sub-fields have given rise to complex, spirited debates and the development of numerous theories. Plus, just as an observation on the overall debate concerning positivism it is worth noting that the claim that all knowledge is scientific knowledge (often a positivist claim) is not itself a scientific claim.

Many social scientists have held that the social sciences should take care to avoid making normative claims and that social scientific explanations should run along the same general methodological lines as those of the natural sciences. Often this is taken to include a univocal notion of causality and the denial that values or moral facts count among the phenomena that can be regarded as having causal efficacy or explanatory significance. People's beliefs about values, or their commitments to certain values can be included among the phenomena to be explained but that does not involve regarding values as items in the explanatory order. The present discussion is critical of such a view and of the putative fact/value distinction on which it is often alleged to rest. I argue that there are very strong reasons to abandon the distinction as it has often been understood by positivist social scientists.

Numerous criminologists are strongly interested in the normative significance of their work. This involves careful reflection on the widely endorsed notion of "evidence-based practice" but also on a broader spectrum of possibilities concerning the aims criminological investigation might serve. As Sparks and Loader say in their co-authored *Public Criminology?*

> Our substantive aim is to describe and reappraise some of the diverse roles, responsibilities and commitments that criminological practitioners have assumed in recent decades, and the ways in which they have responded to, and sought to shape, the changing ways in which crime is understood and acted upon in the wider world of politics and culture.[6]

They are analyzing ways that criminologists regard the role of their research results with respect to public discussion, policy formulation and implementation, and how criminal justice should be understood. Sparks and Loader identify a number of basic positions regarding that understanding and they say their focus "is on understanding criminological *engagement*."[7] They formulate "five styles of criminological engagement" in order to undertake their explanatory and interpretive project.[8] Whatever one's view of the appropriate form of criminological engagement it is a normative conception and it might also include a view of how values are to figure in criminological explanation. This is not to say that every criminologist should engage in practice or try to shape public policy debates. But there are significant ways that normative conceptions are connected with empirical inquiry and explanation.

One of the main considerations in favor of the view defended is that *normativity is pervasive in human activity* and in contexts of many kinds, and the understanding of normativity provides a strong case against the putative fact/value distinction as understood by positivist social science. Normativity has a crucial role in the understanding of moral considerations but there are very important forms of non-moral normativity as well. A fact/value distinction can obscure them or push us into misrepresentations of them. It is important to recognize that if valuative judgments can be supported and justified by factual considerations, or if factual considerations can have ethical significance then making sound, defensible valuative claims involves cognitive content that is not a feature of merely emotive valuation. The latter does not issue in *claims* or *judgments*; emotive valuations are more like exclamations. They do not assert anything.

I do not want to suggest that normative claims and the explication of normative considerations have so far been absent from the social sciences. Criminology includes many different approaches and there are numerous debates about how to understand norms and values, and also about what the norms and values guiding policy should be. In the Introduction to *A Reader on Punishment* Duff and Garland point out some differences between penological studies and the sociology of punishment. Of the former they say that, "Its primary concern has always been to monitor the practices of penal institutions, tracing and evaluating their effects, and suggesting ways in which institutional objectives might be more efficiently achieved."[9] They remark that though it now has a critical dimension "most penology takes the existing institutions for granted, and situates itself within them, so that more radical questions about alternative ways of responding to crime or administering punishment tend not to be part of its research agenda".[10]

> The sociology of punishment, in contrast, is less closely tied to the existing institutions and more willing to raise basic questions about the ways in which society organizes and deploys its power to punish. Its main concern is not to promote the efficient functioning of penal institutions, but instead to explore the relations between punishment and society, to understand how punishment functions as a social institution, and to trace its broader role in social life...[11]

They observe that, "sociologists also examine the relations between normative theories of punishment and the social, political, and economic contexts in which they emerge"[12] and Duff and Garland point out numerous respects in which various investigations include such considerations.[13]

Nonetheless, there is a widely held view among social scientists that either making valuative claims is not a proper part of their investigative and explanatory project, or if valuative claims are made they are not to be regarded as scientific or as empirically justified. Many social scientists remain committed to positivism. They maintain that there are facts, and there are valuative responses, feelings, and expressions but what is valuative is not explicated or justified in any integral way by the facts. Again, the facts might have a causal role in explaining someone's valuative judgment but they are not justificatory. I am not arguing that moral judgment should be part of all criminological studies. Nor am I arguing that all criminological investigations should be explicitly aware of whatever moral significance its results might have. However, moral considerations can have a place in empirical explanations and excluding them from such explanations can stunt our understanding of the empirical phenomena we investigate. Moral considerations need not be part of every empirical account but neither should they be excluded from every empirical account as somehow "non-empirical."

One of the "risks" run by positivist commitments in the social sciences is that they deny to the social scientist a factually informed basis for making valuative judgments. Those commitments deny the possibility of a rationally justified project of arriving at valuative claims on the basis of the facts. As Duff and Garland put it, "normative philosophy must take account of penological and sociological studies if it is to ground its arguments successfully and apply them to the actual world."[14] In many cases numerous bodies of factual information are relevant to understanding the normative features of an institution, policy, or practice. The effort to make sound, supportable valuative judgments can only be helped by an enlarged understanding of social, political, and economic considerations, as well as by facts about the values and attitudes of parties involved in the contexts studied. However, values cannot be easily "read off" the facts. There is every reason to believe that stubbornly persistent moral and political debates will always be with us and that disputes about the valuative significance of specific factual considerations will be a crucial part of such debates. But an *a priori* declaration that the facts cannot inform values is neither philosophically well-grounded nor helpful.

It seems that there is a steadily growing interest in the social scientific study of morality and the sorts of theorizing and conceptual elucidation required of social scientists. In "New directions in the anthropology of morality" Cassaniti and Hickman write, "[t]he increased use of morality in anthropological scholarship demands greater attention to how the concept is being wielded in our discipline and calls for us to develop bodies of research that investigate morality in relation to other domains of lived experience."[15] Moreover, there is increasing recognition that fluency with moral concepts can make a constructive contribution to empirical investigations. In *Moral Laboratories* Mattingly writes, "A virtue ethics portrait of the moral as related to practices of cultivating virtue also resonates with anthropological studies of how the moral is *learned* and negotiated in important domains such as the family."[16] Through understanding persons' conceptions of what is worthwhile, important, significant—their conceptions of the good—we can acquire a much more complete and textured understanding of their motives, perspectives, concerns, emotions, and behavior. That involves a grasp of how values figure in people's lives, and in ways that simply cannot be captured and expressed by the positivist conception of values. Mattingly quotes Laidlaw, who wrote, "The claim on which the anthropology of ethics rests is not an evaluative claim that people are good: it is a descriptive claim that they are evaluative."[17] Though the focus here is on issues of criminal justice and on criminology some of the main claims about the relations between facts and values apply in much the same way to other social sciences and other topics.

It is almost always the case that research and scholarship in numerous disciplines can be broadly characterized as reflecting the prevalence of specific research programs and their methodological and explanatory perspectives. Yet, what is taken for granted at one time might seem very nearly exotic or at least implausible to researchers of a different era. For present purposes it is enough to note that social scientific explanation can be a very complicated project involving several issues at different levels and from diverse angles of approach. For present purposes we need not pursue the issue of what is involved in theory-change or whether theory-change is a rational process, and in what respects. I acknowledge fully that the question of how best to understand the valuative significance of the phenomena studied is also a challenging and complex undertaking. It is not part of the present view that if we get ourselves free of the fact/value distinction the moral significance of the facts will suddenly be disclosed. But the complexity and difficulty of the task that remains does not condemn us to some form of relativism or some other result that puts enlarged and deepened understanding out of reach. We can see the task more clearly and we can see that *there is a task* when we recognize that moral judgment is not factually untethered and semantically and epistemically unguided by the phenomena being studied.

I have noted that among anthropologists and criminologists at present there is increasing interest in the study of morality in ways that are not circumscribed by positivist strictures. The views developed here are congenial to that interest. They are responsive to the willingness to articulate conceptions of moral value and moral considerations as though understanding them actually can help us understand actions, practices, and institutions and what we ought to do. In this book I do not defend a particular approach to moral theorizing and make a case for understanding moral concepts and moral judgment in highly specific ways with the exception of a brief discussion in Appendix I. I certainly have commitments of those kinds and to some extent have developed and defended them in other works of mine.[18] But my concern here is to show that the case for excluding normativity, and moral normativity, in particular, from the explanatory project of criminology is actually quite weak.

Chapter 1 discusses the pervasiveness of norms and the significance of the grasp of norms to the intelligibility of human action. Part of the importance of understanding the pervasiveness of norms is that it helps us also understand the roles of moral considerations in people's behavior and in the explanation of that behavior. However, normativity extends much more widely than just the moral context. The chapter is not focused primarily on the fact/value issue; it is focused on normativity in a broader sense, one that provides a larger framework in which the fact/value issue is situated. Even if the claim of the pervasiveness of normativity is true there remains a genuine question about whether criminologists should regard the illumination and explanation of moral matters as an appropriate part of the social scientific enterprise. The discussion of norms and rule-governed behavior in the first chapter is background needed for the arguments and analysis concerning moral considerations in later chapters. Norms are both more ubiquitous and much less mysterious—as objects of empirical investigation—than is sometimes supposed. Chapter 1 explains how and why they are found throughout human activity and are not intractably problematic for empirical study. An examination of the roles of rules and norms in human behavior generally can help with the explication of several fundamental issues concerning criminal justice. These include the rule of law, the relation between morality and law, and the normative significance of actions and practices in the context of criminal justice.

Chapter 2 focuses on the notion of the rule of law, especially in regard to liberal democracies such as the U.S. and U.K. and other Anglophone countries. With the background supplied by Chapter 1 we will be in a position to interpret more adequately debates about the rule of law and the normativity involved. The notion of the rule of law involves important issues concerning authority and legitimacy and it is a way to connect the very general notion of norms with the notion of values, something that is especially important with regard to liberal democracies. Even if the liberal democratic rule of law is not (or not any longer, anyway) regarded as a way for the state to enforce or impose a specific moral view there are crucial respects in which the rule of law needs to be morally intelligible. Fuller's "internal morality" of the law is an important contribution with regard to that issue. Also, Hart's views (as well as others') have figured prominently in the debates about the rule of law. The notion of the rule of law is quite complex, even if there is stable agreement on the basic institutions of a political order, and significant debates concerning it continue. We will be concerned mainly with how it is understood in the Anglophone political/legal tradition.

The moral intelligibility of the rule of law involves numerous aspects that are responsive to the fact that it is the rule of law for voluntary, rational agents. Even if that leaves wide open the question of whether this or that specific moral view should be reflected in the rule of law it commits the rule of law to several significant features. That the context is one of voluntary, rational agents implies numerous, significant normative constraints in its own right.

Chapter 3 discusses some of the most relevant elements of Hume's philosophy. That might seem an abrupt transition. However, Hume's thought has had a considerable influence on the social sciences and the view of the relation between facts and values. In addition there are important differences between the way many positivists understand his significance and the way others understand it. If the interpretation of Hume's view regarding facts and values presented in this book is plausible then what many social scientists regard as Hume's significance to empirical social science and especially to the study of moral values and moral judgment needs to be reconsidered. The differences between the interpretations provide a helpful center of gravity for much of the discussion.

Hume is, by any plausible measure, one of the heroic figures of modern empiricism and he is also widely regarded as a source of the putative fact/value distinction. I will argue that the positivist lens through which Hume is often viewed actually distorts his view regarding facts and values in some respects, and that his skepticism regarding moral rationalism is not also skepticism regarding morality. Not only did Hume explain how moral considerations can be genuine and authoritative in the ways first-order moral experience takes them to be, he presented a basis for the empirical study of moral values, judgment, and experience. He was indeed, a critic of moral rationalism and intuitionism but he was not a skeptic regarding morality. It is not as though Hume's view completely undermines the character and significance of norms as discussed in Chapter 1 and Chapter 2. There are ways in which Hume exposed difficulties concerning normativity but the difficulties are mainly difficulties for rationalist interpretations of norms, not for the presence of normativity in how we think and judge things.

My aim is not to directly defend Hume's account of moral value. But once some of the less plausible aspects of the positivist view are set aside the way is open for his and other accounts of moral considerations and moral judgment to be examined in relation to empirical investigations. In fact, critique of the fact/value distinction shows how and why a reading of Hume that emphasizes the naturalism of his view of moral value is actually a more plausible interpretation. For present purposes we can characterize naturalism as the view that—regarding *what there is*—there are only the objects, properties and processes in the natural world and the world of artifacts created out of it, and—regarding *knowledge*—the world is explicable in broadly empirical, *a posteriori* terms. Knowledge is attained through the study of that world on the basis of methods that rely on empirical investigation and not *a priori* conceptual analysis or theory-construction. While we will not pursue a study of naturalism in depth we will note that there are numerous conceptions of naturalism. It is helpful to reconsider the way Hume has been interpreted so that we can see how his philosophy contains resources for what we might call "skeptical naturalism." This is especially important to the discussion of the relations between facts and values.

Chapter 4 presents a critical treatment of relativism. I distinguish some different forms of relativism and argue that in general relativism is both untenable and unhelpful; it does not make any illuminating contribution to explanation. At the same time, it is understandable that many social scientists should find relativism congenial. It can appear to non-judgmentally accommodate the diversity of societies' values and perspectives, and there clearly is a considerable diversity of views across time and across space, and even within the history of a single culture. However, I suspect that sometimes inquirers mistake the fact of diversity for the truth of relativism. The former might not even be a source of evidence for relativism; what is crucial is what *explains* the diversity of beliefs, conceptions, commitments, and so forth. Empirical, social scientific investigation of morality need not succumb to relativism nor imply it. That is important in regard to the significance of comparative studies. In addition, value-pluralism does not provide a source of evidence for relativism. The chapter will discuss why not.

By *diversity* I mean the fact of difference; different ethnicity, different religions, political and cultural perspectives, and so forth. By *pluralism of value* I mean the view that (i) there are multiple sources or grounds of value. For example, one might argue that virtue, rights, autonomy, welfare, and liberty are distinct sources of value. Another sense of "pluralism" is the view that (ii) individuals and groups have different and incommensurable conceptions of a good life, of worth and significance, and meaning. In a diverse society there may be considerable pluralism, but maybe not. Those two senses of pluralism are not mutually exclusive. Pluralism regarding value might maintain that there are multiple sources or grounds of value and they are not commensurable or reducible. With respect to that sense of pluralism, valuative judgments often need to integrate or grasp relations between different values without some single, overarching principle or criterion shaping all such judgments. With respect to the second sense there can be complex social and political challenges given the different commitments people have. In a pluralistic society—one in which there are different conceptions of a good or meaningful or well-led life, it is likely that there is a good deal of diversity. Also, a society might be diverse in some respects but there could be a largely shared view of fundamental values, and in that respect the society might not be especially pluralistic.

Chapter 5 considers the ways that empirical criminology on the one hand and philosophy on the other can be mutually informing, focusing on some illustrations from recent criminology. For example, studies undertaken by Alison Liebling on the "moral performance" of prisons and by Anthony Bottoms on desistance bring explicit, systematic attention to bear on the morally significant aspects of criminal justice that they explore. Their work, as well as work by others, is discussed as providing especially helpful illustrations of empirical but non-positivist investigations taking up the challenge of explicating moral features of what they find.

There is increasing recognition of the integral role of normative and evaluative considerations in criminological investigations and many of those investigations are relevant to important issues of moral psychology, normative ethics, and understanding the role of values in human action. That is true of the works that are discussed. Moreover, some of the work of contemporary criminologists fits without forcing into the tradition of the British Moralists.

That is a tradition in which both sensibility and sociability have especially prominent roles in moral life and moral explanation, and we can see that being reconstructed in the work of some criminologists. I do not want to press the affinity too hard but much of the work from the past (works by Hutcheson, Hume, Smith, for example) and much of the recent work can be seen as centrally involving the empirical elaboration of important moral phenomena with an emphasis on sensibility and sociability. It is interesting to see affinities between the sort of approach to understanding morality pursued by some contemporary criminologists and the work of early modern British moralists even though it does not seem that there is any direct influence or intentional borrowing.

Chapter 6 recapitulates some of the main themes of the book through a survey of the several layers of normativity that have been distinguished. It is not an attempt to articulate a highly specific architectonic of the normative issues in criminal justice. Instead, it identifies some of the chief normative issues and indicates ways they are related to each other. This chapter explicates some of the most challenging issues of criminal justice in terms of disputes over the adequacy (in terms of effectiveness and in moral terms) of a broadly liberal-democratic political order such we find in the Anglophone nations (though there are non-trivial differences between them). One of the main issues that occur across multiple layers of normativity is the question of how and where to ascribe *responsibility* for key features of criminal justice. Responsibility for offending is not the only responsibility that matters. There is responsibility for criminalizing various behaviors, responsibility for policy, responsibility for law enforcement and prosecution, for engaging with reintegrating former prisoners, and so forth. There are difficult issues concerning the ways responsibility is constrained by various circumstances and concerning the remedies for serious defects in criminal justice. The issues require us to look at the several layers of normativity and the ways they are related to each other. The chapter is a way of highlighting how fully empirical and normative study is needed, and also how *study that is empirical and normative* is needed. The chapter concludes with a discussion of restorative justice, an approach that has been implemented to varying degrees in Anglophone countries, and whose proponents believe can help with remedying defects of criminal justice aggravated by the prevailing political order and the ways its values resonate through the various layers of normativity.

The **Conclusion** brings the discussion full circle, recapitulating the gains that can be made by moving on from positivist doctrine concerning the relation between facts and values, and commenting on the ways both philosophy and criminology can gain from increased mutual attention. The issues are especially important to the political and intellectual culture of a liberal democracy. That form of political order should be responsive to explanations and understandings that have been arrived at through careful, empirical, critical, investigation. It is a form of political order in which it is crucial that citizens have an understanding of the authority by which law is made and enforced and an understanding of the rights and the rules integral to criminal justice. That is to say, it is crucial that citizens should understand and endorse the chief forms of normative governance of the legal institutions and procedures of their society.

It is possible to have vast factual knowledge and be morally vicious and depraved. Moral knowledge cannot be *read off* of the facts, but there can be an understanding of the moral significance of facts. It is not a grasp of something detached from and independent of the facts nor is it a matter of certain moral conclusions being inferred from the facts. It is appreciation of how they matter.

Moreover, it is a mistake to imagine that moral theory is brought to the facts about criminal justice, as though it is a format or a pattern that can be "applied" to various criminal justice contexts. Moral thought does have distinctive characteristics and moral judgment is not *nothing but* something else, for example, whatever norms and ideals happen to be predominant in a society at a given time. Instead, moral thought should be regarded as articulating the moral significance of criminal justice phenomena. It is possible to study those phenomena without attending to their moral significance, and for many purposes that is a perfectly appropriate thing to do. But that does not mean that their moral significance is present only in a discretionary way, as though we can decide whether and how they matter morally. The moral reality of criminal justice (however we interpret the metaethics of that reality) is present—as is the moral reality of other contexts—on account of what the facts, acts, institutions, and practices are. It is not something that we "construct" and then laminate onto value-neutral facts. We figure out what morally matters and in what way, in living in a world of facts and engaging that world and responding to it affectively and cognitively. In important respects moral thought needs to be guided by the facts and it is not an exercise that can be conducted separately from the facts we want to understand.

Criminological investigations can help us clarify, connect, and "test" philosophical conceptions of action, responsibility, legitimacy, desert, trust, dignity, and other matters crucially important to society and politics. Criminological issues raise important questions concerning important matters of moral psychology and the ways members of a society regard themselves and others in addition to key issues of moral practice. The study of those issues is an inexhaustible empirical resource for applying, refining, revising, and integrating our understanding of normative considerations. Philosophical conceptions of the relevant issues can be generous in return, helping to clarify, sharpen, and lend conceptual precision and theoretical coherence to social scientific investigations.

A society or a culture will reflect certain perspectives on account of the ways they are transmitted through education, for example, and through intellectual culture whether or not they are addressed explicitly and in detail. It is reasonable to think that several decades of positivist social science have influenced the ways that people in general, not just researchers and scholars regard the relations between facts and values. Versions of relativism seem to have a good deal of currency, especially among the educated. Perhaps this can be explained in part by the influence of certain explanatory perspectives that have had a prominent place in disciplines such as economics or anthropology or sociology, in each of which there have been numerous currents of thought denying that there are objective valuative considerations. Also, there have been several decades of critique (or simple rejection without much argument) of the notion of objective values or of value judgments having rational grounds. There are several avenues of approach through which views critical of objectivity have been more or less "at home" in the social sciences.

The fact that some criminologists have acknowledged how important it is for criminology to develop fluency with ethical matters is very encouraging. In many cases they are working their way toward elaboration of ethical concepts from within empirical studies. I hope to show that a way of understanding Hume on facts and values—a way that seems to have considerable currency in the social sciences—is neither the most satisfactory interpretation of Hume nor a plausible view in its own right. Hume is quite clear about his view of moral value not undermining what we take to be the genuineness and authority of moral considerations. It is important to keep that in mind in interpreting his view. That is one of the bases for claiming that his understanding of the relation between facts and values is actually not the understanding that many have assumed was the "lesson" to take from Hume.

Notes

1 Metaethics concerns the metaphysics, epistemology, and semantics of moral value. It can be distinguished from normative ethics (theories of what is morally right and wrong) and moral psychology (examination of attitudes, motivation, relations between sensibility and cognition, etc.). Metaethics concerns the status of moral value—as objective or not, as requiring a realist or antirealist interpretation, etc.
2 David Garland, *Punishment and Modern Society: A Study in Social Theory*, Chicago: University of Chicago Press, 1990, p. 24.
3 George Steinmetz, "Positivism and Its Others in the Social Sciences," from http://read.dukeupress.edu/book/chapter-pdf/625455/9780822386889-001.pdf, p. 30.
4 Ibid., p. 37.
5 I have in mind the U.S., U.K., Australia, Canada, and New Zealand. They share a great deal at fundamental levels of politics and law but also exhibit differences, especially socially and in regard to policy.
6 Ian Loader and Richard Sparks, *Public Criminology?* Abingdon: Routledge, 2011, p. 27.
7 Ibid., 28. Italics in original.
8 Ibid., p. 28.
9 Antony Duff and David Garland eds., *A Reader on Punishment*, New York: Oxford University Press, 1994, p. 21.
10 Ibid., pp. 21–22.
11 Ibid.

12 Ibid., p. 22.
13 Ibid., p. 23.
14 Ibid.
15 Julia L. Cassaniti and Jacob R. Hickman, "New Directions in the Anthropology of Morality," *Anthropological Theory* 14 (3): 2014, pp. 251–262, p. 252.
16 Cheryl Mattingly, *Moral Laboratories*, Oakland: University of California Press, 2014, p. 39.
17 Ibid., p. 11. Mattingly quoting James Laidlaw, 2014, p. 3.
18 See, for example, *Choosing Character: Responsibility for Virtue and Vice*, Ithaca: Cornell University Press, 2001; and "Metaethics and Teleology," *Review of Metaphysics* 55(1): September, 2001, pp. 41–55; "The Fact/Value Distinction and the Social Sciences," *Social Science and Modern SOCIETY* 50 (5): September/October 2013, pp. 560–570; "Meeting the Challenges to the Universality of Virtue," in *Virtues and Virtue Education in Theory and Practice: Are Virtues Local or Universal?* eds. Catherine A. Darnell and Kristján Kristjánsson, Abingdon: Routledge, 2020, pp. 26–40.

Chapter 1

Rules, Norms, and Values

Issues concerning norms and normativity are pervasive in the contexts of human activity and institutions. Of course this includes criminal justice contexts. In addition, a discussion of normativity generally will be a helpful background for the later discussion of moral considerations. Criminal justice has multiple, significant connections with social, political, and economic considerations and that makes many issues of criminal justice unavoidably normative in morally significant ways. For example, the relation between criminal justice and distributive justice can be recognized as highly important, whatever one's political commitments happen to be. Likewise, there are numerous perspectives on what considerations should be the basis for criminalization and what is the justification of criminal sanction. It is not difficult to see that those issues involve normative considerations including some moral considerations. That is unavoidable in a context in which the state intentionally deprives persons of liberty and imposes burdensome, undesirable conditions on people while at the same time important rights are to be respected.

Once we free ourselves from various positivist commitments—a liberation for which there are very good reasons—we will see that empirical criminology can be illuminating in regard to several morally significant issues of criminal justice. In addition, moral thought can contribute to criminology in constructive ways that are not mere editorializing. I do not just mean that criminologists can have interesting moral views about the issues they study; rather, there are significant ways in which criminology and moral theory can inform each other. There are issues of moral psychology, issues concerning attitudes and sensibility (for example, resentment, gratitude, dignity, anger, forgiveness, and respect) as well as crucial issues concerning agency, practical rationality, motivation, and self-conceptions that can engage with criminal justice issues in helpful ways. And the empirical investigations criminologists undertake merit the attention of moral philosophers on account of how the empirical work can help clarify, refine, and elaborate important moral considerations.

DOI: 10.4324/9781003037323-2

1.1 Some Background to the Issues

In introducing the discussion of normativity it will be helpful to make some remarks about developments in philosophy during the last several decades and how those have shaped some recent and contemporary currents of thought relevant to conceptions of normativity. In the Introduction, we noted that the logical positivism of philosophy is not exactly the same as the positivism of social sciences. However, the latter was heavily influenced by the former and some objections to the former are relevant to the latter. Some of the notable trends in twentieth century philosophy are very much in evidence regarding our topic. Over several decades, philosophical positivism has been subject to robust critique. That does not mean that some other specific view is currently ascendant. There is not just one (or two or three) philosophical approach or doctrine shaping recent and contemporary philosophy. English-language philosophy is much more pluralistic in method and in focus than during the period of logical positivist predominance. It is true that among philosophers it is widely thought that the positivist project that looked so promising in the nineteen thirties and forties is not tenable, and its aspiration cannot be fulfilled. But that does not mean that efforts at revision and repair are hopeless or that the view should not be studied carefully.

For almost any philosophical approach or overall way of seeing the problems of philosophy it is possible for refinement, revision, and response to objections to go on even after many philosophers have abandoned the particular view in question. Philosophy is thinking that is relentless in the sense that distinctively philosophical issues are not resolved by the discovery of a particular empirical fact, and there is nearly always a genuine role for careful reconsideration of presuppositions and implications. (Philosophy is thinking that is relentless but it is often also fashion-driven and that can give misleading impressions of what is tenable and what is not.) But the overall positivist project really has been subject to several formidable objections and some of the philosophical views positivism seemed to discredit have been shown to be quite resilient and not so easily dismissed.

Among the most important objections to positivism were doubts about the analytic/synthetic distinction, a distinction significant for positivist views of both language and epistemology. Also, there were objections connected with important insights regarding the underdetermination of theory by evidence in ways that raised significant challenges for positivism. Even if one was not convinced by Quine's formulation of these objections it was possible to see that they pointed to what could be significant vulnerabilities in positivist doctrine. In addition, notions of metaphysics and modality, including notions of necessity, possibility, contingency, and also regarding causality have all been reconsidered. Philosophers developed conceptions of *a posteriori* necessity and nomological necessity that defied the positivist constraints grounded in analyticity. In the nineteen-seventies Kripke, Putnam, and others elaborated metaphysically realist views and essentialist theses. Forms of realism—metaphysical, essentialist, moral, semantic—were again being regarded as positions to take very seriously in philosophical debates though there is no place in a positivist universe for many such views.[1] There have been several decades of critical response to those developments as well. Philosophy has developed in numerous directions, and via several approaches that had earlier seemed excluded by positivism's claims about what there is to be done among the tasks of philosophy.

Relations between epistemology, metaphysics, and philosophy of language were being explored, sometimes in quite new ways, but sometimes in ways that had roots deep in the history of philosophy, for example, in Aristotle or John Locke. Much that had been philosophically ruled out by positivism for several decades was reappearing, supported by sophisticated critiques of the alleged excluding considerations, as well as strong reinforcing considerations of their own. This was not just a matter of switching back to older philosophical views but a recognition that dismissal of the views had been much too swift and summary, and their insights were deeper and more complex than had been thought, and modern approaches to analysis and language were enabling contemporary philosophers to more fully appreciate the depth and complexity.

Many positivists had regarded the history of philosophy as scholarship, not part of philosophy proper. Philosophy, they held, is a form of analysis, and it has a central concern with the question of cognitive meaningfulness. Basically, they regarded the history of philosophy as a long stream of errors until they arrived, tidied up the language of science, and brought philosophy to an end. The retrieval of the history of philosophy as a serious part of philosophy and not just a source of examples of philosophical blunders has made a great many conceptual resources and insights available, which had been of no interest to the positivist program. There are many insights and arguments that have significance that extends beyond the particular circumstances in which they were first articulated. (The notion that there are necessary *a posteriori* truths and that they have a crucial place in the scientific intelligibility of the world is found in Aristotle.[2] A distinction between real and nominal essences and the ways we run up against limits to our possible knowledge of real essences is in Locke. And so forth.)

At the same time numerous criminologists have been connecting their work with philosophical conceptions and concerns. This is a way to acknowledge the philosophical aspects of the issues they are investigating and I would argue that it is also a way of seeing how those investigations can be instructive with regard to those philosophical aspects. Criminologists such as Anthony Bottoms, Richard Sparks, Alison Liebling, Ian Loader, and others have been making the case for more integrated attention to normative issues and empirical issues. They have been doing this through their own work, arguing for greater integration and also undertaking work that integrates normative and empirical considerations, while being fully alert to a number of difficulties and problems. There are very challenging questions regarding the methods appropriate to studying the moral aspects of criminological issues. These include important, substantive arguments concerning what idiom of moral description and explication is to be employed. After all, people have different guiding moral views and not just different views of the empirical study of morality. Also, there are challenges in regard to the explanation of human action and whether there is a role for agency in that explanatory project. That, of course, is connected with issues concerning voluntariness and responsibility, and those are notoriously difficult, disputed matters in philosophy.

In trying to be faithful to positivism, the explanatory projects of some social scientists have short-circuited what could have been illuminating explanations of morally significant issues. Normativity is undeniably a feature of all sorts of human activity. Rather than look past it or claiming that the notion of a norm is somehow non-empirical (and thus, can be safely ignored) it would be better to try to explicate how and why normativity is pervasive in the human context. Clarity about that will enable us to see more clearly the ways that normativity and values figure in the context of criminal justice.

1.2 The Pervasiveness of Rules and Norms

We made some preliminary comments about the pervasiveness of rules and norms, and we need to follow through with further elaboration of the significance of that pervasiveness. Rule-following is found in a great many contexts, including contexts in which rule-following does not involve persons explicitly thinking about the relevant rules. There are of course many situations in which "following" is something like going step by step according to instructions or directions. Consider, for example, when a person is first learning how to do some specific thing, such as changing the oil in an automobile or preparing and cooking a soufflé. Later on, once the person has acquired the know-how, explicit attention to the guiding considerations and steps is needed much less. But a vast amount of rule-following behavior is not recipe-like rule-following but rather, it includes a disposition of *knowing how to go on* without explicit step-by-step reference to guidance.

The later Wittgenstein presented a view that enables us to see the ways that understanding the meanings of words and using the relevant concepts correctly are connected through the notion of *rule-following*. This is not limited to the notion of rule-following that applies to compliance with instructions or with rules understood as elements of a codified procedure. Rather, he explored the notion of rule-following in a sense that showed that the use of concepts and the exercise of rationality generally are rule-governed in a normative sense.

Wittgenstein's thought figures in many ways in these issues because he is widely seen as *having made normativity respectable again*.[3] Many philosophers have interpreted his later work as showing that the use of concepts and the use of language in general are normative matters. The rule-governed behavior of making judgments and communicating intelligibly is normative in a way that is ineliminable. This normativity is not a question of there being values as some sorts of entities, perhaps apt for a Platonist ontological interpretation. Neither is the rule-governed activity of thought, discourse, and meaning explicable in terms of a psychological mechanism, or some particular fact of the matter in the mind or brain. We will elaborate on this point below.

In addition, the rules governing the use of terms and concepts typically are not fully codifiable. Wittgenstein was articulating an approach to understanding these issues that is a way between both ontological inflation and naturalistic reduction. His thought was a direct and robust challenge to any of several broadly Cartesian dualisms of thought and world, or of mind and nature (whether or not they took the form that Descartes gave that dualism). We are not immaterial substances with some sort of regular causal interaction with the natural world. Yet, neither are we fully assimilated to the natural world, being just especially complex physical entities with only physical properties. Each of those views—the dualistic ones and the reductive ones—had given shape to epistemology and other parts of philosophy for many centuries, each attempted resolution giving rise to familiar, stubborn difficulties. Wittgenstein's thought motivated many philosophers to reconsider the formulation of the issues, and to recognize that the rules and norms through which thought, perceptual judgment, deliberation, and decision are intelligible are not just a subset of the causal laws governing the natural world, nor are they features of a separate substance somehow interacting with the natural world. The greatly enlarged philosophical focus was directed to the normative character of thought generally. (Of course, epistemic justification involves normative considerations but it is not the only normative aspect of thought.) This is not to say that the longstanding problems of mind and body and of the relation between thought and object were either resolved or explained away. But the new direction of philosophical thought offered valuable resources for formulating and addressing philosophical issues in some new ways.

Moreover, if the use of terms and concepts generally is normative, then if there is a special way in which the normativity of moral judgments is worse off than normativity in general, it has to be *shown* and cannot be taken as a datum. There is rule-following involved in judging that, "The horses broke out of their enclosure," in the sense that the coherent use of the concepts (and terms) involved in the judgment is rule-governed. Only certain things count as horses, and only certain events count as "breaking out from" an enclosure. Rule-governance is involved in "It is wrong to harm someone just out of jealousy" and not only because it is a prescriptive claim. It is indeed a moral judgment or it could be said to be a moral rule but the chief point here is that the coherent, correct use of the relevant concepts is rule-governed. Is there some special way that the use of the concepts in that judgment is problematic because *wrong* is (in this case) a moral concept? I do not mean that this point about ethical discourse was made explicitly by Wittgenstein.[4] Nor am I trying to illustrate the claim that the metaethical status of moral properties is unproblematic. It is something more ordinary and familiar. Namely, the point is that for each of the statements above there is a thick, familiar, inescapable context of judgments, perceptions, rule-governance, and shared responses which is their setting in the overall activity of making claims and giving reasons. And it is in those contexts that we find the criteria for the correctness or mistakenness of them.

Moreover, the point about normativity taken from Wittgenstein's thinking has been employed by both realists and antirealists. (Not by all of them of course, but by many.) In Chapter 3 we will discuss the significance of this more fully when we take up some metaethical issues. Normativity was increasingly recognized as a key feature of the intelligibility of thought and meaning rather than as some additional feature of the already understood intelligibility of thought and meaning.

Thus, normativity—if not always *moral* normativity—is found throughout human activity. Normativity is not limited to contexts in which people are thinking about values, permissions, or commands. The notion of appropriate norms or of something being in agreement with the relevant norms has application in a great many contexts. It applies to a great many contexts in which it would be awkward or inappropriate to speak of following directions or instructions. In addition, it is not the case that rules can *always* be fully specified or that a norm can be articulated in exhaustive detail. What—in exhaustive detail—is the rule (or the rules) governing the use of the term "spring" or "bank"? Rule-following does not imply that there are fully specified rules or that going on to use a term in new ways has to meet fixed criteria. Nor is rule-following reducible to behavioral regularity. A regularity might be nothing more than coincidence, a pattern of this-then-that; but rule-following generally involves going on in a specific way because doing so *counts as something specific*, a move in the game, a sentence with a clear meaning, or fulfilling the conditions for being an action of type T in certain circumstances. In rule-following behavior the person non-accidentally proceeds in a certain way through a grasp of what-it-is-to-Ø where Ø is some specific type of action or way of using a term or concept.

A highly general notion of rule-following applies to a remarkably wide range of human activities, from language use to specific practical skills of all sorts, whether wood-working or composing literary works or planning a military operation. (Despite the huge number of ways that a literary work might be composed *not just anything* can count as composing one.) The point is not that each of these is an activity for which there is a codification of rules, but that the coherence and intelligibility of the activities depends on the ways in which they reflect rule-following.

Having acquired some fluency with a given term or concept involves rule-following in the sense that the person has some grasp of how to go on using the term or concept appropriately in new cases. Using a term improperly or in a completely inappropriate context are ways of violating the rules for the use of the term, and we can often detect such mistakes even if we cannot specify in a fully exhaustive way the rules that have been violated. Taking some time to discuss rule-following and norms and the fact that they are found throughout the many contexts of human activity is helpful background for the discussion of the relation between facts and values. Discussing rule-following in the context of human action, and especially in regard to acting in accord with laws, Andrei Marmor writes

> When we follow a rule, however, we regard the rule itself as a reason for doing what it requires. Rules have a normative significance; the existence of the rule is something that figures in our practical reasoning, it is something that counts in favor of doing what the rule requires.[5]

Rule-following has a much wider role, in the ways suggested, but even in those roles in which there does not appear to be normativity involved, rule-following makes the difference between doing something (or using a term or a concept) correctly and doing something incorrectly. Rule-following is closely connected with acting for a reason. When asked why one has so many documents on their desk the reply could be: "I'm organizing the materials for the meeting because it will be a full agenda and being well-organized will help us get through it." That is an unexciting example of acting for a reason but a perfectly serviceable one, and at the same time it is an illustration of rule-following behavior (i.e., putting together a meeting agenda.)

When a child has just been introduced to the term "hibernation" it is important to offer some guidance with regard to the proper use of the term. The cat napping in a warm spot on the sofa is not hibernating. The baby, though she sleeps a great deal, is not hibernating. Bats, skunks, and many bears hibernate but a child could hardly figure that out just by looking at them or knowing what they eat or in what parts of the world they live. With a young child who is just learning the word "hibernation" it is probably not important to distinguish between hibernation and other forms of dormancy but it is easy to imagine a somewhat older child being interested in the difference. There are contexts in which the difference matters and the terms cannot be substituted for each other as though synonymous. (There are contexts in which the differences between grass, a bush, and a tree matter even if, as far as a great deal of scientific explanation is concerned, those distinctions are unimportant. That they are all *plants* is what matters to a biologist.)

In general, learning the meaning of a word is a matter of acquiring an ability to use the word correctly in sentences, situations, and contexts that might differ from that in which the person first became acquainted with the word.

That involves grasping rules for its use though often that is not the same thing as learning a fully specifiable, fixed definition. Giving a definition helps clarify important aspects of the rules governing the correct use of a term but there is more to those rules than just a definition. Otherwise, imaginative new uses would be ruled out, as we say, and extending the use of a term to new contexts might always appear to be erroneous.

When one learns a game, coming to grasp the rules of the game is a matter of grasping relevant norms; they are norms for what counts as *a move in that game*. What counts as a "move" or a "play" and what counts as scoring a point or advancing a piece in the game; those too are matters of grasping norms, and satisfying those norms involves rule-following. In addition, there could also be said to be norms for *excellent* play. That introduces an evaluative aspect. For example, it might be that if a player consistently scores more than one hundred that counts as being very skilled, or one's skill level is high on account of capturing more than six of one's opponent's pieces. A great many activities for which there are criteria of understanding or criteria for levels of performance involve norms. There are also many activities that are governed by rules that do not involve standards of excellence; for example, borrowing books from a library. Still, learning to engage in the activity involves a grasp of the relevant rules and we regard returning books on time as the norm with respect to borrowing library books. We might learn that in this community 97% of borrowers return books on time; that is a norm just in terms of frequency of people following the relevant rule correctly. It would be awkward and somewhat misleading to say that a small percentage of borrowers borrow books badly, but being repeatedly late in returning books is a way of violating the expected norm of conduct.

There is also a use of "norms" that does not apply to rational behavior or the activity of human beings. Various types of geese migrate south for winter. In that context the "norm" is a statistical notion and does not involve any understanding or grasp of meaning on the part of the geese or doing something correctly in contrast to incorrectly. Human beings are capable of acting for reasons, acting on the basis of understanding, *following* norms, instantiating them, and they are capable of activity that has moral significance. Thus, in the context of human activity norms often do have a valuative aspect. We can do things well or badly; we can choose appropriately or inappropriately; and our decisions, actions, and responses can be, in many cases, *morally* right or wrong, or can be morally apt or irrelevant, or well-suited or inappropriate. In those respects—separate from the notion of statistical norms—normativity is found throughout our lives. (I am not suggesting that there is no such thing as animal cognition. Indeed, there seems to be quite a lot of it. But it is not the same as human cognition nor is it just a somewhat less robust version of human cognition. The ways that birds find seeds they have buried as a food supply for winter is an entirely different business from what is involved in humans storing food as a supply for the winter and remembering where they put it. For one thing, humans conceptualize it as food and as being stored. The operations of perception, memory, preparation for a season when food is scarce—and the concept *planning for winter*—are not strongly alike in the two cases.)

Anthony Bottoms, in the course of arguing that, "if they are to be true to their calling, all criminologists have to be interested in morality" quotes anthropologist Meyer Fortes who wrote

> The capacity and the need to have, to make, to follow and to enforce rules are of cardinal importance for human social existence...For without rules there can be neither society nor culture; and what I am arguing is that it was the emergence of the capacity to make, enforce, and, by corollary, to break rules that made human society possible.[6]

Bottoms goes on to remark, "Inevitably, the rules (including the prohibitions) in any given emerging group or society will be based on the developing social norms (or positive morality) of the group in question."[7] In the article quoted, Bottoms focused on compliance and the relevance of normative considerations to compliance, and he distinguished between habitual compliance, prudential compliance, and normative compliance. He noted though, that even "habitual compliance may also contain a valuable latent normative content."[8] Also, "good socialization may have valuable long-term effects in producing normative compliance, even though the norms may not, for much of the time, be consciously articulated by those who have been subject to such socialisation."[9] Bottoms was talking about the integral role of moral norms in the context of criminal justice, and we will have a good deal to say about that in what follows.

In fact, *thinking*, the exercise of rationality, is a pervasively rule-governed activity and not just in the sense of involving valid inference. Thinking involves rule-governedness in the use of concepts, rules governing relations between propositions, and a complex repertoire of other rules. Nonetheless, most of the time we just carry on reasoning, using words meaningfully, and (more or less) understanding things even though we do not have a clear picture of just what it is to "stay on the rails" and to be successfully rule-following in the many ways that are integral to thinking. We might point out certain formal logical fallacies when critiquing or correcting someone's reasoning but becoming rationally mature is not a matter of explicitly being taught a body of rules for thinking. That we can grasp such rules indicates that we have rational capacity and our thinking is already rule-governed. We might be taught a number of formal rules and we might be taught various definitions especially if there are specific contexts in which exact usage is required. That might be the case in various legal documents or contracts or various sorts of agreements.

In the 1920s there were international conventions such as the Washington and London Naval Treaties concerning the number and size of naval vessels various signatories were permitted to build and have in their fleets. There were explicit distinctions between capital ships (and their allowable tonnage), secondary ships (also with a ceiling on tonnage per ship), and fixed ratios of numbers of ships for the signatories. But the rules for the use of a vast number of terms and concepts are not laid down in a way that is fixed and exhaustive. Or the rules for the use of a term might be fully defined in a particular context but the term has multiple uses and many of those are not governed as strictly. A food-item might fulfill the criteria for being X-free (e.g., caffeine-free or sugar-free, or fat-free) according to government standards though there is actually a small amount of the item in the food.

What would show that a person has learned the meaning of a word? Almost certainly the best evidence is that the person can carry on in the use of the word, using it correctly in novel cases. And what would show that the person has a grasp of the relevant *concept*? Much the same thing; i.e., correct use of the word typically indicates a measure of fluency of understanding the concept in question. It is very rare that we actually engage in concept-karaoke, making statements we have memorized by their sound while having no idea what is actually meant by the concepts involved. If the individual can provide a dictionary-like definition, that could be additional evidence but we are each (appropriately) regarded as knowing the meanings of a very large number of words without being able to give more than quite fragmentary definitions of them. (Ask someone at random if they are able to use the word "penguin" coherently, and then ask the person to define "penguin.") Moreover, someone might memorize a dictionary definition but not actually be able to use the term successfully. In general, we are able to use the term and employ the concept in ways that are coherent and appropriate, ways that are rule-following, even though (with the exception of a minority of words) there aren't fixed, fully adequate codifications of the meanings of words or explications of concepts.

Commenting on this Stanley Cavell wrote:

> We learn and teach words in certain contexts, and then we are expected, and expect others, to be able to project them into further contexts. Nothing insures that this projection will take place (in particular, not the grasping of universals nor the grasping of books of rules), just as nothing insures that we will make, and understand, the same projections. That on the whole we do is a matter of our sharing routes of interest and feeling, modes of response, senses of humour and of significance and of fulfilment, of what is outrageous, of what is similar to what else, what a rebuke, what forgiveness, of when an utterance is an assertion, when an appeal, when an explanation—all the whirl of organism

> Wittgenstein calls "forms of life." Human speech and activity, sanity and community, rest upon nothing more, but nothing less, than this. It is a vision as simple as it is difficult, and as difficult as it is (and because it is) terrifying.[10]

For rational creatures the normativity of rule-governedness is an integral feature of thinking, understanding, and knowing what we mean even when we cannot articulate that knowledge in codified form. We are rule-following in all sorts of departments of life, and it is when people are *not* rule-following or when we cannot recognize the rules they are following that discourse and behavior are unintelligible to us, perhaps appearing irrational. Cavell points to the complex fabric of normativity that is assumed in the ordinary business of living, acting, and interacting with others in all sorts of ways. As he says, judgments of similarity, rebuke, forgiveness, explanation, and we can add gratitude, resentment, admiration, considerateness, encouragement, commanding, asking, threatening, compassion, and a host of other aspects of action and experience—those are all elements of a form of life and we could hardly imagine our lives without them though we cannot fully specify the rules for each. They are integral to the practices and attitudes constitutive of the lives we lead. In some sense, they are among what we know best and most intimately though we cannot say exactly what each includes.

Using words correctly generally does not involve thinking about the rules for correct usage but it does involve following rules. How else could correct usage be described? It is not as though there is a particular mental image or occurrence that somehow indicates that usage. A town official might point out to another local administrator, "No, we don't say that the mayor's plan for expanded bicycle-paths downtown is *invalid*; we would say it is unfeasible or not workable or in some way flawed; validity concerns other matters, usually concerned with the steps toward official approval." Then the official might go on to explicate the distinctions in mind. This might lead to the administrator then having a better grasp of the rules for "invalid" in that context though the overall use of the term is still not a matter of having a complete and unrevisable formulation in the mind. (In most cases the rules for correct use are not fully given by the term's definition.) Sometimes "following a rule" is analogous to what is involved in a referee noting that someone deliberately tripped an opposing player in a league-sanctioned football game. That kind of tripping is "against the rules" and there are additional specific rules regarding how a foul of that type is to be addressed. It is a situation that is covered by the rules, we might say. The rules can be "looked up" in an authoritative manual of the rules of the game. But a great deal of rule-following is not quite like that.

It is important to see that the rule-following involved in correct use of language is not simply a matter of habit interpreted in strictly behavioral terms.

In addition, knowing how to carry on correctly in the use of a concept is not a matter of being in a certain specifiable psychological state, as though there is a specific state one is in each time the word "bank" is used (correctly). Again, it certainly is not a matter of picturing something in the mind or considering some mental item. Whatever brain-states might have something to do with the usage of a term those are not what a person refers to in order to check if the term is being used correctly.

In developing this insight John McDowell indicated that no finite psychological state *could* explain what it is to grasp a rule for the use of a concept such that one can go on using it and can understand it when others use it. We manage to "stay on the rails," as it were, in employing words and concepts but that does not mean there is a complete map or plan of the rails or that we somehow stay on the rails by focusing on some state of mind that we use as a guide to thinking. It is a mistake to insist that there is what he calls "the deductive model" of rationality, such that any correct use can be shown to follow with deductive validity from a universal formula functioning as the major premise in an inference. He wrote:

> Now it is only this misconception of the deductive paradigm which leads us to suppose that the operations of any specific conception of rationality in a particular area—any specific conception of what counts as doing the same thing—must be deductively explicable; that is, that there must be a formulable universal principle suited to serve as major premiss in syllogistic explanations.[11]

It is not as though the coherent, meaningful use of words and concepts depends on our ability to map out the rails on which their use runs. And, anyway, those rails would need to be understood; we will have not made any advance in the explanation of rationality but just moved sideways, adding some more territory on which parallel rails would need to run. Acknowledging the sense of vertigo that this may induce, he added,

> The thought is: there is not enough there to constitute the rails on which a genuine series of consistent applications of a concept must run. But in fact it is an illusion to suppose that the first horn of the dilemma yields a way of preserving from risk of vertigo.[12]

When someone understands a word or is able to employ a concept that is not because there is some picture in the mind or other mental item that provides the measure or some sort of codification for whether a word is being used correctly. We do not need to do any self-inspection of our minds to see if we are using a word correctly. (What could we be looking for?) Even when we are remembering something it is not a matter of looking around "internally" until we spot the item for which we are searching. Also, regarding meaning, if we were to check an internal dictionary we would have to know which entries to "look" at and the rules governing the use of all the terms involved.

The relevant rule isn't some locatable "item" in the mind. One can know what "add 2" means, and can do that anytime one is asked or needs to do so. But there isn't some entity, image, or other item in the mind that governs every instance of "add 2." I don't look inside myself and compare my attempt to add 2 to an "add 2" icon, image, or guide (or contrast it with the "add 3" icon) to make sure that when I add 2 doing it matches that mental icon. One might think that because rules have such a central and important place in rationality it must be the case that thinking coherently is largely a matter of following specific rules in some self-aware manner. Yet, as McDowell pointed out:

> Rationality requires consistency; a specific conception of rationality in a particular area imposes a specific form on the abstract requirement of consistency—a specific view of what counts as going on doing the same thing here. The prejudice is the idea that acting in the light of a specific conception of rationality must be explicable in terms of being guided by a formulable universal principle. This prejudice comes under radical attack in Wittgenstein's discussion, in the *Philosophical Investigations*, of the concept of following a rule.[13]

There might be numerous tests for whether a person grasps a concept and the person might grasp some of its uses but not grasp some other uses. Or the person might be competent with the concept's literal usage but not understand metaphors in which it has a place. Even in the case of what looks like an example of a rule with a fully fixed, definite meaning—for example, the case where someone is learning the meaning of "add 2"—we do not consult some item in the mind or some psychological mechanism that provides exhaustive guidance for the use of the term. And, besides, we would have to validate that bit of consultation. (In discussing these matters I do not mean to suggest that there is nothing going on in our minds and our brains when we try to remember something or wonder if this new use of a term is an appropriate use of it. Instead, I mean that we do not look around in our heads, in order to find this or that item—a mental picture, a definition, etc.—as though the items are the carriers of meaning.)

One important upshot of this is that rule-following and norms are hardly to be considered exotica or something that could not be a feature of the empirically ascertainable world. They are not in the room in the same way that tables and chairs are in the room but they inform a great deal of human behavior, and the intelligibility of behavior typically depends on grasping the norms informing it. That is not to say that there is no causal explanation of that behavior. Rather, the point is that understanding *what behavior it is*, the very identifying description of what is being done (or refrained from) is likely to involve recognition of the rules that can specify for us what it is for a bit of behavior to count as Ø-ing, whatever it is that fills-in the blank. Whether that was an excellent example of Ø-ing or whether doing that was an excellent thing to do in the circumstances involve additional considerations. But even the basic business of conceptualizing the behavior in some determinate way involves some grasp of norms. In addition, there are activities that are norm-governed in ways that involve specific methodological considerations. Empirical investigation is one such activity (or group of such activities). Notions such as justification, coherence, explanatory, and other notions indispensable to science are normative notions.

1.3 The Space of Reasons, the Causal Nexus, and Norms

There is a significant distinction that applies to a great deal of rule-following in the context of human activity. Consideration of it here will help with understanding the rule of law and the views elaborated by Fuller and Hart, for example, and several other important normative considerations. This is the distinction between "the space of reasons" and "the causal nexus." It is significant for the way it enables us to explicate the difference between a *rational justification* and a *causal explanation*, and also for the way it helps illuminate internalizing norms and helps explain human actions in terms of norms.

Kant famously highlighted the distinction between the sphere of rationality and understanding on the one hand, and that of a naturalistic causal order on the other. He was emphatic that laws of reason are distinct from laws of nature—causal laws. The latter, he held, are deterministic, a property that does not apply to rational norms. Necessity in that sphere has a different form. In the space of reasons normativity governs. The moral law, as Kant understood it, is perhaps the most familiar example of rationality in contrast to causal relations and the laws governing them. The distinction applies in a highly general way, not only in Kant's philosophy. As John McDowell noted, commenting on the "space of reasons" as formulated by Wilfred Sellars in his "Empiricism and the Philosophy of Mind,"

> Sellars is here endorsing a version of the thought that the concept of knowledge belongs in a context that is, in at least some sense, "normative."[14]
>
> At an important moment in "Empiricism and the Philosophy of Mind,"[1] he writes that "in characterizing an episode or a state as that of *knowing*, we are not giving an empirical description of that episode or state; we are placing it in the logical space of reasons, of justifying and being able to justify what one says".[14]

When we characterize a state as a state of knowledge, when we claim that an *epistemic* fact obtains, we are making a point about justification rather than causality. The notion of the space of reasons is relevant to numerous contexts, all of them contexts in which normativity has a role. McDowell remarks near the beginning of the paper (§5):

> [T]he idea that epistemic facts can be analyzed without remainder—even in principle—into non-epistemic facts, whether phenomenal or behavioral, public or private, with no matter how lavish a sprinkling of subjunctives and hypotheticals, is, I believe, a radical mistake—a mistake of a piece with the so-called "naturalistic fallacy" in ethics.[15]

In the introduction to the second edition of his *Mind and World*, McDowell remarks:

> We might say that to place something in nature on the relevant conception, as contrasted with placing it in the logical space of reasons, is to situate it in the realm of law. But what matters for Sellars's point is not that or any other positive characterization, but the negative claim: whatever the relations are that constitute the logical space of nature, they are *different in kind* from the normative relations that constitute the logical space of reasons.[16]

The issue of how to understand the space of reasons is very important because of how it is related to normativity and meaning. McDowell writes

> Modern science understands its subject matter in a way that threatens, at least, to leave it disenchanted, as Weber put it in an image that has become a common-place. The image marks a contrast between two kinds of intelligibility: the kind that is sought by (as we call it) natural science, and the kind we find in something when we place it in relation to other occupants of "the logical space of reasons," to repeat a suggestive phrase from Wilfred Sellars.[17]

Sellars was not simply renaming the items on which Kant focused in making his distinction between a law of reason and a causal law. That latter distinction is certainly relevant to what Sellars had in mind but Sellars and McDowell are referring to something much broader than the moral law or one or another principle of pure understanding in Kant's philosophy. The breadth of the space of reasons has to do with meaning and intelligibility in general. One need not be committed to Kant's epistemology to recognize the distinction between the space of reasons and the realm of causal law. (To be fair to Kant, he maintained that the space of reasons extends to thought in general, not just moral thought. I focused on the moral law in Kant because of how emphatic he is that it cannot be a causal law.)

Mind and World also includes extensive discussion of the philosophy of Donald Davidson and in a passage especially relevant to the points just made McDowell wrote

> Where I use the Sellarsian image of the space of reasons, Davidson talks of "the constitutive ideal of rationality"; but the idea is clearly the same...So Davidson's mutual interpreters must come to their cognitive task already equipped with a sense of the layout of the space of reasons, a substantive conception of what "the constitutive ideal of rationality" requires.[18]

The spheres they govern are different in a basic sense, the one being an order of normativity and meaning and the other not. There is a causal relation between throwing a piece of chalk with great force against the wall and the chalk breaking. The relation between acceptance of a proposition and the propositions that justify acceptance of it is not causal; it is normative, concerning (better or worse) *grounds for*. Speaking of the space of reasons is not reference to a realm of strange entities. It is discourse concerning the normativity of rationality. That normativity is not limited to epistemic justification. The logical, justificatory, or explanatory relations between propositions, whatever the context, are different from the causal relations between events or between objects. Even if there are causal relations involved in how we come to accept propositions there are normative aspects to the issue of whether accepting them in those ways is justified. It is not as though the justificatory aspect can be eliminated or reductively translated into something non-normative.

In the overall way in which the world "works" there are not normative relations between events, and propositions are not causally related to each other. A vast number of propositions concern causal relations but the events themselves are not logically related. Their *descriptions* might be; if X has a scar, then X was injured or wounded at some time in the past, and the scar is indicative of the injury having healed to some extent. A scar and a birthmark differ in their etiology. Scars appear where wounds have healed (to some extent) and birthmarks do not require having been caused by injury. The meaning of "scar" might imply "healing from having been wounded or injured" but that is a semantic relation. Scars are not caused by semantics. We can speak of logical relations between propositions that are *about* events but the events are not logically related.

Sellars's distinction between the space of reasons and the causal nexus is especially helpful because it is not confined to just one specific epistemological view but is consistent with several epistemological theories. It is important that we cannot somehow reduce either the order of propositions or the order of events to the *other* order, claiming that, ultimately, there is really just one.

Empirical features of an object have a causal role in regard to assertions about that object in the respect that the properties of the object can cause us to have specific perceptions. But the issue of whether that assertion is true or is false is a matter that arises in the space of reasons. Asserting the claim (even if only silently to oneself) "That tomato is red" in a particular context is not fully intelligible as *nothing more than* an effect of a particular cause, viz., having a visual perception of a tomato. There is a causal relation between the tomato and one's faculty of sight (and numerous other capacities and organs), and that results in a person perceiving the tomato as red but the red of the tomato does not (in a straightforward, unqualified sense) cause me to know that it is red; it causes me to *see* it as red, and seeing it as red (given my understanding of the concept *tomato* and the concept *red*, being in normal light, with my eyes open, etc.) is a reason for believing it is red. If I have a correct grasp of the concept *red* and the concept *tomato*, and I am reliable regarding certain norms of belief-acceptance I can claim to be justified in believing the tomato is red. The truth of that belief depends on causal facts and on norms of belief-acceptance. (We can assert that point without also committing to a Cartesian notion of ourselves as epistemic agents with specific epistemic responsibilities such that there is a role for volition in belief-acceptance and we are not to accept any proposition that is less than clear and distinct.)

Making moral judgments is a norm-involving activity in the space of reasons. The explication of the involvement of facts and norms is discussed more fully in Chapters 3 and 4. At the present stage my main concern is to have outlined an account of why normativity is not only not mysterious, it is essential to *thought* and activity generally. In addition, we will see that the normativity of moral considerations is not just a matter of emotive expression. This is not a metaphysical claim about what basic types of entities exist. It is a point concerning the intelligibility of thought. Moral life, the making of moral judgments, and giving moral explanations—all of that occurs in the space of reasons. Or, at least it does so when we give any thought to our moral views and judgments. No matter how important aspects of sensibility are to moral judgment there is a fundamental sense in which morality is possible only for rational beings, for beings that can be responsive to reasons.

That does not commit us to moral rationalism regarding the content of moral judgments or regarding moral motivation. There are roles in the space of reasons for receptivity, sensibility, imagination, desire, and other aspects of our overall nature. If we think about what unites people in a common moral world it is certainly plausible to think that sensibility and the enlargement of concern and responsiveness to the conditions and circumstances of others have an important role. That can be the case even if there is a sense in which moral considerations are rational, involve cognitive aspects, and are not purely expressive. It is not difficult to overstate a dualism of reason and affect, or of cognition and emotion. For various analytical and explanatory purposes such dichotomies can be useful though it is a mistake to think that such dualisms reflect an actual clean-break or fixed line of separation between those aspects of our nature. Though human beings are animals for whom desire, passion, and emotion figure in much of what we do and in what matters to us, we are *rational* animals, and even the exercise of our physical capacities is guided in considerable measure by what we think worth doing and our evaluation of desires, feelings, and sensibility generally.

Consider a person's character and the sorts of dispositions constitutive of character. They include cognitive and agential dispositions and also dispositions of sensibility and receptivity. A person can have various non-deliberative but voluntary habits, for example, tending to roll up one's sleeves when one is sitting down to work at one's desk. Or, the person might hum much of the time when not engaged in conversation. But there are also rational habits, such as always checking to see that the backdoor is locked before going to bed or checking the readings on a medical device a family member needs to be using. Maybe one night the backdoor is supposed to be left unlocked for someone arriving quite late. You might have locked it—out of habit—but it is not a mindless habit. It was acquired and sustained for good reasons.

One of the chief reasons it is important to pay attention to one's own habits and patterns of activity is that they can lead to the formation of dispositions that are then very difficult to change. Dispositions can reflect valuative commitments, perspectives, attitudes, and ways of responding, and those are aspects of one's nature that are not merely episodic or situational. Acquired dispositions substantially shape what one *is like*, in regard to states of character. This includes patterns of emotionality, the sorts of concerns and interests that shape one's motivations, the sorts of justifications and explanations one typically proffers, and the person's self-awareness and self-conception. We sometimes admonish others or are admonished by others—"you don't want to make a habit of that"—and often the main message is that, if you carry on acting that way you may come to think that acting that way is acceptable or may find it second nature to do so, but there are good reasons not to act that way. Perhaps it is unfair or selfish or inconsiderate or otherwise objectionable. If we think of a human being's primary nature as the capacities and abilities that are distinctive and characteristic of human nature, then second nature comprises the specific forms in which one's capacities and abilities have come to be disposed. One's developed states of character are elements of second nature. Adult states of character constitute the individual one has become, and one's own choices, reactions, and passions have a crucial role in *what one is like* as an adult.

As Aristotle noted, one would have to be insensible—quite remarkably and persistently distracted or inattentive—to fail to see that acting a certain way is likely to form a disposition to act that way. Like activities cause like states, and that fact is basic to a great deal that human beings do intentionally, as when they set out to acquire a skill or develop an ability in a specific way or practice with a view to performing better, as in a sport or playing a musical instrument or making pastry or painting. Some people *are* insensible, very inattentive to the development of their own dispositions, in that respect, but that does not diminish their responsibility. It may be that they have been unfortunate in how they were habituated but the misfortune is aggravated by their negligence—it has not been impossible for them to have paid more attention. Even with respect to those who are not self-aware in an alert, searching way it is reasonable to expect them to have some awareness of their motives, attitudes, and evaluations.

On this issue of the dispositions constituting character, i.e., one's second nature—John McDowell writes: "One's formed practical intellect—which is operative in one's character-revealing behavior—just is an aspect of one's nature as it has become."[19] Rationality is not fully assimilable to the causal order of natural phenomena; it is not as though all of one's acquired dispositions can be explicated exhaustively in causal terms. At the same time "[t]he concept of second nature registers that we do not need to conceive practical reason as subject only to formal constraints."[20] Practical rationality involves a great deal more than formal logical validity. McDowell writes:

> What it is for the practical intellect to be as it ought to be, and so equipped to get things right in its proper sphere, is a matter of its having a certain determinate non-formal shape, and a practical intellect's coming to be as it ought to be is the acquisition of a second nature, involving the moulding of motivational and evaluative propensities: a process that takes place in nature.[21]

This is a way of acknowledging an important role for a certain understanding of naturalism in regard to practical rationality. It is not a form of rationality that is wholly separate from empirical aspects of human nature. We acquire our dispositions through experience, the shaping of desires and sensibility, and through acting in all sorts of contexts in the empirical world. There are some formal constraints on the proper exercise of practical reason; rationality unavoidably involves formal considerations of consistency and validity. But the exercise of our capacities for practical rationality takes place in the empirical world and its contents and how its features impact us. If we call this "Aristotelian naturalism" to distinguish it from "mechanistic naturalism" the point is not to reinstate a teleological conception of nature but rather to acknowledge that even rationality is shaped in various respects by the activity and experience of rational agents in the empirical world. It is not a re-enchantment of nature but an acknowledgment that nature and rational agency are not utterly distinct worlds, without any degree of mutual influence.

One reason to mention these issues here is that doing so helps us to see that the ways that values and valuative judgment figure in our lives are not confined to subjective or emotive expression or otherwise set apart from reasoning, reasons, and cognition. Describing abstract, formal features of practical reasoning does not capture and express the multiple aspects of character that are involved in the person's understanding, interests, responses, and in how the person decides and judges. When we characterize the person with practical wisdom we do not just describe what sorts of judgments that person makes; we say what that sort of person *is like*. Deciding and judging, and making valuative judgments (including moral ones) involve more than just emotive or expressive aspects of our nature.

Numerous criminologists have taken on the issue of normativity directly. I comment on some of those criminologists briefly here to illustrate how non-positivist notions, especially concerning norms and values, have been shaping recent important criminological studies. Anthony Bottoms, commenting on the powerful influence that the fact/value distinction as understood by many positivists has had, writes: "That difficulty can be simply stated: it concerns the question of how, if at all, from a positivist perspective one can give any serious weight to moral judgements."[22] Bottoms follows Hart in distinguishing between "positive morality," the actual first-order moral beliefs and commitments of some social group, and "critical morality," the moral principles used in critiquing first-order morality—actions, practices, institutions, and he goes on to say of the work of Sir Leon Radzinowicz, "A clear implication of Radzinowick's analysis is that criminologists interested in morality must—if their work is to be comprehensive—consider questions both of positive and critical morality."[23] Simply because of the role of moral beliefs and judgments in many of the contexts studied by criminologists, the study of them is crucial to understanding many criminal justice issues. Otherwise, numerous factors of considerable importance—whatever one's view of the relation between facts and values—would be left out. The role of moral considerations in issues studied by criminologists raises the question of the *relation between normative theory and explanatory methods and conceptions*. Bottoms and other criminologists (e.g., Richard Sparks, Ian Loader, Nicola Lacey, Alison Liebling) have pursued that question in depth in recent years.

Loader and Sparks note that

> Anthony Bottoms has, in somewhat cognate vein, combined patient, multi-method empirical enquiry into criminal behavior and crime patterns in urban contexts and the operation of criminal justice institutions and preventative programs, with an explanatory ambition that links criminological and social theory...He has also developed in various ways that idea that criminology is a moral enterprise...as well as being able to think in policy terms about the import of his work.[24]

In "The relationship between theory and empirical observations in criminology" Bottoms remarks, "Doing criminology, in short, necessarily entails some engagement with normative issues, and it is for that reason that a brief discussion of normative theory is included later in this chapter."[25] Indeed, later in the paper, following a detailed discussion of several aspects of theorizing and methodology in criminology, he writes

> In short, normative analysis in criminology is emphatically not the unintellectual pursuit that positivism made it out to be. It can involve extremely intricate philosophical analysis, and this analysis can intersect with, and be illuminated by, empirical research at many points. ...Normative analysis has not often been included in previous discussions of the theory/research relationship in criminology; in the future it needs to be more centrally located in such discussions.[26]

A somewhat different approach to the relation between empirical considerations and moral judgment is articulated by Pettit and Braithwaite. They have argued for an important relation between normative conceptions and explanatory accounts. They write: "any normative proposal should be subjected to the test of seeing whether it points us towards a plausible explanatory category."[27] And,

> any explanatory category—or at least any that is based in a story about human psychology—should be subjected to the corresponding test of seeing whether it directs us towards a plausible normative ideal: to an ideal that people can be brought, on reflection, to find significantly attractive.

Pettit and Braithwaite argue that, "in doing social theory we should look for an adjustment between normative and explanatory categories of analysis and that, if we do so, we are likely to reach a higher level of performance on both fronts."[28] "Normative theory without explanatory theory is empty; explanatory theory without normative theory is blind, often dangerously so."[29]

They want to show "how the normative argument that republicanism provides is buttressed or likely to be buttressed by an argument that derives from the explanatory significance of the republican ideal of non-domination."[30] This is part of the defense of their theory of freedom as non-domination and their republican conception of political order. Whether or not we endorse their particular view there are important relations between valuative views and explanatory conceptions. We can only see that clearly if our sight is not obscured by a putative fact/value distinction, at least in the way it has been understood by many positivist social scientists. As we will see again when we discuss the notion of the rule of law, many of the normative debates concerning criminological studies are not, as it were, valuative accessories to the substantive, empirical studies. The normative issues are among objects of empirical investigation and how we understand values can make a substantive difference to what we recognize as the explanatorily important facts. Pettit and Braithwaite "argue that normative theory is improved by being responsive to good explanatory theory and vice versa. There is nothing as practical as a good philosophy and the best philosophy is informed by practice."[31]

Alison Liebling's study of the "moral performance" of prisons is an extensive, in-depth exploration of valuative features, and it places them centrally in the explanation of a great many empirical phenomena. Such studies show that it is not only possible to undertake empirical investigation of moral aspects of prison life and prison culture but also that our best understanding of them almost certainly depends on comprehension of those moral aspects. In many respects the most important impact of many policies, practices, and circumstances is their moral impact, the differences they make to attitudes, self-conceptions, motivation, persons' regard for each other, willingness to cooperate and trust, or dispositions of suspicion and distrust, contempt or respect, and so forth. One of the unwelcome results of taking it for granted that morality is subjective or that there are no factual moral considerations is that possibilities for an illuminating grasp of numerous moral aspects of criminal justice are simply overlooked.

One of the most normatively significant issues concerning criminal justice is the rule of law. A conception of the rule of law presupposes and implies key points regarding political order, legality, legitimacy, political obligation, and the exercise of state power. The conception of the rule of law is central to an overall view of legality and criminal justice. In many discussions of criminal justice the notion of the rule of law goes undiscussed or is taken for granted. With regard to some issues and with regard to certain modes of inquiry and investigation, that can be appropriate. But in the present project it is vitally important to explicate the notion of the rule of law and its distinctive normative features.

The discussion so far positions us to take up some fundamental issues concerning the rule of law, and the normativity it involves, especially the normativity of the liberal-democratic rule of law, given its prevalence in the Anglophone world. We need to include a discussion of the normativity of the rule of law as part of an overall framework within which we can address key issues concerning the relations between facts and values in the context of criminal justice. We turn to the rule of law in Chapter 2.

Notes

1 See, for example, Quines's "Two Dogmas of Empiricism" and other essays of his in *From a Logical Point of View*, and the papers in *Ontological Relativity and Other Essays*. Several of those are among his most influential critiques of the analytic/synthetic distinction and some of the central doctrines of logical positivism and they raise key issues concerning the underdetermination of theory. In the final few decades of the twentieth century there was a very large-scale retrieval of realism/antirealism disputes in several philosophical contexts. Saul Kripke's *Naming and Necessity* was very influential in that retrieval. See, also, Hilary Putnam, *Mind, Language and Reality*: Philosophical Papers, Volume 2. The reconsideration of metaphysics and philosophy of language was occurring along with much broader study of the history of philosophy. Thus, there was critical pressure being applied to logical positivism from several different angles of approach.

2 See, for example, Aristotle's *Posterior Analytics*.
3 Wittgenstein's *Philosophical Investigations* was a key work in regard to this issue.
4 Wittgenstein, at the conclusion of his "Lecture on Ethics," writes:

> My whole tendency and I believe the tendency of all men who ever tried to write or talk Ethics or Religion was to run against the boundaries of language. This running against the walls of our cage is perfectly, absolutely hopeless. Ethics so far as it springs from the desire to say something about the ultimate meaning of life, the absolute good, the absolute valuable, can be no science. What it does say does not add to our knowledge in any sense. But it is a document of a tendency in the human mind which I personally cannot help respecting deeply and I would not for my life ridicule it.

Reprinted in Stephen Darwall, Allan Gibbard, and Peter Railton eds., *Moral Discourse and Practice*, New York: Oxford University Press, 1997, pp. 65—70, 70.

5 Andrei Marmor, *Philosophy of Law*, Princeton: Princeton University Press, 2011, p. 47.
6 Anthony Bottoms, "Morality, Crime, Compliance and Public Policy," in *Ideology, Crime and Criminal Justice*, eds. Anthony Bottoms and Michael Tonry, Portland: Willan Publishing, 2002, p. 24.
7 Ibid., p. 25.
8 Ibid., p. 34.
9 Ibid.
10 Stanley Cavell, *Must We Mean What We Say?* New York: Charles Scribner's Sons, 1969, p. 52.
11 John McDowell, "Virtue and Reason," *The Monist* 62 (3): 1979, pp. 339–340, 331–350.
12 Ibid., p. 340.
13 Ibid., p. 337.
14 John McDowell, "Sellars and the Space of Reasons," *Analysis* 21 (8): 2018, pp. 1–22, p. 1.
15 Ibid., p. 1.
16 John McDowell, *Mind and World*, Cambridge: Harvard University Press, 1994, p. xv.
17 Ibid., p. 70.
18 Ibid., p. 185.
19 John McDowell, "Two Sorts of Naturalism," in *Virtues and Reasons: Philippa Foot and Moral Theory*, eds. Gavin Lawrence and Warren Quinn, Oxford: Clarendon Press, 1995, pp. 149–179; p. 167.
20 Ibid., p. 167.
21 Ibid.
22 Bottoms, "Morality, Crime, Compliance and Public Policy," 20–51, p. 22.
23 Ibid., p. 24.
24 Loader and Sparks, *Public Criminology?* pp. 127–128.
25 Anthony Bottoms, "The Relationship between Theory and Empirical Observations in Criminology," p. 92.
26 Ibid., p. 106.
27 "Republicanism and Restorative Justice: An Explanatory and Normative Connection," in *Restorative Justice: Philosophy to Practice*, eds. Heather Strang and John Braithwaite, Aldershot: Ashgate, 2000, pp. 145–164, p. 145.
28 Ibid., p. 161.
29 Ibid.
30 Ibid., p. 153.
31 Philip Pettit and John Braithwaite, "Connecting Philosophy and Practice," in *Restorative Justice: Philosophy to Practice*, eds. John Braithwaite and Heather Strang, Aldershot: Dartmouth Publishing Co., 2000, pp. 203–220, 203.

Chapter 2

Norms and the Rule of Law

The notion of the rule of law is crucial to the political and legal order of a liberal democracy. Given the importance of individuals' rights and liberties in a liberal democracy, in conjunction with the meaningful degree to which citizens may participate in the political process the legitimacy of the political/legal order depends on citizens respecting the rule of law in the sense of endorsing its fundamental principles and norms. In a liberal democracy the rule of law is not to be understood as whatever form of rule-governed coercively backed authority the state can exercise. That the institutions and proceedings constituting legality are recognized as legitimate is an important feature of a liberal democracy. At the same time it is possible for there to be widely shared concerns about the practices of law enforcement. There can be various objections to practices and features of policy and procedure even if those are not part of a fundamental rejection of the political/legal order. That is to say, the values and principles shaping the rule of law might be regarded as worthy of people's respect and endorsement while there are serious doubts about whether those values and principles are realized effectively. Of course, it is also possible for concerns about the practice of law enforcement to run sufficiently deep to motivate skepticism regarding the legitimacy of the rule of law. Concerns of that kind can be critically important to a society's view of criminal justice. Before going directly into discussion of the rule of law we should make some general remarks about reasons for action and the basic norms of a political order.

2.1 Actions, Reasons, and the Normativity of the Legal Order

In a well-ordered society the policies and practices of law enforcement have the rule of law as the guiding, informing authority to which they are responsive. For example, as Bottoms and Tankebe observe:

> a police service that seems either ineffective, or biased against a particular ethnic group, might reasonably be considered by some citizens to have

DOI: 10.4324/9781003037323-3

> lost the moral right to exercise power. For example, the main concern of the *Black Lives Matter* movement in the United States has not been the fairness of the process leading to police decisions to shoot African Americans, nor even the legality of police violence. Rather, what drives this movement is a deep concern and resentment about the unfairness of the very disproportionate representation of African Americans as victims in fatal police-civilian encounters.[1]

This is emblematic of wider concerns about the legitimacy of various institutions, agencies, and policies, and skepticism about whether the frequently avowed commitments and ideals of the basic political order are effectively realized. If they are not realized then there is another layer of questioning about what impedes that realization and how the impediments can be removed. That can become a deep question of legitimacy and whether the ideals and fundamental institutional arrangements should be endorsed. At present in the United States there is widely shared concern about practices of law enforcement but that is not automatically also rejection of the rule of law. Lack of trust in the police and doubts about the legitimacy of the rule of law can reinforce each other. But concerns about the one are separable, at least analytically, from concerns about the other even if they occur together frequently.

Before going into the various reasons people might have for complying with the law we should make some brief observations about the use of terms such as "reason," "intention," and "motive." Sometimes it seems that they can be used almost interchangeably but in other cases distinguishing them can be crucial. Often when we ask "Why did A do X?" or "What was A's reason for doing X?" the question can be ambiguous between asking what the person intended and asking what motivated the person. Thus, a response might identify what was intended by the action; for example, she was trying to win back Jim's affection. Or, the appropriate response might concern the agent's motive, such as "she is a very jealous person." Her affection was alienated and she insisted that it was the other woman's fault. That is what triggered the jealousy that moved her to act, but what she aimed to accomplish was a restoration of a special place in Jim's affection. In some contexts it is important to be as clear as possible about whether we are discussing a motive or an intention, and it is possible for each of those to be part of the explanation of the reasons for an action. There is not a fully fixed doctrine for the use of those concepts but clarity can be crucially important. When we are discussing a person's reasons for action depending on the context of discourse we might want to distinguish carefully between (i) what the person intended, (ii) for what reason was that intended, and (iii) what motivated the agent to do that. If a host asks angrily of a very late arriving guest, "And what is your reason for being more than an hour late to this party?" it is not difficult to imagine responses that highlight motives, or highlight intentions, or that highlight aspects of an action; for example, "I stopped to pick up a person who seemed to be wandering in a daze on the side of the road, and got that person the required sort of help. That can take a while, and it seemed more important than arriving at the party on time."

Another point, one that will be important when we discuss moral considerations, is that in many action-explanations there is a crucial—if implicit—role for a person's desires. If we ask someone "Why are you taking an umbrella?" or "What is your reason for taking an umbrella?" the response might be, "It's supposed to rain later." That belief is only a reason if the person also *desires to stay dry*. "What motivated you to take an umbrella?" sounds a little bit odd but a straightforward answer would be "I desired to stay dry." If it is someone who just never carries an umbrella then maybe in this case there is some interesting difference. "Oh, I wasn't planning to use it but I wanted Miriam to have it for her walk home. It is supposed to rain later." Here, the person's reason was to be helpful to Miriam and the person's motive was considerateness. Human action is such that it is generally appropriate to recognize the *reasons* for which people act in a two-fold sense including (i) what the person takes herself to be doing, i.e., what type of action is it, and (ii) what motivated the behavior.

It might seem that action always requires desire; that desire is needed if the agent is to be moved to act. However, that does not mean that desire is always a felt experience or that it has a distinct identity as a mental state. If someone says, "I stayed to help and sacrificed my own chance to audition for the part because I wanted to do the right thing; staying and helping was the right thing," that need not mean that the person had any distinctive, felt experience of wanting to help. Rather, given this individual's character, she saw that helping was the right thing to do and that was reason enough to be motivated to do it. In this case, that the agent wanted to help is consequent upon the agent's understanding of what she ought to do. There isn't a want as an independent source of motivation, an identifiable episode in the person's mental history.

We should also note that *there are numerous different kinds of action-guiding considerations*. People often do what they most strongly *desire*. However, in many cases they pursue what they take to be in their *interest*. That is not the same as doing it because one wants to or desires to do it. Much that is in our interest we do not desire to do; and much that we desire is not in our interest. Sometimes people act in specific ways in fulfillment of a *religious obligation*. Sometimes people act in ways responsive to *cultural convention*. For some persons the fact that an action is *morally right* (or at least they believe it is morally right) is a reason to act. And, that an act is *what the law requires* is another type of action-guiding consideration. These are different sources of action-guiding norms, and the acceptance of norms is often an important part of the explanation of action, whether we are explaining a move someone makes in a game, an action that merits moral evaluation, or fulfilling a legal requirement.

In those cases where persons do things because the law requires them there can be different sources of motivation for that compliance. It might be that the person obeys the law mainly out of respect for the relevant authority. Perhaps this is someone who generally complies with authority or perhaps this person regards the rule of law as meriting respect. It could also be that the person wishes most of all to avoid prosecution and she obeys the law to "stay out of trouble." Some persons might obey the law because they believe it would be shameful to be regarded as a criminal. It is not that they care only for their reputation but they might know themselves well enough to be quite sure that being seen as a criminal would be painfully shaming, something they wish to avoid. An agent might think that some laws—including the one in question—make appropriate, justifiable demands. This person might see the law here as having a sound point in regard to protecting people from harm. A liberal-democratic political order does not require citizens to have only certain specific motives for complying with the law. It could be that several different normative bases need to be mentioned to specify the grounds people have for obeying the law. However, a key feature of a liberal democracy is that people should be able to comply with the law because they recognize it as endorsable, as legitimate. We turn now to that issue.

Most people do not need criminal law to inform them that murder, hostage-taking, kidnapping, robbery, unprovoked assault, and many other types of conduct are *wrong*. It might be that anyone who is not morally disordered in a serious way recognizes them as wrong and regards the legal prohibitions as making moral and legal sense. As Duff puts it, "[we] can express this point by portraying the law, not as *prohibiting* the central kinds of *mala in se*, but as *declaring* their wrongfulness." Taking the rule of law seriously involves recognizing that one may disagree with some matters of law but still see that such disagreement is not, as such, an adequate basis for flouting the law or for regarding obedience to law as a discretionary matter (assuming that the cases in question are genuinely disputable rather than quite egregious examples of bad law).

> In such instances, what the law says to those who dissent from the stand it takes is not simply and unqualifiedly that the conduct in question is wrong, but rather that this is now the community's authoritative view. Even if they dissent from its content, they have an obligation as members of the community to accept its authority—to obey the law, even if they are not persuaded by its content, unless and until they can secure a change in it through the normal political process.[2]

Duff discusses the issue of compliance with the law in a liberal state at some length and he argues that in a liberal state it is crucial that citizens recognize the law as informed and guided by values they endorse. In a liberal state people are *citizens*, not *subjects* and it is important that they can regard the law as common law. "It embodies the shared values and normative understandings of the community. It flows not from the will of a separate sovereign but from the traditions and practices of the community."[3] His view is that the law of a liberal state needs to be common law in the sense that "The voice of the law is (or aspires to be) the voice of the community addressing itself, the voice of all the citizens addressing one another and themselves. It speaks of what 'we,' the community, require or demand."[4] Criminal wrongs are those "on which the community as a whole can and should take a stand, through the authoritative voice of the law. Second, such wrongs merit a public, communal response."[5] In addition, "Citizens should obey the law not just because it is the law, but because it marks a reasonable attempt by the legislature to serve the common good."[6] He says that, "[t]he legislature's task is not to impose its own will on the population, but to give more adequate and practicable expression to the values that already structure the community's life and understanding."[7]

Most people who have been raised with even modest attention to basic moral decency and sociability, and who are not habituated to reject any authority other than themselves, will feel little temptation to kill, kidnap, or degrade others, or to steal from them, spread malicious rumors about them, and so forth. There are malevolent people and there are plenty of people who seem to be morally stunted, having little empathy or compassion, and barely taking into consideration the rights or welfare of others. But they do not seem to be the majority and it would be remarkable that the complex texture and dynamic of civil society would be sustainable if most people were like that.

It might be that in several areas, such as drug use, prostitution, and pornography there is less convergence of judgment. But as Andrew von Hirsch notes:

> That dissensus exists in modern societies on some legal and ethical issues is undeniable: witness the ongoing debates about abortion and drug use...However, if we turn our attention to the core areas with which the criminal law should deal—the prohibition of victimizing acts of force, theft, and fraud; and the enforcement of certain basic duties of citizenship such as the payment of taxes and the preservation of the environment—there appears to be a greater degree of agreement.[8]

Moreover, in a polity recognizable as morally decent it is likely that the great majority of citizens will not only be law-abiding but they will also be law-abiding *because* they find many of the action-types that have been criminalized abhorrent. "In the U.S. and U.K. most people comply with the law quite regularly. It would seem that they don't generally calculate whether to comply, but instead, just do not find many criminal acts strongly tempting." In a liberal polity there may be more rather than fewer points of friction about what should be a criminal offense, but in some respects that friction can be tolerated and it is indicative of a kind of flexible, resilient strength rather than being destructive of social order and the rule of law.

Duff argues that a liberal polity, common law, public wrongs, and legitimacy are elements of an integrated set of key considerations. He writes:

> A conception of criminal law as a law for citizens depends on a democratic political theory, to argue that a legitimate criminal law requires a political community whose members share the status of citizen; citizenship being understood roughly as equal, mutually respectful participation in the civic enterprise.[9]

The values of the public sphere in such a polity include

> norms about how citizens should treat each other, which gives us a basis for an idea of public wrongs—of wrongdoing that violates the polity's defining values; and this then gives us a basis for an idea of criminal law as a formal way of identifying and responding to such wrongs.[10]

We can see already, just having begun exploring the issue of the rule of law that it has several normatively significant aspects, and this is clear whether or not we endorse Duff's particular view. A legal positivist is likely to articulate the normativity of the rule of law in a different manner even if the positivist regards constitutional democracy as the form of political order for which there is the best case. It might appear that the legal positivist has a much thinner notion of the normativity of the rule of law. The positivist might have little to say regarding the notion of persons as having a civic responsibility to recognize the state as legislating in their name, and the importance of recognizing the dignity of persons as an important constraint on what sorts of laws are justifiable. Hart's positivism is normatively richer than Austin's, for example, but it is still legal positivism, and contrasts with views such as Duff's.

Anglophone countries share a common law heritage. That is not common law in precisely the same sense as Duff articulated but it is certainly related to it. A core element of a common law tradition is that considerable weight is given to the rulings arrived at by courts in contrast to a legal system in which law is explicitly spelled out in detail in a legal code. Commenting on the influence (in Britain) of Sir Edward Coke (1552–1634) and Matthew Hale (1609–1676) Mark Tebbit writes:

> Both were major figures in the law at a time of a revolutionary conflict that was to culminate in the 1688 settlement, which would transform the relationship between the monarch and the representative parliament. The theories of common law articulated by Coke and Hale overlapped extensively, but their under-standing of the nature of law diverged in significant ways. For both of them, law was the accumulation over many

> generations of judicial wisdom which commanded reverence...However, for Coke...the common law was the embodiment of eternal and unchanging principles of natural justice. For Hale, it was in a state of slow organic evolution.[11]

Also, some of those who contributed to the Declaration of Independence and Constitution in the U.S. appealed to the wisdom of the common law tradition in a sense that straddles what Duff emphasized and what is noted just above. In the *Federalist Papers*, "[a]s Publius tells us, constitutional constraints mean little without the support of popular opinion."[12]

> The ultimate conformity of our institutions with the norms of legality and the limits of permissible discretion depends on a populace capable of supporting a tolerable balance of rules and discretion, and of making judgments in particular cases (distinguishing a Lincoln from a Nixon, for example).[13]

The point is that the rule of law in a liberal state depends on citizens having certain dispositions and commitments. This does not mean that citizens need to be especially virtuous and strongly dedicated to exercising their virtues in the political context but the rule of law and its especially valuable features are not just "there," or in place because there is a written record of the laws and judicial decisions. The reality and efficacy of the rule of law in a liberal democracy depend on a durable grounding in the attitudes and concerns of citizens.

That is an especially important part of the notion of a common law tradition. As Stephen Macedo remarks, "Like colonial juries before them, American courts have long been independent sources of political judgment that help both check legislative tyranny and foster popular education and principled political dialogue."[14] That is not possible unless citizens have an abiding sense of the significance of their own commitment to the rule of law. An example of this is Judge David Bazelon's suggestion that there could be a very important role for jury nullification as a response to injustice. Instead of seeing it as a form of waywardness or populist ideológical excess he writes, "Rather, I view nullification as an important means of 'bring[ing] to bear on the criminal process a sense of fairness and particularized justice.'"[15] That, too, is one of the possible merits of common law jurisprudence. Bazelon made the point in the course of arguing that the social and economic inequalities and injustices in U.S. society, and also in its criminal justice system, are sufficiently severe that jury nullification could be a visible form of democratic moralizing pushing back against injustice.

He was making the point in the course of arguing that there are really just two "polar positions" regarding the administration of criminal justice, and they are the "law as external constraint" view, and the "law as a moral force" view. In the latter citizens recognize criminal law (including the proceedings of criminal justice) as informed by morally justified values. Rather than being focused on encouraging habits of compliance mainly as a matter of preserving order, as is the case with "law as external constraint" he says that in the "law as a moral force" view order is

> based on the internalization of control, that is, on the members of the society obeying the law because they personally believe that its commands are justified. Thus, this view demands that the law facilitate the internalization process by becoming a moral force in the community.[16]

Actually, Bazelon's view is disputable in some important respects that do not figure in his discussion, at least in the particular article being quoted. He suggests that there is the "order has priority" view and the "law as moral force" view but does not acknowledge that between them there could be other views shaped by the notion that while the law should be morally intelligible (and not make unreasonable demands on persons, and not require them to do things they cannot do) there is an important difference between the law's moral intelligibility and the law being an enforcement of morality. Bazelon does say that the notion that "no act should be made criminal if it is not viewed as immoral" does not mean that all immorality should be criminalized. However, he argues that "if moral condemnation were the basis for criminal sanctions" we might expand the conception of excuses and mitigating factors on the basis of facts about someone's social circumstances or poverty or alienation from the society's prevailing values on account of deprivation or exclusion because of bigotry.

What Bazelon's view seems not to take into account is that the invitation to an enlarged sense of what is morally relevant to the decisions juries must make opens the door to moral values and views he would find appalling as well as those he would find appealing. There are arguments in favor of many more cases going to trial before juries, and there are reasons why the almost industrial scale and pace of plea bargains is regrettable. But there is no assurance that juries exercising more moral discretion will result in better quality justice. There is not only the issue that juries might do a poor job of exercising moral judgment—for all sorts of reasons. There is also the concern that the pluralism of society, while perhaps strongly desirable in its own right, could result in all sorts of inconsistency, with decisions being made on many different grounds, some relevant, some not.

Overall, inviting juries to remedy social or economic justice through a kind of discretion in the context of criminal justice is potentially a much more complicated matter than Bazelon suggests. But he does raise the question of the relation between criminal justice and other aspects of justice very effectively. That is an unavoidably normative issue, and normative considerations of numerous kinds are involved. Perhaps the main point is that the question of whether we should seek at least a partial remedy of social and economic injustices through criminal justice is a more complex and contestable matter than Bazelon suggests.

Juries can nullify and in that sense they can let conscience be their guide. A prosecutor has a measure of discretion and can decide not to indict if the accused behaved in a way that actually seems justified but as Heffernan notes, "[p]ublic vindication is not achieved."[17] And since "judges should not resolve cases on the basis of a specific conception of social justice, one must ask why prosecutors and jurors should do so."[18] And at least under current rules and policies "federal judges are prohibited under their sentencing guidelines from even considering a defendant's socioeconomic background when imposing a sentence."[19] The sort of discretion with freeing defendants of liability that Bazelon advocates motivates objections on grounds of procedure and also offers no assurance that the "right" values will prevail from the overall diversity of moral views and conceptions of a just society.

The criminal law of a liberal polity can be understood as informed and oriented by norms, including valuative norms that need to be intelligible to, and (largely) endorsed by the persons to whom they apply. They are shared norms regarding permissions, requirements, and prohibitions that apply to members of the community and they also reflect and shape ascriptions of responsibility that are appropriate to persons. Intelligible norms are crucial to our ability to form reliable expectations about how people will act and how they will react to our own conduct. "General rules foster the virtues of reliance, predictability, and stability: by reducing variance in individual cases, they allow individuals and associations to plan their lives and avoid running afoul of the law."[20] "Perhaps most importantly, rules help us avoid errors arising from the prejudice, ignorance, and incompetence of decision makers."[21] While rules might constrain "truly virtuoso performances and fine-tuned treatment...we also avoid suffering the idiocies, corruption, and abuse that will occur when knaves and fools have leeway."[22]

The space of reasons as it concerns the social world and relations between persons in a political community is given contours by the rule of law. One important aspect of the rule of law in a liberal democracy is that taking the rule of law seriously involves recognizing that one may disagree with some matters of law but still see that such disagreement is not an adequate basis for denying the authority and legitimacy of the rule of law (assuming that the cases in question are genuinely disputable rather than quite egregious examples of bad law).

In the U.S. issues such as abortion, gun ownership, and various types of drug possession and use seem to be nearly perennial fixtures of public debate about criminalization. The prevailing attitudes might shift over time but the issues can remain disputed. For example, many states in the U.S. are currently much more permissive regarding the possession and use of marijuana than say, ten years ago. Also, the prevailing attitudes regarding same-sex marriage seem to have changed—in a strikingly abrupt manner—in recent years.

From being an out-of-the-question proposition in the thinking of much of the public, it has been quite widely accepted or at least tolerated across much of the nation. Popular opinion over issues such as abortion, prostitution, and pornography might remain sharply divided but the overall social and political culture does accept many types of behavior that even a relatively short time ago would have been anathema in the view of a great many people. A stable liberal polity in which the society is genuinely civil—or at least, *generally* civil—will be one in which people are willing to live with some laws they do not endorse personally but they believe that the rule of law in general is legitimate and has authority that should be respected.

A vast amount of the activity and interactions, and the transactions that are constitutive of civil society depend on dispositions of trust and trustworthiness. Those dispositions are indispensable for a genuinely civil society. Yet, they do not arise naturally; they need to be shaped, habituated, encouraged, and sustained. (We have seen how threats to them can do very serious damage and cause real divisiveness in society. Consider, for instance, China's repressive smothering of democratic politics in Hong Kong.) Illiberal and repressive politics depend heavily on force and frequently on the unpredictable use of force, as a way of intimidating people into obedience. They discourage trust and trustworthiness, which are dispositions crucial to the spontaneity and the wide range of voluntariness exercised in civil society. Where people have extensive freedoms, and where there is broad scope for people to lead their lives in ways they wish, it is vitally important that people not only do not impede or harm others but that they should be willing to regard others as generally acting in good faith and "playing by the rules," i.e., respecting the relevant norms.

In a liberal polity there may be more rather than fewer points of friction about what should be a criminal offense. Generally that friction can be tolerated and it can be indicative of a kind of flexible, resilient strength rather than being destructive of social order and the rule of law. How likely is it that any liberal democracy that is not an isolated, culturally, ethnically, and religiously homogeneous community will be free of controversial issues? If the society is genuinely pluralistic and actually admits and accepts persons from different cultures, races, religions, and so forth it would be amazing if there were not some persistently disputed matters and also others that might be less enduring but nonetheless arouse strong feelings and sharp disagreement.

In the immediately preceding paragraphs there is repeated mention of values and the importance of a liberal political/legal order reflecting values that citizens (generally) endorse. This is the case even if the law does not attempt to enforce morality in any comprehensive way, or seek to criminalize all behavior that is thought to be morally wrong. There are respects in which morality has a regulative role with regard to law even if the law is restrained in regard to the enforcement of morals. Its regulative role concerns some of the most fundamental features of a legitimate conception of the rule of law.

2.2 Political Culture and the Rule of Law

This issue is complicated and involves conceptual and empirical elements. For example, Devlin's view in *The Enforcement of Morals* is not simply the claim that unless there is shared religion underwriting morality a society will disintegrate and become very unstable. Jeffrie G. Murphy has suggested that Devlin was

> exploiting a tension within liberalism itself—the tension between the value of individual liberty, on the one hand, and the value of democratic rule toward utilitarian ends on the other. Devlin is not a legal moralist. He is rather, a utilitarian, democratic cynic with some controversial empirical views. Utilitarian because he regards social harmfulness, in some very extended sense, as the only factor relevant in justifying a criminal prohibition. Democratic because he believes that the majority has a right to have its preferences enacted into law absent some compelling reason why they should not be. Cynical because he believes the social importance of a moral belief is not a function of its truth or reasonableness but is solely a function of its pervasiveness and the degree of emotional intensity with which it is held.[23]

Whether or not we agree with Murphy's suggestion regarding the interpretation of Devlin it is plausible to recognize a tension within liberalism, a tension between liberal accommodation of diverse views, values, and perspectives on the one hand (and not enforcing morality), and democratic majoritarian politics on the other. Pluralist democracy can require a constantly adjusted interaction of different sources of political pressure.

James Fitzjames Stephen, whose *Liberty, Equality, Fraternity* was a robust response to Mill's *On Liberty* counts as a liberal theorist though he held views in which the moral solidarity of society (generally supported by religion, though he was not writing directly in defense of religion) is regarded as crucial to society's order and stability. He argued that unless there are firmly held, widely shared moral views a society would be subject to powerful, disintegrating forces and that would make it impossible for people to pursue their ends and lead their lives with any confident prospect of success.

It seems plausible to interpret him as a Hobbesian at a fundamental level, and he held that morality ultimately depends on coercion of a sort. There is, he held, "(1) Coercion for the purpose of establishing and maintaining religions. (2) Coercion for the purpose of establishing and practically maintaining morality. (3) Coercion for the purpose of making alterations in existing forms of government or social institutions." And he said: "My book contains no religion whatever. It is not in any sense of the word a sermon or a set of sermons. It expresses no opinion of my own upon religious questions."[24] However, he believed firmly that belief in a future state is crucial to morality, and in that respect, society is dependent on morality and morality upon religion. He wrote: "[m]y present object is to...show both that the prudence of virtue (as commonly understood) depends upon the question whether there is a future state or not, and that the question what is the nature of virtue, understood as the course of conduct which becomes a man, also depends on it."[25]

This is a very unsentimental view, that of a lawyer and civil servant, someone who has considerable experience reflecting on people's motives, aims, and patterns of conduct. It is a view worth considering at least in the sense that it is a reminder that the space of reasons insofar as it concerns the actual character of the socio-political order might differ in significant respects from our ideal conception of that order and of how we conceptualize citizens and what they are like most fundamentally.

Stephen counts as a liberal in a pre-twentieth century sense. He was a staunch defender of common law and the notion of British citizens having rights and liberties protected against violation even by the monarch. He held that Parliament had powers that could not be diminished or suspended even by the crown, and that there are procedural guarantees guarding against arbitrary and extra-judicial treatment. He was not a liberal democrat in the mid- and late-twentieth century sense but that latter view—involving numerous welfarist components and egalitarian commitments—developed from the former. In many respects it was a response to what seemed the inadequacies of "Classical" liberalism, even after that form had become more democratic than its nineteenth-century version. Still, the two views, Classical liberalism and welfarist liberalism, developed out of some common roots.

A.V. Dicey is a good source for what was a widely held view of the merits of common law classical liberalism. Dicey, in contrasting the common law of England with legal traditions on the European continent wrote: "During the eighteenth century many of the continental governments were far from oppressive, but there was no continental country where men were secure from arbitrary power. The singularity of England was not so much the goodness or the leniency as the legality of the English system of government."[26] He contrasts English legality with the "royal lawlessness" prevalent on the Continent. Of the English he said, "With us every official, from the Prime Minister down to a constable or a collector of taxes, is under the same responsibility for every act done without legal justification as any other citizen."[27] Whereas, "in countries like Belgium, where the constitution is the result of a legislative act...in England...the constitution itself is based upon legal doctrine."[28] "[I]n England the so-called principles of the constitution are inductions or generalisations based upon particular decisions pronounced by the Courts as to the rights of given individuals."[29] He commends the political and jurisprudential culture of the U.S. in remarking that "the statesmen of America have shown unrivalled skill in providing means for giving legal security to the rights declared by American constitutions. The rule of law is as marked a feature of the United States as of England."[30]

The emphasis in Dicey's view is on the source of legality and the way that legality is protection against arbitrariness, much more than on whether the legal/political order promotes the public welfare in ways that are effective and fair. For Dicey, the fact that no one is above the law is vitally important. "Royal lawlessness" is tantamount to precious little rule of law in Dicey's view. Martin Krygier notes that A.V. Dicey "focused on three distinctive elements of the British institutional order"[31] and these were (i) the inability of authorities to exercise arbitrary power, (ii) that rank or condition make no difference to whether a citizen is subject to the rulings of the courts, and (iii) the rulings of courts are the basis of constitutional principles, unlike in the U.S., with its written Constitution. (However, the U.S. is to be counted as a common law nation because of the significance of judicial rulings to the validity and interpretation of laws.) Overall, the U.K. and U.S. share important elements of a common law jurisprudential culture. One could move from the one to the other and quite easily recognize the likenesses in the rule of law in each, even if procedurally there are some notable differences.

The notion that citizens of a liberal state should all be "free and equal," in the expression widely used in recent decades, is not part of Dicey's view except that the equality he had in mind is *being equally subject to the law*. That might seem much too narrow, and there are numerous ways that it is compatible with many forms of inequality. However, it is important to note that the notion of being equally subject to the law even if not fully equal according to the law was a significant step in diminishing arbitrariness in the ruling power. Equality in ways that have something directly to do with distributive shares, e.g., making it a principle that such inequalities should be diminished, came later with further democratizing of liberalism and then developing a welfarist orientation. All of these are normative matters of the first importance.

Reflecting on these matters is one way to consider whether the Harm Principle on its own could be adequate as a basis for determining what is to be criminalized. Is a Legal Positivism that faithfully adheres to the Harm Principle a genuine possibility? If not, what else is needed for a real possibility? There is an extensive range of views regarding this issue. If one looks at the literature on criminal justice in a liberal democracy and, in particular, the literature on the aims and justification of punishment, one finds that there are many different views, all claiming (plausibly) to be rooted in some of the same fundamental principles. They present different elaborations of what is needed for those principles to be realized though they claim common sources. Roughly, the views range from libertarian and classical liberal views at one end of the spectrum, to more social democratic and also communitarian-republican views at the other end.

If one's values are more social democratic than liberal-democratic then a sense of community and commitment to community welfare might make shared values an important social bond. For instance, Antje duBois-Pedain writes

> Our fundamental constitutional values commit us to treating each other as creatures of intrinsic value. This gives rise to a concern for the welfare of every member of the polity. At the most general level, this commits us to shaping our institutions of public life such that they will not be harmful or disadvantageous to individual members of the polity but will rather help them in leading productive and fulfilling lives.[32]

And she says, "The welfare orientation of all state action must also register in how we design our criminal justice system."[33] duBois-Pedain's view involves a conception of society that differs from many liberal conceptions and involves a thicker conception of the community overall having a shared sense of what is crucial to living well, and a shared sense of what is required of the society—as a political community—to enable people to live well. My point is not that liberals tend to have a more atomistic view of society. Maintaining that the scale and scope of the reach of government into people's lives should be carefully limited does not imply specific claims about the character of society and modes of mutual recognition and interaction. In fact, a liberal could argue that liberalism *makes possible* the richest and most diverse and textured possibilities for civil society, in part, because of the essential role of voluntariness and persons pursuing forms of interaction and community. Defenders of liberalism need not have atomistic or unsociable dispositions or proclivities. They might be skeptical about the prospects for the *state* making people's lives better by being more fully and directly engaged in their lives, but that is a quite different claim.

The point about atomism and also the charge that liberalism encourages narrowly self-interested, acquisitive dispositions might be explainable in part by the emphasis that many theorists in the early modern period put on the importance of private property. Many contemporary critics of liberalism cite private property as an important factor in people becoming self-interested and unconcerned with overall social welfare. The result is that, for a great many people, their primary concern is with either the accumulation of wealth, consumption, or both. However, the importance of property in liberal theory is understandable on the basis of how ownership, having control of property, even a very modest amount, gives one a kind of standing and offers one a kind of protection, at least in the sense that the state or the king cannot simply take it from you, leaving you destitute and utterly dependent.

If property-less, one's dependence is complete. In addition, economies became more commercial and then also more industrial, and land was no longer the primary or sole basis of wealth and the character of economic activity changed in numerous ways. Wealth remained highly important but it is not as though greed or unconcern for the welfare of others was invented by commercial economies and industrialization. The defense of private property and its political importance did not imply or uniquely cause acquisitiveness or callous self-interest. Perhaps at all levels of wealth and poverty it appeared that self-interest was becoming steadily more powerful because many of the rich wanted to become richer and many of the least well-off had to do whatever they could to avoid abject poverty. In addition, rather than remaining on the land generation after generation, without any realistic aspiration for a different future people now had to make a living in terms of wages, and large numbers of people were (and are) in a very disadvantageous position in that regard. To be sure, there was a great deal of unfairness and the political influence of money replaced the political influence of land. It became necessary for people to seek property and wealth in a way that was not the case for the majority in a feudal socio-economic order. On the one hand, people had to pursue ways of making a living that involved making money; they were drawn unavoidably into the "cash nexus." On the other hand, more and more goods were available and the standard of living for a great many people rose, significantly if not always steadily or evenly. The combined impact of railroads, the steamship, canned goods, the telegraph, scientific agriculture, postal systems and many other innovations made an enormous difference to how people led their lives, often for the better. In much of the world people's lives were no longer irreversibly fixed by one's status at birth and connection to the land.

In the U.S. immigrants maintained various ties to others sharing ethnic and cultural heritage. This had a substantial impact on the character of civil society in the U.S. through literature, drama, newspapers, cuisine, religious life, and so forth. Assimilation, consumerism, and the vulgarizing and coarsening of popular taste were going on at the same time as the development of a pluralistic, very diverse society. New York City, for instance, has undergone several waves of immigration with different groups at different times having a pronounced impact on the cultural life of the city during the last century and a half. The size of its overall population (perhaps on account of geography) has remained fairly stable for decades while the demographics of the city have changed again and again.

Still, it is frequently held that a liberal state will be one in which society will be atomistic with citizens lacking concern for the welfare of others. In developing her account of the type of polity best suited to the conception of punishment she defends Nicola Lacey writes:

> The main adjustment which I shall make to the liberal assumptions on which many modern theories of punishment are constructed is in adopting a view of humans as essentially, necessarily and primarily social beings. In other words, in speaking of the ideal planning or construction of a society, we cannot take our conceptions of what is right or just from any idea of what would be chosen by individual moral agents deciding to get together and form a society afresh.[34]

She also remarks on:

> the falseness of the dilemma set up by traditional liberalism between personal autonomy and social good: because of the relationship between autonomy and a certain range and quality of possible lives, and because the value of the exercise of autonomy depends to some extent on the background social environment, any straightforward opposition between personal autonomy and welfare or social good can be seen to misrepresent the moral situation.[35]

The notion that liberal politics regards the rights and liberties of individuals, and also the development of capacities for deliberation, accountability, and self-determination as centrally important does not necessarily imply a socially unconcerned individual. We should remember that much of the impetus for early modern liberalism came from the interest persons had in freeing themselves from the various corporate structures and social statuses that shaped and limited so much of the social world. People wanted to be free of all sorts of social structures that had limited their freedom. Liberalism's focus on the rights and liberties of the individual reflects the importance of the individual's dignity and autonomy, not necessarily a perspective that is unconcerned with the social world and relations with other persons. There is no need for one particular type of economic model of a person's rationality and concerns to be treated as telling us all there is to know about what people are like and what matters to them.

Liberalism is a view about the political/legal order and not directly about the character of social relations. Granted, different forms of political/legal order have implications for the character of social relations. But the matter is not as straightforward as it is often portrayed to be. A liberal state could be a political order providing for extensive openness for civil society thereby encouraging and supporting numerous forms of solidarity and community but on voluntary bases. In the periods of early modern liberalism there was an emphasis on protecting against arbitrariness and the lawless powers of rulers on the one hand, and protecting persons' rights and liberties on the other but in many respects that was also a time during which there were strong communal ties of various kinds and society was hardly atomistic. For instance, consider the character of the social world, religious, and community life in Britain during the English Civil Wars. Important steps toward Parliamentary supremacy and at least some characteristics of an early form of liberal state were being taken but the society was still one in which the importance of religious community and "local" rule over many governmental and social affairs was very pronounced. (Plus, many people regarded Cromwell's army as no less unwelcome and tyrannical than the King's army.) Some of the pre-modern forms of local governmental administration (various courts, the magistrates, and so forth) still exist. It was also a period during which commerce was developing rapidly and forms of economic activity were changing society rapidly.

A liberal-democratic political order can at least provide some regular, institutional protections against governments behaving arbitrarily, showing blatant favoritism, granting monopolies, being enormously wasteful, and so forth.[36] Granted, even liberal democracy is no guarantee against that. It is not as though a liberal political order tends to be guided by wisdom. In many cases, the sorts of corruption to which it is vulnerable do a good deal of damage to people's lives. Lobbyists, the political process and the bargains it produces, or the inattention of regulators are appropriate objects of blame in a liberal state, and many issues of public welfare go unaddressed or are starved of adequate resources. Yet, how much assurance is there that public administration will not be wasteful, corrupt or otherwise a costly, unaccountable mess...that more of the state makes for a better society? This is not to say we should *expect* the state to be inefficient, profligate with the public treasury, and much more responsive to corrupting interests than it should be. But it is no more correct to assert that *of course* the state will act in ways that are firmly guided by a sound conception of the public good than it is to summarily criticize a liberal state for bringing it about that very large numbers of people are narrowly self-interested and lack concern for fellow citizens. The notion that socially important issues are *of course* addressed and managed more effectively and fairly the more the state is directly involved is not clearly and convincingly supported by historical evidence though there are significant examples of the state pursuing the common weal effectively or at least helping to avoid or recover from crises of various types. (These might include financial and banking crises, crises in regard to failures of major utility companies, crises arising from one or another essential industry being horribly mismanaged, and natural disasters, among others.)

Sometimes, after a very damaging storm, there are news stories about citizens rescuing neighbors and strangers, or traveling a great distance to help; and some observers lament that "ordinary citizens have to do the government's job. Where were the state agencies?" Often, government agencies plan poorly, or fail to be prepared in appropriate ways, or their response is confused and disorganized in ways that clearly are grounds for legitimate complaint. However, that ordinary citizens volunteer to help each other is a fine thing. Sometimes, when citizens rush to help others or extend themselves in generous ways it is not mainly because the state has failed; it is because those people care about others and about their communities. It is certainly appropriate that the state should have primary responsibility in addressing various emergencies and disasters. At the same time we might also find a very generous, constructive response on the part of many members of the public. That is to be welcomed and we sometimes find that even in societies characterized by consumerism, greed, and narrow self-interest many people defy the characterization.

One reason there is a point in considering such matters is that the character of social relations and prevailing societal attitudes can have a significant impact on criminal justice. There are, of course, other very important factors shaping the administration of criminal justice. Still, it is influenced by the public's views of their responsibilities, their sense of what it is reasonable to expect of citizens. Also, the prevailing attitudes that people have to various issues such as law enforcement, crime and punishment, and how offenders and former prisoners should be regarded and treated can influence the state's policies. In this context we do find reason to be very concerned that overly punitive attitudes and widespread unwillingness to support and assist former prisoners (among other troubling attitudes) have motivated policies of very dubious merit regarding criminal justice. Moreover, if a state enacts law and implements policies that make it (needlessly) very difficult for offenders and former prisoners to succeed as participants in civil society that can be both very unfair and counterproductive. Such impediments damage individuals and civil society, and can also perpetuate unhelpful societal attitudes.

2.3 Moral Intelligibility and the Rule of Law

To return to the main theme in this chapter, it is impossible to understand criminal justice in a liberal democracy without considering numerous views of the relation between law and morality and different conceptions of the rule of law and political legitimacy. All of which is to say that it is impossible to understand criminal justice in a liberal democracy without a grasp of the texture of several sources of normativity. This is not (only) because there are inevitably relevant moral considerations; that's true. But it is also because the notion of a political order, and especially one in which freedoms, voluntariness, responsibility, and legitimacy are regarded as significant is, among other things, a complex institutional arrangement of normativity.

It is crucial that the institutional arrangement and what it most fundamentally requires of people should be "morally intelligible." That does not limit the arrangement to just one form and I certainly do not mean that only one specific moral theory can be the basis of the form of moral intelligibility needed. Instead, the chief point is that certain general conditions should be satisfied, and those conditions have mainly to do with the fact that persons are rational agents able to recognize norms as appropriate or satisfactory or as inappropriate or unsatisfactory reasons for action.

One of the most familiar formulations of such conditions is Fuller's notion of the "internal morality of the law." The sense in which I borrow the notion is that there are various conditions on any rule that is to be recognized (properly) as a law. Fuller says that law is "the enterprise of subjecting human conduct to the governance of rules."[37] Thus, legality has an internal morality concerned with the ways in which "a system of rules for governing human conduct must be constructed and administered if it is to be efficacious and at the same time remain what it purports to be."[38] I am not suggesting that Fuller's conditions are all that is needed to explicate legality in a liberal-democratic rule of law but they are plausible as requirements needing to be met by any rule that is to be recognized as a law. They illustrate many of the kinds of things that need to be taken into account when formulating a conception of legality for a liberal democracy. Nothing could be a law, a genuine legal requirement, if it involves requirements that no rational agent can meet. Laws are a class of norms, and they are norms governing some of the most significant ways in which people act and interact in the space of reasons. Even if one endorses a legal positivist view there are various conditions on the norms for legality in a liberal democracy.

Matthew Kramer writes, "Squarely unmistakable is the dependence of the rule of law on the existence of norms that are general in their application. Maybe not quite as obvious is the dependence of the rule of law on the existence of norms that are general in their address."[39] Kramer notes that Fuller "did not include the generality of address within his first principle of legality" and Kramer argues that it is important to include it.[40] "Norms general in their address as well as in their application will be operative whenever any institutions of governance are operative."[41] Again, the main concern here is not whether Fuller's list of features of the law's internal morality is exactly the right list. We could argue about whether generality should be included or whether it is implied or presupposed by one or more of Fuller's conditions. But that would be an argument concerning an important detail, not the larger issue about laws being rules for rational agents.

Should we say that a set of rules constitute laws even if some of the rules do not apply generally and the rules are enforced on a completely discretionary basis? That, actually, is not so far off from what happened in Germany in the nineteen thirties with Hitler's rise to power and then, over the next decade, his commandeering of all final authority, even judicial, so that *he was the law*. He even had that step "legitimized" by process during the Second World War though, of course, it was a sham process. Securing the agreement of state agencies and institutions to a mode of governance that is arbitrary and for which there is no remedy or recourse (which is what Hitler did with respect to the courts during the war) does not bring legitimacy with it. Suppose that, in addition to all power being in the hands of one person, the exercise of that power is unrestricted such that anything could be commanded and required, even if it is a practical impossibility to do what the law requires. Even if there is enthusiasm or at least acceptance of this form of government it cannot be an example of a valid or legitimate rule of law. Being accepted is not sufficient for legitimacy. The rules do not reflect a conception of legality that guides their formulation and underwrites their acceptability if they really are just expressions of one person's (or one small group's) will. In that sense there might be norms that fail to meet conditions for legality though those in power call them "laws." Perhaps that could be regarded as a form of unchecked legal positivism. Or if positivists reject that conclusion they would—like Hart—recognize that there are at least some background constraints on what can count as law even if this is not a matter of deriving law from moral principles. Not just any set of enforceable norms could be a system of law.

Fuller noted that, "Austin defined law as the command of a political superior. Yet he insisted that 'laws properly so-called' were general rules and that 'occasional and particular' commands were not law."[42] That suggests that Fuller did recognize the significance of generality of address, but it also shows that even in Austin's view law is not properly just *anything* whatever that a political authority might command. Kramer writes, "As the set of conditions that obtain whenever any legal system exists and operates, the rule of law is per se a morally neutral state of affairs."[43] However, he goes on, "It therefore lacks any intrinsic moral standing. All the same, when the rule of law is operative within a benign regime, its moral value goes beyond lending itself to worthy uses."[44] This is not the same as Fuller's notion of the internal morality of the law though it need not conflict with it, as can be seen in what Kramer says about the way values are reflected in the law. Rather a lot that is normatively significant is included in the relevant notion of benign regime.

> Instead of merely being instrumentally valuable, it furthermore becomes expressive of the very ideals which it helps to foster. Its basic features take on the moral estimableness of those ideals, for the sustainment of the rule of law in such circumstances is a deliberate manifestation of a society's adherence to liberal-democratic values.[45]

There are moral features of the rule of law in an overall sense having to do with procedural, formal aspects of law because norms for a human institution need to be such that they do not make irrational, impossible demands. More than just logical consistency is required. It would not be logically inconsistent for a norm to require anyone whose surname begins with a vowel to be an indentured servant to someone whose surname begins with a consonant. That would be an offense against the rationality required of norms but not on grounds of a purely formal, logical defect. What possible rational basis could there be for such a norm? If the freedom and equality of persons is to be supportable as a core commitment of liberal democracy a norm such as the one suggested cannot be acceptable. It is inconsistent with the commitment to freedom and equality—both equality before the law and equality in other senses—even if not self-contradictory. There are strong reasons in favor of regarding certain values and principles as fundamental to a legitimate rule of law; and we find those as elements of broadly liberal-democratic (and social democratic) political orders.

Similarly, the *promulgation* of norms is necessary. There is a kind of pragmatic inconsistency if not formal inconsistency in norms not being made public. In that case people are expected to fulfill the norms but they are not informed about what they are. Not being promulgated results in a failure of moral intelligibility. It is one of the ways to fail to respect persons as rational. And so on with regard to Fuller's eight conditions. As Kramer notes, the satisfaction of such conditions "is a morally cherishable expression of commitments to the dignity and equality of individuals."[46]

In Kramer's view a set of rules fulfilling Fuller's conditions will be morally intelligible—i.e., the rules will not offend against the rationality of the people whose behavior they are to govern—but that on its own does not mean that the rules are themselves morally substantive. As Kramer observes, "Especially in any sizable society, the rule of law is indispensable for the preservation of public order and the coordination of people's activities and the securing of individuals' liberties; but it is likewise indispensable for a government's effective perpetration of large-scale projects of evil over lengthy periods."[47] Even tyrannical, repressive regimes claim legality for their practices. That is generally one of the more cynical and perverse features of such regimes. However, as we noted above, "when the rule of law is operative within a benign regime, its moral value goes beyond lending itself to worthy uses."[48] The sorts of requirements articulated by Fuller are responsive to the rationality of persons and when the rules meeting the requirements are connected with ends and values integral to liberal democracy then the rule of law—as we saw Kramer put it—"becomes expressive of the very ideals which it helps to foster."[49]

For example, we noted that promulgation is necessary so that people can know what is prohibited, what is required, and what is permitted. That is a requirement of the ability of a rational agent to plan and anticipate. "When a regime does not promulgate a legal mandate, it withholds those crucial opportunities. [Those are opportunities to know what one's options are.] Hence, even if the unascertainable mandate itself is fair, the regime has shown disrespect for the people whom it governs."[50] Also, as Kramer notes, "Intrinsic to the Rule of Law is that every person will normally be able to act in such a way that he can avoid any violations of the law."[51] He wrote:

> To mark the distinction between the jurisprudential conception of the rule of law and the moral-political conception, I shall henceforth use upper-case letters to designate the phenomenon encapsulated by the later conception: "the Rule of Law." Although the rule of law is of course fully consistent with the Rule of Law and is indeed a vital prerequisite of it, the latter goes beyond the former.[52]

Kramer distinguished the conception which "belongs to the domain of legal philosophy rather than to the domain of political philosophy"[53] and the "Rule of Law," which is a "moral-political conception."[54] (He indicates the difference by the use of lower-case letters in the one and upper-case letters in the other. Except for when I quote Kramer I will not be following his convention regarding upper-case and lower-case forms of the expression.) "The rule of law, as the realization of the necessary and sufficient conditions for the existence of a legal system, is itself morally neutral."[55] There are not any actual, institutionally realized legal systems that are *only* legal systems and accordingly they lack moral-political significance. We can recognize Kramer's distinction for certain analytic purposes but any actual system of law we would regard as supportable will inevitably have moral-political features, even if one tries to explicate it in terms of legal positivism. In particular, concerning freedom and equality, and also valuatively significant procedural elements will be aspects of a supportable rule of law. We should comment briefly on those.

As Jeremy Waldron points out, mainly formal conditions of the rule of law run the risk of overlooking procedural elements of it. Waldron emphasizes the importance of procedural elements and the ways in which argumentation and proceedings of certain kinds are crucial to the rule of law. Think of the ways that court proceedings are centrally important to the rule of law. He includes such features as

A. a hearing by an impartial tribunal that is required to act on the basis of evidence and argument presented formally before it in relation to legal norms that govern the imposition of penalty, stigma, loss, etc.;
B. a legally-trained judicial officer, whose independence of other agencies of government is assured;
C. a right to representation by counsel and to the time and opportunity required to prepare a case;
D. a right to be present at all critical stages of the proceeding;
E. a right to confront witnesses against the detainee;
F. a right to an assurance that the evidence presented by the government has been gathered in a properly supervised way.[56]

If people are to be free and equal in ways that are meaningfully reflected in practice and in what legal and juridical authorities can actually do and can require, conditions such as those indicated by Waldron seem to be required. That suggests that these procedural considerations are an important link between formal and morally substantive aspects of the rule of law. Whether or not these can be derived from the formal features of the rule of law in a liberal-democratic political order or whether they follow logically from propositions about the fundamental values of such an order is not an issue we will pursue here. It is important to observe that they can be integrated unproblematically with the formal and substantive elements of such an order and they have a clearly discernible important role.

If the significance of procedural considerations was not explicitly recognized by Fuller it certainly comports with his view inasmuch as he noted that his conditions are crucial to respecting the dignity of intelligent agents; it is only for such agents that there could be such a thing as a rule of law. That is one fundamentally important feature of the normativity of the rule of law and political order. Intelligent agents are not mere things; they act for reasons; and they can think and decide on the basis of normative considerations, and having that capacity is a basis for respect owed to them. And Waldron writes: "I think what Fuller said about the connection between his formal principles and dignity can be said even more about the connection between procedure and dignity."[57] Moreover, as Waldron notes, the dignity concern is not an integral part of a positivist conception of law, and that suggests an important defect. "A fallacy of modern positivism" Waldron writes, "is its exclusive emphasis on the command-and-control aspect of law."[58] The rule of law, according to Waldron, is not just a matter of acting regularly in conformity with rules; it involves "highly proceduralized institutions in which procedural rights and duties of all sorts are oriented to allowing the application of determinate rules to be established fairly and minutely with ample opportunity for contestation."[59] "Courts, hearings, and arguments—those aspects of law are not optional extras; they are integral parts of how law works, and they are indispensable to the package of law's respect for human agency."[60] Procedural rules specify what "moves" are permissible within the space of reasons mapped by legality in a politically legitimate order.

Whether a nation has a written constitution as in the U.S. or, like the U.K., does without one, it is clear that the common law tradition regards procedural considerations as crucial. They are essential to the protection of rights and liberties. There is additional confirmation of this in studies of persons' attitudes toward political/legal institutions and practices. There is strong evidence of the importance people attach to fair procedures in regard to perceptions of the legitimacy of the political/legal order. Trust is especially important in regard to police and policing in a liberal democracy. Tyler notes that the effectiveness of legal authorities "depends ultimately on their ability to secure voluntary public compliance with their directives."[61] The rule of law and the enforcement of law need to be regarded as serving the public interest and protecting individuals, not as forms of coercive imposition on people's freedoms. That is one important reason why "issues of legitimacy need to be explored from the public's perspective."[62] Of course theorizing about legitimacy, the rule of law, and how they are related is crucial, as well, but as a practical matter the public's attitudes are especially important.

The emphasis on dignity suggests a substantive element of the rule of law in addition to whatever formal and procedural elements it may include. Corey Brettschneider argues that dignity is indeed a substantive value and he favors an "expanded conception, which adds nonarbitrary treatment to dignity," and he claims that, "the moral basis of the rule of law should be respect for dignity."[63] He adds that, "the procedure-independent value of dignity might require additional limits on procedures. I call these limits the substantive guarantees of the rule of law."[64] Much can depend on what we build into the notion of dignity. Even if we do not regard dignity as the primary moral basis of law, it certainly is to be included among a small number of bases. Dignity has a good claim to being a normatively indispensable feature of the rule of law.

The views summarized thus far are not clearly rivals; in important respects they overlap and each can be seen to be articulating something that is important to the others. What is at the root of all of these conceptions is that the rule of law is law suitable for rational, intelligent agents who are free and equal, and are to be respected as such. That fact is crucial to what we regard as a possibly valid rule of law, and its significance resonates through notions such as dignity, equal standing, the importance of persons being informed, the publicity of the laws, being formally arraigned, non-arbitrariness, and limits on state powers. Establishing a legitimate rule of law of the type discussed clearly is not just a matter of certain rules, requirements, and procedures being put in place. It depends considerably on the political culture of the society. (This is connected with the issue of trust, mentioned above.) As Martin Krygier points out, "[o]n their own, the legal institutional features so often identified with the rule of law are not up to the task"[65] of effectively actualizing the rule of law. If the members of a society lack generally stable dispositions to respect the relevant procedures and institutions, and dispositions to regard them as fundamentally important to leading the kinds of lives they wish to be able to lead, just promulgating certain rules and establishing certain institutions (such as courts) might fall well short of achieving justice.

If people are not accustomed to regarding mutual respect, rights, judicial independence, and acceptance of judicial proceedings as vitally important there simply will not be the rule of law even if there is a written constitution and specific items in it defining and authorizing powers, practices, and procedures. That is almost certainly part of why the development of the liberal-democratic rule of law, where we find it firmly established, took centuries. There is abundant historical evidence (much of it quite recent) that it is extremely difficult for a society to construct the institutions and cultivate the attitudes for a liberal-democratic rule of law if there are no roots of such things in their own experience and aspiration. Negotiating the relevant space of reasons and regarding the normative architecture of such an order as both desirable and feasible need to be learned. Where there has been no such learning, it is unlikely in the extreme that such an order can be imported.

History also provides plenty of evidence that elements of the liberal-democratic state can be undone with alarming rapidity if there is not a stable mooring in the dispositions of citizens. In the political cultures of many parts of the world we do not find a steady, resolute aspiration to realize the broadly liberal-democratic rule of law. (There have been two periods in just the last one hundred years during which several European nations seemed to establish liberal-democratic political orders and then, within a couple of decades, more or less sell it out to corruption, various forms of expanded and authoritarian state power, and reversion to illiberal forms of ethno-nationalism. Or, in cases such as the Baltic states and some eastern European states some nations are victims of the brutal strategizing of powerful, ruthless neighbors.) The accounts of the collapse of numerous nascent liberal democracies are complicated and involve many particular historical circumstances. However, it would be a serious error to assume that liberal democracy is surely what nations across the world would strive for if the conditions for it could be created. There is plausibly genuine, durable liberal-democratic political order in a minority of the world's nations.

The main concern here is to characterize the rule of law as (i) essentially normative, at least if it is to be understood in the context of a broadly liberal state, and to emphasize the fact that (ii) its being normative is integrally connected with it comprising rules for rational agents. The rule of law maps an important aspect of the space of reasons for rational agents, an aspect that is essential to those agents participating (even if only by membership) in a political order.

Also, our discussion of the rule of law is compatible with several different views about the relation between law and morality. Whether the law should enforce morality and to what extent remains a question open to diverse answers even if there is firm agreement on the conditions above. Yet, the rule of law should meet certain broadly moral conditions just insofar as the laws are *laws for rational agents*, and are meant to protect the rights and liberties of those agents. Laws in a liberal democracy are not only generalizations about what happens or predictions of what will happen; they are also rules for governing the exercise of agency by persons, by rational agents.

For example, though Hart was a positivist he wanted to distinguish his view from Austin's positivism and its focus on command and compliance. According to Hart, Austin's view oversimplified (in some problematic ways) both law and compliance. Hart distinguished between habitual behavior and rule-following, a distinction that was important to his critique of Austin's legal positivism. Something done on a quite regular basis might be an example of a habitual behavior while in other behaviors the agent is engaging in them on a regular basis but doing so in a more *explicitly* rule-governed way. In discussing Hart's view Mark Tebbit writes:

> activities, however, such as attending religious ceremonies on a certain day or at a certain hour, or selling flags for charity on another day, in addition to having an observable external aspect, also have an internal dimension. With such activities, they are not just habits, the participants are adopting or accepting it as a rule that they should do such things. In other words, they are internalising the rule, making it a rule for their own behavior. This involves the crucial feature of the acceptance of the rule, and it is accompanied by a "critical reflective attitude" towards ones' own activity.[66]

In theorizing about law and the character of legality the notion of rule-following has been especially prominent. In this context the rules are (generally) specifiable, and a finite, adequate formulation can be produced. In addition to specifications articulated in statutes in a common law system the rules can develop and change on the basis of legal rulings. The ruling is a way for a specific determination of a rule to be achieved. With regard to a great deal of criminal law obeying the law is not mainly a matter of following highly specific rules but rather, *not* engaging in certain kinds of acts because of their wrongfulness. Internalizing a prohibition can leave a very wide open field for permissible conduct.

Hart and Fuller had a long-running debate over the extent to which moral considerations are integral to legality, Fuller arguing that there is an "internal morality of the law" essential to it, and Hart arguing that, while there is a "minimum content of natural law" that is really just a way of describing law's responsiveness to important features of the general condition of human beings. (Altruism is finite; resources are finite; anyone can be vulnerable and lack perfect security; and so forth). These are not so different from the conditions that Hume mentioned as providing the need for rules of justice in his discussion in the *Enquiry Concerning the Principles of Morals*. Hart was reluctant to regard the responsiveness of law to those conditions as a matter of substantive moral content in the law. In that respect, his view is reminiscent of Hume's characterization of the conditions that motivate a concern for justice. If benevolence or resources were infinite, what need would there be—Hume argued—for rules of justice and rules governing the ownership and transfer of property? If there is desperate, unrelieved scarcity and no prospect of adequate distributive shares, what efficacy could rules of justice have? Everyone would be primarily concerned with their own survival, Hume argued. Despite their differences rule-following is centrally important in each of their views. We can argue whether Hume is drawing the only conclusion that can be drawn but the main point was to observe the similarity between Hume's empiricism and Hart's Legal Positivism. They both recognize the normative significance of various factual considerations, and the significance of those normative considerations. (I leave aside the question of whether the Humean-Hartian claims about the predicament of human beings are essential to a sound conception of the rule of law.)

Hart regarded Austin's view as having a too-thin notion of habitual obedience or compliance, one that does not distinguish between mere regularity of behavior and internalization of a rule. Hart's example of a driver slowing to a stop at a red traffic light is meant to indicate that difference. The red light is not just an antecedent sign that the driver will stop; it is a signal understood by the driver who has internalized the rule that one is to stop at a red light (for a reason). In some contexts it could make sense to say that the red light *caused* the driver to stop. (Suppose someone does not know that there is now a traffic light at that intersection. That person might ask, "I thought he was in a great hurry. What caused him to stop at the intersection of Pitt and North streets?" But even that would actually mean, "Why did he stop?" asking for a reason, not a cause.) The light is not literally the cause of stopping but the occasion for it for a person who understands the rules governing the operation of motor vehicles. Hart's distinction between primary and secondary rules is crucial to his account and his is a form of positivism in which more than command, coercive power, and a habit of obedience are involved in law. As Fuller says, "Hart is bent on rescuing the concept of law from its identification with coercive power."[67]

That attempt at rescue has something important to do with the law being recognized as a set of norms by those to whom the law applies. Hart is reluctant to commit to the extent that Fuller commits to an "internal morality of the law" but Hart, too, appreciates that the fact that laws are rules for rational beings has very significant implications regarding what kinds of rules are to be acknowledged as laws. As mentioned above, Fuller's claims concerning "the inner morality of law" are not supposed to guarantee that the law should be an enforcement of morality. Rather, they are meant to show that there are fundamental respects in which law needs to be morally intelligible and those respects are not consistent with a strictly positivist view of law.

In Fuller's view

> legal morality can be said to be neutral over a wide range of ethical issues. It cannot be neutral in its view of man himself. to embark on the enterprise of subjecting human conduct to the governance of rules involves of necessity a commitment to the view that man is, or can become, a responsible agent, capable of understanding and following rules, and answerable for his defaults.[68]

It is doubtful that Hart would find much that is objectionable in that claim though he is reluctant to concede the degree of moral inflection Fuller insists on. Fuller makes more of the rational requirements on the possible internalization of rules that is necessary for law but Hart's positivism is to be distinguished from Austin's in large measure on account of the role of internalization of rules in Hart's view. The debate between Hart and Fuller highlights the crucial role of norms in the civil existence of human beings. Whatever causal explanations are also relevant to understanding that existence (and there are many such causal considerations) they are not fully exhaustive. There is a core of rational normativity that cannot be reductively analyzed away. Just the fact that human beings are rational agents already implies a central role for norms, given that human beings conduct a great deal of their activity on the basis of understanding rules constitutive of those various types of activity.

There is the thin, Austinian positivist version, highlighting command and compliance; there is Hart's richer positivism, one that is responsive to some key facts about human beings such as the fact that benevolence is finite, as is the power of any person's will, and the fact that despite differences in strength it is possible for just about any person to overmatch another person, given ingenuity and circumstances. Fuller argued that there is more to a system of law and its legitimacy than being in accord with whatever a Hartian rule of recognition regards as valid. Fuller says, "What I have tried to do is to discern and articulate the natural laws of a particular kind of human undertaking, which I have described as 'the enterprise of subjecting human conduct to the governance of rules.'"[69] Regarding Hart's view he wrote, "A legal system, he asserts, is not 'the gunman situation writ large.' But if the rule of recognition means that anything called law by the accredited lawgiver counts as law, then the plight of the citizen is in some ways worse than that of the gunman's victim."[70] And, "Hart's own distinction between the 'gunman situation' and a legal system…contains no suggestion of any element of tacit reciprocity. Instead, the distinction runs entirely in formal or structural terms."[71] Fuller argues that Hart's rule of recognition does not involve a basis for persons subject to the rule of law in question to regard that rule of recognition as actually, effectively conferring validity on the laws.

Fuller emphasized what he took to be the essential role of various attitudes and durable dispositions of reciprocity between lawgiver and those subject to the law. "There is no doubt that a legal system derives its ultimate support from a sense of its being 'right.' However, this sense, deriving as it does from tacit expectations and acceptances, simply cannot be expressed in such terms as obligations and capacities."[72] At least with the gunman there is generally the understanding that if I give him my wallet or my money he will not kill me. With regard to the rule of recognition, given the extent to which Hart wants to exclude substantive (broadly moral) considerations from his view, the rule of recognition, as one critic has put it, actually amounts to little more than, "treat the general orders of the boss and no-one else as authoritative."[73]

Earlier we took note of Duff's claims about the respects in which the legitimate rule of law for a liberal polity needs to be common law. Duff wrote: "The law does not address the citizens in the voice of a separate sovereign who exercises power or authority over them. It speaks in their own voice, in the language of their own values."[74] "The voice of the law is (or aspires to be) the voice of the community addressing itself, the voice of all the citizens addressing one another and themselves."[75] He also notes that in its classical formulation (Coke, Hale, Blackstone) "the idea of the 'common' law transcended the distinction between statutory and nonstatutory law."[76]

These debates involving Austin, Hart, Fuller, Duff, and many others concerning law and the rule of law are debates about the character of the distinctive normativity appropriate to legality. Even if we settle on a thin, command-and-comply understanding of legality that is still a position occupied in the space of reasons. However detailed and illuminating the causal stories of how this or that system of law came to be, and how it "works," as a system of law it concerns normative considerations and the ways those are understood to have authority. That cannot be reductively analyzed away, displaced entirely by causal patterns and dispositions. The conception and identity of what is being referred to in speaking of the rule of law depends on the grasp of normative considerations.

The rule of law is an issue of the first importance with regard to any political order. It is quite clear that for a liberal democracy (and also a social democracy or any constitutional democracy) the rule of law is crucially important to the legitimacy of political authority and to citizens' sense of political obligation. The rule of law includes fundamental elements of the political order through its identification of fundamental institutions and offices and their powers, their relations to each other, and whatever recourse persons have when they believe their rights have been violated. In addition, basic elements of criminal proceedings—all the way from apprehension and arrest to imposition of sanction, or parole or probation reflect values and norms that are aspects of the rule of law. The form that civil society takes can be strongly influenced by the character of the rule of law because of how the rule of law shapes people's activities, interactions, and modes of association.

In a liberal democracy the state has coercive power but individuals' rights and liberties are not concessions that the state grants. Rather, one fundamental role and justification of the state is that it protects people's rights and liberties according to explicit procedures and in ways that are defined as involving definite limitations. Normativity shapes the political sphere through the pervasiveness of considerations of justification and legitimacy. Whether this is explained by a hypothetical social contract, the tradition of common law, or an actual, historical constitutional moment as in the U.S. when its Constitution was ratified, it is the normative significance of legitimacy that is being explained. Nineteenth-century legal positivism sought to explain legality without invoking considerations of natural law, moral theory, or any sources of authority or justification external to a factual state of affairs including command and compliance. Positivists excluded prescriptive considerations but later thinkers, such as Hart, who wanted to preserve positivism also saw the need to revise it. Hart's approach for quite modest morally substantive commitments included distinguishing primary rules and secondary rules. This can be seen as a way to avoid identifying a source of normativity by dividing rules into first- and second-order, and distinguishing them by function rather than by substantively normative grounds. However, even that approach acknowledges the unavoidability of normativity insofar as the distinction performs a normative function.

With this discussion of rules, norms, and laws as background we are in a better position to undertake an examination of the relation between facts and values. This is a large topic and the discussion is not intended to be comprehensive. We do not have to undertake such a study in order to make some key points regarding the issue's place and importance in social scientific investigation and explanation. Chapter 3 focuses on Hume's influence on the way the relation between fact and value is understood. This focus is chosen because of the way Hume's thought is widely held to be a crucial source for the most familiar positivist understanding of the relation between fact and value, namely, that a prescriptive conclusion (an *ought*) can never be inferred from descriptive (fact-stating, what *is*) premises.

Hume did not regard his critique of moral rationalism as undermining either the genuineness or authority of moral considerations or as rendering empirical study of them less than scientific. For one thing, Hume was, after all, an important moral theorist in his own right, and it would be odd for him to have developed the view of morality we find in his works if he believed that his critique of rationalism left moral judgment nothing to be except person-relative expressions of feeling. He offered an account of moral value and moral judgment that was apt for elaboration in empirical terms after sweeping away what he took to be the chief errors of moral rationalism. Hume is widely regarded as having "shown" that claims about what one *ought* to do cannot be derived from claims about what *is* the case, and that part of his view is often interpreted as a basis for excluding moral matters from empirical social science. Examining his view and its later influence will be helpful background for going directly into the relation between facts and values, the project of Chapters 4 and 5.

Notes

1 Anthony Bottoms and Justice Tankebe, "Procedural Justice, Legitimacy, and Social Contexts," in *Procedural Justice and Relational Theory*, eds. Denise Meyerson and Catriona Mackenzie, Therese MacDermott, Abingdon, pp. 85–105, 91–92.
2 Antony Duff, *Punishment, Communication, and Community*, New York: Oxford University Press, 2001. p. 65.
3 Ibid., p. 59.
4 Ibid., p. 60.
5 Ibid., p. 61.
6 Ibid., p. 65.
7 Ibid., p. 59.
8 Andrew von Hirsch, *Censure & Sanction*, New York: Oxford University Press, 1996, p. 105.
9 Antony Duff, "Responsibility, Citizenship, and Criminal Law," in *Philosophical Foundations of Criminal Law*, eds. R. A. Duff and Stuart P. Green, Oxford: Oxford University Press, 2011, pp. 125–150, p. 138.
10 Ibid., p. 139.
11 Mark Tebbit, *Philosophy of Law: An Introduction*, Abingdon: Routledge, 2017, pp. 21–22.
12 Stephen Macedo, "Rule of Law, Justice, and the Politics of Moderation," in *The Rule of Law NOMOS XXXVI*, ed. Ian Shapiro, New York: New York University Press, 1994, pp. 148–177, p. 161.
13 Ibid., p. 161.
14 Ibid., p. 151.
15 David Bazelon, quoting himself from his dissenting decision in n. 32 United States v Dougherty, 473 F.2d 113, 1142 D.C.Cir. 1972. The passage is in David Bazelon, "The

Morality of the Criminal Law," *Southern California Law Review* 49: 1975–76, pp. 385-405, p. 397.

16 Bazelon, "The Morality of the Criminal Law," p. 387.

17 William C. Heffernan, "Social Justice/Criminal Justice," in *From Social Justice to Criminal Justice*, eds. William C. Heffernan and John Kleinig, New York: Oxford University Press, 2000, pp. 47–83, p. 74.

18 Ibid., p. 74.

19 Ibid., p. 70.

20 Macedo, "The Rule of Law, Justice, and the Politics of Moderation,", p. 154.

21 Ibid.

22 Ibid., p. 155.

23 Jeffrie G. Murphy, "Legal Moralism and Liberalism," *Arizona Law Review* 37: 1995, pp. 93–94.

24 James Fitzjames Stephen, *Liberty, Equality, Fraternity*, Cambridge: Cambridge University Press, 1976, p. 35.

25 Ibid.

26 A. V. Dicey, *Introduction to the Study of the Law of the Constitution*, Indianapolis: Liberty Fund Edition, 1982, p. 111.

27 Ibid., p. 114.

28 Ibid., p. 116.

29 Ibid., p. 117.

30 Ibid., pp. 118–119.

31 Martin Krygier, "Four Puzzles About the Law," in *Getting to the Rule of Law: NOMOS* L, ed. James E. Fleming, New York: New York University Press, 2011, pp. 64–106, p. 66.

32 Antje du Bois-Pedain, "Punishment as an Inclusionary Practice," in *Criminal Law and the Authority of the State*, eds. Antje du Bois-Pedain, Magnus Uluang, and Petter Asp, London: Hart Publishing, 2017, pp. 199–228, p. 220.

33 Ibid., p. 220.

34 Nicola Lacey, *State Punishment*, Padstow, Cornwall: Routledge, 1988, p. 171.

35 Ibid., p. 179.

36 During the first couple of years of the Second World War Hitler gave numerous enormous gifts of money and large estates to various generals, in addition to the promotions he gave them, as this was a way of both rewarding them and securing their support. "Hitler never completely trusted the army, and saw such promotions as a means of binding senior officers to his will even if they disapproved of Nazi ideology." Richard J. Evans, *The Third Reich at War*, New York: Penguin, 2009, see especially pp. 494–495. This was an example of arbitrariness in the extreme, and without regard to public interest.

37 Lon Fuller, *The Morality of Law*, New Haven: Yale University Press, 1964, p. 96.

38 Ibid., p. 97.

39 Matthew H. Kramer, *Objectivity and the Rule of Law*, New York: Cambridge University Press, 2007, p. 111

40 Ibid., 111.

41 Ibid., p. 112.

42 Fuller, *The Morality of Law*, p. 97

43 Kramer, *Objectivity and the Rule of Law*, p. 102.

44 Ibid.

45 Ibid.

46 Ibid.

47 Ibid.

48 Ibid.

49 Ibid.

50 Ibid., p. 151.

51 Ibid., p. 159.
52 Ibid., p. 143.
53 Ibid.
54 Ibid.
55 Ibid., p. 143.
56 Jeremy Waldron, "The Rule of Law and the Importance of Procedure," New York University School of Law Public Law & Legal Theory Research Paper Series Working Paper No. 10-73. Posted: October 8, 2010 Last revised: November 4, 2010.
57 Jeremy Waldron, "The Rule of Law and the Importance of Procedure," in *Getting to the Rule of Law*, *NOMOS* L, ed. James E. Fleming, New York: New York University Press, 1991, pp. 3–31, p. 15.
58 Ibid., p. 22.
59 Ibid. p. 17.
60 Ibid., p. 23.
61 Tom R. Tyler, *Why People Obey the Law*, Princeton: Princeton University Press, 2006, p. 71.
62 Ibid.
63 Corey Brettschneider, "A Substantive Conception of the Rule of Law: Nonarbitrary Treatment and the Limits of Procedure," in *Getting to the Rule of Law*, ed. James E. Fleming, New York: New York University Press, 1991, pp. 52–63, p. 53.
64 Ibid., p. 55.
65 Krygier, "Four Puzzles About the Law."
66 Tebbit, *Philosophy of Law*, p. 38.
67 Fuller, *The Morality of Law*, p. 177.
68 Ibid., p. 162
69 Ibid., p. 96.
70 Ibid., p. 139.
71 Ibid.
72 Ibid., p. 138.
73 F. Schauer, *The Force of Law*, Cambridge, MA, and London: Harvard University Press, 2015, p. 160, p. 44 in Tebbit.
74 Duff, *Punishment, Communication, and Community*, p. 59.
75 Ibid., p. 60.
76 Ibid., p. 59.

Chapter 3

Hume's Moral Philosophy and His Contested Legacy

3.1 Some of the Philosophical Contours of the Issues

The discussion so far has focused on some of the chief features of the civil context as a context shaped by reasons and norm-governed activity of many kinds. Also, we have considered some of the values and principles relevant to understanding the rule of law in a liberal democracy. Our discussion provides a way of answering a skeptic who says, "I've never seen a norm. Where would one have to go to see something so exotic? People might have various beliefs about norms but social scientists do not encounter norms as such among the phenomena they study." We can point out that just by virtue of participating in a coherent conversation, one in which words are being used in appropriate, meaningful ways one's behavior is governed by norms. They are hardly exotic, if part of what "exotic" means is that the thing is rarely encountered and is radically unlike anything with which we are familiar in our experience. It is true that one does not encounter a norm in just the same way as one encounters a desk or a sandwich, but linguistic competence, the ability to describe things coherently, following someone's reasoning, and recognizing behavior as an instance of some specific type all involve grasping norms.

Are there good grounds for adhering to the positivist division between facts and values or can values be "at home" in empirical criminology? The discussion of normativity is helpful as background to that issue. Also, Hume is a crucial figure regarding the issue and we will discuss his view at some length. One of the conclusions we will reach is that even if there are respects in which objective values are problematic those respects do not diminish the significance of norm-governance, and neither do they diminish the significance of moral values. There are ways of understanding Hume that leave moral values intact, so to speak, and approachable by empirical methods, even if the values are not to be regarded as items in the objective order of things.

This might come as a surprise to those defending a fact/value distinction. They are likely to deny that a moral claim actually expresses a judgment at all, an assertion of what is the case, and instead, moral judgments are to be interpreted in expressivist, non-cognitive terms. Hume is widely regarded as

DOI: 10.4324/9781003037323-4

a key thinker concerning these issues, for the way he developed an empiricist account of knowledge, one that distinguished between matters of fact on the one hand, and valuative responses and feelings on the other. We will look carefully at Hume's view to try to be as clear as possible about what he took himself to have shown.

A widely held positivist insistence on a fact/value distinction is anchored in the view that moral terms have only emotive meaning and no cognitive meaning. For the use of a moral term there is no basis in the facts that *shows* in some demonstrable way whether the term has been used correctly or incorrectly. There is just a difference in attitude. Thus, the norms governing moral discourse are expressive norms. If someone insists that Pol Pot was one of humanity's great benefactors—and the person seems to know what those words mean—and this person is unmoved by facts about Pol Pot's murderous cruelty and central role in causing a vast amount of human suffering, and so forth, we can only hope that this person somehow undergoes a change of heart. If positivist-based emotivism is a correct account of moral value then neither of us is making a moral judgment of Pol Pot that is either sound or unsound, and based on any factual considerations.

The positivist reading of Hume is widely thought of as having driven values out of the empirical study of human activity and the social world except in a thin, emotivist sense. Actually, Hume was a moralist, and had important, substantive views about moral value and moral judgment in ways that he elaborated empirically. He is an important figure regarding substantive moral theory in the tradition of British Moralists despite his skepticism regarding moral rationalism and objective values. It is not as though he thought there was no empirical study of valuative issues. His claim in the *Treatise* that "ought" statements are not derivable (or have never been *shown* to be derivable) from "is" statements does not imply that morality is off-limits for empirical investigation or even that factual considerations have no important role in moral judgment.

Regarding ethics, A.J. Ayer, an influential twentieth century positivist philosopher, wrote: "What we are interested in is the possibility of reducing the whole sphere of ethical terms to non-ethical terms. We are enquiring whether statements of ethical value can be translated into statements of empirical fact."[1] This is a nice, clear articulation of what I have referred to as the semantic focus of logical positivism and its implications for ethics. He goes on to argue that ethical concepts are unanalyzable; they *cannot* be translated into statements of empirical fact. However, in his view, this is because "they are mere pseudo-concepts. The presence of an ethical symbol in a proposition adds nothing to its factual content."[2] According to Ayer, in making ethical statements we are "merely expressing certain moral sentiments."[3] These sentiments *matter* to us, and we also care that others should agree with us and are moved by our moral responses and attitudes. Emotivists argue that (i) there are no objective values and moral claims are not cognitive claims, and (ii) even if there were objective values they would be idle in the respect that something being the case cannot, in its own right, have any prescriptive significance. Moral judgments are meant to be action-guiding, not fact-stating, and moral facts or objective values would have no action-guiding prescriptivity. Thus, both in regard to ontology and in regard to motivation, there is no case for objective values.

Positivists claim that no realist conception of moral values can supply a plausible account of the expressive function of moral judgments and the ways in which they influence, and are intended to influence, action. Positivists need not deny that moral values matter a great deal to people. They deny that moral judgments *refer to objective considerations or have cognitive content*. That might seem to undermine the ways in which they matter but positivists are satisfied for mattering to be a purely expressive, non-cognitive phenomenon.

What about evaluative judgments regarding artifacts for which there are specific functions? Are evaluations of those also without a factual basis? If someone's refrigerator needs repair frequently and it cools poorly and is expensive to operate, is it semantically, rationally open to that person to still insist that it is—in its current condition—a *good* refrigerator? No, actually it isn't. Suppose the owner is using the refrigerator as a way to block the draft from a broken window, and suppose it does that job pretty well. The refrigerator is not operating well as a refrigerator but it is being put to use in another way, and it is succeeding in that other way. Still, it is not a good refrigerator. Nor is it a good "window closer." With artifacts there are purposes, proper uses of them; they are *for* something. In that sense there are fact-based judgments of whether they are good or poor examples of whatever type of artifact they are. A positivist could agree that there are conventions governing the evaluation of many artifacts but those conventions are expressive rather than cognitive. The evaluations depend on what human beings' interests and aims happen to be. It is not as though there are some artifacts that are part of the inventory of the world apart from human interests and aims and for which there are objective bases of evaluation.

Thus, a defender of the fact/value distinction could say that with artifacts there are factual bases for evaluating them because we define what they are for. There are evaluative conventions. The only sense in which values are involved is in terms of persons' desires or intentions regarding the artifacts. However, a human being is not *for* anything and cannot be conventionally defined as having a specific end convincingly. Even if persons have intentions and they design strategies for living, and organize their ends and interests in ways meant to enable the fullest realization of those ends and interests there still is not something a human being is *for*. Perhaps in specific roles and responsibilities there are some fact-based evaluative grounds. We can say what is involved in being a good librarian and how that differs from being a good operating room nurse, and from being a good pastry chef, or composer, and so forth.

Even in those cases the bases of evaluation are all conventional. That is what makes them possible.

What about being a good parent or a good citizen? Those might seem to be examples of fact-based valuation. However, the valuation of a citizen will have something to do with the political community or the political order that is presupposed. (Aristotle addressed the question of the relation between the good citizen and the good man.) Even being a good parent could be said to depend on culturally relative factors. The defender of a fact/value distinction could allow that there are a great many context-dependent factual bases of valuation in the sense that this or that group accepts such-and-such norms regarding prescription and evaluation, but the defender denies that the norms are fact-based if "fact-based" means that the valuative judgments are implied or semantically necessitated by factual considerations. The defender of the fact/value distinction can recognize that there are contexts in which numerous valuative judgments are regarded as normative, as reflecting stable, widely accepted conventions. But they are only conventions and they are not truth-evaluable, not correct or mistaken in an objective sense.

Of course, it is possible to use artifacts for purposes other than their conventionally defined purposes. One can use a wooden-handled hammer as a piece of firewood if one is desperate to keep a fire going; one can use (an upturned) sturdy trashcan as a chair if it is needed for that purpose. Even though human beings can perform many functions that nothing else can perform there is no human function in the sense of a final, intrinsic end according to the expressivist view. But the claim that there are objective values or objective moral considerations does not, in its own right, imply or presuppose that there is an intrinsic human function or *telos*. One could be a moral realist independent of such claims.

Someone can be a good (or bad) librarian, or bus driver, or astronaut, or calligrapher or landscape architect on the basis of conventional norms and it can be argued that being a good father is also a matter of conventional norms. If someone is the biological father of twenty-seven children that does not make him a good father or even good at *fathering* unless all we mean by fathering is "contributing as a male to human offspring." What about being a first-cousin? With respect to being a first-cousin there does not seem to be a way to plausibly spell out a function or responsibility even in strictly conventional terms. First-cousin is a relation, not a role. However, in a particular culture there could be specific norms concerning that relation. In aristocratic and royal family trees it can be a quite important "position." Suppose someone argues, "being a good father involves taking responsibility for raising a child, showing the child loving attention, providing care and guidance, seeing that the child's needs are met, that the child is protected, and that the child develops as an alert, healthy individual." Those (or criteria similar in many respects) might seem to be objective, non-conventional bases for judging someone a good father. Now we are edging our way onto moral territory.

Even if there is no distinctive human function or end it could make sense to insist that criteria relevant to fathering are not *wholly* conventional or stipulated. We can formulate a conception of a flourishing childhood and develop a conception of fathering (or parenting) suitable to it.

However, it could be argued that despite the stability and generality of many (cultures') conceptions of fathering, still the criteria really are not fully objective. Even if there is wide agreement on key features of a well-lived human life and the role of the male parent in such a life the agreement is just that; it is a matter of contingent convention rather than criteria with objective status, and the agreement is a matter of likeness in attitude rather than cognition of facts. Or, so a defender of a fact/value distinction might argue. Part of what might be involved in the arguments concerning this issue is whether there are objective criteria for good fathering that are distinct from those for good parenting. Perhaps there are objective considerations regarding the latter (or at least disjunctive sets of such considerations) but it does not matter whether the conditions are fulfilled by fathers rather than mothers.

What about the explicitly moral context? It might be said that the valuation of honesty, compassion, trustworthiness, and justice as virtues reflects a pro-attitude but not a cognitive judgment. Evaluating dishonesty, cruelty, and callous inconsiderateness as vices reflects a negative attitude; it is disapproval but not a cognitive judgment. Someone might "use" a baby as a doorstop, and we would find that appalling but the positivist would insist that our objection is not based on cognitively grasping that treating a baby as a tool is morally wrong while the other person (incredibly) thinks it is just fine to do so. Even if it's not hurting the baby and because the baby is not yet mobile, the arrangement "works" pretty well, we still think it is terrible. It is a very strongly endorsed convention that babies are not to be treated merely as physical objects or instruments. It reflects a widely shared, durable attitude but that expressive meaning is all the meaning it has in regard to values. Or, so one view of the matter would have it.

3.2 Some Relevant Metaethics

Since the nineteen fifties and sixties there have been multiple waves of critique of emotivism and prescriptivism (versions of expressivism), ranging from Philippa Foot's essays in *Virtues and Vices* and Iris Murdoch's *The Sovereignty of Good*, to a significant retrieval of virtue-centered ethics encouraged by influential works by G.E.M. Anscombe, Peter Geach, Rosalind Husthouse, and Alisdair MacIntyre, and the articulation of various forms of realist metaethics by John McDowell, Nicholas Sturgeon, David Brink, and others such as David Wiggins who developed a number of lines of argument against non-cognitivism.[4] The work in virtue-centered ethics restored topics in moral psychology to the agenda of many moral philosophers. Also analyses of agency, character, moral sentiments, and topics such as resentment, friendship, respect, weakness of the will, forgiveness, courage, and others were more widely pursued. Numerous thinkers returned to Kant's moral philosophy and that has developed into a powerful influence in contemporary moral philosophy and political philosophy. To be sure, there have been significant defenses of antirealist metaethics, powerful claims on behalf of skepticism regarding moral realism, critiques of virtue-centered ethics, and plenty of critics of Kantian moral theory. Moreover, there are sophisticated versions of contemporary expressivism (though they are sophisticated in ways that have depended to some extent on non-positivist developments).

The way that Hume's moral philosophy is understood is a good example of this. Hume's philosophy has been interpreted in some different ways and some of the contemporary interpretations emphasize different features of it than those that positivism highlighted. Hume remains a powerful critic of moral rationalism and moral realism but the appreciation of him involves a good deal more than highlighting his insight concerning the alleged mysterious character of deriving an *ought* from what *is*. One overall upshot of these developments is that it is clear that the alleged fact/value distinction merits reconsideration.

We will devote some space to discussion of moral naturalism on account of how influential it has been in recent decades and because of how it is related to Hume's view. For realists and antirealists alike there has been a striking resurgence of interest in naturalism as a position regarding epistemology, moral value, aspects of philosophy of language and philosophy of mind, and other issues. In the first few decades of the twentieth century the critique of ethical naturalism was among the most prominent issues of metaethics. At the time, realist intuitionists and positivist emotivists—who agreed on almost nothing else—were sharply critical of naturalism, each view claiming that there cannot be an analysis (or definition or reduction) of moral terms in non-moral, naturalistic terms. The prevailing notions of naturalism that were thought to be the chief targets at that time—classical Utilitarianism and some versions of Social Darwinism—might seem to us to be less than the best that naturalism can present in making the case for naturalistic ethics. Indeed, several more philosophically defensible versions of ethical naturalism have been developed. In any case, G.E. Moore's formulation of the "naturalistic fallacy" set in motion several decades of significant metaethical argumentation and theorizing even if few philosophers followed Moore in defending the view of moral value he developed.

During the last fifty years several versions of naturalism have been developed and defended. They exhibit a striking range and variety. At one end of the spectrum there is scientistic naturalism and, at the other, there are interpretations of the later Wittgenstein's thought as a form of naturalism. By "scientistic naturalism" I mean the view that the facts disclosed and described by physical science are all the facts that there are. They 'tell' the entire "story" of what there is, what it is like, what we know, and so forth. This seems an implausible view inasmuch as it needs to somehow provide an account of propositional and other attitudes that human beings have (e.g., believing that_____; hoping that______; fearing that_____; and so forth) along with all of psychology and conscious experience—and mathematics. This is not the place to undertake an evaluation of the view though it is important as holding down one end of a spectrum of versions of naturalism. A very different conception of naturalism highlights the importance of practices, social interaction, and "forms of life" as understood in Wittgenstein's later thought. Wittgenstein's insights and formulations of issues seemed to break free of the confining formulations of many philosophical issues. This refocusing of attention did not employ the apparatus of various familiar dichotomies, such as mind and body, primary and secondary qualities, analytic and synthetic, idea and object, and others in familiar ways. The way in which Wittgenstein redirected attention to actual practices, responses, and finding meaning without separating thought and behavior, or locating understanding in a specific idea or mental state, and so forth seemed to many philosophers a basically anti-metaphysical, naturalistic project. Wittgenstein's urging that we look carefully at actual practices, at the ways that human beings respond to the various uses of language, and how discourse is connected with what we actually do seemed to be both non-metaphysical and non-scientistic. It gave impetus to the "ordinary language" movement in philosophy and a transition away from earlier conceptions of philosophical analysis and semantics.

There are any number of versions of naturalism between the scientistic and the Wittgensteinian. As Barry Stroud pointed out in his American Philosophical Association Presidential Address,

> When we look at this most recent enthusiasm for what its proponents call "naturalism, " I think we find that, whatever they are excited and optimistic about, it is not naturalism as such. With two exceptions that I will mention in a moment, I think there is nothing in naturalism alone that is sufficiently substantive to be philosophically controversial. What is usually at issue is not whether to be "naturalistic" or not, but rather what is and what is not to be included in one's conception of "nature." That is the real question, and that is what leads to deep disagreements. And as far as I can see, those disagreements are not themselves to be settled by what can be recognized as straight-forwardly "naturalistic" means.[5]

Naturalism had become so attractive to so many philosophers that it seemed as though just about any position that did not involve a role for God or for immaterial substances could claim to be naturalistic. There are several views that clearly do merit the name and the way in which some elements of Hume's philosophy are interpreted as naturalistic seems quite plausible, as we will see.

There are very diverse interpretations of Wittgenstein's thought, ranging from a sort of behaviorism at one end to a form of linguistic idealism at the other. (Both ends seem to me overstated and mistaken.) In fact, there are respects in which Wittgenstein's later thought has been found congenial both to realist and to antirealist metaethics and to forms of naturalism suitable to each of those views. For the antirealist, Wittgenstein's anti-Platonism and anti-rationalism fit with a non-scientistic naturalism. For the realist, Wittgenstein's later philosophy can help explicate a non-relativist conception of judgment and virtue without Platonist and rationalist commitments.

As we noted in Chapter 1, some of the most important aspects of the debate in metaethics in recent decades can be diagnosed as a dispute between a basically Aristotelian position and a basically Humean one, in respect of the overall philosophical anthropology and metaethics shaping the positions. On both sides, the influence of Wittgenstein is evident. Insights and arguments from Aristotle play an important role in some of the most able defenses of the role of virtue in moral judgment and moral psychology. And Hume has had a powerful influence on some recent forms of antirealist moral judgment. It took a few decades of criticism of expressivist ethics for those views to develop.

In the middle decades of the twentieth century, positivism's ethical view developed beyond the emotivism presented by Ayer. The prescriptivism that was formulated recognized that universalization is an important mark of ethical judgment, and there is a role for reason at least in the sense that if a person judges one action to be a good action, then it is incumbent on that person to also judge a qualitatively exactly similar action (in similar circumstances) as good. That is a requirement of consistency and it is a crucial acknowledgment of a role for rationality in valuative judgment. Otherwise, we pretty much have abandoned coherence. The requirement for consistency is not limited to the moral context. Any valuative judgment needs to meet that standard. R.M. Hare made the point about rational consistency in valuative judgment as follows:

> Suppose that either P is a replica of Q or Q of P, and we do not know which, but do know that both were painted by the same artist at about the same time. Now there is one thing that we cannot say; we cannot say "P is exactly like Q in all respects save this one, that P is a good picture and Q not." If we were to say this, we should invite the comment, "But how can one be good and the other not, if they are exactly alike? There must be some further difference between them to make one good and the other not."[6]

Consistency requires similar responses to similar situations, even though there is no objective value entailed by, identical with, or constituted by naturalistic facts and properties in Hare's view. Consistency is a basic norm of rationality. There is a coherent general structure to moral judgments even though the judgments express responses or stances rather than reporting the cognitive detection of value. Rationality cannot be a source of knowledge of good (or whatever value is in question); there is nothing to know. Yet, it is a requirement concerning the formal character of evaluative judgments.

This might strike us as having a kind of Kantian resonance, and to some extent it does have that. Hare's view can be seen as responsive to Kant's argument that morally valid maxims of action must be universalizable; it must be possible for any rational agent to endorse the maxim. Kant's concern regarding the moral validity of maxims was not, "What if everyone did it…i.e., acted thusly?" but "Could any (and every) rational agent recognize the validity of the maxim?" The only way for the answer to be affirmative is if the maxim satisfies an *a priori* test of rational universalization, a test that is independent of what individuals happen to feel or desire. Those latter considerations are subjective in a person-relative way and cannot provide a basis for a practical requirement that is universal and necessary. According to Kant, universality and necessity are the features that constitute moral objectivity. He argued that the "common rational knowledge" (an expression occurring numerous times in *The Foundations of The Metaphysics of Morals*) of morality recognizes that moral requirements involve a distinctive and categorically imperative character. Any rational agent can be aware of the difference between inclination and obligation as sources of motivation, and any agent can see that moral obligation must be independent of inclination. In Kant's view, for a maxim to be morally valid it must be universally endorsable on a rational basis. Hare's own moral views were more utilitarian than Kantian. Hare did not believe that rationality on its own indicated what is morally required but his metaethics included the requirement of rational consistency. In that recognition prescriptivism acknowledged a formal role for reason in ethical judgment though as an expressivist view it, like its emotivist predecessors, denied that there is any substantive rational knowledge of value.

Someone who denies that there are objective values could be just as firmly committed to values as anyone else. To endorse a fact/value distinction does not imply that the person has no moral commitments. Positivists can be morally committed in morally admirable ways, and it is part of their view that moral judgments have practical, action-guiding significance. Nonetheless, to put the matter bluntly, according to emotivism and prescriptivism disputes concerning moral matters are not to be resolved by substantive reasoning. Whatever sorts of considerations might have influence, their influence is not a matter of cognitive content. Hume's distinction between facts and values rested, in large part, on his recognition that moral judgments are *practical*, and he wondered how a belief, a cognitive state could be action-motivating. He was not advocating a form of nihilism or amoralism. Nihilism and amoralism are something else altogether. Expressivism does *not* commit one to claiming that moral judgments are of no significance or import though it explains them without reference to moral facts.

Suppose we say to the person who used the baby as a doorstop: "That is incredibly inappropriate and wrong. It shows an utter lack of proper regard for a human being, especially one that is not yet able to decide and act independently. It indicates a grotesque failure to acknowledge the line between *things* and *human beings*." And suppose the person then says, "All right; I get it. That really was a stupid and inappropriate thing to do. Now that you've reacted so strongly I can accept that it was wrong of me to do that." The change is not a matter of the person now having a true moral belief or having an improved moral understanding. There is no moral cognition and in that respect, there are no moral beliefs (which can be true or false). It is just a change in attitude.

Factual beliefs can have a causal role in changing a moral attitude, but there is no rationally specifiable relation of *meriting* the change. In this way we can imagine a positivist-minded investigator doing an in-depth study of the moral values and conduct of members of a particular society without considering at all whether those views and the conduct are worthy of praise or condemnation. The investigator might have his or her own views about that, but also believe that it is crucial to maintain a studied neutrality in order to conduct an objective study of moral values. Is that the sort of objectivity that makes for a scientific comprehension of the values of that society?

We can distinguish a couple of issues here. One of them is whether a positivist conception of morality is best suited to understand another community or group's moral beliefs and practices. The other issue is whether in striving to be objective the investigator should make no moral judgments of the behavior, commitments, institutions, and practices of the people studied.

It is not at all clear that a positivist view of morality is well suited to understand another group's moral beliefs and practices. In fact, it could involve a systematic distortion of them. This is because it will analytically decompose moral judgments in ways that might depart, possibly quite radically, from what the people studied mean when they make moral judgments. Understanding a group's morality might involve formulating explanations that depart from how the persons studied to see their own beliefs and practices. It is plausible to think that having a grasp of their conceptions and terms of evaluation is also an essential part of understanding them even if it happens that much of what they believe is false or is best interpreted as a projection of values. A scientific methodology might involve showing that there are significant explanatory factors that are not part of the self-understanding of the people studied or that their morality includes false or confused beliefs. But presupposing a fact/value distinction could be a way of systematically misrepresenting people's beliefs and commitments because it precludes appreciating any rationally substantive norms that might inform the beliefs and practices of the persons studied.

It is not clear that an utterly neutral account is the only sort that has explanatory merit. It could be that the morality being studied includes unjustified and deeply troubling (morally perverse) elements. Imagine studying the moral views of Ante Pavelic and the Ustashe movement in Croatia before and during the Second World War. That ideology was a form of ethno-religious fascism like Nazism in many respects. Even if certain views and commitments differed from those of Nazism many of its policies were almost indistinguishable, especially in regard to anti-Semitism, and the brutal treatment of various other minorities. (In fact, the Croats' brutality even troubled the SS to some extent but mainly on account of lapses of discipline and not for moral reasons.) There could be various social scientific, explanatory purposes served by a strictly descriptive view of the ideology and behavior. But it would seem that what is most important to understand is how vicious and murderous views and policies come to be widely endorsed. What is it that is more important in the study of such movements and their behavior? Understanding it requires exercising at least some moral thought. Strictly descriptive understanding, a record of what the people were for, and what they were against, amounting to little more than a list of pro- and con-attitudes, would not be sufficient as an illuminating explication of their behavior.

There are many possible corrupting and distorting factors. I am not suggesting that a morally sound and illuminating account is easily achieved. But neither is it something altogether external to the social scientific project. James Laidlaw writes:

> Of central significance is what, following Bernard Williams...I shall refer to as "the ethnographic stance," the anthropologist's aim of gaining an imaginative understanding from the inside of a set of ethical concepts and of a form of life, and to learn to use and think with those concepts and participate in the form of life, without, as a pre-requisite for doing so, having to adopt its concepts and values as his or her own.[7]

Pursuing Williams's point Laidlaw emphasizes that what is needed is to integrate the successful ways in which "some philosophers have been quite good at capturing the way in which ethical concepts cannot exist other than as woven into a way of life"[8] with "the fact of ethical diversity."[9] This is to see the explanatory project as having an important role for ethical thought. In fact without ethical thought being involved it is difficult to see how an understanding of the morality of those being studied can be achieved. The study of morality involves

> *taking seriously* the forms of life we describe: regarding them—and therefore describing them—as something we learn from as well as about; and it involves learning to think with as well about its concepts, such that they become resources in our own critical reflection and self-constitution.[10]

The primary challenge is not, "How can we ensure that no ethical thought of our own is involved in the study of the society's morality?" but "What concepts enable us to understand and explicate the morality and the people we are studying?" and certainly some of our own ethical concepts could have a significant role, even if they are revised along the way because of what we find. This is not to say that numerous explanatory considerations—many of which might not be in the awareness of the people studied—do not also have a critically important role. Extensive reference to historical factors, social and economic factors, and religious considerations might be essential in explaining aspects of the beliefs and ideals. However, moral beliefs and ideals are not external to the agents whose values they are, coming to be their values as a result of processes in which endorsement and rationally aware commitment have no role.

Granted, voluntariness in this context is not a matter of choosing from among a number of clearly distinct alternatives at a particular moment of choice. Even in pluralistic societies though there are people who change their valuative commitments most people do not undertake a systematic, focused review of their moral commitments with a view to arriving at a careful decision of what to endorse. Instead, in many cases values are developed as second nature through the ways people are encouraged, rewarded, and praised and how they are criticized, blamed, and punished. That is compatible with the beliefs and ideals being voluntary in that voluntariness does not require altogether unconditioned, fully explicit choice, as though selecting from a menu of options. One is still negotiating the space of reasons through voluntary undertakings even if a great deal of what one does is done by second nature or by habit without critical reflection. Being rational does not mean (and certainly does not require) that persons exercise their critical capacities and capacities for inquiry and assessment with a high degree of rigor all of the time. While thinking critically and having an alert, inquiring disposition are vitally important aspects of rationality, the exercise of rationality does not require each of us to pursue an adequate proof or justification for everything we accept.

In addition, voluntariness does not require some form of contra-causal, unconditioned agency. Voluntariness involves the capacity for reflection on one's aims and motives for action-relevant judgment, the ability to critically consider and revise reasons for acting and for the point and significance of possible courses of action. Whether, and to what extent, persons exercise those capacities can be an important aspect of their moral life. But a great deal of voluntary activity is a matter of persons being self-moving—uncoerced, unconstrained—but not also studiously self-examining. The fact that as young persons, we are guided largely by others does not render our behavior involuntary; it is an aspect of how our voluntariness is habituated. Some people are guided and habituated to be self-determining to a high degree while many are not, and some remain impulsive and careless in ways that are both imprudent and pose a risk to others. But those persons, too, are acting voluntarily unless there are specific reasons to conclude otherwise. Everyone is influenced by whatever circumstances they are in; and everyone is influenced by the actions and attitudes of others, persons we did not choose to have in our lives. And some people are much more fortunate than others. But misfortune as such is not a form of compulsion. In addition, in many contexts even just being compliant involves voluntariness; the compliance is generally not coerced even if there are incentives for it and disincentives for non-compliance. States of character, temperament, and natural propensity can all figure in the way a person acts, and those are not ways in which voluntariness is diminished; they are factors influencing how it is exercised.

A child reaching for a cookie is acting voluntarily even if it is not the same as the voluntariness of the parent who is considering whether to send the child to an afternoon playgroup a few days each week. The latter involves deliberation and choice in ways that are not yet abilities of an infant or toddler. Voluntariness is not simply "on" or "off;" it needs to be developed and it can become more fully guided by reasons and consideration. A thirty-year-old who has a somewhat volatile temper, acts imprudently, and seems to give little careful thought to consequences should not—for those reasons—be considered less voluntary or less responsible than someone who has virtues that contrast with those vices. In most cases the vices are not afflictions, unavoidable interferences with voluntariness. The actions of a person with moral vices might be less thoughtful, considered, and deliberate than those of a person with virtues; but that hardly diminishes responsibility. Indeed, the person is responsible for acting *like that*, in ways that exhibit the vices mentioned.

A great deal of habitual activity is norm-governed. In many cases this is a matter of agents knowing what is expected or required and not needing to think it through explicitly. In some cases it is a matter of having learned how to do some specific form of activity, such as riding a bike or how to knead the dough for a particular type of bread. Once learned, the person can do these things by "second nature," but can also give reasons for various aspects of what is being done, if asked to do so, even if ordinarily the person is not explicitly thinking about how it is done. On the other hand, one's conduct in a committee meeting might be governed by multiple sets of norms, by rules of order, by-laws, and more specific norms for specific issues being addressed. In that case, one might be very aware of the relevant norms and the reasons for behaving in certain ways. Overall, habit and normativity are found together throughout human activity.

We have argued that normativity is pervasive in the human world, if for no other reason than the fact that thinking and using words meaningfully in ways that are consistent involve normativity. Also, we make valuative judgments regarding artifacts; that is a context involving normativity. We evaluate natural phenomena in some ways also. We refer to that "healthy, century-old oak tree" and we might observe that, "the older female elephants at the zoo seem more energetic and alert and just more happy overall since the previously sick one—and now healed—has been returned to the group " and so forth. Natural entities can be evaluated in numerous ways, and we might insist that even though plants and non-human animals do not *make* normative judgments, normative judgments apply to them *on factual bases*. Whether a tree is healthy or not is not only a matter of some convention we adopt; it is also a matter of biology. And none of us knows quite what it is like to be an elephant but we can tell—at least to some extent—from behavioral and physiological indicators whether an elephant is healthier than before the treatment it underwent and how the other elephants respond to being reunited with it.

We often use terms anthropomorphically, as when we say that "that whale was so angry that it attacked the boat" or "adult male penguins are amazingly resolute and selflessly devoted when tending eggs for weeks and weeks amid blizzards and plummeting temperatures" or "meerkats will accept an expelled member of the family if that member makes a proper show of submission to the individual in charge." Those all include terms that do not apply literally, mainly on account of the fact that those creatures cannot understand their own behavior through anything like the conceptualization articulated by the linguistic formulations of the examples. We actually have little accurate idea of what the whale was "thinking." Did it mean to drive the boat away, or was it aware of the difference between people and boat; was it protecting other whales, or was it sending a warning…or what? We try to make the behavior intelligible by describing it in a specific way even if we really do not understand the situation from the whale's perspective. That is an entirely different form of life and it does not share the "space of reasons" with us. As Wittgenstein observed, "If a lion could speak, we could not understand him."[11]

Perhaps an exponent of the fact/value distinction will argue that we are in an analogous situation with respect to moral values. The positivist might argue that we organize moral experience, and make various types of conduct morally coherent by talking about it *as though*, among the things in the world, there are moral values, and human beings respond to them in various ways. But there are no such values. We use language purportedly referring to moral values but the latter do not exist to be grasped any more than meerkats have a grasp of submission or loyalty or forgiveness or community solidarity conceptualized in a way that is intelligible to us without analogy, simile, or metaphor. The structure of moral discourse is such that it could "support" moral values if there were some; but there aren't any except in the sense of non-cognitive attitudes.

Thus the non-cognitivist view might be that it *seems* to us as if moral judgments make assertions, but they actually have only expressive meaning. However, as Cassaniti and Hickman remark in "New Directions in the Anthropology of Morality," "moral judgments are widely (and perhaps universally) experienced as cognitive judgment and not solely as aesthetic and emotive judgments" and "moral judgments are also experienced as aesthetic and emotive judgments and not solely as cognitive judgments."[12] In moral life and moral experience it certainly does often seem that we are making substantive claims and not merely expressing attitudes. They refer to "humanity's propensity toward moral realism" and that is an important part of the case they make for a form of pluralistic realism.[13] Whether or not one reflectively endorses the realism, they are making an important point about the phenomenology of moral life and experience.

Even J.L. Mackie, who presented a powerful case against objective moral values on ontological, epistemic, and motivational grounds recognized that the phenomenology of first-order moralizing with which we are all familiar seems to point to objectivity and a realist interpretation of moral value. He did not think that the most powerful case against moral realism was the primarily semantic/conceptual case (the version of analysis as indicated earlier in the quotation from Ayer) that was a key feature of positivism. Almost fifty years ago in *Ethics: Inventing Right and Wrong* Mackie argued that the common sense view of the world, the view we have prior to systematic scientific investigation and philosophical reflection presupposes that there are objective moral values but that view is mistaken, it is false. However, he argued that the question of whether there are objective moral values cannot be settled by a project of philosophical *analysis*, which is the strategy positivists had undertaken. It is, he thought, an ontological question, a question of what kinds of entities there are. Mackie held that though the phenomenology of moralizing makes it seem that there are objective values in fact this first-order phenomenology is mistaken. Mackie argued that we cannot conclude that there are no objective values just by considering concepts or criteria of meaning, analogously to the way we can know that an object cannot both be a triangle and a square, or cannot be both entirely red and entirely black just by considering the relevant concepts.

The realist/antirealist disputes concerning moral value go on unabated. While there is a sense in which the core issues are what they have always been, and the main positions are variants of positions that have been taken in many periods of the history of philosophy the debate is not pointless, nor does it fail to "get anywhere." In each generation there are developments regarding philosophy of language, epistemology, metaphysics, and the relations between philosophical theorizing and empirical sciences. Indeed, the present book is centrally concerned with the last-mentioned relations. The various developments bring with them helpful illumination and they involve novel insights. Moreover, some of the directions in which criminology (and the anthropology of morality) is developing are directly relevant to philosophical concerns regarding morality. We will say more about this and illustrate these claims in later chapters.

3.3 Hume's Naturalistic Morality

In the course of defending what he takes to be a basically Humean projectivist account of moral value Simon Blackburn also has claimed that from the first-order perspective, from the perspective of being an engaged participant in morality, it seems to us that moral values are real. Moral discourse has the form and force of assertoric practice though the account of morality does not require objective values. In saying, "Causing people needless suffering just for one's own pleasure is wrong" we take ourselves to be talking about the wrongness of that sort of pleasure-taking, rather than talking about our attitudes. Blackburn argues that *of course* we take the world and things in it to be the objects of our moral attitudes and judgments. The objects of our attitudes and feelings are the objects of concern. Our direct interest is not just the psychological states that have them as objects. It is true that we make moral judgments because of the sensibility we have; affect underlies ethical judgment. Yet, in making moral judgments we are judging acts, situations, and people's characteristics; we are not talking about our feelings. Blackburn puts it this way:

> From the inside, the objects of our passions are their immediate objects: it is the death, the loved one, the sunset, that matters to us. It is not our own state of satisfaction or pleasure. Must projectivism struggle with this fact, or disown it? Is it that we projectivists, at the crucial moment when we are about to save the child, throw ourselves on the grenade, walk out in the snow, will think, "Oh, it's only me and my desires or other conative pressures—forget it"?[14]

He is right about that; no one, except in a very contrived and affected frame of mind, abhors cruelty *and* at the same time, thinks "but not really, because after all, it is not *really* wrong." We do not accompany our moral judgments, not even *sotto voce*, with antirealist disclaimers.

Blackburn takes his view to be basically Humean. We do take the world to include moral values (at the first-order level) but reflection shows that sensibility projects responses and attitudes, and it is really affective responsiveness that is the basis of values. However—and this is crucial to his view and his reading of Hume—when, upon reflection, we make that acknowledgment we do not conclude that values are mere feelings, or that morality is illusory or subjective in a person-relative way. Rather, the view is that projective values are *all that moral values need to be in order to be genuine*. We don't come to a point where we conclude that values are not real; we reflectively discover that the reality they need is projective. As Blackburn says, "It is because of our responses that we say that cruelty is wrong, but it is not because of them that it is so."[15] "What makes cruelty abhorrent is not that it offends us, but all those hideous things that make it do so." His view is that "there is only one proper way to take the question 'On what does the wrongness of cruelty depend?': as a moral question, with an answer in which no mention of our actual responses properly figures."[16] When we make moral judgments we are not making judgments about our feelings; we are saying, for example, that *cruelty* is wrong, and we certainly do not mean to convey that the wrongness of cruelty is not genuine, that it is just a matter of feelings.

That is a way of blocking the unhelpful reply that asks, "What if someone has a different sensibility? That person will have different feelings. Doesn't that mean that values are subjective in a person-relative way?" It does not mean that at all, and even Hume was explicit about the way that moral judgments involve a universal perspective. To regard a judgment as a moral judgment involves *not* taking it as merely person-relative. More than two hundred and fifty years ago Hume, speaking of the moral agent, wrote: "He must here therefore depart from his private and particular situation, and must choose a point of view common to him with others; he must move some universal principle of the human frame, and touch a string to which all mankind have an accord, and symphony."[17] Universality—because of how it can reflect impartiality—is a crucial aspect of a moral judgment. Hume regarded humankind as the group to which moral judgments apply. And he was clear in claiming that when we make moral judgments we are not just disclosing a personal attitudinal response. What sort of significance could moral judgments have if that was all they amount to?

Part of Blackburn's reply to the claim of group-relativity and by implication, person-relativity of values was to make the point that, "if everyone comes to think of it as permissible to maltreat animals, this does nothing at all to make it permissible: it just means that everybody has deteriorated."[18] While there is no question of looking at the wrongness of cruelty from a standpoint outside of ethics and trying to ascertain from there what facts make it wrong there is no question of moral judgments being relative to the feelings or attitudes of individuals or being interpreted in relativist terms. (This is one of the places where the influence of Wittgenstein can be detected. The language game of morality we might say does not depend on some *other* language game for its authenticity.) An important connection that this kind of view has with our earlier discussion of norms is that the view asserts that moral discourse reflects concerns and involves topics that can be characterized as constituting a recognizable and important mode of activity in our lives. We just saw that Blackburn wrote, "there is only one proper way to take the question 'On what does the wrongness of cruelty depend?': as a moral question, with an answer in which no mention of our actual responses properly figures." He is pointing to the fact that moral experience and participation in moral life are fully integral aspects of our lives, and they involve reason-giving, reflective criticism, and judgments from a point of view that is not merely personal. We engage in moral *thought*, and we can consider our moral views, what is in favor of them, and what follows from them. Given that Blackburn defends projectivism, it is significant that he denies that it is our actual responses that are determinative of judgment. There is moral thinking to do, and moral judgment is not simply a matter of what my affect or attitude happens to be on *this* occasion of judgment. There is a role for moral reasoning, elaboration, refinement of view, and attention and insight.

As we have indicated the metaethics that McDowell defends differs in important respects from Blackburn's. Nonetheless, there are some fundamental points on which they are largely in agreement. For example, compare the passage above quoting Blackburn to this from McDowell:

> No doubt the self-scrutiny of an ethical outlook can take note of independent facts about the layout of the realm of law, when they are relevant. But that is not to say that we can reconstruct the idea of genuine ethical demands on us from materials that are naturalistic in that sense. The idea of getting things right in one's ethical thinking has a certain autonomy; we need not conceive it as pointing outside the sphere of ethical thinking itself.[19]

The agreement, even across a metaethical divide, that ethical thought is to be treated as having standing, as it were, in its own right, and it is not to be understood as dependent upon or somehow subordinate to some other form of thought is significant. (Again, a Wittgensteinian resonance.) In part, it is a way of acknowledging that ethical thought is within the space of reasons, governed by norms concerning reasonableness, and it is not merely reactive, merely an expression of affect best explained in strictly causal terms even when interpreted projectively. While McDowell was not speaking about Hume's moral theory in the quoted passage it is clear that the critique of rationalism so important to Hume was not meant to render moral judgment thoughtless, spontaneous attitudinizing.

Blackburn's understanding of Hume avoids the most serious defects of some of the more familiar ways of reading Hume and Hume's significance with regard to the fact/value distinction. Blackburn's reading of Hume is projectivist but it is also naturalistic in a way that we do not find among the positivists. Understanding Hume in more naturalistic terms rather than narrowly positivist terms seems closer to Hume's own view and also yields a much more plausible view in its own right.

Hume would have regarded the notion of person-relative values ("everybody has their own values") as entirely implausible and without explanatory merit. What could be the point, the significance of moral judgments if they are nothing more than person-relative exclamations with no supporting considerations others could recognize or criticize? There would be no reason for anyone to regard them as anything more than noise coming out of people's faces or simple, baseless preferences.

Hume also wrote

> When [one] bestows on any man the epithets of vicious or odious or deprave he the speak another language [than that of self-love] and expresses sentiments in which he expects all his audience are to concur with him...If he mean therefore to express that this man possesses

> qualities whose tendency is pernicious to society, he has chosen this common point of view, and has touched the principle of humanity in which every man in some degree concurs.[20]

He almost certainly overstated the universality of moral judgments when he wrote:

> Would you know the sentiments, inclinations, and course of life of the Greeks and Romans? Study well the temper and actions of the French and English: You cannot be much mistaken in transferring to the former *most* of the observations which you have made with regard to the latter. Mankind are so much the same, in all times and places, that history informs us of nothing new or strange in this particular. Its chief use is only to discover the constant and universal principles of human nature, by showing men in all varieties of circumstances and situations, and furnishing us with materials from which we may form our observations and become acquainted with the regular springs of human action and behaviour.[21]

Still, the passage makes an important point in Hume's moral philosophy. Hume regarded morality as consisting of judgments made on the basis of propensities that are human, that are shared by people universally.

He wrote:

> But the sentiments, which arise from humanity, are not only the same in all human creatures, and produce the same approbation or censure; but they also comprehend all human creatures; nor is there any one whose conduct or character is not, by their means, an object to every one of censure or approbation.[22]

It is an antirealist but also anti-relativist view. As we pursue discussion of the fact/value distinction I will argue that, in some important respects, the wrong lessons have been taken from Hume's famous articulation of the mystery alleged in deriving an "ought" from what "is."

In addition to the emphasis on universality Hume also acknowledged a role for matters of fact in moral judgment. He held that "in order to establish laws for the regulation of property, we must be acquainted with the nature and situation of man; must reject appearances, which may be false, though specious; and must search for those rules, which are, on the whole, most *useful* and *beneficial*."[23] As he put it in the *Enquiry Concerning the Principles of Morals*, "every quality of mind, which is *useful* or *agreeable* to the *person himself* or to *others*, communicates a pleasure to the spectator, engages his esteem, and is admitted under the honourable denomination of virtue or merit."[24] Those positive responses have a key role, but they are responses to matters of fact. Factual considerations need to be taken into account. There aren't moral facts but there are facts relevant to moral judgments.

Also, in Hume's view there is scope for moral reasoning and moral argument. It is an important part of his view that the distinctions that seem important to moral judgments—distinctions between sound and unsound judgments, superficial vs subtle moral discrimination, vulgar judgment vs discerning judgment, defensible vs indefensible judgment—all of those are genuine. That is part of what I meant above in saying that the Humean asserts that moral considerations have all the authority and genuineness we typically regard them as having. Humean morality is not morality-lite, or a simulacrum of genuine morality. It is all that morality needs to be, including criticism and revision of moral views.

Hume wrote, "Those who have denied the reality of moral distinctions, may be ranked among the disingenuous disputants; nor is it conceivable, that any human creature could ever seriously believe, that all characters and actions were alike entitled to the affection and regard of everyone."[25] If I had judged someone a selfish coward because he left the scene of an accident but I then learn that he had made sure the injured person would survive and then went to find a physician he knows not far from the scene of the accident—the only doctor within ten miles—my moral judgment changes on the basis of my new factual beliefs. Hume did not argue that the facts themselves have moral significance, "in their own right," as it were; but a moral judgment is coherent, relevant, and appropriate on a basis of the facts. He wrote:

> But though reason, when fully assisted and improved, be sufficient to instruct us in the pernicious or useful tendency of qualities and actions; it is not alone sufficient to produce any moral blame or approbation...It is requisite a *sentiment* should here display itself, in order to give a preference to the useful above the pernicious tendencies...Here therefore *reason* instructs us in the several tendencies of actions, and humanity makes a distinction in favor of those which are useful and beneficial.[26]

Something other than cognition is needed for prescriptivity and for a person being effectively motivated to act. But that does not mean that there is no role for facts in moral judgment. In Hume's view someone who finds it morally acceptable to degrade and humiliate others is not just someone with values different from our own; that is someone with wrong, indefensible values. Such a person provides an example of morally wrong judgment and of cruelty or depravity, not an example of moral diversity. Hume's metaethics is not intended to hollow out morality or disclose respects in which moral judgment is less than what it seems to us at the level of first-order participation in moral life.

A realist will of course have significant objections to the view and to the claim that Hume's account encompasses all that is needed for moral values to have the authority we take them to have. It might seem that a realist view of moral value requires, as Blackburn puts it, an "external reading." In that case, as Blackburn says, there would be "a fact, a state of affairs (the wrongness of cruelty) whose rise and fall and dependency on others could be charted. But antirealism acknowledges no such state of affairs, and no such issue of dependency."[27] According to the antirealist (well, *some* antirealists) there is no question of looking at the wrongness of cruelty from a standpoint outside of ethics and trying to ascertain from there what facts make it wrong. However, realism can agree with that. A realist can hold that the objectivity of moral considerations depends on (supervenes) non-moral facts and properties, but is still something real in its own right, and that within ethical thought itself we can find the appropriate sort of objectivity. According to numerous realist views the objectivity of moral considerations is no worse off and no less genuine than the objectivity of other types of considerations. Objectivity has to do with how claims are justified and there are compelling considerations for a great many ethical judgments.

Though Hume asserted that reason is and can only be the "slave of the passions" he did not mean that in the sense that factual considerations cannot have any impact on how we value things. Often, when Hume is discussing *the rational* he means it in the rationalist sense, in a sense that concerns rational *demonstration*, logical derivation from premises that are known with certainty. He is quite severe regarding the ways rationalist claims—in his view—are overstated and overconfident. But not every employment of facts is a matter of rational *demonstration*. He did allow that facts can make a difference to valuative judgments in the way suggested above. Coming into possession of some new facts can alter one's valuative judgment of a situation or an action. There is no rational demonstration of what ends human beings should pursue or what is the best kind of life for human beings. But that does not imply that there is no role for facts concerning what is useful and agreeable. How could such judgments be made without facts supporting them? If we think moral judgments should be demonstrable the way theorems in geometry are, we have a mistaken view of morality. And a realist can concur on that point.

We might compare Hume's view to Weber's insofar as the latter held that our commitment to one or another "ultimate value" is arbitrary. There are numerous different "value spheres" (religion, familial, political, economic, scientific, aesthetic, and erotic) and those spheres can be in tension with each other without there being a rational basis for resolving such tensions. Weber held that values can have a causal role in regard to human conduct and that understanding values in that role requires hermeneutic methods. However, interpretivist methods can still respect a fact/value distinction in that our explanations of social phenomena are to be value-neutral. Values can shape various aspects of human conduct and they can have an impact on what issues we decide to investigate and try to explain. But values are ultimately subjective and relative. They are not even underwritten by the sort of non-relativist considerations that Hume points to as supporting the phenomenology of moral life. Weber's interpretivist view is worth mentioning here for the sake of indicating that important difference from Hume. Weber is a source for relativist treatments of moral value along with an instrumentalist conception of the role of rationality, one that differs from Hume's reason-as-slave-of-passions on account of the fundamental arbitrariness of values in Weber's view.

It is important to see how and why Hume's rejection of moral rationalism results in a form of subjectivism that is neither relativist nor indifferent to facts. There are versions of antirealism that can agree with realism that the relation between facts and values is not limited to arbitrary or thoughtless affect or person-relative subjectivity. Hume's is one such version. Hume wrote: "The one [reason] discovers objects, as they really stand in nature, without addition or diminution: The other [taste] has a productive faculty, and gilding or staining all natural objects with the colours, borrowed from internal sentiment, raises, in a manner, a new creation."[28] The "new creation" is not illusory or merely in the imagination. Part of what Hume means here is that though aesthetic and moral judgment involve a projective aspect, judgments of taste and moral judgments are not of some lesser status than judgments concerning matters of fact. The new creation is as much a part of the world of experience and action as anything else. Moral life is not "as if" there were real values; our morality is genuine morality. We do not grasp moral values the same way we grasp truths of reason, the truths of arithmetic and geometry, for example. But they are not mere figments, either. This was captured by Blackburn's interpretation but many readers of Hume draw the more radical—and less plausible—conclusion that moral values are subjective in a way that disqualifies them for being considerations in moral *thought* and that so distances them from facts that the latter seem to have no significant relevance to moral value.

Hume wanted moral notions to remain anchored in empirical considerations but that does not take the form of reductive analysis showing that moral significance is actually *nothing-but* something non-moral. There is the "new creation." The fact that he could not see how there could be a valid inference from what *is* the case to what *ought* to be done did not stop him from articulating a moral theory and explanations of how moral judgments are made and what are the elements of moral motivation. He did not conclude,

"Well, that's it; there is no such thing as a supportable claim about what we morally ought to do, or morally ought to prohibit. Not only that, this means that moral judgment and reasoning are untethered from factual considerations about people's characters and their circumstances. Moral judgments are just emotive and not truth-evaluable, and there is no shared basis for ascertaining whether they are correct or incorrect, appropriate or just plain unreasonable, etc."

It is also helpful to keep in mind that Hume, as was the case with others among the British Moralists, regarded sociability as fundamentally important, and in ways that shape the subjectivism of his view. Concern for the welfare of others, interest in how others perceive us, enjoying diverse forms of interaction with others—all of this was fundamentally important to Hume. His moral view was not a form of person-relative subjectivism.

In most moral discourse we are not, as it were, reporting how we feel. We are making points about what we believe is morally unacceptable or morally required, points about what people should and should not do and why. And we take moral evaluation to be quite different from just plain-old preference. It is easy to imagine someone saying, "I just don't know how those kids can enjoy skateboarding down the railings next to flights of steps; it just looks dangerous to me." That remark indicates that the speaker does not share a certain enthusiasm shared by some teens. It would strike us as quite troubling for a person to say, "I just don't know why people think it's wrong to spray lighter fluid on homeless persons' belongings and then light them on fire. Homeless people and their disgusting possessions are worthless and don't deserve any better." How could anyone think that such a view and such conduct are acceptable? Part of what strikes us as evident in this judgment is its universality; when and where would it be all right to humiliate and dispossess persons right there on the street *because* those persons are thought to be worthless? That is not exactly the same as claiming that the objective wrongness of the conduct is evident. We might want to say that as well. However, that raises important and difficult questions about the epistemic status of moral value. But a Humean need not conclude that the rightness or wrongness of that kind of act is a matter of personal sensibility. It is wrong, and any morally decent person agrees.

3.4 Hume and Prescriptivity

Another significant aspect of Hume's view of morality has to do with the motivational efficacy, the practical significance, of moral considerations. He held that a belief or a cognitive state (i.e., taking it to be the case that such-and-such) does not have any motivational efficacy in its own right. We can be moved to act only by affective or appetitive states. Passions and desires can motivate action, and without them, our beliefs would have no practical significance. That is a way of formulating a distinction between facts and values; facts lead to no action unless conjoined with desires or passions. Without the latter, we would have no inkling of prescriptivity. Just as importantly, Hume argued that moral discourse is often meant to *influence action*. Typically, when we say that something is morally wrong we are not only reporting our judgment but we also mean to discourage persons from acting that way. When we note that a state of character, honesty, for example, is admirable, we mean to commend honesty to others. That behavior should be influenced by it is a crucial feature of moral discourse. We are not just indicating what our own evaluative view is.

To Hume, the practical significance, the prescriptivity of moral discourse could not be explained in rationalist or cognitive terms. How is it, he thought, that believing something to be the case could *move* anyone to *do* anything? If someone says, "I'll get something to eat. I am suddenly hungry" it is not just the fact that the person believes he or she is hungry that motivates getting some food. It is *desiring to eat, feeling hunger* that motivates it. Suppose one says, "It's the belief that by eating I will cease to be hungry that motivates me to get some food; thus, I am motivated by a cognitive state and not an appetitive state." It is true that the belief that eating will relieve one's hunger has a role in motivating the action. However, it is still the case (Hume and many others would argue) that what lends that belief motivational efficacy is its relation to the desire to relieve hunger. If someone is about to leave the house and says, "I see it's raining. I'll take an umbrella" what goes unspoken (but is necessary to explain the umbrella-carrying behavior) is that the person *desires* to stay dry or wants someone else to be able to use the umbrella to stay dry. The oft-quoted passage in the *Treatise* concerning the obscurity of the inference of an *ought* from what *is* makes the point about prescriptivity by emphasizing that Hume had never seen the actual inferential structure by which prescriptive conclusions follow from descriptive premises. Hume was *not* showing that there are no fact-involving bases for moral evaluations. He was making a point about the prescriptive powerlessness of matters of fact and beliefs about matters of fact, when considered on their own.

The significance of the way that Hume distinguished factual discourse from prescriptive discourse is sometimes misinterpreted. This could be due, at least in part, to some of the specific commitments of twentieth-century logical positivists and their considerable influence. The passages in the *Treatise* in which Hume points out that he has several times noted that authors pass from claims about what is the case to claims about what ought to be the case or how one ought to act, without explaining how that inference is valid, constitute a *locus classicus* for many defenders of the fact/value distinction. It is often referred to as though it is obviously compelling and no additional argument or analysis is needed to make the case that the facts cannot be the basis for valuative judgments. Regarding an important rationalist sense Hume was clear in arguing that they cannot be such a basis. But that is not the only possible role for facts. Hume himself observed their relevance to moral judgments.

In addition, as we indicated above, it was important to Hume (and to other British Moralists, such as Smith, Butler, and later Mill) to understand human beings as *social* beings, and as beings to whom relations to others and how people see and regard each other are especially important. It is helpful to appreciate the larger intellectual context of the British Moralists. It saves them from the narrowness of later philosophical preoccupations. Hume and Adam Smith, for example, both regarded sensibility and sociability as crucially important to human beings' lives and to morality. And Hume's critique of the role of reason was focused especially on some rationalist theses regarding the claims of reason. If those are not the only terms through which the action-relevant role and efficacy of reason can be interpreted Hume's critique might leave various other theses intact. (For instance, there is the broadly Aristotelian conception of practical rationality in which there is a different relation between reason and desire than the one with which Hume was primarily concerned. Granted, the Aristotelian view might seem just as problematic to Hume, but the grounds of objection would be somewhat different, given that it is not the same conception as that of the rationalists.)

Adam Smith, too, made extensive reference to empirical considerations in the explication of moral judgment. Sympathy had a central role in his view and in Hume's, though Smith's elaboration of the role of sympathy differed from Hume's in some important ways. Nevertheless, the reason to mention the likeness between Hume and Smith is that both of them understood moral experience, moral motivation, and moral judgment in ways that involve attitudes and responses to others and to situations that are much more complex than being just pro or con. Smith used the term "sympathy" to "denote our fellow-feeling with any passion whatever."[29] He did not limit it to pity or compassion, and the broader notion had an extensive, fundamental role in Smith's understanding of morality. For example, he wrote:

> We readily therefore sympathize with the grateful affection which he conceives for a person to whom he has been so much obliged; and consequently applaud the returns which he is disposed to make for the good offices conferred upon him. As we entirely enter into the affection from which these returns proceed, they necessarily seem every way proper and suitable to their object.[30]

He went on: "In the same manner, as we sympathize with the sorrow of our fellow-creature whenever we see his distress, so we likewise enter into his abhorrence and aversion for whatever has given occasion to it."[31]

This is not the simplicity of a pro-attitude or a con-attitude of the sort that was central to mid-twentieth century emotivism. Smith went into considerable detail explaining the propriety of this or that specific response, and the bases for the suitability of one or another attitude. His discussion of the fundamental roles of gratitude and resentment is a very effective example of the analytical and empirical texture of his view. He wrote: "To us, therefore, that action must appear to deserve reward, which appears to be the proper and approved object of gratitude; as, on the other hand, that action must appear to deserve punishment, which appears to be the proper and approved object of resentment."[32] That, of course, is just a summary statement. But it is clear from Smith's treatment of the pertinent issues of moral psychology that his view is responsive to the potentially quite considerable complexity of moral judgment. In his view there is a great deal more to moral normativity than just the expression of an attitude.

Moreover, Hume and Smith not only drew extensively upon empirical considerations, they also were very alert to the developments going on around them in economic life, social life, aesthetics, letters, law, and political thought. They understood morality in a way that recognized how powerfully actual social institutions and a diverse range of features of the social world influence morality. D.D. Raphael said of Smith's view, "Straightforward moral judgments about our own actions, according to Smith, are built up in the mind as a reflection of the attitudes of society, mediated especially in childhood through the influence of parents, teachers, and schoolfellows."[33] Sympathy and moral imagination are "trained" and developed through awareness of how others see our actions and awareness of the motives and responses of others. Smith himself uses the language of dividing oneself into two persons in the examination of one's own conduct, "the spectator, whose sentiments with regard to my own conduct I endeavor to enter" and "the agent, the person whom I properly call myself, and of whose conduct, under the character of the spectator, I was endeavouring to form some opinion."[34] This is not context-domesticated relativism, the view that the norms and values people happen to accept are the only basis for whether moral judgments are correct or mistaken. In Smith's view people remain capable of critical, reflective judgment and reasoned revision of their views. Hume also took the realities of the social world to be vitally important to understanding morality and moral judgment. Empirical considerations—about sensibility, about what people find useful and agreeable, and about the significance of practices for society overall—are crucial, and moral requirements cannot be ascertained on an altogether *a priori* basis.

Another reason it is helpful to see Hume in relation to predecessors, contemporaries, and some of the thinkers influenced by him in later generations is that it can remind us of some widely shared perspectives and concerns. Many of those thinkers were responsive in a number of ways to the rapidly developing recognizably modern world and the features of social life and civil society. Some of the same basic notions are quite visibly present in Mill's *Utilitarianism*; the emphasis on the "social feelings," the priority of regard for our own welfare but not in an egoistic manner, and the durable concern for the welfare of others, and how it can be enlarged and elaborated. Looking at the lengthy history of a rich tradition of British Moralists—roughly from Hutcheson (or Hobbes) to Bentham—we can more clearly see how Hume fits in it not only as a critic of moral rationalism but as an important source of thought concerning moral value, judgment, and motivation being studied by the methods of empirical science.

As David Wiggins has remarked:

> Hume's interest in morality was that of a moral scientist or as one would now say moral psychologist. His first question is not the question of the vindication of duty (that question can arise later), but the question of

how natural beings such as ourselves can have arrived at the point where we can even think the refined and complex thoughts we do think about morality and its requirements.[35]

That is a way of seeing Hume as someone who was bringing into view a broadly naturalistic, empirical science of morality. It seems fairly clear that Hume did not see himself as engaged in a project of denying that there can be any scientific study of ethics, and denying this *because* ethical discourse is merely emotive. Hume sought to fit morality into the overall project of inquiry along the lines of scientific thought that is *both* fully alert to skeptical concerns *and* able to offer the prospect of genuinely explanatory accounts of the natural and social world. Hume's attention to the is-ought relation is an especially effective illustration of what he regarded as the exaggerated claims on behalf of reason. But in drawing important conclusions from that important case we should not ignore other elements of his account of moral life. There is no evidence that he thought it is enough to interpret moral claims just in terms of attitudes of being-*for* and being-*against*.

3.5 Normativity and Naturalism

It is plausible to see Hume as defending an empirical study of morality in naturalistic terms. "Naturalism" is a very broad heading and there are many conceptions of naturalism. The various versions agree that there is no "first philosophy," no *a priori* conception that yields knowledge in its own right with regard to whatever it is that is understood in naturalistic terms. One might endorse naturalism regarding some classes of entities and areas of experience but not all. Naturalistic epistemology maintains that knowledge is a phenomenon that can be understood in terms that assimilate it to the natural world. Theories of naturalized epistemology typically involve causal accounts of knowledge, explicating epistemic justification in terms of reliable processes of (true) belief-acquisition. Naturalism does not automatically commit the theorist to explanations in terms of natural selection but it is hardly surprising that many naturalistically-minded theorists strive to show how the process of evolution by natural selection has an important role in what they are explaining.

Some forms of naturalism focus on what there is, some focus on how we can know, and there are forms that explicitly address both issues. There are forms of naturalism that focus on issues in philosophy of mind, seeking naturalistic accounts of consciousness, belief, volition, and a wide range of mental states. While naturalistic views reject any role for entities, agents, and processes that are not constituents of the natural world, the world studied by the sciences, not all forms of naturalism are *scientistic*. Scientistic naturalism is the view that only entities posited by the sciences exist, and that any knowledge of reality is knowledge acquired through the methods of the sciences. Often, this includes a commitment to physicalism as well. In this view what there is and what it is like is reducible to the most fundamental sciences. Thus, if there are moral facts and properties they can be shown to be identical with non-moral facts and properties of the kinds studied in the physical and biological sciences. (The reductionism need not be analytic, conceptual reductionism. It can be synthetic, *a posteriori* reduction.) If one's view is that there are moral facts but those can be reduced to non-moral facts and properties, and thus, that is how they are among the possible objects of scientific investigation, that is scientistic naturalism. Moreover, scientistic naturalism would include a conception of the mind such that all mental phenomena and processes can be explicated in the vocabulary of the physical sciences. Mind and even consciousness are not categories requiring a vocabulary and modes of understanding that are not fully within the natural sciences. The naturalist with regard to mind will not countenance entities, events, and processes distinct from what the methods of the sciences can capture and explain.

Scientistic naturalism is perhaps the most extreme form of what McDowell calls "bald naturalism," "which aims to domesticate conceptual capacities within nature conceived as the realm of law."[36] (Of course, he means *causal* law.) And, "according to this approach, we can reconstruct the structure of the space of reasons out of conceptual materials that already belong in a natural-scientific depiction of nature."[37] There are numerous other forms of naturalism and in some, phenomena such as moral facts and properties are said to non-reductively supervene on natural facts and properties. While not all versions of naturalism are physicalist and reductionist we can say that naturalism is anti-rationalist and anti-metaphysical.

It is sometimes argued that we can make a case for regarding Aristotle's ethics as naturalistic. Granted, his conception of nature is different from the modern conception but Aristotle was not a Platonist about Good, and he clearly believed that excellent human activity and the pleasures that accompany it are only achievable through a process of acquiring a second nature of a certain kind, one informed and oriented by the (human) virtues. Thus, in that regard, he understood human good as intimately connected with human nature, which itself is a kind-specific nature, one that is actuated through the activities of leading a life. That is not "bald naturalism" and it is not Quinean naturalism or Humean naturalism. But it is plausible to understand Aristotle's ethics as naturalistic in a broad sense.

Hume was a naturalistic thinker in the sense that he regarded causal explanation arrived at by empirical inquiry to be the fundamental form of explanation in the natural and social contexts. Hume held that "All reasonings may be divided into two kinds, namely demonstrative reasoning, or that concerning relations of ideas, and moral reasoning, or that concerning matter of fact and existence."[38] He maintained that complex ideas can be made clearer and more fully understood if we

> perhaps, attain a new microscope or species of optics, by which, in the moral sciences, the most minute, and most simple ideas may be so enlarged as to fall readily under our apprehension, and be equally known with the grossest and most sensible ideas, that can be the object of our enquiry.[39]

This is very close to what we saw Ayer presenting as the central claim of positivist epistemology. I am not disputing that Hume did indeed regard the analytical decomposition of complex ideas into simple ideas as a central plank of his epistemological platform. Instead, I have been urging that when we are interested in understanding Hume's view of moral judgments we need to acknowledge additional elements of his view, in particular, claims about whether he held that the examination of moral ideas "analyzes them away," so to speak, leaving only pro- and con-attitudes.

Hume did say that, "Complex ideas may, perhaps, be well known by definition, which is nothing but an enumeration of those parts or simple ideas, that compose them."[40] That makes it sound as though all complex ideas can be reduced to simple ideas, which are copies of impressions combined in various ways to create complex ideas. But while Hume's moral thought is explicitly committed to empirical methods—he calls empirical thought "moral reasoning"—when he turns to morality he finds that there are roles for considerations other than just the analysis of complex ideas into simple ideas. These other considerations have a crucial place in understanding moral judgment and how values figure in our lives. Thus, he was anxious to show that there is an empirical, non-rationalistic account of how and why justice matters in the ways that it does, and why ownership of property is politically important. He understood moral ideas in a complex context of human concerns and interests, and not only attitudes of favoring or opposing.

One way to interpret Hume as having a naturalistic view is to see that he regarded human nature as providing us with propensities, sensibility, and dispositions that provide a basis for moral concern and moral responses. (Recall the quotation from Wiggins.) Hume of course lived before Darwin, and Hume was not concerned with the evolutionary origin of human sensibility but there are ways in which we can see the mutual relevance of Hume and Darwin regarding moral naturalism. Darwin developed a naturalistic account of how beings with the sensibility needed for morality, and with the capacity for addressing cooperative needs and challenges concerning coordination came to be. We can see how evolution by natural selection could be the process that "brings" morality into the world. That does not mean that the substance of morality can be "read off" of the naturalistic process of evolution but it is a way for natural history to be strongly relevant to the morality humans have developed.

This was understood by T.H. Huxley nearly one hundred and fifty years ago. He wrote, "I have termed this evolution of the feelings out of which the primitive bonds of human society are so largely forged, into the organized and personified sympathy we call conscience, the ethical process."[41] The ethical process, which is itself made possible by the process of natural selection by which the human species came to be is, he thinks, in conflict with what he called the "cosmic process," the constant, lethal struggle for existence. A crucial part of the ethical process is that by which

> It becomes impossible to imagine some acts without disapprobation, or others without approbation of the actor, whether he be one's self or any one else. We come to think in the acquired dialect of morals. An artificial personality, the "man within," as Adam Smith calls conscience, is built up beside the natural personality. He is the watch-man of society, charged to restrain the anti-social tendencies of the natural man within the limits required by social welfare.[42]

Reading just the quoted passages gives the impression that he is basically putting a Humean (or maybe Smithian) theory of moral sentiments on an evolutionary basis. Huxley's view, however, included another insight, and one that is crucial to his view of the relation between natural history and human society.

Huxley argued that the capacities we have for both virtue and vice are products of the process of evolution by natural selection. He noted that:

> as the immoral sentiments have no less been evolved, there is, so far, as much natural sanction for the one as the other. The thief and the murderer follow nature just as much as the philanthropist. Cosmic evolution may teach us how the good and the evil tendencies of man may have come about; but, in itself, it is incompetent to furnish any better reason why what we call good is preferable to what we call evil than we had before.[43]

We do have good instrumental reasons to approve of and encourage some habits as moral habits rather than immoral habits. They enable us to prosper, they reduce insecurity, they promote trust and mutual concern and assistance, and so forth. The more we encourage the "ethical process" the less likely we are to make true the "gladiatorial theory of existence"[44] for which some Social Darwinists claimed to find support on the basis of the natural facts. However, with respect to what should be the norms of moral life, the theory of selective advantage is incomplete at the crucial point, the point where we need to consider what those features of sensibility and those motivational tendencies should count for in rationally warranted actions and responses. *The causal account of the origin of sensibility does not itself supply the norms of morally well-ordered sensibility*. The causal account of sensibility does not provide guidance regarding the space of reasons concerning human good. It does not provide guidance to moral *thought*.

The adaptive merits of a complex repertoire of behaviors do not, on their own, constitute ethical merits even if there is substantial overlap between what is adaptively selected and what is ethically endorsed. We still need ethical thought to ascertain what the norms should be. Natural selection "made" creatures such as we are; creatures capable of responses, motivations, and concerns that can be shaped into moral life and experience. But selective advantage is not the basis of moral norms. The natural process is just that; it is a causal history. Morality does not appear on the scene until persons have conceptualized behavior, the motives of behavior, and its results in certain ways articulated in the space of reasons. The normativity of morality is not fully assimilated to the norms of the evolutionary process.

I mention Huxley because his insight regarding the relation between naturalistic explanation and moral reasoning is especially striking for someone who was such an energetic champion of Darwin's theory of evolution by natural selection. Moreover, the central insight of Huxley's paper continues to be relevant. In addition, Huxley's view illustrates the claim that we cannot read morality off of the natural facts, and yet, that does not mean there is no basis for making reasoned moral judgments. He did not see our predicament as a dilemma of "competition for existence or relativism" with no other genuine options.

In recent decades several versions of moral naturalism have been developed and there are important differences between them. Some, such as Blackburn's projectivism are antirealist but not thinly emotivist. The view developed by Nicholas Sturgeon is a form of moral realism, in which there is a naturalistic account of moral facts. He argues that we should accept that there are moral facts given their genuine role in moral explanation even if the account is not reductionist or physicalist, or otherwise assimilated to natural science.

Some recent philosophers who are skeptics with regard to moral values have taken a different approach to the issue, arguing that supposed moral facts have no explanatory role and thus, there is no reason to include them in our conception of what there is. They are not a necessary part of any explanation of any phenomena, and we can dispense with them. Gilbert Harman wrote:

> The observation of an event can provide observational evidence for or against a scientific theory in the sense that the truth of that observation can be relevant to a reasonable explanation of why that observation was made. A moral observation does not seem, in the same sense, to be observational evidence for or against any moral theory, since the truth or falsity of the moral observation seems to be completely irrelevant to any reasonable explanation of why that observation was made.[45]

Why is that? Because in order to explain the moral judgments people make:

> It would seem that all we need assume is that you have more or less well articulated moral principles that are reflected in the judgments you make,

> based on your moral sensibility. It seems to be completely irrelevant to our explanation whether your intuitive immediate judgment is true or false.[46]

In critically discussing Harman's view, and making a case for the explanatory contribution of moral values Nicholas Sturgeon wrote:

> His claim is not that if the action had not been one of deliberate cruelty (or had otherwise differed in whatever way would be required to remove its wrongness), you would still have thought it wrong. It is, instead, that if the action were one of deliberate, pointless cruelty, but this did not make it wrong, you would still have thought it was wrong.[47]

In Harman's view no moral facts are needed to explain people's reactions, attitudes, and actions and this is because the only facts that are needed in order to explain your thinking the act is wrong are facts about your moral sensibility and the moral principles to which you are committed. The presence of the property *morally wrong* or the fact that an action is morally wrong is not what explains your judgment that it is wrong.

Sturgeon argued that moral facts do indeed have an important role in explaining moral and non-moral phenomena. For example, (though this is not an example Sturgeon used) how else are we to explain Fred and Rosemary West's torture and murder of several young women in England except to say that Fred and Rosemary West were depraved, and morally degenerate? Their vicious states of character had a role in explaining the actions they performed. Even according to the positivist there might be considerable convergence in people's attitudes toward the Wests. Who *doesn't* find them depraved, degenerate, and wicked? But for the subjectivist or relativist all there is to the story is that they might happen to be the objects of widely shared attitudes and responses but they and their actions have no moral properties except in the sense that a great many people happen to agree in their responses to them. There is no further account of what it is that we find so awful about such people and their acts. It is attitude all the way down.

Sturgeon pointed out that if no moral facts are needed to explain moral judgments, then presumably they are not needed to explain the behavior that is being morally judged. He maintained that such a view is quite implausible. How could persons have the features that Hitler or The Wests had and not be morally rotted? Moreover, the fact that a person is virtuous may well be part of the explanation of why she is held in high esteem and asked or elected to fill positions of responsibility or authority. The fact that a social and economic arrangement is just may well be part of the explanation of why it is stable and why people regard it as legitimate. Far from being unneeded, moral facts, it can be argued, are a familiar and essential part of our understanding of the world. In Liebling's study of the "moral performance" of prisons she found that where treatment of prisoners was more humane, and relations with staff more congenial and mutually respectful, the overall mental health and attitudes of prisoners were better. The evidence seemed to show that the moral features have explanatory significance. The main issue is not whether they have some peculiar nature of their own but whether our best understanding of the world (including various kinds of facts, acts, and situations) involves reference to moral facts.

In also making the case for moral considerations having a genuine explanatory role, Peter Railton has argued that moral facts supervene on natural phenomena. He wrote:

> Where is the place in explanation for facts about what ought to be the case—don't facts about the way things are do all the explaining there is to be done? Of course they do. But then, my naturalistic moral realism commits me to the view that facts about what ought to be the case are facts of a special kind about the way things are.[48]

He says, "In the spirit of a naturalized moral epistemology, we may ask whether the explanation of why we make certain moral judgments is an example of a reliable process for discovering moral facts."[49] It seems the answer is yes, making careful, considered moral judgments surely is part of a reliable process of ascertaining moral facts. What is the best explanation of why there is strong opposition to trial by ordeal in the world's constitutional democracies? Is it not fairly clear that this has something to do with facts about what is in people's interests, what are appropriate and effective ways of gathering evidence and examining witnesses, and facts about what are rational strategies of belief-formation and acceptance, all of which together (with other facts) provide a quite compelling explanation for the claim that trial by ordeal is morally *wrong*? We ought not to torture people to ascertain guilt or innocence. Why should we treat that as less than a fact?[50]

In what sense is Hume's moral theory naturalistic? It appears that he did not endorse naturalism of the form defended by Sturgeon or Railton. He was not defending naturalistic realism. The respect in which Hume's view can be characterized as naturalistic is made clear by recalling the basic distinction he made between relations of ideas and matters of fact. Regarding the former, Hume clearly rejected rationalism, and the only analytic truths he recognized expressed—in his terms—"relations of ideas" and he insisted that those had no content or meaning regarding "matters of fact or existence." They say nothing about what there is, what it is like, and how it interacts with anything else. Hume did not use the terms "*a priori*" and "*a posteriori*" or "analytic" and "synthetic" but his view maps onto those categories as they are generally understood. His view is one of the sources for such a distinction. It seemed impossible to him that conceptual analysis alone, just thinking through the implications of some concept or proposition, could give us any contentful beliefs about what there is and its features. It also seemed impossible to him that the perception of some event or a belief about some matter of fact could logically entail the existence of any other matter of fact. The world is not held together by logic, and we cannot attain knowledge of any item in it or aspect of it through the exercise of reason alone. Hume was a fierce critic of rationalist realism, and he maintained that it is only through the "experimental" (i.e., empirical) method that we attain any true beliefs about matters of fact and existence, and those beliefs depend ultimately on impressions and not logical relations. In that regard, in his insistence on experience as the only source of beliefs about the world, and in his insistence that the relation of cause and effect is the chief way in which matters of fact are related to each other he can be said to have adopted a broadly naturalistic account of factual belief and the acceptance of claims about factual matters.

Hume's "sceptical solution" to doubts about necessary relations between matters of fact rests on a naturalistic conception of the operation of the mind in regard to matters of fact and on psychological habits doing the work, so to speak, where rational justification does not.[51] Hume held that the project of understanding morality needs to be pursued by the same "experimental" (i.e., empiricist) method that is employed in understanding natural events and processes. In regard to the philosophical method overall his manner of addressing fundamental issues highlights causal accounts and minimizes the role of rational justification in a formal, demonstrative sense.

In regard to moral values Hume held that we are to look to sensibility and our affective responses to actions, persons, and situations, and we are to explain moral judgments in terms of what we find useful and agreeable but not in a narrowly ego-situated way. Hume was clear that moral judgment involves considering things from a general or impersonal perspective. He clearly rejected what we might call "vulgar subjectivism" and he also rejected relativism. Hume can be said to endorse ethical naturalism in the sense that he regarded moral value, moral judgment, and moral motivation as accessible to us through empirical investigation. He regarded empirical methods as fully adequate to the explanation of morality. His philosophy includes considerable resources for moral judgment and moral thought even though he rejected moral facts and objective moral values. Interpreting his importance mainly in terms of formulating the fact/value distinction and as showing that moral considerations are unrelated to facts can be quite misleading.

My main concern here is not to defend Humean moral theory but to present a certain interpretation of it in the course of explicating some of the philosophical issues most relevant to the relation between facts and values. Whether a realist or antirealist conception of moral considerations has the strongest case, and whether moral considerations should be interpreted naturalistically or in non-natural terms are not questions I am directly attempting to answer here. But I do hope to have offered an interpretation of Hume that is both faithful to him and has some plausibility in its own right. If I have done that then we can see how it is that Hume could be both a champion of the is/ought distinction and a moral thinker for whom facts are relevant to valuative judgment though the latter are not derivable from the former. Positivist social scientists have sometimes interpreted Hume's empiricism in a way that has more radical implications than he appears to have countenanced. He clearly did not think that the fact/value distinction limited moral judgment to thinly emotive expression unguided by factual considerations.

Even if our interpretation of Hume is basically sound we still need to look more closely at relativism. A great deal of social scientific study has endorsed relativism and it seems to be widely regarded as the only plausible option. Upon examination, the case for it comes apart in ways that leave little prospect for reconstituting it. In addition, the putative fact/value distinction has been thought to point the study of morality in a relativist direction. We need to look carefully at the content of relativism and the case for it.

Notes

1 A.J. Ayer, *Language, Truth and Logic*, New York: Dover, 1952, p. 104.
2 Ibid., p. 107.
3 Ibid.
4 This group of philosophers does not constitute a school, and there are numerous significant differences in their views. However, they all elaborated conceptions that included elements antithetical to expressivist views and non-cognitivism.
5 American Philosophical Association, "The Charm of Naturalism," *Proceedings and Addresses of the American Philosophical Association* 70 (2): November 1996, pp. 43–55.
6 R.M. Hare, *The Language of Morals*, New York: Oxford University Press, 1964, pp. 80–81.
7 James Laidlaw, *The Subject of Virtue*, Cambridge: Cambridge University Press, p. 45.
8 Ibid.
9 Ibid.
10 Ibid., 46, italics in original.
11 Ludwig Wittgenstein, *Philosophical Investigations*, 3rd edition, trans. G. E. M. Anscombe, Pearson, 1953, p. 223.
12 Cassaniti and Hickman, "New Directions in the Anthropology of Morality," p. 253.
13 Ibid.
14 Simon Blackburn, "How to be an Ethical Antirealist," in *Essays in Quasi-Realism*, New York: Oxford University Press, 1993, p. 176.
15 Ibid., p. 172.
16 Ibid., pp. 172–173.
17 David Hume, *An Enquiry Concerning the Principles of Morals*, ed. L.A. Selby-Bigge, Oxford: Clarendon Press, 1975, Sect. IX, Part I, p. 272
18 Simon Blackburn, "Errors and the Phenomenology of Value," in *Essays in Quasi-Realism*, New York: Oxford University Press, 1993, p. 160.
19 McDowell, *Mind and World*, p. 81.
20 Hume, *Enquiry Concerning the Principles of Morals*, p. 222.
21 Hume, *Enquiry Concerning Human Understanding*, ed. L. A. Selby-Bigge, Oxford: Clarendon Press, 1975, p. 83.
22 Hume, *Enquiry Concerning the Principles of Morals*, Sect. IX, Part I, p. 273.
23 Ibid., Sect. III, Part II, pp. 194–195.
24 Ibid., Sect IX, Part I, p. 277. Italics in original.

25 Ibid., Sect. I, pp. 169-170.
26 Ibid., Appendix I, p. 286.
27 Blackburn, "How to be an Ethical Antirealist," p. 173.
28 Hume, *Enquiry Concerning the Principles of Morals*, Appendix I, p. 294.
29 Adam Smith, "Of the Propriety of Action," in *The Theory of Moral Sentiments*, eds. D. D. Raphael and A. L. MacFie, Oxford : Oxford University Press; Glasgow edition. Reprinted Liberty Fund Press (1982), I. i.I. 5, p. 10.
30 Ibid., II. I. 2. 4, p. 70.
31 Ibid., II.i.2.5. p. 70.
32 Ibid., II.i.I.2, p. 68.
33 D. D. Raphael, *Adam Smith*, New York: Oxford University Press, 1985, pp. 41–42.
34 Smith, *The Theory of Moral Sentiments*, III, I.6, p.113.
35 David Wiggins, "Categorical Requirements: Kant and Hume on the Idea of Duty," in *Virtues and Reasons*: *Philippa Foot and Moral Theory*, eds. R. Hursthouse, G. Lawrence, and W. Quinn, New York: Oxford University Press, 1995, pp. 297–330.
36 McDowell, *Mind and World*, p. 73.
37 Ibid.
38 Hume, *Enquiry Concerning Human Understanding*, Sect. IV, Part II p. 22.
39 Ibid., Sect. VII, p. 41 ed. Eric Steinberg. Indianapolis: Hackett Publishing Co., 1977.
40 Ibid., Sect. VII, Part I, p. 41.
41 T. H. Huxley, *Evolution and Ethics*, D. Appleton and Co., New York, 1899, p. 30.
42 Ibid., p. 79
43 Ibid., p. 80.
44 Ibid., p. 82.
45 Gilbert Harman, *The Nature of Morality*, New York: Oxford University Press, 1977, p. 7.
46 Ibid., p. 7.
47 Nicholas Sturgeon, "Moral Explanations," in *Essays on Moral Realism*, ed. Geoffrey Sayre-McCord, Ithaca: Cornell University Press, 1988, p. 250.
48 Peter Railton, "Moral Realism," in *Moral Discourse and Practice*, ed. Stephen Darwall, Allan Gibbard, and Peter Railton, New York: Oxford University Press, 1997, pp. 137–166, p. 147.
49 Ibid., p. 155.
50 Ibid.
51 One way to understand what Hume means by a skeptical solution is to see that he explains the basis of confidence in our ability to make moral judgments and the relevant distinctions despite the fact that rational justification of them is not forthcoming. Various natural propensities and forms of responsiveness that are rooted in our empirical nature make those sorts of judgments possible and there is no reason to believe that the underwriting supplied by nature will somehow or someday fail to meet that need. No urgent search for justificatory grounds is needed.

Chapter 4

Relativism and the Study of Morality

In Chapter 3 we considered reasons to interpret Hume's moral philosophy as a form of skeptical naturalism, in large part because that enables us to highlight features of his view that he took to be most significant. He was a moral skeptic, if by "moral skepticism" we mean the denial that there are objective moral values. But he was not a skeptic if we mean by that that there are no grounds for distinguishing correct from incorrect moral claims, or for regarding some moral judgments as sound and appropriate and others as unsupported and implausible. He held that there are naturalistic considerations relevant to such distinctions. Hume did not take the denial that there are objective values to have some of the implications often ascribed to it. In this chapter we discuss issues concerning relativism chiefly because it is often associated with the denial of moral objectivity.

Many social scientists are moral relativists, and one might think the positivist interpretation of fact and value implies or at least supports moral relativism. I will argue that relativism, in whatever manner it is motivated, is not well-supported by the sorts of grounds often suggested as supporting it. In addition, it has little or no explanatory merit; it does not enlarge or deepen our understanding. Overall, the case for it is very weak. But moral relativism is not the only form that has been influential in the social sciences. A more general conceptual relativism has also had a good deal of currency and I shall argue that the case for it is also very weak. We will say a bit about that before going directly into the discussion of moral relativism. That will be a way to address some epistemic issues relevant to basic questions about relativist thinking generally.

4.1 Why is Anyone a Relativist?

It might seem that there is a strong case for conceptual relativism, for the view that there is no strategy for arriving at an objective conception of the world, and that we (whoever "we" happen to be) are always, and necessarily, confined to conceptual schemes through which we describe and explain the world. Indeed, one might think that positivism—or at least certain versions

DOI: 10.4324/9781003037323-5

of it—is congenial to conceptual relativism, for example, if one believes that the data of sense perception do not uniquely determine any specific way of conceptualizing the world. One might argue that multiple, competing but not fully commensurable conceptual schemes are consistent with the data of experience and there is no rationally decidable approach to ascertaining which theories are most truth-conducive. This does not mean that any set of concepts is as good as any other. A set of concepts might be so general and so lacking in capacity to make distinctions and categorize things that it is explanatorily worthless or near-worthless. "It's because of nature" and "It's because of God" are both unhelpfully, maximally general hypotheses, supposing that "it's" refers to anything whatsoever. If we imagine that they are left at that level with no further elaboration or specification they each explain nothing. Without further elaboration, neither of them even rules out the other. In fact, what is sometimes the case is that a set of concepts applied to a certain context of inquiry is found to be inconsistent with concepts that we employ elsewhere and find to be quite helpful in arriving at explanations and predictions. There can be good reasons to accept one way of understanding rather than some other. Criteria for evaluating conceptions, theories, and explanations need not themselves be arbitrary or merely stipulative.

Relativism might seem to be a way of not dismissing unfamiliar ways of understanding the world, and one might think that there is no standpoint from which a conclusive assessment of a conception of the world can be made. Or if one argues that for whatever conceptions and theories are accepted at a given time there is a causal explanation pointing to factors other than independent norms of rational justification that could be a way of trying to show that epistemic norms themselves are the results of causal rather than rational processes. The effect would be similar to conceptual relativism though the causal-explanatory character of the view just mentioned distinguishes its focus from some forms of relativism. The causal-explanatory approach might be what we are left with if relativism is true though it motivates some awkward questions about its own epistemic authority. In any case, one especially important point regarding relativism is that to say that any set of concepts is just as good as any other guts the notion of "just as good as" of any sense. It is left an empty notion.

However, someone might be led to relativism by the thought that there is no sideways-on perspective on the relation between concepts (or judgments) on the one side, and the world on the other. We cannot compare what we *think* (how we take things to be) with *what is the case*. We are always within the realm of concepts, descriptions, and categorizations; thus, the best we can strive for is greater integration, coherence, and explanatory interrelations yet even the best of such efforts cannot bring us closer to the truth. Or one might argue that the process of theory-change is not amenable to any measure of whether a succeeding theory is more truth-conducive and genuinely explanatory than the one it succeeds.

Regarding that issue I will quote Israel Scheffler at length, discussing Kuhn's notion of paradigms and of theory-change. After making several points concerning the implications of Kuhn's view for the language of scientific theorizing and the possibility of common meanings across theories, of the possibility of the shared relevance of observations, and of the comparability of theories with regard to explanatory content, Scheffler writes:

> The breakdown of observational community and of the community of meaning, and the consequent rejection of cumulativeness seem to remove all sense from the notion of a rational progression of scientific viewpoints from age to age. If contemporary theoretical alternatives cannot be compared and evaluated with respect to their factual accuracy and comprehensiveness, neither can succeeding theoretical alternatives be thus compared and evaluated. The genesis of a new theory cannot be backed up by an established methodology of justification, such as is presupposed by the standard view; indeed, the very distinction between justification and discovery breaks down as well.[1]

He then goes on to make a case for why those results need not be accepted and how they indicate an untenable conception of science. An important part of the argument has to do with how the Kuhnian (antirealist) view precludes crucial features of scientific theorizing and explanation, such things as independent, public controls, and shared conceptions of truth-conducive methods pursuing an understanding of a public, shared world. Scheffler regards the set of implications of Kuhn's view as "a *reductio ad absurdum* of the reasonings from which it flows."[2]

It must be said that the metaphysical, epistemological, and semantic issues relevant to questions about objectivity and the realism/antirealism debate generally are very complex, involve multiples angles of approach, and we are not pursuing them in depth here. The present treatment is very brief and summary. But it is worth mentioning here at the start of this chapter that if one assumes that objectivity just cannot be attained by a theory because the ways we conceptualize the world constitute barriers to actually encountering what there is, what it is like, and what happens, that assumption is doubtful. It is not clear what is gained by it in regard to explanation, and moreover, there are multiple reasons in favor of a non-relativist interpretation of conceptualizing the world. If it is suggested that conceptual relativism indicates a meritorious form of epistemic humility it can be replied that there is plenty of humility in striving to be responsive to the authority of truth rather than "constructing" the world in ways unguided by it.

The debates concerning metaphysical and epistemological realism and antirealism, as well as debates about theories of truth, are longstanding, complex, and interrelated in various ways, and debates about the status of theoretical entities in scientific theorizing are connected to all of them. Adding to that the question of how best to understand theory-change makes for a formidable philosophical agenda, one much too large to even summarize here. However, I will suggest that relativism faces serious problems—of its own making in an important sense—and we can ascertain some very good reasons to reject it even discussing the issue at a very general level. Moreover, our interest in relativism here has to do with whether it is an appropriate perspective regarding moral issues studied by criminological investigation, and that will be our focus.

In the course of arguing that criminologists cannot distance themselves entirely from moral and political issues by claiming to study the world rather than being engaged directly in action, Anthony Bottoms presents his "Key Proposition II," which asserts that "there is indeed a real world, and that criminologists cannot avoid engagement with the world, whether they like it or not (and some do not like it much)."[3] This is a realist claim but it does not imply that there is no role for theory and for conceptual constructions through which phenomena are understood. It does not take constructivism to the extreme: "Since all observations are, admittedly, 'constructions,' some have argued that *empirical research findings are therefore always simply another 'construction,' with no particular claims to validity*."[4] Such a view, Bottoms remarks, results in relativism, which is to be sharply contrasted with realism. There is a

> real world that is available for observation and interpretation, and a very important test (though not the only test) of any theoretical account will be whether it interprets that real world more accurately and convincingly than do other theoretical accounts—for which purpose, the results of empirical research will have to be taken into account by the theorist.[5]

Theoretical conceptualization and the fact that observation is always *under a description*, for example, do not confine us to a kind of conceptual relativism. When we test hypotheses the categories and classifications of entities and properties that our theory commits to do not themselves determine which hypotheses will be confirmed. As Scheffler noted, "[c]ategorization provides the pigeonholes; hypotheses makes assignments to them."[6] And "[o]bservation may be considered as shot through with categorization, while yet supporting a particular assignment which conflicts with our most cherished current hypothesis."[7] Theory and the construction of explanations can be responsive to what is found in ways that enable us to revise and refine theories and explanations so that they are more truth-conducive. The fact that much is contributed by our own conceptual choices and the shape of our interests does not mean that what the world is like in its own right is beyond epistemic reach.

For our purposes the central issue is that the fact/value distinction might be taken as a basis for moral relativism, and indeed moral relativism has been widely held by social scientists, often on that basis. The view that there is no valid logical inference from what is the case to what one ought to do has been widely regarded as basically conclusive concerning the relation between facts and values. However, among philosophers the mid-to-late twentieth century critique of emotivism and prescriptivism involved a reconsideration of the meaning of moral concepts that motivated a reconsideration of the relation between facts and values and supplied materials for a strong case against moral relativism.

In the middle of the twentieth century Philippa Foot drew attention to ways in which the alleged separation of descriptive and prescriptive meaning defended by positivism is actually quite implausible, with implications for meaning that are decidedly problematic. We might not notice these problematic features because there is often a high degree of moral agreement. With the agreement we might not be alert to the implications of the division of meaning into descriptive and prescriptive. But if we look closely at the implications they do seem odd, even when there is not disagreement about the evaluations of things. And what is problematic is not confined to moral discourse; it is found also in other forms of discourse in which there is a role for normativity or evaluation. For instance, Foot considered whether there are limitations on what one can intelligibly take as an object of pride. After all, if descriptive and prescriptive meanings are independent of each other perhaps there are no such limitations. If evaluation is not fact-based but a matter of attitudinizing then perhaps the attitude could be adopted to just about anything. Can one take pride in the fact that the sun is approximately ninety-three million miles from earth, or in the fact that per unit of volume, granite is heavier than cotton, or the fact that millions of human beings have diabetes? Is it true that, when we are speaking of attitudes and normative contexts, there is no factual governance of our responses and attitudes?

It is not just that these are improbable objects of pride; pride makes no sense in such cases. Could one be despondent over the fact that Neptune is smaller than Jupiter or indignant over the fact that 107 is an odd number? (If someone had bet a lot of money on what turned out to be the losing side of these propositions that person might be despondent. But the despondency is over losing the bet, not the facts in their own right.) If one says to the psychiatrist, "Doctor, I am despondent over the fact that 107 is an odd number," we would not expect the reply to be, "I'm finding that there is a lot of it about, though it is usually 109 that troubles people. I wonder what is different about your case."

When we turn to the moral context there, too, we can ask about whether there are constraints regarding intelligible moral judgment, about the relation between the facts and moral thought. Can moral valuation take just *any* facts as its object? It can if there is only a contingent relation between facts and prescriptions (or normative judgments). Can moral prescription accompany facts without there being any rational relation between the facts and the prescription? If that is true then we should be able to attain an understanding of a moral term, "good" for example, without the understanding requiring any factual content, without any specification of what it is that is being said to be good. Not just anything could be a moral norm.

In Foot's view

> The crucial question is this. Is it possible to extract from the meaning of words such as 'good' some element called "evaluative meaning" which we can think of as externally related to its objects? Such an element would be represented, for instance, in the rule that when any action was "commended" the speaker must hold himself bound to accept an imperative "let me do these things."[8]

That's what prescriptivism would say. Foot went on:

> I wish to say that this hypothesis is untenable, and that there is no describing the evaluative meaning of "good," evaluation, commending, or anything of the sort, without fixing the object to which they are supposed to be attached. Without first laying hands on the proper object of such things as evaluation, we shall catch in our net either something quite different such as accepting an order or making a resolution, or else nothing at all.[9]

Basically, Foot was asking, could a person understand what fairness, benevolence, or honesty is without also understanding that each of these is (generally) morally good, and that its goodness has a basis? Can we really specify the contents of these concepts and then ask a *separate* question about our stance or attitude toward those contents? (Is it an open question in *that* way?) Is moral judgment a matter of choice or decision in that way? Can the facts "take" or "accept" just *any* stance, or do they seem to have a certain kind of moral significance in their own right? What looked like a plausible move, the move that told us that there is something inscrutable and strange about moral facts, now looks as though it is based upon a contrived and distorting distinction. All of the attempts at analytically decomposing judgments into descriptive elements and a pro-attitude, or commendation, or a prescription (or their negative counterparts) distort the way we actually understand such discourse. We learn what things are morally good and which are morally bad in ways that involve informing the understanding and not exclusively through a training of affect. The latter is genuinely important but it is not all that is included in the meanings of moral terms. Affect is directed at certain objects and is responsive to certain objects; those "directions" are fact-guided, at least if affect is be intelligible, appropriate, reasonable rather than merely occurrent with an antecedent but not a basis.

In their focus on semantic considerations the emotivists and prescriptivists stressed the fact that we often use moral discourse to influence people. They highlighted (correctly) a function of the discourse while claiming (incorrectly) the discourse had no cognitive content as prescriptive. In saying of something that it is a malicious, unjust thing to do to someone, part of what we mean is that the person to whom we are speaking should see it that way too because of the features to which we respond so negatively. It is quite right to emphasize the practical import of moral discourse but the fact/value distinction left the practical significance of moral language without an intelligible relation to the facts that are being evaluated.

There is more to the meaning of good than a pro-attitude. What makes something a good X depends on what kind of thing X is. The goodness of a really efficient gas turbine for a locomotive is explicated quite differently from the goodness of a particular soil for growing certain crops. Of course there are certain highly general features of things that are good; often this concerns efficacy at performing a function, or meeting certain needs. The notion that good can always be specified mainly in terms of a pro-attitude is quite implausible. Not only do the criteria for the application of "good" differ with what is being spoken of, but in many cases the link with what our attitudes are is either quite thin or it actually gets things backward; we have a pro-attitude to various things *because they are good*. If a particular institutional arrangement and set of policies governing its operation are fair to all those affected by them that is a very strong reason for thinking them good.

The considerations just discussed are among those that have been used in arguments against moral relativism. If there are rationally intelligible relations between facts about something and the evaluation of it we at least know that pro-and con-attitudes are not altogether untethered. But couldn't one still defend moral relativism on other grounds?

It might seem so; moral relativism has had a considerable presence in the social sciences and for several reasons. Many social scientists insist that the diversity of cultures and their norms provide overwhelming empirical evidence that there are no objective moral considerations, moral principles, or moral values. The fact that there are different cultures with very different values and attitudes and practices does not, in its own right, show that relativism is true in regard to morality. But in conjunction with the persistence of different norms and attitudes, and stubborn disputes over what would count as establishing the objectivity or universality of moral values, many investigators conclude that moral values are always relative to a society, a period, or a culture. The view is that there are no objective moral values for human beings to strive to know, to encounter cognitively. Sometimes additional support for this view is claimed on the basis of moral values not being among the things that scientific methods ever discover. If the social sciences are to be genuinely scientific it is crucial to acknowledge that there is no moral knowledge, or knowledge of morality except insofar as moral systems can be studied scientifically. This is part of why many believe that Hume's view supports relativism, even though he did not maintain that position. That the scientific study of morality does not bring us any closer to objective moral values is one of the implications of positivism. We might have a much more sophisticated understanding of how societies come to have the moral values they have, and how people's moral beliefs figure in their actions and in their practices. *We might achieve enlarged understanding of morality but not enlarged moral understanding.*

According to positivism there is no such thing as the latter and that is one of the reasons many social scientists are led to relativism. It appears that there are empirical reasons (largely concerning diversity, non-agreement, and disagreement) in favor of relativism, epistemological reasons (lack of rational justification), and broadly sociological reasons (how people come to have their values) in the respect that a person nearly always internalizes many of the society's prevailing norms. Being enculturated into valuative stances is a highly general feature of human life. The combination of those factors might appear to make a formidable case in favor of moral relativism.

There are also political/moral reasons why many persons endorse moral relativism. It is widely held that it is an important *political* matter to accept that different groups have different moral views, and that a just society accommodates such differences to a considerable extent and respects the different values of other societies. Part of the appeal of liberalism, as a form of political order, is that it limits the role of the state in moral life and permits more rather than less moral independence for individuals. A broad exercise of state power in enforcing morality could be at odds with equal respect for persons, and equal respect for different valuative commitments. Of course, in criminalizing certain types of conduct the state and its citizens are indicating that some actions are morally wrong and prohibited because wrong. However, not all criminalization is on grounds of moral wrongness, and not all moral wrongness is a basis for criminalization. If the state regarded its authority to extend to the enforcement of morality in general that would almost certainly make for an oppressive presence of the state in people's lives. Many moral matters, even quite significant ones, just are not among the appropriate concerns of a liberal state. If the person who has long been your best friend surprises you with a very hurtful act of betrayal, that is morally objectionable but there is no role for the state in the matter (unless blackmail, theft or violence, for example, are involved).

We should note that in many cases it is the *liberalism* of a liberal-democratic state that accommodates a diversity of views, not primarily its democratic character. The diversity will be reflected in its democratic character but democratic majorities—as Mill suggested—can be oppressive, single-minded, and intolerant of different perspectives, values, and commitments. We might wonder how a state could be democratic if it did not tolerate and respect differences. The short answer is that unless the democratic character is also committed to the protection of extensive rights and liberties, democratic populism can result in all sorts of ugly illiberal politics.

The liberal-democratic political/legal order makes it possible for different groups and outlooks to engage in generally peaceable political bargaining and compromise. That form of political order tolerates a range of perspectives and valuative commitments, and potentially many different conceptions of a well-lived life. In a country such as Australia or the United States or in the United Kingdom there is likely to be considerable diversity in people's views about how to lead their lives and diversity in interests, aims, and values.[10] There are regional differences, ethnic and cultural differences, and while certain views and values might be the prevailing ones it is possible for non-conformists, so to speak, to lead lives in a variety of different ways without the state demanding conformity.

We should make clear how the notions of diversity and pluralism are used here. By *diversity* I mean a variety of ethnic, cultural, national, and religious backgrounds and commitments. The fact that there are many differences in heritage does not automatically translate into differences in valuative commitments. A society could be diverse but there could be a high degree of agreement regarding values. *Pluralism* is distinct from diversity and it has a number of senses. One kind of pluralism is pluralism of moral value; i.e., there are multiple values each with its own ground or source. For instance, autonomy as a value might not have exactly the same ground as welfare or the right to free exercise of religion, or the right to own private property. Another sense of pluralism has to do with a society being pluralistic in that there are people with different valuative commitments, different conceptions of what makes for a good or worthwhile life. That might or might not be explained by the diversity of ethnic and cultural heritage. It is conceivable that a society could be fairly homogeneous in ethnicity but pluralistic with regard to the values people seek to realize in how they lead their lives. A society could be diverse without being pluralistic, and could be pluralistic without being especially diverse. Some societies, such as in the United States, are both diverse and pluralistic, and the pluralism concerns the multiple sources of values *and* also people having many different conceptions of what makes for an excellent life.

Where there is a genuine commitment to liberal values and principles there will be toleration and appreciation of a pluralistic civil society. Members of different groups might find the values and attitudes of some other groups objectionable but will be willing to tolerate them, acknowledging a difference between "finding objectionable" and "being harmed by." Moreover, appreciation of the freedoms of an open, pluralistic civil society could provide people with good reasons to want to preserve the liberal order; they will recognize the mutual support between the political/legal order on the one hand, and the character of society on the other. An open, dynamic civil society does not develop in just any political order. And if people have little or no experience with a liberal order they might have little interest in an open civil society, preferring a more homogeneous, unchanging, highly familiar form of social and cultural life. In many countries with little heritage of liberal democracy there is also only modest enthusiasm for a more open society or for tolerating pluralism. Authoritarian and other types of illiberal political cultures are generally hostile to increased diversity or pluralism, and often are keen to preserve their cultural heritage in ways that exclude others.

If a society is largely homogeneous ethnically, religiously, and culturally, say, five million mostly middle-class Lutherans, it is not likely to be highly pluralistic and not likely to struggle with tensions due to differences in cultural outlooks. There might be a number of somewhat different perspectives and attitudes represented among the population and there may be a history of including such differences to an extent. Thus, it might be democratic and it might claim to be open and tolerant but without having been tested by some of the realities of pluralism. A society could be diverse but not very pluralistic if, for example, there has been a history of assimilation of different groups and especially if members of those groups wanted to assimilate.

One might think that diversity and pluralism suggest a basis for relativism. That is not the case. We noted that one sense of pluralism concerns different and potentially incommensurable conceptions of what makes for a worthwhile, well-led life, i.e., different guiding conceptions of good in the context of leading a life. That is not exactly the same as moral relativism though they might seem similar. Moral relativism maintains that the rightness of moral values, principles, or ideals is dependent on what a group happens to accept. The criteria for moral judgments are all domesticated to, relative to, whatever principles and values are in fact accepted. There is no neutral or impartial or perspective-free standpoint from which these things can be assessed. Just as we cannot attain a sideways-on perspective to compare our scientific theories to the world we cannot attain a sideways-on perspective that enables us to look at the relation between a group's moral values and the world, observing where each ends and the other begins. This (as well as conceptual relativism), is a form of antirealism.

I have characterized moral relativism in terms of morality being domesticated to the values and norms that a society or a community *happens to accept* because that way of putting it makes it clear that a society or a culture's moral values and ideals are contingent in the sense that there is no objective necessity providing a justificatory basis for moral values. There is no anchor or ground for moral concepts and moral evaluation external to whatever anchors or grounds the group in question endorses or accepts. These can differ across groups and can differ for a group across time. No group is in a position to have a more objectively accurate or adequate mode of moral evaluation than any other group.

It is possible that there are causal explanations for a group's moral values in the respect that various conditions (natural, historical, adaptive, social, and so forth) appear to explain why that group or society endorses the values it endorses. But the way they understand their values might involve no reference to those conditions, and members of the society might vehemently reject causal, functional, empirical accounts of their values. They might insist on the truth of what their culture values, and reject any claim that there is some other explanation for their commitments. Perhaps they are mistaken in that rejection of causal explanations; still *from their valuative perspective* what they take to be the ground of their values is the way their values matter to them. They might not regard their values as a consequence of conditions over which they have had little control. If it is pointed out to them that some of their values can be explained in terms of the social functions they serve they might reject such suggestions as an affront to their values, their agency, and their commitment to the truth.

In any event there can be various relations of mutual support between conceptual, cultural, and moral relativism. Each type highlights ways that our conceptions, our investigations, and our values do not correspond to the way the world is *anyway*, i.e., apart from how we describe, conceptualize, and evaluate things. Relativism maintains that there is no criterion or measure that we could apply to assertions to ascertain whether they are getting the world right, as it were. Moral relativism seems to have attracted a great many adherents and many of its adherents seem to think it is obvious or nearly obvious that moral relativism is true, in large part, on account of the diversity of moral views and practices and the lack of agreement that we find both historically and in the contemporary world. Plus, if values are not fact-based or fact-supported that might seem to be an additional reason for thinking moral relativism is a correct view. Many positivists might reason that if values are not fact-based and thus, scientific investigation will not enable us to attain any moral knowledge, then perhaps social scientists should try to maintain a studied neutrality regarding morality.

In discussing trends and developments in criminology Anthony Bottoms writes:

> Part of the strong legacy of positivism to British (and other) criminology has been a deep suspicion, in many "main-stream" criminological circles, about any kind of political or moral engagement on the part of criminologists...That view must, however, now be regarded as unsustainable; for the concept of "crime" itself, and the kind of criminal justice system that given society develops, must necessarily be the product of political and moral choices. Moreover, even the most careful, dispassionate, and rigorous criminological research can have political consequences.[11]

One could argue that criminological research has moral and political significance but it is not the job of the social scientist to make moral or political judgments, or if one does make such judgments it should be clear that they are not claimed to be justified by the results of research in anything more than an expressivist sense. But why all this insistence that moral judgment cannot be supported or guided or criticized or revised on the basis of knowledge and reasoning? If it is undeniable that normativity pervades the subject matter it would seem the responsible course is to consider carefully what sort of moral significance one's research could have. A declaration of relativism is not a way of advertising one's impartiality; it might indicate a refusal to engage in moral thought.

Or maybe not; of course, people can reflect upon and criticize the prevailing values and relativism is not an impediment to people considering their (and other's) values and being motivated to revise their commitments. However, according to relativism reflection and criticism never connect with objectivity. At the first-order level it might *seem* that it does. People argue vigorously about moral matters, giving reasons, presenting evidence, and regarding the issues as very important. In our moral experience it certainly can seem that objective values are at stake. We saw both Blackburn and Mackie observing that the phenomenology of morality is not different from what it would be if there *were* objective values. Relativism does not somehow dilute moral experience. But if one is methodologically committed to relativism on the grounds that there are no objective moral considerations even one's reflections cannot claim any epistemic merit. Nor would one regard anyone else's moral view as having any epistemic merit.

Perhaps relativism appeals because it seems to support a kind of epistemic and moral humility. It can seem a way of embracing moral and epistemic toleration of communities and cultures with very different ways of understanding the world and different values. It is a way of not taking a verdictive stance and not using the results of one's inquiry as a basis for evaluation of other ways of conceptualizing moral value. In addition, human intellectual history is littered with "certainties" that turned out to be less than certain and, for that matter, not even true. Relativism might seem to be a form of epistemic humility in that theories are overthrown, ways of seeing the world are displaced by other ways, and so forth. The same is true of moral views. Why should we think that we, now, are attaining a kind of understanding that will not be displaced by another?

4.2 Relativism and Moral Explanation

The critical response to moral relativism is similar to that regarding conceptual relativism. With regard to the latter the reality that is the object of understanding is never fully exhausted by our conceptions, theories, and explanations, and there are always reasons to pursue investigation further and to seek precision, integration, and accuracy without limit. We are to be responsive to the authority of reality, so to speak, and are not free to portray reality as a construction for which there is no objective measure. With regard to morality we also do not have a complete, fully elaborated conception of moral requirements and the moral significance of all kinds of facts, acts, practices, and situations. Morality is frequently interpreted in terms of rules and principles, yet it can be more illuminating to focus attention on the various modes or forms of moral significance. There are different forms of engagement with different kinds of ethical considerations and that is often overlooked.

Christine Swanton refers to what she calls "modes of moral responsiveness (or acknowledgement)."[12] She writes:

> They include not only promoting or bringing about benefit or value, but also honouring value (roughly, not dirtying one's hands with respect to value, e.g. by not being unjust in promoting justice), honouring things such as (appropriate) rules, producing, appreciating, loving, respecting, creating, being receptive or open to, using or handling appropriate things in appropriate ways.[13]

That brief passage reminds us that it is a drastic oversimplification to think of morality almost exclusively in terms of rules—requirements and prohibitions—and in terms of some single, fundamental value, and in one sort of response to that value. Moral experience and moral life are more textured than that. While we often focus on one primary value as the focus of attention in a situation it is often the case that good judgment involves appreciating the co-presence of numerous values. In a situation that requires courage it can be the case that compassion and justice are required as well. Or when honesty is required there might also be the need for courage and generosity, and so forth. Moral life is not lived one value at a time in nice, neat units or episodes. We do not encounter moral issues one at a time, each with a natural language label like a name plate under a painting in a museum. Even if one is committed to a primary, highly general value such as human welfare, it is almost inconceivable that just the one value will be adequate to address all moral matters. Or, if someone really does approach morality in that way that person will have a distorted and inadequate grasp of moral significance.

A virtuous person will exhibit numerous types of response, engagement, ways of interacting with others, restraining one's emotions, extending oneself, and so forth. This is one of the reasons virtue-centered ethics often acknowledges that ethics defies codification. Virtue-centered conceptions of ethics are often very sensitive to the variety of ways that value figures in our lives, the plurality of the values, and the need for judgment if we are to make excellent decisions. It is not as though the virtuous agent knows one thing really well or does one thing really well, unless we characterize that in very general terms such as "being responsive to good."

This is not the place to build a case for a virtue-centered conception of ethics. (I discuss this a bit further in the Appendix.) However, as just suggested, we should note that one of its merits is its alertness to the complex character of moral value, and also to the significance of the sort of attention and awareness the agent has. Iris Murdoch made much of the importance of *attention* in *The Sovereignty of Good* and that was a very valuable insight. We often overlook the importance of just being morally attuned, noticing morally relevant features of actions and situations, and exercising some care in how we see morally relevant considerations related to each other. This is often a quasi-narrative type of discernment; finding a moral "story-line" in what we are considering. (Look at the way Murdoch develops and illustrates the notion of attention.) Moreover, developing that ability requires fluency with moral concepts and a developed sensibility that is not just reacting to things but in conjunction with conceptual fluency gives us a kind of sensitive moral discrimination. A person might be very conscientious but in the absence of discrimination and conceptual acuity enabling the person to appreciate what is morally relevant the conscientiousness might amount to little more than clumsy seriousness.

Whether one's moral theory is committed to realism or, as in Hume's case, antirealism, there is equal scope for morality having a complex texture. That is one of the things that are often missed by explicating moral judgments in terms of pro- and con-attitudes. An emotivist could claim that of course morality is complex and textured but ultimately moral judgment is expressive and there are really only the two fundamental attitudes. But there are good reasons why that is much too reductive. Plus, as was shown earlier, if there is not an intelligible relation (which does not have to be logical, i.e., deductive derivation) between the facts about something and the attitude toward it then the significance of moral complexity can become muddled or pointless.

A reflective person who comes to settle on moral relativism and is aware of that as a second-order stance, is not then rationally required to regard her own views and moral commitments as some sort of play-acting. The second-order relativism might not disturb first-order moral seriousness. For relativism there is a sense in which it is true that what *seems* important is not objectively important, and what *seems* choiceworthy is not objectively choiceworthy, and what matters most does not objectively matter at all. But pain still hurts, failure remains frustrating, having friends continues to be gratifying, and one's plans and interests might lose none of their attraction and significance on account of the second-order view. Given that, we might wonder whether relativism actually makes any difference. If the phenomenology is unchanged then what is accomplished by leaving Plato's Cave, so to speak, rather than just staying there? Why should importance, worth, and mattering depend on objectivity? Plus, we have seen Hume argue that the lack of rational justification of our moral commitments does not erase their authority or genuineness.

However, we also saw that Hume was not a relativist and he thought it very important that moral judgments should be made from an impartial standpoint and not from a perspective domesticated to this or that group. That is because of how moral values differ from mere preferences and from approvals and disapprovals that do not involve crucial distinctions between sound and unsound judgments, and between supportable and arbitrary choices. Moral judgment, Hume argued, is not "local" and does not reflect just any expression of sensibility. There is a distinct moral perspective and it is possible to revise and refine moral judgments on the basis of facts, even in Hume's view.

There are some respects in which relativism *is* very problematic. We quoted Blackburn who insisted that in moral experience we do not have a thought of a type that says, "but it's only me and my feelings so, really, what difference does it make whether I help when I can or the person just suffers and dies?" First-order moral experience *seems* realist, and Hume and Blackburn both argued that moral experience does not need to be rationally vindicated as realist in order to be genuine morality. However, we also looked briefly at views such as McDowell's, which hold that there can be a role for sensibility in moral responses without that being indicative of antirealism or non-cognitivism. It is not as though a defense of moral realism can allow no constitutive role for affect and desire. For a paradigmatic conception of their inclusion see Aristotle. What is crucial is to see that even the realist (or most realists, in any case) is not claiming that the encounter with moral value is just like our encounter with physical objects. The moral properties of facts, acts, and situations are (argues the realist) no less genuine and no less accessible to cognition than the fact that bovine creatures are mammals, the fact that acorns are edible (by humans) if tannin is removed from them, the fact that magnets attract iron, the fact that cocoa is high in fiber, and the fact that there are many more men than women in China. Those facts and features of things have to be conceptualized to be recognized, and while many non-moral facts might be directly observable that is not the distinctive criterion of objectivity. Granted, moral considerations do involve sensibility and prescriptivity, and in that dual respect they differ from the fact that Douglas Fir trees typically grow taller than apple trees. But the difference is not one that renders objectivity impossible for moral considerations.

Why would it be the case that the repertoire of capacities of cognition, perception, sensibility, and reasoning that is employed in thinking and judgment generally cannot be employed in moral thought and judgment? To "see" that treating the children at the birthday fairly does not require giving every child the same size piece of cake (because some of the children are two years old and some are seven years old) is a moral judgment of a sort, and it involves no exotic faculties. To be sure, the moral antirealist will not agree with the realist on the *status* of moral considerations, but can agree that moral experience and moral considerations can have a kind of complexity that frequently requires developed, experience-educated sensibility and the exercise of judgment. Actually, there are antirealist views (Hume's is one of them) that are alert to moral complexity. There is the metaethical debate about whether they have the "right" to help themselves to that complexity, but that is another matter. Need a social scientist who is a moral antirealist impressed by Hume's reasoning conclude that one of Hume's lessons is to treat morality as merely expressive in a way that involves only spontaneous affect? No.

There are, though, important arguments against ethical non-cognitivism, and we will take a brief look at one of the critiques. In "Truth, Invention and the Meaning of Life" David Wiggins sought to show that there is a kind of incoherence in the non-cognitivist view of value. He noted that a feature of the phenomenology of moral life is that human beings "crave objective reasons"; we strive after things, aspire to things, care about things, etc., because of what *they* are—we cannot genuinely take it that the point and the value are projected by us onto them.[14] As he puts it, we cannot treat our appetitive states or states of valuing in isolation from the things they are directed at—the world must be involved—the objects of these states must be equal partners with the states. Various facts are significant in diverse ways because we see meaning and worth as a matter of the properties of things in the world. What reality includes is a crucial basis of what matters and why.

Wiggins argued that one of the faults in the non-cognitive view is that —"the non-cognitive account depends for its whole plausibility upon abandoning at the level of theory the inner perspective that it commends as the only possible perspective upon life's meaning."[15] That is the source of a kind of incoherence. From the inner perspective outcomes or results matter; but at the level of theory we see that they do not. From the theoretical perspective life is objectively meaningless but from the inner or lived or practical perspective we seek good reasons, objective considerations to support our valuations. The theoretical perspective regards our volitions as pointless, but no one could rationally and psychologically maintain such a view at the first-order level. The facts matter to us and to the ways we think things matter. Wiggins says, "the non-cognitive view always readdresses the problem to the inner perspective *without itself adopting that perspective*."[16] It cannot adopt it, because it has to remain unaware of the outer view, and hang onto its illusions of meaning; and that is where the incoherence is most evident.

Wiggins diagnoses a serious weakness in non-cognitivism, and by implication relativism. He has identified a reason non-cognitivism cannot coherently map the space of reasons concerning value. The problem Wiggins is highlighting is independent of the sorts of issues that get bogged down in "competitive culture" and "toleration of diversity" debates. The problem has to do with the fundamental conceptual/logical architecture of the view, an issue that has nothing to do with "that's *your* logic," as though logics can simply be invented to suit different interests and contexts. The relation between the "inner view" and the "outer view" is fraught in a way that renders the position untenable. He says, "no attempt to make sense of the human condition can really succeed if it treats the objects of psychological states as unequal partners or derivative elements in the conceptual structure of values and states and their objects."[17] And, pressing further the difficulty for the non-cognitive view of value Wiggins writes: "For no appetitive or aesthetic or contemplative state can see its own object as having a value that is derivative in the special way that is required by the thesis that all non-instrumental value resides in human states of satisfaction."[18] Non-cognitivism regarding value involves a conflict between the inner view of value on the part of the agent and the agent's reflective conception of value, a conception that renders the inner view counterfeit.

4.3 Relative to What?

There is a structurally similar problem for relativism. Reflection on its commitment to the notion that moral judgments are correct or incorrect only relative to the values and norms that members of a group happen to accept shows that such acceptance could never confer the sort of authority and genuineness of our valuative conceptions seem to have when we engage in valuative judgment. If we just never think about whether the norms are defensible, supported in ways that can be articulated in a set of reasons perhaps the problem is muted. But the defect in the position does not go away if we avert our minds from it. The relation between first-order valuative experience and judgment on the one hand and our theoretical perspective on that same issue on the other is problematic in a way that might render the position untenable. Persisting in the view after taking note of the difficulty would be rationally suspect.

There is another difficulty for relativism, one that is more clearly and directly motivated by it. How are we to discriminate and specify the relevant groups to which values are relative? For any individual there could be an enormous number of groups to which that person belongs. Consider a particular U.S. citizen. Suppose that individual is a Caucasian, lapsed Catholic, of mainly German ethnicity but partly Irish, lower middle-class, with a skilled but not professional occupation, lover of opera and 1940s-era noir films, former smoker, craft-beer aficionado, who is active in steam-engine restoration projects, and his girlfriend is trying to get him to take up ballroom dancing. That is just a start. There are many additional ways the person can be described and many different purposes for categorizing the individual. It might seem that many such categories are superficial or not especially important in regard to understanding the society in which the person lives or the person's morality. But there are any number of ways membership in one group can affect participation in others and a description on its own generally cannot reliably signal whether it is explanatorily significant or not.

It could be argued that there need not be some especially basic group to which a person's moral views are related, and that for different explanatory purposes different groupings can be highlighted. In fact, regarding some criminal justice issues, such as desistance, for example, it could be especially important that the person increasingly identifies with certain groups rather than others. But rather than illustrating the relevance of relativism that seems to diminish its explanatory purpose. What is important is that the person is responsive to certain *values*. Those might be especially important in a specific context or group but it is the values that make the difference to the prospects for a law-compliant life. Relativism mistakes the multiplicity of contexts for the relativity of values. Everyone's life, or nearly everyone's life is lived in a multiplicity of contexts and there can be different norms in them. But the values and norms that seem prevalent in a context are neither *ipso facto* morally authoritative nor should it be assumed that they are unrelated to the norms in other contexts. It is not as if fairness always requires the same conduct or that what fairness consists in is exactly the same in a context-indifferent way. Moreover it is certainly possible that in a given context the prevailing understanding of fairness or generosity, for instance, is corrupt and lacks moral justification.

In addition, spending part of the day or part of one's life in a different context in which different norms are the dominant ones does not mean that the person is now in a different moral world. Values are not put on and then shed the way that costumes for a theater performance are. Fairness in the context of a personnel evaluation at one's job might not be exactly the same behavior as fairness in distributing a medical resource in short supply at the county health clinic. That does not mean that fairness is relative, it means that being fair requires responsiveness to particular circumstances. A person who is fair, for whom fairness has become a reliable disposition and a constituent of character does not have different virtues of fairness, one for each of those different contexts. Rather, that person appreciates that what is owed to whom on the basis of fairness is not always the same thing. This illustrates what we were saying above regarding the merits of the virtue-centered approach. But even if one does not adopt that approach the relativist interpretation of moral values remains problematic.

It appears that reference to *any* group whatsoever could be seen as indicating moral relevance but that will rob morality of general significance. As just observed, in different contexts different considerations might be especially important. Domesticating values to groups is incompatible with the generality of moral judgment. There is no non-arbitrary way to specify the relevant contexts. The relativist might argue that in fact, generality is what is in doubt, and we should accustom ourselves to the reality that values are always relative to specific groups. Accustoming ourselves to that will enable us to achieve a focused understanding of valuative judgment in all sorts of specific ways that would be impossible if we insist on the generality of moral judgment.

Accordingly, it might seem that the notion of traditions might have a centrally important role in morality, a role in place of supposedly universal notions of rightness or virtue or moral good. With the notion of tradition we can explore just about any society's moral values, beliefs, and practices in a coherent way without worrying about showing how those are reflective of or connected with much more general conceptions, principles, and values. Also, the notion of tradition might seem especially well suited to explorations of ethics in which the notion of virtue has a key role. It might seem very plausible that conceptions of virtues should be local to cultures, to traditions, to worlds of practice, to certain social and political forms, and so forth. It seems plain that in different cultures—and at different times even within a particular social world—there are different conceptions of what count as ethical virtues and different notions of virtuous practice. Perhaps conceptions of virtue reflect rival, or at least, strikingly different views of human nature or at least human excellence. In recent decades works such as MacIntyre's *After Virtue* and *Whose Justice? Which Rationality?* have helped restore tradition as an important explanatory notion in (philosophical) ethics, and those works might seem also to make the case for relativism of virtue. Conceptions of virtue might seem "local" to specific traditions.

However, while the notion of tradition is indeed helpful to the articulation of ethical views, and perhaps virtues, in particular, we should not take the step from the importance of tradition to the endorsement of relativism too swiftly—or at all. For one thing, the notion of tradition does not imply or presuppose relativism. Tradition can be understood in terms of the transmission of beliefs and practices, as a mode of sustaining perspectives and values and types of knowledge without any specific connection with relativism. It is a mode of social and cultural continuity. As such, it could also have a connection with objectivity in the respect that a tradition could be a mode of access to what is objectively the case rather than a mode of thought and practice to which people resort when there is no objectivity or truth to which thought and practice can aspire. We might have a tendency to associate tradition with the *traditional*, as in a traditional society, one that remains largely insulated against modernity, internal critique, and reflective self-evaluation. However, to assume that being traditional in that sense is integral to the notion of tradition is a mistake. It is perfectly appropriate to speak of "the scientific tradition," or "the tradition of legal positivist thought," the "tradition of constitutional democracy" each of which is open to critique, refinement, and adjustment, and internally motivated forms of criticism.

Perhaps those seem like exceptions to a general rule that tradition really is most often associated with something other than objectivity and something much more like relativism. However, the latter is not a conceptual or logical link and there are also ways in which traditions can penetrate each other and there can be a deepening or broadening of understanding as a result of interaction between traditions. Maybe that does not happen as regularly as we would wish and perhaps traditions are more often in situations of conflict and cultural competition. Still, the mode of transmission that is characteristic of tradition, and the way tradition provides a kind of integration and coherence to beliefs and practices can be consistent with illuminating interaction.

There is an important respect in which human beings *need* traditions, in the sense that independence from tradition— genuine, complete independence from it —is not a real option for human beings on account of their social nature and the ways that they tend to learn, whether we are speaking of practical tasks and ends or more theoretical undertakings. The acquisition of concepts, the development of conceptual fluency and practical skill and achieving excellence, while they may all exhibit striking marks of individual distinction, are basically rooted in modes of activity and learning that involve tradition or, at the least, stable forms of habituation.

Commenting on MacIntyre's views regarding tradition Laidlaw remarks:

> if disentangled from MacIntyre's moralizing meta-narrative and the exclusive claim of his "Tradition" to be the only legitimate mode of moral life, there is nevertheless much that is helpful in MacIntyre's account: the notion of a good or excellence internal to a practice and of the pursuit of ideals through socially instituted and habituated practices, the importance of narrative understanding and reasoning, and the idea of ethical traditions being constituted in part through ongoing argument. All these have the potential to illuminate a great deal of ethnographic material.[19]

Again, it is possible for a tradition to be a mode of access to objective considerations. That does not mean that *of course* it does provide such access. However, depending on the content of the tradition those educated and habituated in a tradition might find that it provides guidance with regard to enlarging and deepening their understanding. There are numerous and diverse intellectual traditions such as the positivist tradition, the common law tradition, the empirical tradition, and the skeptical tradition, for example. Perhaps they are not traditions in just the same sense as traditions of a traditional society but a meaning tightly tied to *traditionalism* is not the only genuine or correct understanding of tradition. A tradition is not automatically or unavoidably a way of being cut off from objective understanding, even with regard to values. The fact that one learns certain ways of formulating and addressing issues when inducted into a tradition does not imply that one's thought will be dogmatic, uncritical, and inflexible. In any case, a tradition is not automatically at fault if persons are dogmatic, narrow-minded, and uncritical of their own views. To be sure, there are some traditions that do seem to be especially impervious to external influence and stubbornly resistant to criticism. But those are not marks of traditions as such.

It is very difficult to see what epistemic or explanatory illumination relativism affords. It lacks a helpfully clear approach to discriminating different groups to which values would be said to be relative, and in general, there is more to be gained by seeing how the values of different groups might share common concerns or mark developments of similar challenges and needs. I am not suggesting that there is a universal morality that will gradually come into view as cultures learn more about each other. There are a great many factors that can affect whether a genuinely shared morality develops, and why it develops. And it is true that frequently it is important to acknowledge real differences and the differences they make rather than trying to assimilate different groups' values into some broader, shared valuative view. However, what is gained by cutting off a valuative view from other valuative views? It might be that the conditions in which a particular society finds itself are quite unlike those found elsewhere and the society has a quite distinctive response to that in terms of its values. But we can understand that without invoking any relativist notions.

Laidlaw's critique of relativism involves an examination of anthropologists' views and attention to philosophical insights, the latter chiefly attributable to Bernard Williams.

> It is nearly always, as Bernard Williams puts it, either too early or too late for cultural relativism too early in a case of two parties between whom there is no contact, and neither of whom therefore can think of itself as "we" and the other as "they," since in such a case no problem has arisen for which relativism might be the answer; too late in cases where they interact to any significant degree, because there are no longer two separate entities (still less two different "worlds") between which relativism might prescribe relations (or rather non-relation).[20]

Laidlaw notes that anthropologists who profess to be relativists often find themselves espousing "performative contradictions"[21] on account of being committed to relativism on the basis of holding in an absolute way values such as "self-determination, tolerance, diversity, racial equality, anti-imperialism, etc."[22]

The more closely relativist views are examined, and the more explicitly explanatory considerations are articulated the less that relativism seems to offer. It is, as Laidlaw remarks, "an incoherent solution to a non-existent problem"[23] though it might have originally been motivated by what seemed insurmountable differences between cultures and a commitment to not impose the investigator's values on those being studied. Much more is to be gained in regard to explanation and mutual coherence by developing a fluency with the values being studied while not insisting that they are utterly alien to other societies or cultures. Indeed, what might be found is that the more one knows about remote cultures (though, it is not certain that remoteness is what matters) the more one can gain insight into one's "cultural home values" and the more that valuative considerations become intelligible, possibly with non-obvious but nonetheless discernible links, analogies, and likenesses.

In any case, suppose one believes that there are numerous, significant values that are universal. And suppose that it is very difficult to actually show that, given the differences between various cultures' values. It could be that, given the way human beings learn about values and come to thoughtful realizations of many valuative matters, the universality of values is something *found* rather than something *given*. Any plausible conception of moral values will include considerable scope for revision, refinement, adjustment, and noting hitherto unnoticed relations, and so forth. There could be room for finding numerous similarities, openings for mutual influence, and common concerns. Why foreclose on that via a declaration of relativism?

Also, it is important to realize that other cultures and people living in other eras have not been trying to be *us* (whoever *we* happen to be). There might be a tendency to regard one's own values as objective and tacitly use them as a measure against which to assess others' values. It is important to guard against that presumption and to be willing to subject one's own values or tradition to reflective criticism while also acknowledging that they are needed as starting points for one's reflections. It is almost certainly more realistic and illuminating to think of morality in terms of the various elements of guiding conceptions of human good(s) and ways of understanding and responding to the valuative features of situations in ways that are shaped by those conceptions. Those might take the form of codification to some extent; moral life almost always involves specific rule-formulated requirements and prohibitions. However, to think of morality almost entirely in terms of rules can be a way of overlooking the fact that it is values that make rules morally significant.

In addition, a great deal of moral life is a matter of making judgments regarding which values are most relevant to a situation. That judgment is where much of the moral work is done. That judgment depends upon the agent's appreciation of the situation. In many cases that appreciation comes easily. For example, one acknowledges that honesty is required, or that gratitude is required, or that sharing rather than taking all is required, and accordingly various possibilities are prohibited. But there is no assurance that situations calling for moral judgment will be that simple and straightforward. Plus, what sharing requires in the situation might take some careful consideration. Even being honest—in a way that is not needlessly hurtful or that does not compromise a confidence, and that involves admitting some moral mistake of one's own in the situation—might require alertness to numerous factors and careful deliberation about exactly what to do. In numerous respects rules come fairly "late" in the process of moral engagement and they are dependent upon a grasp of the situation.

Those considerations are among the reasons that virtues are especially important to the understanding of morality. Virtues (in the sense most relevant here) are states of character that are good to have because they enable a person to act well. They enable a person to act in ways that are worthwhile and that contribute to a well-led life. States of character can be dispositions of sensibility and desire ordered in accord with what reason understands to be good. For example, *courage* enables a person to manage fear, face risks, and be resolute in the face of challenging circumstances. *Temperance* keeps a person from excesses of indulgence that can be ruinous to health or that can involve reckless expense or greed. *Fidelity* and *honesty* are important to developing and sustaining relations of trust and to being able to rely on each other and being able to cooperate—things that people inevitably need. We can characterize many virtues in terms of rules or generalizations but the actual exercise of virtue often involves much more than just following a rule.

Granted, the concept *virtue* might seem especially well suited to helping elaborate moral relativism. It is obvious that different cultures and different periods have regarded different dispositions, responses, and behaviors as virtuous. Moreover, it can be a challenge to ascertain whether in a given case there has been a continuity of context but a change in what count as virtues, or the change has been on a more fundamental level and there is cultural discontinuity. In either case relativism might seem apt for addressing the diversity of conceptions of virtue and the traditions associated with many of them. One might wish to press the case for relativism further, insisting that notions of human good or goods are especially suited to relativist interpretation. While many conceptions of human good will be easily recognizable and will seem plausible several might seem strange or dubious. A very different society, perhaps a highly traditional, pre-industrial (but contemporary) society might have a conception of virtues that seems very remote from our conception.

It is important to distinguish between genuinely and deeply different conceptions of virtue on the one hand, and very different circumstances, needs, and preoccupations on the other. Any society will fashion some approach to caring for the very young and for the very old. It might be that many of the differences are not primarily a matter of the two cultures having utterly and irreconcilably different values, but instead, different ways of meeting their different conditions. This need not be a way of saying, "We all value the same things. It is just that those values are reflected or realized in different ways." Sometimes the values really are quite different. But we should be alert to the level of generality at which we are describing things, and aware of the sorts of contrasts and comparisons plausible at that level. There might be significant but unobvious similarities.

James Laidlaw writes, "In following Durkheim in equating morality with the social, anthropologists have often deemed practices and processes 'moral' simply because and insofar as they have the effect of strengthening collective cohesion, and values 'moral' just because they are shared, or collectivist in content."[24] He went on to add:

> It is easy to see, therefore, why insofar as anthropology inherited Durkheim's conception of the social, morality should have seemed simultaneously at the centre of its concerns, because an essential part of how social life gets constituted, and yet impossible to keep in focus, because once framed as a question narrowly of what are the collectively sanctioned rules and how do they come to be obeyed (or not), it becomes just another dimension of the master-problem of Durkheimian sociology, the explanation of how "social control" is established over unruly individual behavior.[25]

It is understandable that morality should be interpreted in terms of the theories with which social scientists elaborate their explanations. Yet, it is important to be responsive to the character of the phenomena being investigated and that can mean having a grasp of whatever is distinctive of morality. As Laidlaw points out in discussing the ways that many anthropologists approach morality mainly in terms of "functional devices of social control"[26]

> Nothing will prevent anthropologists from rediscovering that moral rules do indeed fulfil such a function, if the question of how this function is fulfilled is yet again asked (e.g. Yan 2011). The point, instead, is to find a way to ask another question. It is not to say that moral life contains no rules; it is to ask what if anything is distinctive about *these* rules: what might be true of the ethical dimension of human life that is not true of everything else?[27]

In Chapter 1 we argued that rules and norms are pervasive features of human life. Understanding the morality of a society or of a specific context within a society can present various challenges and difficulties but the intelligibility of the moral norms involved does not require somehow grasping something altogether unlike the other norms realized in, and guiding people's behavior. It might be very difficult to grasp some of the moral norms in ways that enable us to fully understand what it is like to genuinely endorse the values and principles they reflect. Still, that does not leave us so distanced that moral imagination fails us completely. We need to negotiate the space of reasons in ways that might be unfamiliar but it is an unhelpful misrepresentation to insist that another culture's form of life is alien in ways that make such negotiation hopeless or make it impossible to achieve a critical appreciation of it.

Moral considerations are one type of action-guiding consideration and there are several others. Reasons for acing based upon considerations of law, prudence, desire, custom, religion, peer pressure, and numerous other categories figure in what people do. In addition, one might do what the law requires because one believes it is a good law, or mainly to avoid drawing the attention of the authorities, or because one is characteristically compliant with authority. There are other motivations as well. There can be a great many combinations of action-guiding considerations and motives. Situations sometimes involve multiple types of urgency, and a person's response to urgency can reveal important aspects of character. There are also the phenomena of weakness of will and of honest self-awareness. The agent might exhibit *akrasia* and/or a measure of dishonesty regarding her motives or the type of action-guiding considerations to which she was responding. In addition, a person's circumstances can have a significant impact on the agent's notion of what is possible, or what is necessary, and why.

The point of this is that it is much too simplistic to consider morality primarily in terms of a set of rules and whether or not persons fulfill the requirements of those rules. Agents might frequently respond to several types of action-guiding considerations simultaneously and their motives might be mixed to some degree. A person with a notable degree of moral integrity will reliably respond to the moral considerations that are most pronounced in a situation but persons of lesser integrity or weak of will might act in ways that result from much more mixed notions of what is important and much more mixed motives.

Having discussed norms, rival interpretations of Hume, and some of the main considerations regarding relativism we are in a position to look at what is meant in saying that empirical criminology and moral philosophy can be mutually informing. In Chapter 5 we focus on some of the recent work of criminologists who are fully alert to the ways that moral considerations can figure in investigating issues of criminal justice and the ways those investigations can be morally illuminating.

Notes

1 Israel Scheffler, *Science and Subjectivity*, Indianapolis: Hackett Publishing Co., 1982, p. 17.
2 Ibid., p. 19.
3 Anthony Bottoms, "The Relationship between Theory and Empirical Observations in Criminology," in *Doing Research on Crime and Justice*, 2nd ed., eds. R. D. King and E. Wincup, Oxford: Oxford University Press, 2008, pp. 75–116, p. 77.
4 Ibid., p. 77, italics in original.
5 Ibid., p. 78.
6 Ibid., p. 38.
7 Ibid., p. 39.
8 Philippa Foot, "Moral Beliefs," in *Virtues and Vices*, Berkeley: University of California Press, 1978, pp. 110–131, p. 112.
9 Ibid., 112–113.
10 Yet, even in liberal democracies there can (and often do) remain various tensions regarding cultural and valuative diversity, and in the Anglophone states there has been a long and still incomplete process of democratization and cultivation of mutual respect. A state's ideals and fundamental commitments often remain only incompletely realized. However, as argued in Chapter 1, a merit of a liberal political order is that it can sustain the conditions for an open, dynamic civil society. It is not clear that a political order in which democracy was the most fundamental value would be in which the freedom and equality of persons is steadily recognized in genuinely effective ways.
11 Bottoms, "The Relationship Between Theory and Empirical Observations in Criminology," pp. 75–116, p. 92.
12 Christine Swanton, *Virtue Ethics: A Pluralistic View*, New York: Oxford University Press, 2003, p. 21.
13 Ibid.
14 David Wiggins, "Truth, Invention, and the Meaning of Life," in *Needs, Values, Truth*, Oxford: Blackwell, 1987, pp. 87–138.
15 Ibid., p. 135.
16 Ibid., p. 136. Italics in original.
17 Ibid., p. 106.
18 Ibid., p. 105.

19 James Laidlaw, *The Subject of Virtue: An Anthropology of Ethics and Freedom*, Cambridge: Cambridge University Press, 2014, p. 79.
20 Ibid., p. 27.
21 Ibid., p. 29.
22 Ibid., p. 28.
23 Ibid., p. 24.
24 Ibid., p. 21.
25 Ibid., p. 22.
26 Ibid., p. 23.
27 Ibid.

Chapter 5

Some Illustrations

In this chapter we will look at some recent criminology as a way of illustrating some of the main points made thus far. This is work that is empirical and, at the same time, concerned with moral considerations. The moral features of institutions, actions, and policies are treated as moral features, and not drained of moral content so that—in the positivist sense—only the facts are included in what is studied. Investigation that is not constrained in that way can help explicate important moral phenomena and also show how moral phenomena themselves can have an explanatory role. There can be a fruitful intersection of empirical inquiry and moral philosophy. The claims that have been made regarding normativity were meant to help build a case for that claim, and here at the opening of the chapter I make some remarks about social scientific study of normativity. Then we look more closely at some examples of criminological investigation that explicitly addresses normative and valuative matters.

Chapter 1 defended the view that even when knowledge of causal considerations and dispositions is enormously helpful in explicating human behavior that is not a matter of one kind of knowledge displacing another or rendering the other merely anachronistic. The formulation of empirical explanations does not render normative considerations otiose or indicative of a humanistic and unscientific perspective. Normativity, I argued, is more constitutive than that in the conceptions of ourselves, each other, and a vast amount of human activity, understanding, and experience. The space of reasons is not a strange and inscrutable "nowhere" inhabited only by confused and misled philosophers. The notion of the space of reasons is a way of indicating that illuminating accounts of thought, understanding, various forms of judgment, and the exercise of rational capacities involve features that are not just complex arrangements of unthinking, unconceptualized events and processes. Maybe, for example, there is much more cognition in nature than we generally imagine, and the natural world includes much more of what many people like to think of as distinctively human. That would not, in its own right, be a reason to conclude that human cognition can be accounted for entirely within terms that include no role for normativity, and that causality can do all the work

DOI: 10.4324/9781003037323-6

that normativists insist on, and can do it entirely without invoking normativity. There would remain a great deal in the human world (philosophy, science, universities, banking systems, air traffic control, writing books, writing poems, political institutions, the rule of law, etc.) that is not *nothing but* a more complex version of what is found in many other portions of nature. Or, rather, it is not clear what is genuinely illuminated by insisting that it is nothing more than a more complex version. In any case, normativity figures in human beings' lives in a great many ways and many of the norms concern many aspects of criminal justice.

Though I will not attempt to summarize the various positions that social scientists have adopted regarding the explanation of norms it will be helpful to take note of some of the main characteristics of the issues and the debates. That will point to additional considerations in favor of non-positivist views.

5.1 Some General Considerations About Norms

Not only are norms present in a huge number of contexts; to a large extent contexts of human activity are shaped by the norms integral to them. Moreover, there are numerous different *kinds* of norms. Even within a given context there can be multiple kinds of norms. For example, there are moral norms. The norm that one is to answer truthfully unless there is a quite special reason not to is a norm concerning honesty, and of course there are many other moral norms expressible in terms of action-types. One is to make promises in good faith; one is to treat others fairly; one is to care and provide for one's children, and so forth. However, there are also norms regarding appropriate and inappropriate ways of feeling and showing various sentiments. Consider, for example, admiration, gratitude, grieving, condolence, celebration, and so forth. Many of what we call "moral sentiments" involve norms.

Sometimes there are genuine feelings involved, sometimes there are not; someone might recognize that it is appropriate to express condolence in a given situation even if the person does not have much feeling regarding the person who has died or the person for whom this is a significant loss. Still, the "decent thing to do" we might say, is to express condolence. It would be a bit harsh to call that "feigning sympathy"; it would be more accurate to say that in this case sympathy is being shown largely as a matter of etiquette rather than being heartfelt. Is this *merely* a matter of etiquette? We might want to say that for the person who really just does not care, it is a matter of etiquette—but perhaps that is because that person is not showing the appropriate moral response. In this case, while the etiquette is welcome it is also a poor substitute for genuine sympathy. There is an appropriate moral response that is not merely etiquette but if a person just does not have that response the etiquette of condolence is better than just evident unfeeling unconcern.

Generally, we do not make a similar distinction between rightly felt and focused *admiration* on the one hand, and making a passable show of it on the other. Admiration differs somewhat from condolence in that respect. It could be that someone fails to admire another because of jealousy or resentment; in that case there are moral sentiments involved and a person can be said to not have the appropriate sentiments. Still, showing admiration does not have the sort of obligatoriness of condolence. *Gratitude* often does, and there are any number of possible situations in which not showing gratitude (even if not genuinely heartfelt) would be a fault and not simply a minor failure of etiquette. Whether or not we have feelings of fondness for our benefactor or have strong feelings of appreciation for what was given there are situations in which gratitude is owed.

Similarly, in the absence of certain sorts of factors we are to congratulate persons on getting married even if privately one has some doubts about the wisdom of the marriage. If those doubts have been undisclosed up to the time of the marriage (and if it would be highly inappropriate to raise them only at the last minute) it is almost always best to congratulate and hope for the best rather than suddenly make known one's doubts. There might be a formal invitation of such doubts in a wedding ceremony but it is probably a widely shared social norm that the invitation is meant in a mainly ceremonial way, and especially if one is not close to the parties getting married. Granted, if I have just arrived at the ceremony and I alone know that the groom is guilty of a massive financial fraud and a blackmail operation I should probably speak up. But that is an exceptional sort of case, one hopes.

There are also more complicated cases, such as those in which a parent never becomes angry over the needless, very bad behavior of their adolescent son or daughter. We might think, "for heaven's sake, do you just let that kid off, no matter what? If it was my kid, I'd be plenty angry over this." This might be a situation in which the norms of one group differ from those of another. Or, perhaps it is a case in which these parents just accept whatever mischief—or worse—their teenage children get into, and they seem incapable of reprimanding or punishing them, with the result that those teenagers acquire some very bad habits. In any case, whatever disagreements there might be over what constitutes good parenting, it is clear that there are at least some norms for the appropriateness of anger even if it is not nearly as clear what form the expression of anger should take. There is also the difference between (i) never becoming angry no matter what the teen does, and (ii) feeling anger but believing it is always wrong to show it, and (iii) feeling anger but concern not to alienate the teen's affection is given priority over everything else, and thus, not showing anger. The number and variety of contexts in which it is reasonable to expect persons to become angry, and the diversity of ways it might be thought one should manage one's anger give rise to a host of issues concerning anger and the norms appropriate to it.

Anger is not an appropriate response to just *anything*, and at the same time there are situations in which failing to become angry—or at least making a show of anger—will seem to reflect poor judgment and a failure to properly appreciate the situation. Anger can be excessive, damaging, and it can cause needless harm. Sometimes a person's anger or the way that it is directed at someone also reflects unfairness, perhaps making the wrong person the object of one's anger or it is plainly disproportionate. There might be significant disagreements with regard to norms concerning the appropriate expression of various moral sentiments and attitudes but it seems quite clear that for many of them the dispute is over the norms, not whether *there are* (or should be) any. When we say to someone, "You've got to learn to control that temper of yours" that presupposes that there are relevant norms.

It would be less plausible to suggest that there are norms for envy, arrogance, and spite. Arrogance and spite are always morally suspect and it is doubtful that there are ways of feeling (and expressing) them rightly, or with good reason. We might have little difficulty understanding someone's envy but that still does not indicate that there is a way of feeling it rightly. Someone might have reason to feel that their own efforts have not been availing and someone else is enjoying advantages that improve that person's life quite a lot. In that case envy might be both understandable and excusable, but that is still not quite the same as being felt rightly. And while we can often understand a person's jealousy we would be less understanding if their jealousy becomes embittered and develops into malicious spite.

We might find it odd that someone does not mourn the loss of a life-partner but if the surviving person's view is, "she lived a very full life and had almost no regrets, and always wanted to be a source of joy to her friends; I won't spoil that gift by being sad" we might understand the absence of mourning. Or if someone's last wish was that friends would come together to celebrate her life and not mourn her death—and that is what her friends do—that is quite different from just seeming not to care very much about the loss. This example might seem to violate some widely held, firmly established social norms but it would not be quite right to say that the deceased person's friends showed a lack of appropriate sadness at her death. Actually, they were respecting her wishes.

The norms with regard to many sentiments and attitudes can involve an element focused on how they are felt and an element focused on the behavioral aspects of them.

We expect someone who has been openly treated in a demeaning way to be angry about it and to resent it. To just accept it or to feel as though it is merited would typically seem to reflect a deficit of self-respect. Adam Smith elaborated a conception of resentment as a sentiment through which the concern for justice is upheld. He recognized that resentment can be toxic and can have an improper object or be felt to an improper degree but he argued that there is a morally appropriate role for resentment and that it is not an inherently or necessarily wrongful or morally problematic sentiment. In addition, there can be forms of behavior appropriate to expressing one's resentment.[1]

What is evident, even from this small number of examples, is that there is a very complex texture of normativity in human beings' actions, and interactions, sensibility, and attitudes. Geoffrey Brennan and co-authors write

> Norms are ubiquitous in social life. Every time we enter a room, open our mouths to speak, walk down the street, conduct a meeting, play a game of cards, write an email, or wage a war, norms are in play. All our interactions with others are mediated by a complex multiplicity of norms. Without norms, it is doubtful that there could be such a thing as a free market economy or democratic politics or indeed society as we know it.[2]

Brennan and co-authors distinguish three categories of norms; there are formal norms (and legal norms are paradigmatic of this kind), norms that comprise moral codes, and social norms. Social norms "are not made, interpreted, and enforced by a central authority."[3] "Nor, (unlike moral norms) do they principally derive their authority from any objectively valid normative principles that they purport to represent. Rather, social norms purport to be somehow authoritative in their own right."[4] Of course, one might argue for a different typology of norms, but in any case, it is evident that there are multiple types of norms, and as Brennan's view suggests, they have different sources and differ in the sort of authority they have.

There are also epistemic norms and their relations to moral and political issues can result in very complicated situations. At present in the United States there is a very public dispute about which norms regarding COVID-19 vaccines should be the decisive ones. Should they be norms based on the safety and effectiveness of the vaccines or should they be political/moral norms? Or, if all the norms have legitimate places in the debate what should be the relations between them? Addressing this situation is proving to be much more contentious and difficult than just about anyone imagined it would be. It might have been widely and confidently thought that public policy should be led by our best understanding of how to contain the pandemic; that and considerations of public health properly have an authoritative place in deciding what is to be done. We are finding that very different views of the matter are also firmly held.

Brennan and co-authors say that they will consider and reject the *norms as practices* view and *the norms as desires* view, two of the most influential conceptions of norms in social scientific theorizing. Rejecting those views, they go on to defend a *norms as normative attitudes* view, "according to which norms are clusters of normative attitudes plus knowledge of those attitudes."[5] This, is, as they say, a non-reductive view.

One of the chief competing views maintains that norms are "grounded upon individuals' preferences and expectations."[6] In that view, developed by Cristina Bicchieri, there are three conditions for a social norm to exist and be followed. The first is that "the individuals involved *believe* it exists and know the class of situations to which the norm pertains."[7] Second, "individuals must have a *conditional preference* for following the norm."[8] The third condition is "the presence of empirical and normative expectations."[9] The notion of preference here is that a person will obey a given norm if she expects others to comply with it, and believes that others expect her to obey the norm.[10]

One of the issues that figures importantly in the debate over a theoretical account of norms has to do with whether, and in what ways social norms require attitudes as well as behavior. It seems quite plausible that at least some social norms would require attitudes as well as behavior; attitudes in their own right have a significant place in the relations between people, and attitudes can be the difference between behavior that fully counts as behavior of a certain type and behavior that does not. Also, there could be contexts in which attitudes are expected or required by social norms even if a person is not independently motivated to exhibit the attitude. As Han Van Wietmarschen says,

> ...it is often important to have norms requiring attitudes or behavior even when the individuals subject to it have sufficient norm-independent reason to conform to the rule. It makes sense to have a legal norm against killing persons, for example, even if most or all individuals have sufficient moral reason not to kill persons. One reason to have such norms is that they may provide motivation to conform to the rule in situations where people fail to be motivated by their moral reasons.[11]

The empirical considerations involved in the approaches mentioned more or less presuppose normativity of the kind characterized in Chapter 1 insofar as the identification of the relevant preferences, beliefs, and rules of behavior depend on the normativity involved in conceptualization. In addition, the explanatory project is rule-governed, norm-informed in a number of ways.

The complex fabric of normativity in the criminal justice context is connected with numerous other contexts; multiple layers and aspects of normativity, and intersections of those layers. Normativity is largely lost to positivism except in terms of causal relations and dispositions that purport to replace it and eliminate its allegedly mysterious character. But as we have noted several times, the identification of causes and effects, and the identification of dispositions—what is disposed, and *to what* it is disposed, and the difference made by the disposition—depend at the least on the normativity of conceptualization. This is not a form of linguistic idealism; the social world is a public world of practice and interaction informed by a community of thought and meaning. And that community is the context in which other forms of normativity, including moral normativity, subsist.

We will look at some examples of empirical investigation engaging explicitly with normative considerations—including valuative considerations. There is a two-fold sense in which valuative considerations figure in these investigations. First, they are an attempt to understand how moral considerations figure in the behavior and attitudes and practices they study. Thus, the investigations regard normative considerations as having explanatory significance. Second, they also show how what is studied is an appropriate object of explanation-informed moral concern and moral judgment. I do not mean that the inquirers see themselves as moral experts dispensing moral wisdom but that they are willing to accept the responsibility of noting matters of moral significance when their investigations lead to them. Normativity and values are treated as among the empirical matters to be investigated rather than being regarded as a distorting lens or unscientific fabrication, and they are also recognized as the basis of a great deal of the significance of what is disclosed by investigation.

5.2 Investigating Moral Life Through the Study of Prisons and Prisoners

Many studies by criminologists investigating a wide variety of issues could be cited to illustrate claims made thus far about the significance of normativity, the possibility of empirical study of morality, and ways that philosophical conceptions have influenced the work of social scientists. As we noted in the Introduction, the history of the social sciences during the last one hundred and twenty-five or one hundred and fifty years is rich with methodological reflection and innovation. Criminological investigations of a number of topics, from several angles of approach could be used to show how normativity is being explored. However, the studies providing our illustrations seem especially well suited to that role. One reason is that they include critical awareness of the philosophical issues connected with normativity and with morality in particular.

Consider the work Alison Liebling has done on the "moral performance" of prisons. Liebling wrote, "[b]y moral performance we mean those aspects of a prisoner's mainly *interpersonal* and material treatment that render a term of imprisonment more or less dehumanizing and/or painful."[12] She noted that the virtues that matter so centrally in prisoners' moral performance—virtues such as respect, fairness, showing concern for others, being helpful, and so forth—are among "the foundation of our social life"[13] and are virtues "that human beings need."[14] Moral performance looks at much more than rules and enforcement and it is centrally concerned with attitudes and modes of sensibility that shape prison life. It also includes the extent to which prisoners are able to regard themselves as agents and not just objects, and the ways in which prisoners find it realistic to think about participating again in civil society upon release.

Features of prison culture and the quality of life in prisons such as the way staff interact with prisoners, the extent to which prisoners are permitted to exercise any judgment, and the extent to which they are given honest, informative explanations of policy and disciplinary decisions all figure in the institution's moral performance. This is a way of acquiring a great deal of empirical data regarding the sorts of relations and modes of interaction that are especially important to people. A prison is an extreme environment even if it is a safe, orderly place in which the prisoners feel as though they are treated decently, and in many prisons the extremes are aggravated by poor conditions and bad treatment. In one sense what the study of moral performance disclosed is what we might commonsensically expect; rates of depression, violence, and feelings of hopelessness are much lower in prisons in which prisoners believe they are treated fairly and are listened to. Humane treatment is good for human beings. But it is important to show that on the basis of a large body of carefully collected empirical data.

Liebling compared the different cultures in five prisons and found substantial differences in staff–prisoner relationships and the prevailing dispositions of the administrative regimes. Those held in prisons where there was little civil interaction or trust between staff and prisoners, where they were shown little respect and felt that procedures were unfair, were more likely to agree with the statement "my time here seems very much like punishment."[15] An important factor, according to prisoners' reports, was whether prisoners were treated with respect and trust, whether they felt stripped of their human dignity, and whether they had the sense that authorities made genuine efforts to take the prisoners' welfare into account. In fact, we could interpret the evidence as showing that it made a considerable difference to prisoners to be included in the space of reasons. Also, the sorts of conditions of moral intelligibility that we discussed in regard to the rule of law—the conditions that need to be met for rules that are to govern the behavior of rational agents—were strongly relevant. Prisoners not only want not to be voiceless and powerless but they also want to be regarded as meriting an environment that includes them as rational agents. That enhances their sense of the legitimacy of the regime and that can help support a habit of compliance.

Several decades ago, writing of prison in the U.S. Gresham Sykes said:

> The rules, the commands, the decisions which flow down to those who are controlled are not accompanied by explanations on the grounds that it is "impractical" or "too much trouble." Some of the inmate population's ignorance, however, is deliberately fostered by the prison officials in that explanations are often withheld as a matter of calculated policy.[16]

In many prisons inmates develop their own rules and regime of self-government. That can be a way to enforce a certain conception of solidarity or at least a form of cohesion in their own terms with "us against them" as its animating principle. Often, in this version of "self-government" there is a hierarchy of authority (and power) among the prisoners and they make it clear that non-compliance has costs, which might include sanctions involving violence or at least intimidation. For some, this is an important source of community and power. For the unfortunates at the lower levels of the hierarchy this can mean that they are exposed to a second source of power and sanction. They are now doubly vulnerable, needing to answer to the prison staff and to other prisoners.[17] And as Marguerite Schinkel has noted regarding prisoners in the U.K., "[b]y accepting the prisoner culture, one of antisocial values opposing the norms of prison staff and society at large, the prisoner has difficulty in adapting to life outside once he is released."[18] Given the ways in which voluntariness, choice, and activity in general are very narrowly constrained, and given the possibility of having to respond to multiple "authorities" perhaps none of which involves respect and concern for dignity, the prison experience is very poor preparation for return to civil society and it can have a damaging impact on one's psychological health and self-conception.

Liebling's study of English prisons found that "the absence of respect and fairness (among other values) is psychologically painful, as other prison studies have shown. Being treated disrespectfully or without dignity generates negative emotions (anger, tension, indignation, depression, and rage)."[19] She reports a prisoner remarking

> The way I look at it, we have no control over our lives. They do our thinking for us, so in that way we have none [humanity]. We're not allowed to think for ourselves in jail; they tell us when to eat, when to go to work; when we can do things.[20]
>
> (Prisoner, Holme House)

Discussing her large-scale study of the moral culture of prisons, Liebling wrote:

> We had become persuaded that the relational aspects of a prison's life, and its linked ethos or culture, were crucial to the prison experience, and yet were not adequately captured by official data collection methods. As one of the prisoners we interviewed put it:
>
> When I first came in, I had no pillow. I approached two officers—they were chatting, so I waited. Eventually, one of them asked me what I wanted. He said, 'You're not entitled to a pillow' and carried on chatting. They were not concerned about me. That seems minor, but it's crucial. It can turn you into a different person.[21]

Liebling reported that

> prisons differ in their moral performance and that, at best, apparently "high performing" establishments only deliver "fairness," "respect," "humanity," and "safety" to a limited extent. The more troubled prisons score very poorly on these value dimensions. There are serious implications of a "differential delivery of punishment" and a "differential delivery of pain," with some prisons being experienced by prisoners as much more distressing than others.[22]

An individual who leads a life in the space of reasons is an individual for whom meaning, worth, and significance are crucial to their activities. Think of the difference between someone who only pursues desires, and who follows whatever happens to be the strongest desire, and someone for whom the evaluation of their desires has a point. This person might generally just pursue what is desired but will at least be alive to the possibility of making judgments of *worth*. This is someone who will want to connect their desires with what they regard as worthwhile or important. In that respect, practical rationality in the space of reasons involves a kind of moral or at least valuative imagination employed in reflective judgment. If such an individual is starved of the occasion and opportunity for that it is hardly surprising that he or she will find that deeply demoralizing. "The absence of any means for meaning-making and identity formation in prison, and the imposition of indeterminate and unthinkably long prison sentences to which these experiences are linked might arguably constitute inhumane and degrading conditions."[23] A very long sentence (decades perhaps) can be demoralizing in the literal sense of diminishing the prisoner as a moral agent. Abilities for rational judgment, self-determination, and interaction with others can go unused or are exercised in only very limited ways. In becoming accustomed to an environment in which those abilities are not used and in which the exercise of them is regarded as a challenge to order and authority can result in the abilities being lost. They cannot be suspended without loss through a lengthy period of being unused.

Granted, some people serving long sentences have committed terrible crimes and are very dangerous people. (They might deserve lengthy sentences but the gravity of their offenses does not justify inhumane or degrading treatment.) But there are many others for whom a long sentence is not similarly justified and they are harmed by conditions that are morally suspect both in regard to considerations of proportionality, and often also just in terms of being harsh and debilitating. In addition to incapacitating prisoners who present a high risk of reoffending and harming others the conditions can also incapacitate prisoners—high risk or not—with regard to the dispositions they need to return successfully to civil society. Even with regard to very dangerous offenders for whom especially strict conditions are needed those conditions should nevertheless meet at least a plausible minimum of moral acceptability.

Many aspects of prison life can be described in moral terms without highly contentious and tendentious claims or interpretation. The sort of investigation Liebling undertook does not depend on a specific, potentially controversial interpretation of moral life and moral experience. It is not as though someone reading the work would think, "That is not a set of moral categories I can imagine using. The very formulation of the issues depends on a moral interpretation that is dubious." Someone might want to explore whether a study focusing on additional or other moral concepts could be as illuminating but it is doubtful that an alternative set of concepts would be motivated by finding the ones used to be inappropriate or suspect in an important way. To a large extent the moral idiom that is employed in Liebling's work is very familiar "common sense" discourse concerning morality.

A notable finding is that many of the values that are especially important in the civil society of a liberal democracy are also values that are highly important to prisoners. She wrote:

> In our quantitative analysis...humanity was strongly correlated with respect, fairness, trust, relationships, and support. What seems distinct about the accounts of the term "humanity"...is the emphasis on *personhood*. In their answers, prisoners linked humanity most Closely to respect—which was often interpreted as "being treated as a human being," where staff "don't talk down to you"; they "treat you as a person of value."[24]

In prison many of the values and norms that are integral to a liberal democratic political order remain of the first importance, or at least they remain important to prisoners who are not already so alienated from moral values that decent treatment will not elicit a more civil response on their part. It seems especially important to many prisoners that certain basic moral considerations should continue to have weight within the prison walls. The standards governing order are obviously different in a prison, and they depend on the security level of the prison, but many prisoners felt that it was crucial that their humanity be recognized, and in many cases this basically just meant showing some small consideration.

In response to questions about humanity one prisoner said

> Here they have a laugh with you, play pool, have a little bet, and they pay up! We bet for chocolate bars. They give you straight answers and help you as much as they can and don't swear unless they're messing about. They see that being in prison is not to punish you more than having your liberty taken away. (Prisoner, Doncaster)[25]

When evidence is gathered regarding features of persons' experience and the character of relations between people that shape an overall atmosphere we see that rather than focusing on the central principle of this or that specific moral theory it might be most revealing to recognize that a familiar vocabulary of sociability and ordinary civil interaction can actually capture and express much that is very significant. The fact that many of the prisoners were able to express themselves in that sort of vocabulary suggests that they had a level of articulation that enabled them to highlight matters of trust and trustworthiness. That might not be as common across prison populations as we might wish, and certainly prisoners for whom gang loyalty or racial solidarity or a code of silence is their anchoring commitment probably would not respond in these terms. Still, it is important that a large, articulate vocabulary of moral concepts is employed in grasping the morally significant features of the prisoners, their situation, the prison staff, and the character of their relations and interactions.

In prisons crowded with violent offenders, many of whom have very poor education, spotty records of employment, and multiple convictions, their primary concerns perhaps would not be formulated in the terms used by prisoners just quoted. In *Reforming Punishment* Craig Haney writes, "It is not surprising that the overcrowded conditions and anti-rehabilitation ethos that characterized the last several decades in American corrections appear to have greatly increased the criminogenic risks that persons must overcome following incarceration."[26] Haney quotes Joan Petersilia's summary of research on released prisoners.

> The average inmate coming home will have served a longer prison sentence than in the past, be more disconnected from family and friends, have a higher prevalence of substance abuse and mental illness, and be less educated and less employ-able than those in prior prison release cohorts. Each of these factors is known to predict recidivism, yet few of these needs are addressed while the inmate is in prison or on parole.[27]

Also, if civil interaction between staff and prisoners is discouraged even if there are few violent or unstable prisoners and there isn't an atmosphere of high tension and fragile order there could be undesirable results for prisoners and staff. Some of the same factors that habituate and shape many of the prisoners' dispositions are likely to have an unwelcome impact on staff as well. We could find that prison staff instructed to have no informal or spontaneous interaction with prisoners and to interact only on the basis of the requirements for keeping order and maintaining security acquire habits and forms of regard for others that will not serve them well when participating in civil society outside the prison. Of course, maintaining order is crucial. But maintaining order is compatible with many different degrees of civil interaction especially if many of the prisoners do not have records of violent behavior.

Much can depend on what the prevailing societal attitudes regarding offenders are. Jonathan Simon identifies key features of a view of crime, criminals, and punishment he calls "total incapacitation," a view he believes is widely held in the United States.

> First, according to the prevailing wisdom, most criminals have a high and unchanging potential for criminal activity, including violence, even if their present offense is not violent. Second, prison can do little to change criminals for the better, but prison can prevent them from endangering innocent people by keeping criminals locked up. Third, so-called penal experts cannot predict which criminals poses the most danger, so long sentences should be given to all. Fourth, any time a criminal leaves prison for any reason, the community becomes less safe.[28]

This is a view in which moral possibility is precluded. In such a view if a prisoner shows signs of willingness to try to reintegrate successfully into free society that might not be regarded as credible, authentic. Instead, it might be seen as a form of manipulation perhaps in the hope of being treated better while incarcerated. If there is only a minimal culture of communication, that will make it very difficult for prisoners to acquire the habits needed for participation in civil society.

The civil society of a liberal democracy depends heavily on people being trusting and trustworthy, on the willingness to interact in a considerable diversity of ways with strangers without first checking their backgrounds or observing them in relevantly similar situations. In the epistemic context we accept the vast majority of what we know (or claim to know, or at least what we believe) on the testimony of others. This occurs in the form of conversational testimony, the testimony of published works, persons regarded as relevant experts, and so forth. Similarly, we accept the word of others when there is something we wish to know about a particular person. There is not much at all that we actually ascertain for ourselves in an epistemically thorough and methodologically rigorous way. For a great many of our beliefs this is not problematic. If we could not accept the testimony of others our lives would almost surely be different—and diminished—in ways it is difficult to imagine. If we believed that we could only accept claims we have actually proven or for which we can present a sufficiency of justifying grounds, and that we are not to act on any claims that do not meet those standards our lives, both intellectual and practical, would be stunted and contracted severely. The acceptance of testimony presupposes a significant level of trust on the one side and reliability (or at least good faith) on the other, and each of us is on each side countless times.

The trust and trustworthiness create the space in which testimony can have authority. That is the basis of important, informal epistemic norms. We rely on those more regularly than we rely on fulfilling formal terms of epistemic justification through our own systematic efforts. Because people (generally, certainly not always) adhere to norms of good faith communication and regard each other as rational a great deal of their interaction consists in a social fabric of normativity rather than exclusively causal interaction. At least that is so in the social world of a stable liberal-democracy. That form of political order both permits and requires a level of trust that is not expected in an authoritarian regime. Where the culture of communication does not permit that sort of fabric to be created the society will become less and less civil. That people are expected to be morally intelligible to each other and more rather than less open in expressing their beliefs and commitments is a crucial aspect of the civility of civil society. Being persistently subject to repressive conditions people can become accustomed to being treated in ways that do not include a mutual concern to be morally intelligible. They will not expect explanations and justifications that are plausible and responsive to their concerns, and they will not expect to be asked what their own views and concerns are. Those do not matter in a repressive regime.

Numerous studies support the conclusion that programs and practices in prison that encourage prisoner engagement, in ways that are democratic, and that genuinely involve prisoners as full-fledged participants will help the most in regard to preparing prisoners to return to civil society successfully. This means that the modes of engagement by staff can be critically important. They need to respond to prisoners and interact with them in ways that diminish the impact of the ordinarily very pronounced differences in freedom, authority, and role that are more or less fixed features of prison life. Discussing the sorts of approaches that seem to work best in regard to helping prisoners transition to free society Stephen Duguid writes

> This not only provides a forum to practice democratic solutions, but allows the outlaw-exile-prisoner the option of adopting the role of citizen, even in its truncated carceral form. Because prisons are structurally authoritarian and dehumanizing it is especially important that staff working in such participatory and democratic programs accept the limitations on their authority that reciprocity implies.[29]

Considerations about legitimacy are no less significant in prison than outside it. That is because a prison too, is located in the space of reasons.

> Legitimacy should be clearly distinguished from "appeasement" or "pleasing the prisoners." Sparks et al. point out that prisoners (often) know the difference between reason-able expectations (that a visit will be preserved) and unreasonable or "unjustifiable" requests ("don't patrol our exercise yard"). These are expectations which can be justified in relation to a wider set of largely shared beliefs about what is reasonable. Legitimacy requires reference to standards that can be defended externally in moral and political argument.[30]

Again, this is further affirmation of the significance of moral intelligibility as a requirement of a human institution. The quotations above from Haney and

Petersilia indicate what sorts of costs there are when there is not a disposition to regard moral intelligibility as a responsibility of those overseeing prisons and prisoners.

The study of moral performance conducted the investigation in a familiar idiom of first-order moral discourse but that cannot be dismissed as importing subjective elements. If one objects that the meanings of many of the moral terms are themselves disputed that is both true and not necessarily a weakness. The study can contribute to the clarification and refinement of moral terms through an ongoing back-and-forth between putative meanings and findings. At the same time that the willingness to employ moral vocabulary in gathering data regarding prison life can illuminate explanatory considerations it also has the potential to highlight aspects of the relevant moral concepts. Seeing how they are meaningful in a setting quite different from familiar everyday settings, but nonetheless, an important setting for which people should have some sense of responsibility can be morally instructive or at least can vivify aspects of meaning we might tend to overlook. It would be a mistake for people to think, "that's not my problem. What goes on in prisons is the business of prison administrators and staff." Prisoners are members of society and the vast majority of them will be released. Thus, in addition to the fundamental moral considerations that apply to them in any case, whether in prison or not, it is prudent for society to consider how the prison experience affects prisoners, most of whom will rejoin society.

The prison environment is one in which significant study of self-conceptions, motivation, notions of legitimacy, the relations between self-respect and respect for (and by) others, and many other aspects of moral life can be studied fruitfully and with implications for our understanding of civil society. Finding out the impact of the prison regime on prisoners' ability to reenter civil society is important if for no other reason than the large numbers of people involved. Also, an in-depth understanding of how prison affects inmates should be treated as part of the study of society rather than study of something outside of society. The willingness to take that seriously would itself be a constructive step in the direction of society taking more responsibility for prison life. The study of the moral culture of prisons and the morally significant aspects of prison life should be recognized as part of the study of society. It is true that prison life is life at an extreme but it is an extreme that is not independent of the society; the confinement to which prisoners are subject is a condition in the society and no less subject to the rule of law and its requirement of moral intelligibility.

5.3 Desistance, Character, and Agency

Anthony Bottoms's work on desistance explores issues in ways meant to explicate their morally significant aspects and also the ways the concept of agency is relevant. He recognizes that many issues studied by criminologists are moral issues and it would be a mistake to always abjure their pursuit on the grounds that to pursue them would compromise the scientific character of one's investigation. Debates about the explanation of human action are directly relevant to desistance and Bottoms has argued that the notion of agency can have an explanatorily significant role. While we have not addressed the debates about agency in this book it is something positivism largely dismisses as unscientific.

For example, in distinguishing his own view from that of Ray Paternoster, Francis Cullen writes

> Whereas Paternoster prefers the study of human agency among adult offenders, I prefer the study of intersecting causes across the life course. As an unabashed positivist, I believe that a human agency paradigm takes us away from establishing the empirical sources of crime, whether that is to be found in biosocial factors or concentrated disadvantage in communities.[31]

After asserting the *non sequitur* that using the concept agency would be to "throw up our criminological hands and to admit that free will is involved and we criminologists have no more to add"[32] he goes on to assert that "[a]ttributing agency and denying causality make a strong criminological case for universal mens rea and for holding all offenders responsible for their acts"[33] and that seems yet another *non sequitur*. There is no reason to think that the inclusion of the notion of agency is to abandon any empirically meaningful approach to explaining action. Rather, it is a way of recognizing that much of human behavior reflects the reality that not all behavior is to be explained on the basis of one univocal interpretation of causality. The way in which one's desire to one day become District Attorney figures in choosing actions differs from the way that one's desire to sit down after walking miles on a badly blistered foot has an explanatory role. It is plausible to consider that desires, attitudes, passions, judgments, and reasoning could all have roles in the explanation of behavior and that those roles might not be one-dimensional. There is a very broad range of types of desires and ways that desires figure in explaining action. Consider the desire to no longer be a gossip and the desire to have seafood for dinner. The phenomenology of those desires differs, the ways they figure in practical reasoning differs, and the gratification one experiences from the desires being fulfilled differs in psychologically and morally interesting ways.

If it is objected, "causality is causality; the complexity or type of the issue makes no difference," that does not hold up well under scrutiny. Thinking about a possible career path, weighing what is in favor of it and what is not, and imagining how it could fit into a conception of the next phase of one's life overall, including relationships with people, the importance of location, and cost of living, and so on...all of that deliberative activity does not simply amount to an antecedent event that is the cause of whatever decision is made.

Rather, a person engaging in such deliberation is negotiating a potentially quite complex landscape in the space of reasons and normative as well as factual considerations go into the deliberation. The deliberation is not a process going on in the person, who awaits its result and perhaps is able to observe some of the process; it is something the person *does*, it is an activity in which the person is *engaged* and the result of it is a determination of how to proceed. That determination can involve aspects of affect, volition, judgment, expectation, and other features that have a crucial role in the exercise of agency in distinctive ways. Getting up off the sofa might involve volition but not in the same manner as in a career-shaping deliberation and decision; unless one regards career-shaping decisions as basically not different in kind from deciding whether to roll over or to get up off the sofa.

A person is not just a locus at which various lines of causal connectedness intersect. A person is capable of weighing considerations, discriminating reasons from episodic passions, and judging the worth or importance of doing X in contrast to not doing it or in contrast to doing Y. Often, agency is involved in the sense that the individual has a temporally extended self-conception as a background to deliberations and choices, and has capacities for judging worth and not just responding to strength of desire. That self-conception can be crucially important to understanding the decision the person makes. Or, it can be a background against which the decision is surprising and not at all what was expected of the person. We then would want to understand what made this deliberative process different and perhaps, "out of character," as we sometimes say. The defender of univocal causality can say that there was some extraordinary causal antecedent that resulted in an unexpected outcome but the drama goes no deeper than that. Sometimes the antecedent is as simple as fatigue or hunger, and sometimes emotional upset or a preoccupation of some sort is what accounts for "out of character" decisions. But, again, causality is causality and there is no need for additional complexity, it might be said. Yes; that might be said. However, such a view takes for granted what actually could be the involvement of a multitude of factors of different types. An emotion, an aspiration, a concern, a self-evaluation, and a fear are not all causal antecedents of the same type, only differing in a way analogous to the way that billiard balls differ—only in their color—while the ways they behave and interact are all characterizable by a few completely general statements. The explanation of much of human behavior and the kinds of interest we have in understanding human behavior often involve considerations other than "what were the casual antecedents of person P doing X?" For one thing, formulating an explanation generally involves presupposing a great deal—about context, how people typically behave, what sort of weight and significance was regarded as at stake by the person acting, what count as responsible and irresponsible ways of behaving in the context, what are the most relevant social and moral norms, and so forth. A vast amount of human behavior is intelligible on the basis of the fabric of norms constituting the situation in which the person acts, and how the person regards (or is oblivious to or actively defies) those norms.

It is widely held that rational behavior is typically explicable in terms of persons' beliefs and desires but both belief and desire can exhibit a good deal of texture. The ways that some are temporally extended and some are episodic; and that some have characteristic "feels" while others do not; and the way that valuative considerations can be an ingredient; all of those can be relevant aspects of practical reasoning and action. Can they be treated as antecedent events according to a univocal conception of causality? The issue is not whether such explanations are often constructed. The issue is whether such explanations are responsive to the various elements actually involved in what the person is doing. Or, is it a systematic homogenization of factors in the same sort of way as when economists treat all values, judgments, commitments, and so forth as preferences so that they have a universally applicable method of explaining behavior?

Similarly, it is possible to treat all human actions as self-interested as a form of theoretical economy. If we interpret all action as ultimately of the same type—preference satisfaction— that can enable us to provide a global, systematic account of human action. And there might be explanatory purposes for which such simplification is desired. But that does not mean that the explanations it produces actually elucidate the phenomena they address. For some purposes it could be appropriate to have highly general, small in number explanatory categories; e.g., treating all actions as caused (in part) by desire, or treating any valuation of any sort as reflecting a preference. But the fact that an explanatory idiom of great economy and generality can be formulated does not assure us that the explanations it yields are actually true of the phenomena we wish to explain, and provide illuminating accounts of them.

In all or nearly all contexts in which we find ourselves we do not think of ourselves as *things* (rather than *persons*) and we do not think of all the constituents of our lives as events arranged into causal regularities in which all of the elements are involved in much the same way—as events. The issue is not whether introspection reveals a substantial self and a clear picture of each of its powers. Instead, the issue has to do with what sorts of concepts are required for an intelligible, plausible account of the things human beings can do, the sorts of concerns that they have, and the integral aspects of their lives (including self-regard and regard for others).

In "Freedom and Resentment" Strawson wrote:

> We should think of the many different kinds of relationship which we can have with other people – as sharers of a common interest; as members of the same family; as colleagues; as friends; as lovers; as chance parties to an enormous range of transactions and encounters. Then we should think, in each of these connections in turn, and in others, of the kind of

> importance we attach to the attitudes and intentions towards us of those who stand in these relationships to us, and of the kinds of reactive attitudes and feelings to which we ourselves are prone.[34]

He went on to say

> The range and intensity of our reactive attitudes towards goodwill, its absence or its opposite vary no less widely. I have mentioned, specifically, resentment and gratitude; and they are a usefully opposed pair. But, of course, there is a whole continuum of reactive attitude and feeling stretching on both sides of these and – the most comfortable area – in between them. The object of these commonplaces is to try to keep before Our minds something it is easy to forget when we are engaged in philosophy, especially in our cool, contemporary style, viz. what it is actually like to be involved in ordinary inter-personal relationships, ranging from the most intimate to the most casual.[35]

His point is not that this proves that determinism is false. Rather, it shows that for a vast amount of human behavior our main interest in its intelligibility is in terms of its place in the complex fabric of human interactions and relations, and the sorts of attitudes that are reflected in persons' actions and responses. That is what is distinctive of the human social world; those features are not part of the social lives of bees, ants, or wolves though there is no question that they are social creatures.

This is not a matter of trying to preserve an elevated metaphysical status for human beings or a power of volition that is not possessed by other natural beings. It is a matter of acknowledging what sorts of concepts are needed to make human behavior intelligible. Consider voluntariness, for example. It is not one thing, either present or absent or either on or off. There are respects in which some of the behavior of very young children—babies, even—is voluntary and there are respects in which some of the behavior of a five-year-old and a thirty-year-old is voluntary despite the fact that the voluntariness of them is not some single feature, exactly the same in each instance. Five-year-old children are capable of voluntary behavior of many types that are not possible for an eight-month-old baby; and a person who is thirty can exercise voluntariness in ways that include aspects not found in the behavior of a child of five. There are kinds of considerations and ways of regarding and weighing them that differ broadly on account of age and experience. If a thirty-year-old person's actions could be explained in the same terms as that of a five-year-old with no difference in terms of the self-conceptions and values involved, the way that the future and the past are connected with the present, and the way that regard for other persons and their situations and perspectives figure in how the individual decides to act that would be shocking and probably disturbing. Granted, there are action-guiding decisions that just do not need to involve all the factors mentioned; if it is a question of whether to have whipped cream on the ice cream dessert that is usually a pretty basic deliberative project. But many of the action-guiding decisions of a thirty-year-old person are not that basic and straightforward.

It might be true that, in a very general sense, beliefs and desires are the basic elements of deliberation but given how many sorts of considerations can come under the headings "beliefs" and "desires" it can be misleading oversimplification to say that that is all that is involved. One's belief that her commitment to be with a particular friend is at this moment a weightier matter than the desire to pursue an opportunity that involves a great deal of travel to places she is very interested in visiting, and the desire to be the kind of person on whom others can count in times of crisis—those are different kinds of considerations than go into the choices a five-year-old makes, even though those, too, are desires and beliefs. The thirty-year-old could be thinking about what sort of person she is to be and the aspirations and imperatives to which she is to be responsive and to be regarded as having authority in her life. Making a distinction between Upper-Case Desires and lower-case desires—the former concerning enduring desires held to be important, and the latter shorter term desires of less weight—does not adequately capture what the decision-making process involves. The deliberative project is a matter of working out a specification of what is the right thing to do, all things considered. To say that the matter is decided by what she most strongly desires leaves out much that is important and is potentially very misleading. (In any case, that would involve sorting desires on the basis of normative considerations concerning significance. Why should intensity alone be decisive; and how would intensity of desire be measured?)

Our lives at the broader social level are pervaded by the normativity of our attitudes, and the ways that those are responses to others and their dispositions, responses, and attitudes. When someone seems to be *incapable* of participation in that normative social order we look for the causal explanation of the inability or the absence of response, or the preoccupation with something irrelevant. Saying that "He took that job in St Louis because he's crazy about Theresa and wanted to be near her" is a quite different type of claim from "He took that job in St Louis because he had a dream that organized crime figures would kill his mother if he didn't take it." (We can assume that this is someone who has no connection whatsoever with crime—organized or not—and there is no plausible reason why anyone in organized crime would single out this man's mother as a victim.) Is "being crazy about" translatable into a purely causal idiom, referring perhaps to a lengthy, detailed description of the man's psychological state, or referring to neurophysiological states of his brain? Suppose some set of brain-states is correlated with this sort of strong passion. However detailed the description of the brain-states that idiom would not help us understand what he is doing and why. That description would not tell us his reasons and how he came to regard them as decisive in his deliberations.

Generally, what we need to understand about people and their actions has to do with how they invest themselves in what they do; and that is the exercise of agency. That is not a way to forfeit explanation; it is a way of indicating that not every explanation is of the same form. If he is following Theresa to St Louis we might also want to know if that is a very imprudent thing to do, or if it means neglecting important responsibilities, or whether it might actually help his career, and so forth. If there is no compulsion or pathology involved then it is likely that an illuminating narrative will be more usefully explanatory than an attempt to identify causally necessitating antecedents. Seeking the latter might involve forcing the behavior into a law-like form when that does not actually provide the contours of the act. If a decision or an action is surprising because of how out-of-character it is we look for possible extraordinary causal factors and/or possible motives and reasons, the latter, while untypical for this person are still considerations within the space of reasons.

Suppose that the recognition of agency as having a role in the explanation of many actions implies that *mens rea* has a role in regard to many actions. There is no reason why *mens rea* would apply to *every* act, *every* episode of human behavior. There is no reason why explanations in terms of coercion, compulsion, duress, insanity, psychosis, and numerous other causes and conditions that defeat voluntariness would somehow become disqualified. In most cases, most of what people do they do voluntarily, even if much is done habitually or in response to directives from superiors in particular contexts or even if the thing is done without explicit, self-aware deliberation. People can acquire *rational* habits, habits for which there are good reasons. When doing the thing has become habitual the rationale for doing it has not disappeared even if in doing it the agent need not think it through step by step any more than the agent needs to think through what to do next once having learned how to swim or to ride a bicycle. There is a cognitive element but that can become habitual. Much more is to be gained by elucidating the various aspects of agency and the forms of its exercise than by eliminating it in favor of causal generalizations that almost certainly require reformulations of phenomena to fit explanatory desiderata rather than our explanatory conceptions being responsive to the features of the phenomena. Taking agency seriously does not mean that no actions are caused, or that everything anyone does they do freely, or that there are not necessary conditions for doing what persons do through the exercise of agency. The point is not that we must do whatever is required to save freedom of the will. The point is that the concept *agency* has a substantial explanatory role in regard to human behavior.

In his study of desistance Bottoms conceptualizes it as involving what he calls a kind of "turning around" rather than a deeper kind of repentance of the sort that Antony Duff includes in his view of punishment and secular penance. Bottoms writes, "I will explore the application to punishment theory of an understanding of repentance as primarily 'turning around'…or 'change of mind or purpose' (that is, as *metanoia*, as standardly translated in English bibles)."[36] Bottoms distinguishes his view from Duff's, in which the notion of repentance has an important place.

Bottoms highlights the way that repentance in the way Duff understands it is backward-looking and the way it generally includes an element of self-evaluation. "By contrast, the primary focus of 'repentance as turning around' is the future state, or future relationship, to which the person repenting aspires. It is recognised that one needs to move in from—and deal with—the past, but it is the future that is of central significance."[37] Thus, "on the 'turning around' concept of repentance, the illocutionary and perlocutionary point of the censure is to prompt not remorse, but a 'change of mind or purpose' towards the behavior required by the 'objective values' enshrined in a justifiable criminal code."[38] Duff and Bottoms are offering different accounts of how agency is exercised in key elements of the process of desistance, or in Duff's view, the process of coming to engage steadily with different values.

Whether this is mainly a backward-looking reconsideration of how one has acted and what it signifies, or this is a more forward-looking consideration of how to project oneself into the future, it involves an exercise of agency. The person's project, whether it is best characterized as repentance or "turning around"—and it might be one in some cases, and the other in other cases—involves imagining possibilities, adopting a perspective, coming to grips with judgments about oneself, and thinking in valuative terms in ways that are not possible for non-agents. "Agency" is not simply a name for whatever-is-going-on. What we briefly described is an example of an exercise of agency and we can see that it involves cognitive considerations, affect, imagination, memory, and interpretation. Not every exercise of agency involves all of those. In considering whether agency is explanatorily helpful we address the question whether the categories of belief and desire on their own are adequate to explain action, and whether valuative considerations as well as desires are needed, and whether motivating self-conceptions are involved. It is not simply a matter of selecting agency as an approach to explanation; it is a matter of what we find is needed for adequate explanations.

In "Desistance, Social Bonds, and Human Agency: A Theoretical Exploration" Bottoms integrates considerations under the headings "self-other differentiation" and "self-other coordination" in developing a view of agency that will help explain desistance.[39] He sees that there are normative considerations that need to be explicated as part of the explanatory project; the normativity is not something that comes 'later,' or is an accessory to the explanation of the phenomena, a kind of dangling epiphenomenon. In a context within the space of reasons it is important to grasp the meaning that action has for the agent while realizing that the agent might have an incorrect or distorted grasp of its meaning. (Perhaps he thinks that moving away and being in an entirely new setting will afford him a fresh perspective on life when actually, he is just following Theresa, being in love with her in ways he just does not acknowledge.) Still, in a great many cases understanding the agent's practical reasoning—even if it is confused, involves false premises, or is otherwise defective—is crucial to explaining the behavior.

Without question people often act on account of strong emotions, compelling desires, or threat, provocation, or other causally relevant factors. But it is not necessary to assume that all human action is best explained by showing it to be causally necessitated. Even when there are very regular patterns of behavior it could be that firmly established dispositions—dispositions to act for certain reasons rather than deterministic considerations—explain the behavior. We should not automatically regard whatever a person does as the causal product of that person's strongest desire, as though *strongest desire* is always what moves a person to act. If we make that an analytic claim it is not empirically contentful. If we treat it as an empirical matter we see that people frequently distinguish between the *best reason* and the *strongest desire*. Agency includes the ability to act for reasons when one's reasons are distinct from one's strongest desires.

Agency is not a spectral something-or-other "inside" a person; it is an ability that persons can exercise in ways that involve various capacities for judgment, receptivity, affect, and cognition. Again, human beings can act on the basis of judgments of worth and in ways expressing certain attitudes as well as various psychological needs, emotional tendencies, and appetitive propensities. Agency is not all-the-way-on or all-the-way-off and the circumstances can help shape the person's capability for agency. A long period of demoralization, severely limited range of activity, and denial of reading materials, interaction with others, and information about the world outside prison can diminish one's agential capacity. In commenting on alternatives to medical approaches to deviance Duguid observes,

> First, and perhaps most important, is the idea that it is through democratic and communitarian interaction that the individuals grow and mature and thereby alter their beliefs, attitudes, and behaviours. Especially important here is the idea that such a process is reciprocally reinforcing, that non-criminal community norms can thrive in a penal setting.[40]

The relevant education in perspective, attitude, motivation, focus of concern and so forth needs to be a process between people and not just a transfer of information or skills from one to another. And there is a role for voluntariness, for agency and engagement in education that can actually help people revise their perspectives and guiding concerns.

At any particular time what a person is like, and what a person is likely to do depend on a complex history of circumstances and causal factors as well as choices, determinations, and ways of pursuing meaning. As noted earlier, agency reflects those various aspects and factors in the ways that we negotiate the space of reasons. We do not always act as agents; in some situations we act reflexively, or we are passive and contribute nothing—as agents—to what is done or what is going on. Being swept down a river with strength well beyond what can be resisted by human effort is one example. Being stabbed in the back, utterly by surprise and without warning is another, and so is an epileptic seizure, especially if the condition is undiagnosed. Also, agency does not occur in pure form, as though anyone is ever completely free of influencing factors, the limits of possibility, and all of the necessary conditions for any human being to act. It is an aspect of human nature concerning our capacities for reasoning, for motivations of various kinds, for end-oriented activity, and valuative assessment. It is through agency that practical reasoning informs and orients human action.

Bottoms says he is "an unrepentant advocate of serious attempts at synthesis."[41] "A good synthesis seeks to weld theory and data together in an ongoing cumulative search for the truth."[42] He recognizes the need to be "open to the insights offered by many theories."[43] The complexity of phenomena can be made more tractable with a willingness to employ a theoretical and conceptual vocabulary that is not limited to just one way of conceptualizing what is studied. Again, while there are no circumstances in which a person is utterly free of all causal factors—at least as necessary conditions—there is often scope for agency. Consider, for example, a person's resolve to desist. Though there might be a particular episode of decision-making the resolve needs to be sustained, needs to be dispositional. That is the only way its end can be realized. Desisting is often *work*, and not just an episode of volition. The sustained effort, the relation of that to a self-conception and to the way it impacts others, and how they respond—all of that can be explanatorily relevant. Integration of elements from different theories has to be done very carefully; it cannot just be an *ad hoc* aggregate of convenience. It has to make good theoretical sense. But why rule that out as a constructive possibility? Doctrinal purity is not so impressive if it fails to be illuminating.

Bottoms recognizes the importance of a conceptually articulate grasp of agency, and he maintains that explanations that are almost exclusively at the level of social factors and institutions are not satisfactory in the respect that they do not register the role of agency.

> First, taking agency seriously *requires* that our research methodology takes full account of the actor's own self-understanding of actions—a dimension that has been singularly absent in much of the positivist-founded research on criminal careers, and even in much recent sociology with its stress on "social action" rather than "action."[44]

The effort to desist can involve an effort to change one's predominant attitudes and perspectives. It can involve trying to modify one's self-regard at the same time that the person is striving for honest self-knowledge. Part of that self-knowledge might be awareness that one cannot do this alone. The support of others is needed, and supportive circumstances are needed. Thus, the person might come to see that agency on his part is crucial, but so too, are surroundings, opportunities, and relations with others. It might be that only after a sustained, successful effort involving some painful self-examination the person realizes that the way he had formerly thought of himself and his abilities was just all wrong and unhelpful and that "agency may be real, but it is constrained, in explanatory terms, by lack of self-awareness and lack of full contextual awareness."[45] He can now see more clearly why his earlier attempts at desistance failed.

Studies of situational crime prevention (SCP) suggest that there is a vitally important role for agency in the sense that those making the effort to desist need to judge what sort of prevention is likely to be efficacious for them, perhaps trying multiple approaches. These might include throwing oneself into some regular, disciplined activity (such as a fitness regime) or changing one's pattern of activity so that there is a greater distance between oneself and the surroundings and the people most closely associated with one's prior offending, or responding to familiar impulses and inclinations in new ways, ways meant to impede follow-through that involves offending. The main point overall, as Bottoms notes, is that "earlier desistance studies, I believe, have not always fully appreciated either the pervasiveness of self-applied SCP among would-be desisters (or, at least, among young adult desisters), or the full significance of such tactics as an important element in their attempts to exercise self-control."[46] It is important that offenders find what will be most effective, given their own particular ways of reacting to opportunities for offending, and what is involved in shaping new patterns of desire, gratification, and self-respect. Bottoms emphasizes the fact that "many offenders—even persistent offenders—are not only willing to consider compliance, they are also actively putting into effect various compliance strategies of their own making."[47]

There is an important connection between the criminological investigations from which our examples have been drawn. A great deal of work studying prisoners' experience and prison life suggests that one of its most demoralizing features is the way that prisoners' agency is diminished. Having very little opportunity to make decisions or to deliberate about anything non-trivial, having very limited types of interactions with others, and in many cases, spending the vast majority of a twenty-four hour day in one's cell has results that extend well beyond boredom. Persons' agential capacities are lost if they are unused; it is not as though those abilities can be suspended indefinitely and then reactivated without difficulty. Also, among the most important exercises of agency are such things as developing an aspiration, a direction in which one wants to shape one's life, and fashioning ways of finding significance in one's activities and experiences. Granted, prison is not likely to be a setting in which this can be pursued in an especially efficacious way. However, some prisoners find that they can use their time in prison to break some especially bad habits, and in some cases, overcome addictions, and others manage to engage in some constructive reflection but for many, as we have already quoted Liebling, "The absence of any means for meaning-making and identity formation in prison, and the imposition of indeterminate and unthinkably long prison sentences to which these experiences are linked, might arguably constitute inhumane and degrading conditions."[48] The conditions in which many prisoners spend years or even decades are the types that undermine the sorts of realized agential capacities one needs to be a successful participant in civil society.

Bottoms wrote:

> Extensive literatures exist on issues such as power and social relationships in high security prisons, but much less attention has been paid to how prisoners in such institutions make sense (including moral sense) of the sentence that the court has imposed upon them, in the context of their having to live in confinement for an extended period of time, and eventually return to society.[49]

Bottoms has observed, "we consider that the whole concept of agency in criminology is currently under-theorised: the word tends to be used without detailed exploration, and rather differently by different authors."[50] Those different uses can be instructive. They are almost certainly not all compatible but each is likely to reflect some explanatory consideration meriting attention. That certainly does not mean that several of them can just be combined but it can provide valuable guidance regarding what sorts of aspects to keep in mind in formulating a conception.

Regarding the role of agency in desistance Bottoms notes that it is significant that regarding persons giving up criminal careers, "desistance will very likely include both individual and 'community' elements, which may interact."[51] And " in the desistance literature there are two important strands: (A) meaningful social attachments (notably marriage and employment); (B) agency and cognitive reorientation."[52] It is not essential that a fixed, unqualified definition of agency is produced. What is more important is a clear articulation of the elements required for an explanatorily effective conception, and the just quoted passage from Bottoms indicates some of them.

Concerns with meaning-making and agency are concerns formulated in an idiom that is foreign to positivist investigation. That does not mean that they are beyond the horizon of methodologically rigorous empirical science. There is a great deal more to do in developing empirically satisfactory approaches to meaning-making and agency but the work is not primarily a way of reductively eliminating them in favor of considerations that are more congenial to positivism. For instance, to try to wring all the normativity out of them would be to miss the point about why and how they matter. Agency, meaning, self-respect, dignity, accountability—those and many other concepts are integral to the lives of human beings or at least lives that twenty-first century Westerners (plausibly) regard as worthwhile and gratifying. Insisting at the outset that "if it is not causally determined it is not explanatory" or worse yet, "it is not real" massively contracts the scope across which we can seek intelligibility. The putative dilemma "causal explanation of action or unintelligible free will" is a false dilemma. Giving (or finding) a rationale for a decision or an action is very frequently a matter of showing the decision or the action to be choiceworthy, desirable, appropriate, or in some way why the agent thought it the thing to do. That is not the same as being understood in terms of preference but much of the exercise of agency concerns an individual's view of that for which there are the strongest reasons. It tells us something about how this person moves about in the space of reasons.

Someone trying to desist from a criminal career might see that the strongest or best reasons are in favor of desisting while the strongest desires point in a different direction. This is not always or simply a matter of competing desires. It can be a matter of whether to be responsive to a value that shapes aspiration or to a desire that would impel the person to act in a different way. Explanations that involve the concept *agency* are not limited to being narratives of one particular action at a time, or one particular agent at a time. Multiple factors and diverse social relations can be centrally involved. What sorts of considerations are explanatory will depend in important ways on what it is we seek to explain. There may be a genuine need to integrate elements of different approaches and theories. For instance, focusing on the concept of states of character could be an important part of the project along with social factors. To what extent is a state of character voluntary? Is there a point at which at least some states of character no longer exhibit any plasticity and they are not amenable to change (except for the types of change that come with aging)? What is the role of states of character in a person's practical reasoning and judgment? What sorts of experience and habituation are required for the formation of specific states of character?[53] How do different states of character reflect a changed view of what norms are authoritative?

Given a person's states of character and given that person's effort to acquire a certain disposition there are specific kinds of considerations the person will typically regard as reasons, as action-guiding. Being truthful or being willing to help, or being self-centered and quite mercenary can be characteristic ways in which persons exercise agency. States of character are often disclosed in action but that does not mean a state of character is a straightforward cause of action. As Bottoms has suggested we might find that an offender in his mid-twenties is more likely to desist if he has a stable relationship with a partner and is able to get some distance from his drinking buddies but it would also help to know how those matters figure in the way that he regards himself. Are they just matters of behavioral discipline and have only instrumental value for him? Or, is he trying to change himself so that he values things differently?

Can we tell when one of those rather than the other is most efficacious? What are the norms that he is now motivated to internalize and how are those shaping his motives? There is an important difference between just staying out of trouble, on the one hand, and trying to change oneself on the other. Acquiring a new perspective might disclose to him that norms he had been flouting are actually quite reasonable and worth respecting. A revision in one's agentic perspective can be important to the account of that person's behavior. These are not all things that "happen to" a person as though he or she is a passive subject or a locus at which several causal chains intersect. These changes often involve effort, changes of perspective and aspiration best understood in terms of agency. Much can be understood through comprehension of the subject's conception of his own agency and changes in his view of accountability.

Debates about agency and how it figures in explanations are longstanding. To some, it seems obvious that there is a respect in which human beings are authors, originating sources of at least some of their actions, while others find this obscure, at best. If we ask ourselves, "What needs to be the case if we are to explain and understand the various types of human behavior?" there will be a role for action that is not fully assimilated to causal law. In a great many contexts it is extremely difficult and even a kind of affectation to think of ourselves in strictly causal terms and as lacking agency altogether. Consider, for example, how we think about and understand friendships, what is involved in pursuing a strong interest as an avocation, or the sorts of literature or music one enjoys most. For each of those contexts it is plausible that there are causal factors and some of those escape our awareness. However, as we describe them in increasing detail and articulate their meaning for us it is very likely that a number of valuative considerations, matters of perspective, and avenues of interest surface as most important in contrast to causes that would show them not to involve any agency. This is not to say that these phenomena are untouched by causal factors or that there are not causes operating on us in ways that do not rise to awareness. However, the ways these matters figure in our lives and the significance they have for us can only be captured and expressed in an idiom reflecting agency, judgment, modes of concern, and so on in ways that are not fully amenable to translation into the language of efficient causes. Without the idiom of agency the normative aspects would be absent from accounts of a vast amount of human activity.

We *of course* think of ourselves as persons, agents many of whose *activities* are not reducible to events. This is not a conceptual choice about which we might just decide to change our minds. Doing *that* would be an exercise of agency. We have concerns and are engaged with all manner of things in ways that are not translatable into the form of causal discourse that is appropriate to natural processes. We do not *choose* to think of ourselves and others as engaging in activity and as responding to other persons in ways that are categorically different from our responses to non-persons. The dense, textured constellation of concepts employed in experience, including concepts such as gratitude, admiration, blame, contempt, pride, trust, forgiveness, resolve, accountability, excuse, and many others are intelligible through the ways they express or ascribe aspects of agency. There are, for example, normative differences between explanations and apologies, or between assurances and predictions. Also, we can be *angry* at having tripped over a stone or *fearful* of a snarling dog, and we can *anticipate* the rigors of frigid weather, and *be relieved* that the storm blew out to sea; but we cannot be thankful or grateful—to the storm—for blowing out to sea in the way we can be thankful or grateful to a person. We can be angry with a person in all sorts of ways that are inconceivable or at least completely inappropriate with regard to a stone. Many of the ways we can be angry with a person involve recognition of the person's agency.

We can feel thankful that finally someone came along the road and can help with our broken down car and thankfulness in this case is basically relief that we are no longer simply stranded and helpless. The thankfulness that we feel toward the person who helps us, either by fixing the car or giving us a ride, is gratitude, which is quite different from relief. In this case gratitude involves appreciation of the person's motives and effort, something just utterly out of place in regard to finally seeing a car slow down to stop and wondering if the driver will offer help. Also, one feels relief and perhaps some excitement that the fund-drive succeeded beyond its target-amount for collection, but feels gratitude to the people who contributed. There are a great many ways agency can be reflected in human activity. Even when we look for causal generalizations to explain human behavior we are likely to be doing so in a way that presupposes a great deal about agency and the sorts of reasons that typically guide human action. Just identifying different types of behavior, different exercises of voluntariness, and different ways that people respond to situations and pursue their interested and values involve presuppositions about agency.

Though we might not account for this by Kant's doctrine of the two standpoints, his view that we necessarily think of ourselves as rational agents and at the same time, as included in the causal order is a critically important insight. In it we think of ourselves as responsive to the law of reason as autonomous agents, while we understand our empirical nature as subject to causal law. Kant's view depends on his transcendental idealism and we might have reasons to reject that. (Recall the point Turner made regarding the transcendental aspect of normativism, discussed in Chapter 1.) Still, it is important that the view captures and expresses the fact that we cannot think of ourselves only and exclusively as *things* inhabiting an order of events. There is so much that is integral to the ways human beings live their lives that is different from the behavior of any non-agents, any creatures whose behavior is fully within the order of causal processes of the natural world—though we, too, are in the natural world. (Think of all of the aspects of the lives of people the Nazis condemned as "useless eaters" as though that is *all* those persons were, namely, useless *things*.) The notion that actually all of the activity that we find intelligible on the basis of how it figures in the space of reasons can be fully causally explained shuts out the normativity integral to the activity to be explained. It is not as though we just have to keep adding complexity to the causal processes. Such a view indicates failure to grasp that the difference between the causal order and the space of reasons is not a matter of complexity. It most fundamentally concerns normativity, not complexity.

The space of reasons is thickly intertwined with the causal nexus; it is not as though the space of reasons is somewhere else, sealed off from and not impacted by the causal nexus. But human beings can act for reasons, for considerations that they regard as *justifying* and as choiceworthy in a sense other than just strength of desire. They can act on the basis of considerations that have (or are taken to have) normative significance. They might exhibit poor judgment; the claims they make regarding justification might be unavailing; and they are often mistaken about what they believe to be the case. But all of that is consistent with the capacity to act in ways that have a normative valence. Whatever causal factors are operating on a person the intelligibility of much of what he or she does is intelligibility in terms of the space of reasons. In a great many cases the vocabulary that describes its elements and highlights what has pronounced importance presupposes various causal facts. For instance, if it is appropriate to forgive someone, that is because that persons has done something wrongful, harmful, or otherwise objectionable. If someone expresses admiration of another person it is at least partly because of that other person's achievements, efforts, or specific qualities exhibited in their actions (possibly including their judgments, responses, and attitudes). In each of these various cases there is a basic role for causal facts but those are not all the facts. One way to see that is to observe that while certain kinds of causal factors are involved in admiration, gratitude, and pride for example, the way those causal factors are involved is norm-determined in the sense that those attitudes have certain appropriate *objects*. Those do not figure only or exclusively as causes. The ways those attitudes are reasonable depends (in part) on their objects.

We drew on some illustrations from criminology in this chapter to help make the two-fold point that (i) there are strategies of scientifically rigorous empirical explanation in criminology that involve normative concepts and considerations, including moral ones; and (ii) in addition to contributing to criminology those strategies of explanation can help enlarge and deepen our understanding of morality and agency. The study of desistance can involve looking closely at resolve, self-awareness and self-conceptions, temptation and self-control, regret and ambition, self-evaluation and responsibility to others. The study of the moral climate in prisons can involve looking closely at some of those same issues and also at ways that trust is sustained, the importance of forms of attention and awareness of others, and how one understands the possibilities for one's own agency, and how those possibilities are influenced by others.

In Chapter 6 we discuss some of the most important normative considerations shaping philosophical articulations of criminal justice, chiefly in the U.S. and U.K. This will highlight some of the layers of normativity that are integral to criminal justice issues and the ways they are related to each other.

Notes

1 I make a case for a morally appropriate form of resentment in *The Liberal State and Criminal Sanction: Seeking Justice and Civility*, New York: Oxford University Press, 2020, and in numerous articles, See, for example, "Adam Smith on Resentment, Desert, and Justice" in Volume 12 of *Adam Smith Review*, ed. Fonna Forman, 2020, pp. 67–84.
2 Geoffrey Brennan, Lina Erikson, Robert E. Goodin, and Nicholas Southwood, *Explaining Norms*, Oxford: Oxford University Press, 2013, p. 1.
3 Ibid., p. 7.
4 Ibid.
5 Ibid., p. 15.
6 Cristina Bicchieri, *The Grammar of Society: The Nature and Dynamics of Social Norms*, Cambridge: Cambridge University Press, 2006, p. 11.
7 C. Bicchieri, "Behaving as Expected: Public Information and Fairness Norms," p. 3. Electronic copy available at: http://ssrn.com/abstract=1082264.
8 Ibid., p. 3.
9 Ibid.
10 Ibid.
11 Han Van Wietmarschen, "Attitudinal Social Norms," *Analysis* 81 (1): January 2021, pp. 77–79, p. 78. This article was brought to my attention by Anthony Bottoms.
12 Alison Liebling, *Prisons and Their Moral Performance: A Study of Values, Quality, and Prison Life*, Oxford: Oxford University Press, 2004, p. 473.
13 Ibid., p. 470.
14 Ibid.
15 Liebling, *Prisons and Their Moral Performance*, p. 348.
16 Gresham Sykes, *The Society of Captives*, Princeton: Princeton University Press, 2007, pp. 74–75.
17 There are particularly harrowing accounts of this in the most extreme forms imaginable in concentration camps during the Second World War. Capos were feared and hated in equal—unlimited—measure, and when camps were liberated surviving prisoners often took their revenge without procedural formalities.
18 Marguerite Schinkel, *Being Imprisoned: Punishment, Adaptation, and Desistance*, New York: Palgrave Macmillan, 2014, p. 82.
19 Liebling, *Prisons and Their Moral Performance*, p. 470.
20 Ibid., p. 225.
21 Ibid., p. 145.
22 Ibid., p. 165.
23 Alison Liebling, "Moral Performance, Inhuman and Degrading Treatment and Prison Pain," *Punishment and Society* 13 (5): 2011, pp. 530–550, p. 545.
24 Liebling, *Prisons and Their Moral Performance*, p. 225.
25 Ibid., p. 224.
26 Craig Haney, *Reforming Punishment*, Washington, D.C.: American Psychological Association, 2009, p. 224.
27 Joan Petersilia, *When Prisoners Come Home: Parole and Prisoner Reentry*, New York: Oxford University Press, 2004, p. 53.
28 Jonathan Simon, *Mass Incarceration on Trial*, New York: The New Press, 2014, p. 23.

29 Stephen Duguid, *Can Prisons Work? The Prisoner as Object and Subject in Modern Corrections*, Toronto: University of Toronto Press, 2000, p. 246.
30 Liebling, *Prisons and Their Moral Performance*, pp. 472–473.
31 Francis T. Cullen, "Choosing Our Criminological Future: Reservations About Human Agency as an Organizing Concept," *Journal of Developmental Life Course Criminology* 3: 2017, pp. 373–379, 375.
32 Ibid., p. 375.
33 Ibid., p. 378.
34 P. F. Strawson, "Freedom and Resentment," in *Free Will*, ed. Gary Watson, New York: Oxford University Press, 1982, pp. 59–80, p. 63.
35 Ibid., p. 64.
36 Anthony Bottoms, "Penal Censure, Repentance and Desistance," in *Penal Censure: Engagements Within and Beyond Desert Theory*, eds. Antje du Bois-Pedain and Anthony Bottoms, Oxford: Hart Publishing, 2019, p. 127.
37 Ibid., p. 128.
38 Ibid., p. 129.
39 See Bottoms, "Penal Censure, Repentance and Desistance," pp. 109–140.
40 This is in the course of discussing the Special Unity at Barlinnie, outside Glasgow. Duguid, *Can Prisons Work?* p. 118.
41 Bottoms, "The Relationship Between Theory and Empirical Observations in Criminology," pp. 75–116, p. 82.
42 Ibid., p. 83.
43 Ibid., p. 82.
44 A. Bottoms et al., "Towards Desistance: Theoretical Underpinnings for an Empirical Study," *The Howard Journal* 43 (4): September 2004, pp. 368–389, 374–375.
45 Ibid., p. 375.
46 Anthony E. Bottoms, "Learning from Odysseus: Self-Applied Situational Crime Prevention as an Aid to Compliance," in *What Works in Offender Compliance: International Perspectives and Evidence-Based Practice*, eds. Pamela Ugwudike and Peter Raynor, New York: Palgrave Macmillan, 2013, pp. 67–86, p. 79.
47 Ibid., p. 85.
48 Liebling, "Moral Performance, Inhuman and Degrading Treatment and Prison Pain," p. 545.
49 Bottoms, "Penal Censure, Repentance and Desistance," 2019, p. 19.
50 Bottoms et al., "Towards Desistance: Theoretical Underpinnings for an Empirical Study," p. 376.
51 Ibid., p. 379.
52 Ibid., p. 381.
53 I have discussed at some length the issue of whether states of character are voluntary and whether in an adult much plasticity of character remains. I argue that there is a significant role for voluntariness in the formation of character and that individuals are typically responsible for at least some of their mature dispositions. My views have changed some in recent years but my fullest treatment of the topic is in *Choosing Character: Responsibility for Virtue and Vice*, Ithaca: Cornell University Press, 2001. The account there involves significant elements from Aristotle's view as presented especially in Books I, II, and III of *Nicomachean Ethics*. While habituation has an important role in shaping states of character there are good reasons for regarding agents as responsible for many of their states of character, in part, because of how individuals habituate *themselves*.

Chapter 6

The Multiple Layers of Normativity

The arguments and analysis offered thus far make a case for seeing the relations between facts and values in criminal justice contexts as more complex and informative than is suggested by positivism. Normativity is pervasive in the human world. In addition, there is more to values-discourse than expressive meaning, and facts often have normative significance. To put the point very directly, the answer to the question, "Where in the world are moral values?" is that they are all around us because many of the facts concerning actions, practices, and institutions are morally significant. (This is the case even if the metaethics is projectivist.) Ethical significance can be found in any setting in which there is human experience and activity.

While it is true that Hume did not believe there are moral facts or objective values he did regard the moral significance of acts, facts, and situations as part of the social reality of human life. He had no intention of "thinning" prescriptive significance in a way that could be interpreted as weakening the claims of moral considerations. His interests in morality, aesthetics, and politics all reflect his concern with normative and valuative considerations in multiple contexts. In this chapter we indicate some of the main layers of normativity in criminal justice as a way of illuminating the interrelations of facts and normativity. The discussion focuses on Anglo-American liberal democracy but the main concern is to show the numerous layers of normative significance of the issues, and how those layers are not altogether distinct from the facts that constitute the issues.

In the course of the discussion some of the most contested and controversial issues concerning the various layers of normativity will be identified. The interrelatedness of empirical and normative aspects in them should be clear. In the final sections of the chapter I discuss briefly the republican form of political community defended by Pettit and Braithwaite, who argue that republican politics with dominion as a central concern has much more to recommend it than the form of liberalism found in the U.S. or U.K. at supporting a political and social culture in which civic virtue and mutual concern for dominion are sustained. They write: "when freedom is construed as dominion, we are forced to take a different view of the formative institutions involved

DOI: 10.4324/9781003037323-7

in creating a suitable system of mutual assurance. We are forced to see them in a positive light."[1] They regard their view as a form of liberalism though they argue that liberty understood mainly in terms of absence (or removal) of impediments to voluntary activity act is an inadequate and too thin conception of liberty, in place of which they put a notion of dominion. Discussion of their view is a fitting way to conclude because of the way they see the normative and explanatory projects as interrelated. In addition, they see their republicanism as connected with restorative justice and the latter merits attention. Could that combined approach offer a more promising prospect regarding the central challenges of criminal justice?

6.1 Identifying Layers of Normativity

The context of criminal justice involves multiple layers or aspects of normativity. One crucial layer of normativity—one that is relevant to criminal justice and to many other matters—concerns the fundamental features of a political order. One way to think of this layer is in terms of the constitutional order of the state (whether or not there is a written constitution). For example, we can consider the main normative features of a liberal-democratic political order, which differ in basic respects from, for example, one-party states, non-republican dynastic succession, and other illiberal forms. In addition, there are different forms of a liberal order, for instance, the classical liberal form, the welfarist form, and various forms shaped by egalitarian commitments concerning distributive shares. Some of the most intense debates regarding the liberal political order concern distributive justice and the way it is understood to impact other aspects of justice. In some states there are programs of social security, a social safety net, and various other sorts of public support though they are not all regarded as integral to the state's basic institutional arrangement. (That would be true of the U.S., for example.) In other states such programs are more firmly fixed features of the state and its responsibilities and the promotion of social welfare is a more systematic and less *ad hoc* national commitment. During the twentieth century several European nations established liberal democratic or social democratic constitutions. The periods following the First World War, then the Second World War, and then following the collapse of the Soviet Union were critical moments in the development of constitutional orders in Europe, many of them broadly liberal in character but not proving to be enduring. (The current situation in central and eastern Europe bears some important similarities to the situation one hundred years ago when liberal democratic forms collapsed after a decade or two.)

Numerous theorists argue that the liberal political order inevitably gives rise to serious problems concerning distributive justice in ways that cause serious inequalities, and those inequalities in turn result in additional forms of injustice. This question of the relation between criminal justice and other aspects of justice is critically important and a normatively rich and complex matter. It concerns forms of political participation, the state's responsibilities regarding the distribution of wealth, resources, and opportunities, and the extent to which we think the conception of the state, the political order should be responsive to various moral ideals and aspirations. In addition, the way that the relation between law and morality is understood, and the way that the relation between citizens and the political order is understood can be centrally important to such concerns. Lacey and Duff (among others) have written on these issues with a view to shaping our understanding of the responsibilities of citizens for the form that criminal justice takes.

The question of the fundamental form of political order includes the question of how the rule of law is to be understood. That is important in regard to the view of political legitimacy, political obligation, and the relation between law and morality. Do we believe that criminal law should be primarily concerned with preventing harm or do we believe we should endorse a more fully moralized conception of the state and the aims of criminal law? Whether we believe the state should have significant moral ambition or quite modest ambition we unavoidably find that we need to address the issue of how to articulate a conception of the moral intelligibility of law, an issue we examined in Chapter 2. Even an austere, positivist (i.e., legal positivist) conception will presuppose at least some basic conditions on what can count as valid law. One might try to develop a theory of law leaving aside matters of political theory but law is always part of a larger political reality and is connected with political ideas and ideals. The form that law takes depends in large measure on the character of that political reality and the relevant ideas and ideals. That will have important implications for the way that law does or does not reflect prevailing moral views. Whether one argues for a version of legal positivism or a version of law that has more substantive valuative considerations integral to how the rule of law is understood involves normativity. Legal positivism is not a norm-free conception of law; such a notion is barely intelligible. Rather, legal positivism's account of normativity differs from that in other conceptions of legality.

There are important debates over whether liberalism can create the conditions for a form of civil society that encourages dispositions of mutual respect and common social concern between citizens. Many critics of liberalism highlight ways that the liberal order tends toward a form of the social world and a form of politics that is inadequately concerned with overall social good. We will discuss some of those views. The ones on which we comment do not call for a radical replacement of the liberal order but for significant adjustments in how the responsibilities of the state and citizens are understood. This is an important debate within the broadly liberal tradition that has been a central part of Anglophone political culture.

Accounts of the rule of law, of legality, and also of the relation between law and morality lead almost inevitably to another layer of normativity. This concerns what is to be criminalized. There is an important political aspect to this in the sense that the sorts of political institutions that are regarded as legitimate, and the conception of their powers and authority are crucial to understanding how decisions are made regarding criminality. Questions about the relation between law and morality are among the most disputed matters concerning the intersection of law and politics, and questions about responsibility for criminalization concern more than just specific details of political bargaining and official steps in the process of legislation. They concern fundamental perspectives on how the state conceptualizes criminality and they concern societal attitudes regarding offenders. We tend to think of criminal responsibility in terms of offending, when in fact, there are several other significant forms of responsibility involved.

They include matters concerning what sort of responsibility a society—its citizens, ultimately—*takes* for criminal law and, by implication, the treatment of offenders. This often goes unmentioned but it is of the first importance because of the ways it can reflect prevailing views about what should count as crimes and how those decisions impact members of society. While legislatures are responsible for statute law, and in common law nations judges' rulings have considerable significance as determinations of law that are important as precedents this does not mean that citizens have no responsibility for law. The legislators are responsive to citizens and judges are not above the law in a way that permits them unlimited discretion. Judges and legislators are ultimately answerable to citizens and they are working "for" citizens. It is not an implausible stretch to say that what the law is and how it is enforced reflects what citizens think it should be. Their responsibility might be indirect and unsystematic but it is considerable.

That is one way in which citizens generally have responsibility for what is criminalized and for the forms and meaning of censure and sanction. This topic is also connected with how criminal liability is to be understood and important questions concerning voluntariness, *mens rea*, excuse, justification, and what it is in an action that constitutes its criminality. To see how important this question is, imagine a system of law in which all offenses are matters of strict liability. We would find that unbearable and deeply unjust. Thinking about what makes it unjust is a way to get some perspective on what we think should be required for criminality.

As just mentioned there is also the normativity involved in sanction. What are the aims and justification of punishment and what forms of sanction do we believe it is appropriate to impose? "Appropriate" here can be a complex matter. It might include considerations of efficacy, of desert, of cost, of collateral consequences, and other matters. This is a large and complex topic and our concern with it in the present book is limited to the fact that it involves normativity in an unavoidable, important way.

The following layers of normativity have been identified: (i) the fundamental political order, (ii) the conception of legality and the way the rule of law is understood, (iii) how criminality is understood and responsibility for what is criminalized, (iv) sanction and its aims, how it is justified, how it is evaluated, and societal attitudes toward offenders. In fact, looking at the various layers of normativity mentioned we can see that they are interrelated in complex ways. Views of sanction presuppose claims and views regarding the way criminality is understood and the character and significance of the rule of law. How the rule of law is understood involves presuppositions regarding the fundamental political order and the relation between law and morality; and so forth. Our views of any one of them have implications, and involve presuppositions regarding the others. Moreover, all of the issues concern relations between criminal justice and other aspects of justice in the overall conception of a just society. We will discuss the relation between criminal justice and distributive justice to a modest extent but criminal justice is connected in multiple ways with multiple aspects of a just society. There is normativity writ large.

The connections between these matters and between criminal justice and justice more comprehensively understood do not mean that all of these matters need to be dealt with jointly all the time. But there are significant conceptual and empirical relations between them and we are better positioned to make genuine progress in understanding each of them through seeing how they are related to the others. The final part of the chapter acknowledges that complex of interrelations through a brief discussion of restorative justice and whether it provides plausible remedies to some of the main concerns regarding criminal justice. That seemed a fitting way to conclude given that the view is explicitly committed to (i) interrelations between explanatory and normative considerations, (ii) the way it connects criminal justice with justice overall, and (iii) with views about the sorts of regard and attitudes people have, and could or should have toward each other.

The issue of pluralism runs through all of the layers of normativity. There are competing conceptions of what are the most significant grounds of value and how we should be responsive to them in organizing institutions and formulating practices. It is perhaps especially prominent in the relation between criminal justice and distributive justice. For instance, there are defenders of the view that because there is considerable distributive injustice some defendants should have diminished liability for at least some crimes. The view is that society and political institutions have ill-served these defendants and there is a place in criminal justice proceedings for at least some remedy of this injustice. For example, some prosecutors and judges believe that many arrestees are reaping the misfortune of their poverty and perhaps are also victims of discrimination so it would be acceptable for those prosecutors and judges to address this social injustice through the proceedings of criminal justice by not prosecuting or by reduced sentences. Is that an example of pluralism at work or is that a distortion of criminal proceedings and a misuse of discretion? This issue is related to the broader issue of whether the liberal political order inevitably gives rise to significant injustices and should be revised in significant respects. Or, at the least, if it is not revised, then exercises of discretion such as that mentioned are justified. The issue has to do with taking responsibility for justice.

6.2 The Liberal State and Responsibility for Criminal Justice

Numerous theorists and investigators have argued that liberalism, at least as understood in the U.S. and U.K. is defective as a political order and though many such critics defend some fundamental liberal principles and values they also believe that liberalism needs to be reconsidered and revised. Nicola Lacey has argued that "liberalism has been slow to develop any conception of public goods or virtues, or indeed any thorough conception of common social values."[2] Accordingly, "if some of the strongest arguments for punishment have to do with the upholding of common goods or public virtues, liberalism will have difficulty in accommodating the best that can be said for that practice."[3] In the final chapter of *State Punishment* she writes:

> I have argued that the strongest possible arguments for punishment can be developed within a communitarian conception which envisages a society genuinely committed to pursuing with equal concern the welfare and autonomy of each of its citizens, and of creating an environment in which human beings may flourish and develop, whilst acknowledging the role of the community in constructing the values and human interests which it seeks to defend.[4]

Defenders of liberalism can argue that the criticism that liberalism encourages a society of atomistic individuals chiefly preoccupied with self-interest and lacking commitment to shared goods and social welfare can be answered. Historically, many defenders of liberalism were concerned to minimize the arbitrariness of state power and they were concerned to diminish privilege, systemic corruption of courts and judges, and to make an explicit commitment to the protection of numerous fundamental rights and liberties of individuals. This was to be achieved through wider participation in the political process, and equal application of the rule of law to all. The courts, too, are crucial. If arbitrariness is not eliminated or at least diminished, then persons' rights are vulnerable. Many who have espoused and supported liberal principles are primarily focused on basic protections of the individual from from coercive, arbitrary (lawless) state power and concerned also with the independence of the judiciary.[5]

Liberalism has been centrally concerned with what sort of rule of law is appropriate to a political/social order in which there are certain rights that need not be conferred and cannot be withdrawn by a political or social superior. Among its chief challenges are specifying the trade-offs between equality and efficiency, and between equality and liberty.

Liberalism is certainly consistent with understanding persons as social beings and as beings to whom common interests and engagement with others in all sorts of ways are highly important. Sometimes the emphasis on the political importance of the rights of individuals and the ownership of property seems to be mistakenly exaggerated into *all that matters* to some defenders of liberalism (and certainly to some critics of liberalism) when in fact, they can have commitments to numerous values, many of which concern social welfare.

Whatever one's view about the appropriate role of the state, as a matter of fact during the twentieth century Anglophone broadly liberal states became more democratic and also more pluralistic, and came to have a much expanded role concerning the welfare of citizens. In Britain, starting with the People's Budget in 1909/1910 and in the U.S. starting with the Progressives and then Depression-era legislation the state became much more involved in welfarist ends and in regard to regulation (and sometimes nationalization) of industries, product standards and safeguards against hazards, employees' protections, anti-monopoly initiatives, and forms of social security and other entitlements. In addition, there was legislation supporting the formation of unions and protection of them against corporate intimidation and violence. The late nineteenth century and early twentieth century was an era of "company towns" in much of the U.S. and numerous firms exercised an alarming level of control over many employees and often treated them very abusively. At the times they were proposed some elements of those reforming initiatives might have been meant to be temporary, to meet short-term exigencies. Some of the Depression-era programs were of that kind. Many others have become regular, enduring, and politically broadly supported responsibilities of the state. That is an important respect in which contemporary Anglophone liberal democracy has more socially oriented aims and commitments than in 1900, for example. In general, there seems to be popular support for much of that expansion of the role of the state though there remain critics who are concerned that far too much is now a matter of public policy and administration by the state.

Until legislation in the early twentieth century Americans generally did not regard the Federal government as having many responsibilities other than defense and customs. At present, even advocates of a much smaller Federal government appreciate that it would be politically impossible to do away with Social Security, for example, various types of regulation of banking, and many of the health and safety standards set by government.

The liberal state has many responsibilities it did not have a century ago and most contemporary liberal theorists accept various welfarist commitments that libertarians and classical liberals might find suspect. Liberalism now is a more pluralist form of liberal democracy than the liberalism of, say, Mill's time. There is little question that society in the U.S., the U.K., Australia, and other Anglophone countries is more diverse than in the past. It is probably true that there is less moral consensus, at least with regard to certain issues, or that the moral consensus that we find is different from what it would have been at an earlier time. (Consider same-sex marriage and inter-racial couples, for example.) The expansion of roles for the state and the increased diversity of the social world have given impetus to difficult questions concerning responsibility in regard to aspects of criminal justice.

On the one hand, a more diverse society and permitting various behaviors that had long been regarded as morally suspect has meant that there is pressure for the state to enact more tolerant laws and stronger protections for members of many groups. On the other hand, those opposed to such changes often object to the state "legislating morality" or permitting immorality and interfering with more "local" legislative authority (as they see the issue) and they see some of their socio-moral practices and attitudes threatened. What one "side" regards as protection of liberty another "side" regards as overreach by the state. It is likely that there will be some persistent disputes over which norms are to be authoritative and over the way that the political culture understands the relation between moral and legal norms. In a liberal democracy such issues are not all resolved once and for all. Moreover, even if particular issues are not persistent it can be expected that at just about any time there will be disputed issues. One of the merits of liberal democracy is that it can allow for important debates about the state's authority and the rights of individuals.

Citizens and the state are jointly responsible for criminal justice in ways that are sometimes overlooked. That is a point developed by Antony Duff, Alice Ristroph, Nicola Lacey, and others, who have emphasized the importance of citizens taking responsibility for the form that criminal justice takes. Lacey writes,

> I will argue that this distinction between environment and agency is in fact more problematic than it first appears. Cases in which environment or socialization fundamentally affects the judgment and reasoning of the individual subject pose, I shall argue, a real challenge to the basis for the practices of responsibility attribution on which legal judgment depends.[6]

She goes on to argue that far too often theorists of criminal law are concerned almost exclusively with formulating the conditions of responsibility regarding offending, and how they are to be met. However, in her view "the normative question whether the conditions of criminal responsibility have been met cannot be answered in the abstract."[7] She argues that it is not as though the character of agency is articulated independent of the purposes of the law and then brought in to be employed in legal contexts. The various aims of the criminal law and criminalization in various contexts have a role in the way criminal law understands the agents it is addressing. She writes

> the question of where responsible agency for the purposes of criminal law begins and ends in difficult cases such as those already canvassed is a matter for social evaluation. It is, at root, a decision which depends on a judgment about the proper purposes of criminal law and about the broader obligations of the state, rather than a question which can be determined

> by an ahistorical metaphysics or, to be sure, by sciences such as psychology or neuroscience.[8]

> Where we draw the line around responsible subjecthood—what we regard as a fair opportunity to conform—is, of course, open to moral and political criticism. But that critique must be based on an explicit defense of certain moral and political values, rather than an appeal to an asocial concept of the responsible subject.[9]

This is an acknowledgment that normativity is inescapable, and it needs to be part of how we understand what the facts are. In the space of reasons it is often the case that accurate or objective description must involve normative considerations; they are parts of *what is the case* and not simply a matter of an attitude toward what is the case.

There is an additional dimension of the issue and it has to do with the ways that the circumstances of people's lives can shape their views of self-determination and accountability. Legislators, police commissioners, prosecutors, mayors, and others who are in positions from which they can influence policy and shape prevailing attitudes regarding numerous issues might have perspectives and patterns of judgment that reflect unfair biases that are not the result of people deliberately trying to regard or treat others unfairly.

> The psychological research can leave us in no doubt of the fact that socialization into certain pervasive implicit biases—notably on the basis of sex, sexuality, and race—is likely fundamentally to shape subjects' interpretation of other people's behavior. This consequently affects both people's propensity (as police officers, prosecutors, judges, or jurors) to label behavior as criminal and, as potential defendants, the likelihood of their misreading behavior in a way which encourages them to engage in potentially criminal conduct.[10]

Those who decide what to criminalize and how criminal conduct is to be sanctioned, and who also decide on policies of law enforcement, strategies of prosecution, and the tone of much of the public political debate are also responsible agents and their role is often overlooked. On the one hand, many such persons have probably been habituated and socialized in ways that encourage ambition, self-determination, attitudes of self-worth, and capability in ways that are, perhaps at most, merely occasional features of the lives of many people living in poverty. Many who have been socialized to achieve, to lead, to seek positions of responsibility might also have been socialized in various biases, including various forms of racial prejudice, and derogatory views of persons less well off than themselves.

It would be a crude form of bigotry to just baldly assert that those who are fortunate or who have opportunities and the means to pursue them are—if white—racists whose success has only been possible because of their unfair and abusive treatment of others. (I certainly am not suggesting that Lacey's view suggests that.) In many cases there just is not evidence of that sort of unfairness or abuse even if one insists that overall social institutions and norms reflect the biases in question. That insistence sometimes reflects the refusal to entertain the possibility that anything *could* count as evidence of fortune without unfairness for members of specific groups. That should be treated as an empirical matter rather than a matter of definition or ideological doctrine.

Still, it is plausible to think that many persons who have been habituated to pursue success and to expect to succeed and enjoy the fruits of success do think of others, who happen to be less fortunate, as less deserving, less capable, and as belonging in their lower socio-economic circumstances. One of Lacey's central concerns is that

> there is a normative question about whether the state, in whose name an attribution of criminal responsibility and criminal judgment is made, has carried out its own obligations. These arguably include a duty to create an environment inimical to the development of prejudices on the grounds of factors such as race, class, sex, or religion and to counter such prejudices, through the education system, the law, and elsewhere, where they nonetheless arise.[11]

That important observation does not suffer from the "there are only victims and villains" way of carving up society. As we noted earlier, it is not as though a discussion of responsibility for criminal behavior is a discussion of offending exclusively and nothing else. In addition, it is clearly possible that different participants in criminal justice proceedings have different notions of responsibility, self-control, answering to authority, and so forth, largely on account of their backgrounds and experiences. "A certain conception of self-direction, in other words, is a culturally specific phenomenon, and moreover one which has to be achieved within the context of certain kinds of social institutions."[12] Criminalization, enforcement of the law, criminal proceedings, and sanction all need to be seen in more fully social terms and as involving responsibility on the part of persons in several different positions.

It is clear that many laws and policies impact different groups in highly disproportionate ways, and why and where that is the case needs exploring. For a great many arrestees, if they were to be told to "hire a really good lawyer and you can beat this charge" that would be blind to the realities of people's circumstances and the affordability of counsel. Moreover, as Alice Ristroph reminds us, people tend to focus just on the offender when, in fact, where there is no criminal law there is no crime even if there is wrongful conduct, and criminal law is a political, collective enterprise and a responsibility of the public. The state "designated this act as a crime and chose to prosecute and punish it. For these public acts, there is collective responsibility. That responsibility should be part and parcel of any theory of criminal responsibility."[13]

An important part of Ristroph's analysis is that "responsibility is a matter of human relationships, of attitudes and practices. One may act alone, but one is responsible in relation to others."[14] She rejects individualist accounts of responsibility. There generally is not a stand-alone fact of responsibility that concerns only an individual and some individual act of that person, and we need to see that "responsibility involves multiple persons."[15] Moreover, holding someone responsible is itself an action for which we are responsible. She discusses Duff's view that fellow citizens must have standing to insist that the accused, in so acting, is answerable to others in the society. Calling someone to account requires having the relevant standing—analogously to the way that forgiving someone requires standing. In most cases, it is for the victim and only the victim to forgive. Duff's view is related to these points about agency and responsibility in that citizens generally are responsible (in at least some important respects) for what the law requires and for the way that criminal justice agencies, practices, and institutions operate.[16] There is a meaningful respect in which citizens are responsible for whether the normative conditions that are to be met by criminal justice are met, conditions concerning fairness in various respects, and the access that persons have to the resources that are to help persons charged with crimes. Responsibility needs to be *taken* and not just *assigned*.

We saw earlier (in Chapter 2) that Antony Duff has argued that the law needs to be perceived as *common* in the sense that it is anchored in the values and endorsement of citizens generally, and that the recognition of law as legitimate, including fairness of opportunity to comply, are crucial features of criminal law. Also, Duff has argued that

> a practice of calling to account presupposes a community to which caller and called belong, within which this process makes sense. More precisely, it must presuppose a linguistic and normative commonality; and a substantial community, though not necessarily one to which caller and called both fully belong.[17]

Alice Ristroph has argued that "the very category crime is distinctively political" and "law is inevitably a collective endeavor."[18] "A theory of crime, or criminal law, thus needs to be attentive to the collective entity that makes crime. Criminal law theory needs political theory."[19] "It is not just punishment, but also criminalization, policing, and prosecution that need to be subject to the analytical and evaluative scrutiny of political theory."[20] Also responding to the narrowness of much of the discussion of the justification of punishment Lacey wrote, "we need to turn our attention to both history, which illuminates the development of ideas over time, and the social sciences, which shed light on the role of criminal law and criminalization in the broader project of governance and in the production of social order."[21] This is a clear endorsement of the notion that the explanatory and normative projects need to be more fully integrated.

These critiques argue that key aspects of criminal justice need to be understood in a normatively rich context of political culture and social world. The normative features are integral rather than accessories to criminal justice. Even if criminal justice has some of its own integral principles the institution and practices of criminal justice need to be appropriately related to other aspects of justice. (Some aspects of this issue are discussed below.) They are not wholly distinct from them and that means that the issue of the normativity of criminal justice could be much more complex than it might seem at first, and that is an important matter for those who wish to defend the liberal democratic political order and those who wish to argue against it.

6.3 Discrimination and Criminal Justice

There are issues concerning the role of wealth and race in all the Anglophone nations even if they are especially pronounced in the U.S. Marguerite Schinkel, commenting on Britain, writes, "[h]igh levels of imprisonment have, along with other social problems, been linked to the level of inequality in a society (Wilkinson and Pickett, 2010)."[22] "Research has also shown a linear correlation between the level of deprivation in neighbourhoods and the number of their residents in prison (Houchin, 2005), indicating that the most disadvantaged are imprisoned disproportionately."[23] In the U.S. the rate of incarceration for blacks is much higher than for whites and for other groups, and blacks in general earn less, have fewer assets than other groups and have higher unemployment rates. So, in the U.S. as well there is a correlation between poverty and prison.

Many critics of the political order in the U.S. argue that it sustains various important forms of discrimination and it involves a deeply unfair form of distributive justice, with implications for criminal justice. Critics often argue that the U.S. should significantly reform distributive justice and that only through reform of distributive justice will the most serious problems of criminal justice be addressed successfully. There are critics who believe that liberal democracy, at least the form of it in the U.S. and some other Anglophone countries, inevitably tends toward economic inequality and as a result, political and social inequality, and systemic corruptions of criminal justice. Some defenders of liberal democracy maintain that distributive shares in the U.S. should be much less unequal. In part, this is so that there are not extremes of poverty but also because diminishing economic inequality can help ensure that there are not extreme differences in regard to effective political participation—the very wealthy having a great deal of political influence and the very poor having next to none. If there is to be political equality, the reasoning goes, the inequalities of wealth need to be diminished. In addition, even some who would preserve key elements of the liberal-democratic order believe that it should have more expansive, systematic welfarist ends and should address the public good in a less *ad hoc*, politically unpredictable manner.

In Canada, Australia, and New Zealand members of indigenous groups are disproportionately represented in arrest rates and incarceration, and even among juveniles there is a disproportion in regard to police surveillance as well as custodial and community supervision.[24] In the abstract of "Racial Profiling, Surveillance and Over-Policing: The Over-Incarceration of Young First Nations Males in Australia" Grace O'Brien writes:

> Historically, countries such as Australia, Canada and New Zealand have witnessed an increased over-representation of minority groups who are exposed to the criminal justice system. For many years in Australia, young First Nations males have been over-represented in the juvenile justice system in all states and territories.[25]

In Britain the Prison Reform Trust notes that "26% of the prison population, 22,683 people, are from a minority ethnic group. If our prison population reflected the make-up of England and Wales, we would have over 9,000 fewer people in prison—the equivalent of 12 average-sized prisons."[26] And,

> Analysis conducted for the Lammy Review found a clear direct association between ethnic group and the odds of receiving a custodial sentence. With black people 53%, Asian 55%, and other ethnic groups 81% more likely to be sent to prison for an indictable offence at the Crown Court, even when factoring in higher not-guilty plea rates.[27]

In all of the countries being discussed there are serious concerns regarding discrimination in law enforcement, in regard to defendants receiving custodial sentences, in regard to the length of sentences (especially in the U.S.), and in regard to how incarcerated persons are treated. William Stuntz noted that the black inmate population in the U.S. "multiplied more than seven times in the last three decades of the twentieth century."[28] There have been disproportionate increases in minorities being imprisoned in the other nations as well. As the number of persons incarcerated rose, the damage to various neighborhoods and communities increased. Stuntz wrote, "[t]he removal from black communities of a substantial fraction of young men and a smaller but growing fraction of young women cannot help but alter those communities' sense of identity, and the mores on which cultural identity rests."[29] Similar observations have been made about the impact of law enforcement and criminal justice policies on First Nations peoples in other countries. O'Brien writes, "According to Allard (2010), two-thirds of First Nations males and one-quarter of First Nations females in the general population had contact with the juvenile justice system, while the proportion of non-Indigenous young people who had contact was much lower."[30] And, "[j]ust as in Canada and

New Zealand, negative relationships between police and minority groups are also a significant contributing factor to the higher incarceration rates of First Nations young people in Australia" (Tauri 2009).[31]

These issues are examples of the complex intersection of different aspects of justice. On the one hand it is fairly clear that reform of aspects of distributive justice is crucial because of how matters of distributive justice have consequences that radiate throughout institutions, policies, and the character of the social world, politics, and economic life. That is an empirical matter, and because of the complex interaction of a large number of factors it can be very difficult to ascertain causes with precision. Still, it is a matter of considerable importance and the results of investigation could help inform philosophical conceptions of relevant normative issues. Moreover, even if there is a widely shared commitment to bringing about a more just society there could be very challenging difficulties regarding how to revise or realize certain of the principles of each aspect of justice in part because of how those principles stand in relation to other aspects of justice. Should we address the social and distributive justice issues concerning relative poverty through the exercise of discretion in the context of criminal justice, or does that result in confused and inconsistent criminal justice? Should prosecutors and judges exercise discretion so that impoverished defendants have diminished liability just on account of poverty? Is that a partial remedy for injustice in distributive shares (supposing that injustice explains or results from the differences in shares)?

In work published in 2017 Lucia Zedner writes, "Criminological research furnishes clear evidence that the criminal process is routinely and radically undermined by the unfair, discriminatory or even errant practices of policing and prosecution."[32] (She was writing of the U.K. though there are similar issues in the U.S.) Critics note that in numerous jurisdictions in the U.S. and in other liberal democracies as well, all sorts of fees and charges are imposed upon persons arrested and while in jail or on probation and these are often imposed on those least able to afford such costs. "For instance, in Germany defendants (unless entitled to legal aid) are, upon conviction, liable to pay court charges, prosecution charges and possible charges for representation of victim-complainants during trial, on top of the costs of their own defence."[33] And in the U.K. as in the U.S. there are serious concerns about the vast majority of criminal cases not going to trial. In the U.S. this is often a matter of impecunious defendants settling for (often disadvantageous) plea deals instead of trial, though they might not understand their rights very well and might be receiving less than genuinely satisfactory legal advice. In the U.K. "[s]ome 97 per cent of criminal cases are heard in magistrates' courts before a panel of three lay judges."[34] While this is in some ways reflective of some of the virtues of the common law tradition, and "lauded as the embodiment of democratic accountability, active citizenship, local justice, and social representation in the criminal justice process"[35] the number of cases has grown so large that ways of streamlining the system are being considered, and those changes raise concerns about the quality of justice. "Despite the government's wider transparency agenda and its wish to make court processes more accessible to the public, moving to adjudication of low level criminal cases by a single lay justice behind closed doors provides little assurance of a commitment to open justice."[36]

It is true that in various respects compliance with the law can be more difficult for an impoverished person, perhaps, even just on the grounds that the temptation to steal might be heightened by want, envy, and resentment of those who have much more. Still, that does not automatically create acute conditions, making for a kind of motivational urgency highly difficult to control. One reason we know this is that very large numbers of relatively badly off people do not commit crimes. Providing an actual, situation-relevant justifying condition is a criterion more difficult to meet than just being much less well-off than others in economic terms. Regarding many cases we can understand persons' anger, frustration, and feelings of not being fully included in society. The perception of the legitimacy of the rule of law can be weakened considerably if a combination of poverty and racial discrimination is part of the situation, accompanied by the unwanted and sometimes abusive attention of law enforcement.

Attitudes toward minorities are an important test of how a society understands justice overall. If there is complacency on the part of majorities that suggests a troubling willingness to settle for justice that does not involve aspiration to ideals. It suggests a willingness to regard some groups as less than full-fledged citizens inasmuch as it is thought that their rights need not be respected. The situations in Anglophone countries differ to some extent in terms of whether the issues concern primarily First Nations or racial minorities, or perhaps a combination. Plus, the histories of minorities in each society differ and that means that the character of alienation or resentment or distrust in each might be different. Still, there is similarity in that issues concerning criminal justice for minorities in each society are closely connected with issues concerning justice more comprehensively understood. Some of the issues mentioned here have motivated advocacy of restorative justice. This seems to some to be an approach that addresses some of the lack of mutual understanding of different groups in the society, and addresses them in ways that can encourage greater trust and mutual respect. Some proponents of restorative justice argue that it is an approach that involves all the layers of normativity in criminal justice in an especially constructive manner.

6.4 A Restorative Approach to Integrating the Layers of Normativity?

How effective is restorative justice at addressing several of the layers of normativity in an integrated manner? In much of the discussion of restorative justice its proponents acknowledge that even should it become more popular and more widely available it is likely to remain an option, with conventional criminal justice remaining as the principal form of criminal proceedings. However, some proponents argue in favor of a conception of restorative justice as part of a reconsidered and significantly reformed criminal justice, the reforms being part of a much wider project of political reform in the direction of a more republican, communitarian conception of a just political order and a just society. John Braithwaite has developed such a view. In Chapter 1, Pettit and Braithwaite were mentioned as an example of scholars who recognize crucially important relations between normative considerations and explanatory accounts. Here we will take a brief look at their view.

One widely discussed example of a transformational approach is the view Braithwaite and Pettit presented in *Not Just Deserts* and numerous articles. In the book they take themselves to be theorizing about liberty but they also see themselves departing from versions of liberalism that are primarily concerned with liberty as the absence of external impediment. Liberty, they argue, can be "interpreted in an asocial or social way. The asocial construal is the liberal one, the social construal the republican."[37] In the version of republican liberty they endorse the notion of dominion is centrally important. The "bearer of dominion has control in a certain area, being free from the interference of others, but has that control in virtue of the recognition of others and the protection of the law."[38] It is important in their view that persons not only have equality with regard to liberty but also that this is "a matter of common knowledge."[39] People need to be able to acknowledge that they have liberty equal to others' liberty as a form of mutual recognition. If this means that the state needs to take on a larger role than in a more libertarian conception, then the state should of course do that.

A person enjoys full dominion, we say, if and only if:

1. she enjoys no less a prospect of liberty than is available to other citizens.
2. it is common knowledge among citizens that this condition obtains, so that she and nearly everyone else knows that she enjoys the prospect mentioned, she and nearly everyone else knows that the others generally know this too, and so on.
3. she enjoys no less a prospect of liberty than the best that is compatible with the same prospect for all citizens.[40]

And finally, "the promotion of dominion is an appropriate target to propose for the criminal justice system."[41] This is a large-scale project of reconstructing the normative order of politics with significant implications for criminal justice and justice generally. In fact, the project reaches all the way to the general structure of moral theory, with a case for consequentialism at the center of the view. Accordingly, they distinguish between a theory having a target and a theory shaped primarily by constraints. (Retributivism is an example of the latter.) Their theory is shaped by aspirations to be realized rather than primarily by constraints to be respected.

Braithwaite understands restorative justice as an appropriate (or indeed, morally required) approach to criminal justice. "Restorative justice is about struggling against injustice in the most restorative way we can imagine."[42] "It is a way of transforming the entire legal system, our family lives, our conduct in the workplace, our practice of politics."[43] In this view "[c]itizen empowerment...should be a higher-order value of restorative justice than, for example, non-punitiveness." Braithwaite says "[m]y approach to the theory of restorative justice is to seek to develop explanatory and normative theories that inform each other."[44] There needs to be traffic in both directions between explanation and normative theory, each being informed, refined, and enriched by the other. (We noted this commitment of Braithwaite and Pettit in our mention of them in Chapter 1.) "*Criminology* is the contemporary discipline most systematically engaged with explanatory theory about injustice. Not only is it impoverished by substantial neglect of normative theory, it also tends to narrow the kind of injustice we are concerned about to crime."[45] And he says that he is a "republican normative theorist."[46] Like Judge David Bazelon (discussed in Chapter 1) Braithwaite believes that "punitive justice is a great disabler of social justice."[47]

Many critics of the liberal state argue that the market economy is a significant source of injustice because of the way it rewards persons who are already well positioned, and many minorities and poor persons are largely condemned to poverty and severely limited social mobility. Plus, when the state privatizes various responsibilities, such as when it permits privatized prisons as a way of reducing the demands on the public treasury or hires private security forces, and so forth this tends to aggravate issues rather than resolve them. There might be uneven quality control, lax oversight of employees' qualifications, and efficiency, and so forth. To some critics what is most objectionable is the state abdicating some of its most important responsibilities, shifting them to the private sector. To others, the market economy overall is regarded as the source of the problem. In any case, discussion of the issue very quickly surfaces the fact that several layers of normativity are involved.

I believe it is reasonable to expect that in the U.S. and the U.K. there will be more policy and programs aimed at assisting persons and making opportunities, skills, and resources available to more people but it is very likely that the market will continue to be relied upon to be the main engine of wealth creation even if there are extensive state programs aimed at assisting those who need support of various types. (The suggestion is that there will be some additional redistribution but not a fundamental reorganization of the economy.) Perhaps the main reason we should not expect fundamental reorganization of the economy is that forms of liberalism—defended on non-consequentialist grounds—in conjunction with the market as the basic mode of economic arrangement, seem deeply rooted in the political culture of the

U.S. (and the U.K. as well). A form of consequentialist republicanism would be opposed by a great many people for a variety of reasons. Some of those would be sophisticated, carefully considered reasons and some are likely to be not very good reasons at all. But for politics to "go consequentialist" (and communitarian, given that there is also that feature of the view in question) would almost surely be regarded by many people as a problematic revision of a widely shared, strongly supported conception of fundamental political values and principles. That is not to say that a consequentialist cannot uphold a conception of rights and liberties but that such a rendering of them would be regarded as a significant revision of aspects of the political culture widely held to be integral. To put the point a bit simplistically, many people would regard trading in Locke so that they could have Mill as a bargain with very little appeal in large measure because of doubts about whether what they value most about a political order could be preserved if interpreted in consequentialist terms.

Some critics of the market object to it on much the same basis that they object to the liberal order; that it involves too limited attention to the public good, it encourages an atomistic society, and encourages motives of greed, gain, and self-interest. In at least some respects it is true that, where there are significant elements of a market economy, "market relations tend to expand into areas of human life which had previously been outside the scope of the market."[48] "'Market relations' here refers not only to the physical activities of exchange, but also to the legal institutions, and even ways of thinking which are characteristic of the market."[49] Elaborating this point, Peter Singer argues that, "if we allow market relations to dominate most or all spheres of human activity, we may no longer be motivationally capable of certain forms of altruism."[50] That seems an implausible overstatement. For example, there is a vast amount of philanthropy and altruism in the U.S. and not all of it is just "trophy-seeking" as in having one's name on a new university library. *Per capita*, Americans voluntarily contribute to charity many times the amounts given by Europeans, and the overall figure for 2019 was $449 billion, and that is separate from corporate giving and foundation giving, which jointly added over $95 billion in the same year.[51] Allen Buchanan has noted that while there is considerable debate over "the scope and validity of the generalization that the market drives out altruism, there is a great deal of plausibility to the more guarded claim that human life would be greatly impoverished if all interpersonal relationships were market relationships."[52] There certainly are grounds for that concern but the notion that the market kills off altruism is just false.

At the same time globally the empirical evidence of market relations and increasing trade improving the standard of living for enormous numbers of people is very considerable. It is also very uneven, and many people toil at very low-pay, often dangerous jobs. They reap little of the reward of those who hire them. However, the combination of the rule of law, respect for rights of private property, a sound currency, and democratic government has very few rivals for making people better off, in economic terms and in terms of the political culture. Multi-year plans for planned economies have a quite dismal record by comparison. Compare the recent performance of the Chinese economy with that of the Great Leap Forward (China's prosperity is largely the result of permitting more market activity while seeking tight political control over it. The Chinese government is, right now, in a phase of increasing political intervention and closer control of the market, largely as a way of keeping the market from diminishing the regime's power.) The regime seems quite concerned with the prospect of the activity of the market leading to demands for political liberty.

Pettit and Braithwaite, in developing a republican theory of criminal justice use the term "dominion" in a way that helps distinguish their view from several forms of liberalism while not disavowing some liberal fundamentals. They say that they "hope that the term has the connotations required to suggest that the bearer of dominion has control in a certain area, being free from the interference of others, but has that control in virtue of the recognition of others and the protection of the law."[53] And, "Perfect liberty will be a condition enjoyed so far and only so far as a person relates to other people, and to the institutions of his society, in a way which gives him a certain sort of power."[54] The view owes a debt to Montesquieu as well as to classical liberals such as Locke. And, they say, "we hope that it ["dominion"] can suggest to modern ears what *libertas* must have suggested to the Romans, 'franchise' to the medievals."[55] "Dominion, freedom in the republican sense, requires more than the bare fact of exemption from interference by others: more than the liberal notion of freedom."[56] They say that liberty is a social status and as such, "whether someone perfectly enjoys liberty will depend not just on how he fares in himself but on how he fares comparatively with others in his society."[57] "Perfect liberty is no longer to be defined on an intrinsic basis as the absence, for example, of any sort of prevention, frustration, or coercion; it is to be defined comparatively or relationally."[58] Standing *vis à vis* others is critically important, as is the *knowledge* that the person has such standing. One of the most powerful criticisms of the liberal order is that standing *vis à vis* others is often very unequal and the effects make a significant difference to persons' overall life prospects. Supposing people are willing to seek a remedy it will require thinking carefully about how criminal justice is related to other aspects of justice, and it will be necessary to consider how several layers of normativity are interrelated .

It is not difficult to see how the conception of republicanism mentioned connects with a conception of restorative justice. Braithwaite writes, "[p]ower imbalance is a structural phenomenon. It follows that restorative processes must be structured so as to minimize power imbalance."[59] "Non-domination does imply empowerment."[60] "Restorative justice programs must be concerned with the needs and with the empowerment not only of offenders, but also of victims and affected communities."[61]

> The republican view would replace the liberal concern replace the liberal concern with harm by a concern with activities that diminish dominion. And it would reject the legal moralist claim that the mere fact that an activity is immoral or is thought to be immoral constitutes a distinct reason why it should be criminalized. But it can, at least in principle, accept the legal paternalist claim that activities which undermine a person's own dominion are matters of concern as well as activities which diminish the dominion of others.[62]

Even if there are not promising prospects in the U.S. and U.K. for transformation on a large scale of the type described by Braithwaite there are contexts in which it could develop a modest record of success. This seems to be the case, for example, in juvenile justice and in regard to indigenous persons' communities. Also, in Northern Ireland there appears to have been real interest in restorative justice succeeding. Perhaps if more people were more willing to address important community issues themselves as active participants, by acting in the community, there could be more successes for restorative justice. In several respects contemporary conventional criminal justice is seriously defective and it is vitally important to invigorate reflection on the legal order and the political culture. But restorative justice could perhaps have some successes in specific contexts and could be part of an improvement of at least some social relations.

Some defenders of restorative justice see it as performing some of the functions of criminal justice only performing them much more effectively. For example, Lode Walgrave writes

> Probably the most important function of criminal justice is as a beacon of social disapproval, to show clear limits which are observable to all. After a crime has been committed, disapproval must be expressed in such a way that it is understood and accepted by all concerned.[63]

There might be less than complete agreement that the communicative aspect of criminal justice is its most important function but its communicative function is certainly important. In a discussion of Pettit and Braithwaite's view of restorative justice Walgrave says that "[t]he communitarian ideal must be inserted into a model of the state."[64] Also, "the aim of restorative justice as a public intervention model is to restore the assurance of rights and freedoms, which is essential for restoring dominion."[65] "Assurance provides the crucial distinction between the social concept of 'freedom as non-domination' and the liberal concept of 'freedom as non-interference.'"[66]

Bottoms, Shapland, and others have raised concerns about the more ambitious versions of restorative justice, not primarily as a critique of the ideal it presents but in regard to clarifying it as having a feasible conceptual architecture. For example, the communitarian aspect of restorative justice is important, and it aims at restoring just relations between members of communities. This could encounter difficulties regarding legitimacy in the respect that there could be numerous conflicts of values, disagreements about the roles of various participants, and quite different views of what would constitute a successful outcome. As Shapland notes, "It is important here, however, to focus upon the importance of the defence lawyer and of adequate representation and advocacy in most human rights legislation."[67] Part of the point of restorative justice is to replace much of the formalism of criminal proceedings administered by the state, and to bring the issues to the level of the individual persons involved, and to have them interacting as equals rather than the issues between them becoming the business of the state and lawyers. Part of what is to be restored is the human relation between victim and offender, in a way that involves a way of seeing and regarding each other directly, as it were, and not through the mediation of state institutions and a carefully orchestrated formality of procedure. Shapland notes that there could be numerous challenges regarding the sorts of protections available to participants, and there could be difficulties with regard to the role of voluntariness. As she says, "[c]onsenting implies the ability to walk out of the situation without prejudice."[68] That is a feature of restorative justice meetings but not of state processes.

It is conceivable that restorative outcomes could be punitive or punitive outcomes might be sought, if not at the outset, then perhaps in the course of the proceedings. There is no assurance that resentment, anger, and distrust can be left outside the room. One of the very concerning features of contemporary criminal justice in several countries (especially the U.S.) is the democratic populism that has supported over-criminalization and over-punishment. Such attitudes could find their way into restorative justice conferences and "communitarianism could be used 'as a façade not only for illiberal populism but also for vigilantism and community despotism' (Dignan and Lowey, 2000:18)."[69] Especially if it is a pluralistic society there is the risk that various constituencies will have narrow rather than broad perspectives and restorative justice conferences might not succeed in encouraging mutual respect and fuller mutual appreciation.

Bottoms observes that there are numerous reasons why restorative justice has appealed to various groups and in several contexts. Plus, there is no shortage of objectionable features of conventional criminal justice, giving people reason to consider restorative justice. At the same time, he expresses doubts about whether contemporary Western societies are likely to accept restorative justice on a wide scale. This is in large part because

> the social mechanisms on which RJ depends work less well in contemporary than they do in traditional societies, because of the different social-structural contexts; hence, a "blanket" delivery of RJ (to all cases in a given category) is always likely to achieve modest and/or patchy results in contemporary societies.[70]

In addition, he believes that there will always be informal versions of restorative justice in families and schools, and other contexts, but those will exist along with conventional, more formal criminal justice.

Walgrave, while sympathetic to the political theory Pettit and Braithwaite have articulated, and supportive of restorative justice, also notes some of the challenges Shapland described. In discussing the role and the form of shaming Walgrave writes:

> But as soon as shaming goes beyond the informal and enclosed environment, there is no longer any control over what "people" at large will do with that shaming process. The risk is that "the public," not being involved in the exchange of feelings and opinions, will adopt a position towards the offence (and the offender) that is relatively unrelated to the reintegrative aims of the process. Stigmatisation of the offender then would become an obvious consequence.[71]

One could argue that during a time of divisive politics and distrust between politically opposed groups—and that characterization applies to several of the Anglophone nations at present—restorative justice could be a way of encouraging greater civility and mutual respect. Or, more pessimistically, one could argue that restorative justice has especially poor prospects in such a socio-political atmosphere. As Walgrave notes, "Some scholars even argue that the decrease of social blaming in the community provokes an increasing need for penal punishment (Boutellier, 1996): because people do not feel blamed anymore, you have to augment the 'objective risks' for potentially criminal behaviour."[72]

If there are significant groups of people that do not feel shamed by being convicted of crimes, and if there are not generally effective reprobative attitudes as a feature of social culture, maybe some punishments need to be augmented for any effective communication to occur. That would be dispiriting but it is a suggestion to take seriously given what might be a weakening of shared moral attitudes or just a weakened notion of morality. That could be another obstacle to restorative justice having more than very modest and local successes though Walgrave makes clear his support of restorative interventions and one of the reasons is that they at least could "have a more reintegrative impact than traditional punishments."[73]

There are many reasons why restorative justice will not become the main or primary form of justice with respect to crime. As hinted at above, these could have to do with urbanization, the mobility of persons, absence of some of the sorts of regulatory and administrative supports the state would need to provide, and uncertainty about whether the sorts of communities that would be well suited to pursue restorative justice will develop. The sorts of socio-cultural infrastructure needed for restorative justice are not widely available and there is lack of agreement about just what the character of restorative justice should be, and what it should aim to accomplish. It might be that many people will not develop the habits and attitudes that would support restorative justice on a large scale. That should not automatically be interpreted as reflecting vices of character or lack of concern with the common good. It might reflect that, but it could also be that many of the features of contemporary society and the ways that social life and forms of interaction are changing are not conducive to restorative justice. If there is a great deal of mobility and many people do not come to feel rooted in their communities the concern for restorative justice aims might be weak, but that does not have to also indicate weak concern for criminal justice

Critics of restorative justice—not necessarily rejecting it, but raising significant practical concerns—point out that Braithwaite's notion of the "democratic pragmatism," which he sees as a positive feature of his approach could make restorative justice proceedings unpredictable in ways that are problematic with respect to expectations, fairness, and consistency. As Shapland notes, "restorative justice, by definition, is created anew each time a set of participants come together to consider that offence and what should happen as a result."[74] That does not mean that the world has to be remade from the very beginning, or that utterly unpredictable results will emerge from each restorative justice conference or sentencing circle, or whatever other form it takes. In fact,

> the extent of democratic unpredictability is constrained—not by the state or the national criminal law in any top-down way, but by participants' normative ideas about justice which they bring to the restorative justice event and which shape both the process and the resulting outcomes.[75]

Restorative justice processes will almost surely have recognizable features regarding the values that are highlighted. Yet, that also makes it "highly unlikely to be transformative towards a different society based on different justice principles."[76] Participants in restorative justice conferences might change their perspectives and see the wisdom or at least plausibility in new ways of seeing things but perhaps not. If restorative justice is an option—probably a fairly marginal one—in what is a largely unreformed criminal justice culture, restorative justice might be very limited in impact, doing some real good where and when it is practiced but for several reasons limited in the scope of its practice.

That conservatism need not reflect bigotry or philistinism. It might reflect a willingness to give the procedures of criminal justice a chance to do their work, and hopefully, do it properly, with many citizens unpersuaded that a significantly different approach is needed or is the key to much better quality criminal justice. If restorative justice is to accompany significant changes in prevailing attitudes and forms of mutual acknowledgment as part of changed responses to offending the transformative task, especially If restorative justice emphasizes democratic pragmatism and decentralization, will be very difficult to set out in detail. Plus, if it remains an option within a much larger system of conventional criminal justice perhaps we should expect the familiar norms and perspectives to continue to resonate in ways that will influence restorative justice. Even if it worked well in some types of cases conventional criminal justice (hopefully, reformed in various respects) would almost surely remain the prevailing mode.

6.5 What Does Experience Show?

We noted earlier that in Canada, Australia, and New Zealand indigenous people often have a fraught and distrustful relationship with police. In the U.S. African-Americans have fraught relations with law enforcement at the same time that crime rates in African-American neighborhoods are often very high and residents feel a strong need for police protection. There has been success with restorative justice proceedings in Northern Ireland, where it has been fairly extensively employed in the context of youth justice and there is an effort at expanding its use in adult justice as well. There is experience with restorative justice in Canada, Australia, and New Zealand and much of that experience has involved indigenous groups. Restorative justice is not yet a mainstream process.

A number of different restorative approaches have been tried in Canada including Holistic Circle Healing, a program through the Toronto Aboriginal Community Council, and circle-sentencing. In each case the approach is meant to involve the community more fully and help the offender feel that he or she is among a group with which some feeling of solidarity or at least trust can be genuine. This is important because in Canada, for example, numerous studies show a "significant race effect on jury decision-making, [as is the case in the U.S. regarding African-Americans] such that jurors perceive same-race defendants to be guilty less often that defendants who are of a different race (Devine & Caughlin, 2014; Mitchell, Haw, Pfeifer, & Meissner 2005)".[77]

As we mentioned earlier indigenous people are incarcerated at disproportionate levels. In Canada between 2005 and 2015, there was a fifty percent increase in indigenous inmates, while the general incarcerated population increased by only ten percent (Sapers, 2015).[78] In addition, studies "support the argument that racially diverse juries engage in a greater exchange of information"[79] and consider evidence more thoroughly. Thus, it would seem that several lines of argument and types of evidence, plus the fact that "many indigenous people feel victimized by the Canadian legal system"[80] provide support for restorative justice practices because of how they would seem to diminish some of the objectionable factors noted.

Canada's Supreme Court has issued a number of rulings explicitly regarding restorative justice, and rulings concerning alternative sanctions—especially in place of incarceration—have explicitly acknowledged the importance of community relations, the interests of offenders, and the reintegrative promise of restorative justice. "The Court also indicated that Parliament's new mandate to sentencing judges to pursue restorative purposes in sentencing should be seen as an attempt to remedy high rates of incarceration in Canada for all offenders and disproportionate rates of incarceration of Aboriginal peoples."[81]

An Australia Bureau of Statistics Report for 2020 shows that

> The Aboriginal and Torres Strait Islander imprisonment rate decreased by 1% from 2,304 to 2,285 prisoners per 100,000 Aboriginal and Torres Strait Islander adult population. As of 30 June 2020:
>
> - Aboriginal and Torres Strait Islander prisoners made up 29% of all prisoners.
> - Male prisoners made up 91% (10,963) of Aboriginal and Torres Strait Islander prisoners.
> - Female prisoners made up 9% (1,134).
> - The median age was 32.1 years.
> - 79% had experienced prior adult imprisonment.[82]

There is a striking disproportion of Aboriginal and Torres Strait Islanders in the prison population. A report from Griffiths University shows that "the Māori in Aotearoa New Zealand are imprisoned at 7 times the rate of the general population."[83]

In the Anglophone world it appears undeniable that there is a problem of very disproportionate representation of minorities in prison. If this is largely explained by high rates of crime among minorities then we need to consider whether *that* problem is explained to some extent by in poverty and poor quality housing, education, employment, health, etc. Restorative justice can be imagined as a way of addressing several layers of normativity. In the most optimistic imagining it encourages a stronger feeling of belonging to the community and having a voice on the part of offenders, and helps overcome distrust of law enforcement. It could also help offenders appreciate how crime looks and feels to victims, and help victims appreciate how it looks and feels to offenders. Thus, it can enable victims and offenders to feel that they belong to one community in which they all have critically important stakes. That could be important to creating a shared sense of being subject to the same norms and standards of behavior. The fact that many people regard the rule of law as unfair (in several respects) is a critically important challenge.

Unsurprisingly, the development of restorative justice has been welcomed by some and regarded with concern and disappointment by others. It will be both important and difficult to develop a body of restorative justice proceedings and sanctions in which there will be widespread public confidence as well as approval by the courts. Some proponents of restorative sanctions are concerned that a growing number of mandatory minimum terms of imprisonment close off what could be important opportunities for restorative sanctions.

Restorative justice can be seen as a way of introducing a constructive form of pluralism into the criminal justice context. When the contexts are those of indigenous peoples who both want to preserve aspects of their culture and also have serious concerns about the aptness and fairness of conventional criminal justice restorative justice can be a way for their values to be more fully respected though not through a completely unchecked, alternative set of justice proceedings. As indicated above, it is likely that there would remain important connections with conventional criminal justice. In addition, given the realities of popular attitudes regarding crime and offenders, as well as powerful political interests and the general conservatism of courts it is likely that restorative justice will find approval only if it is fairly clear how conventional criminal justice can be reasserted in the restorative process.

The public would need to be educated to understand that restorative processes are not a matter of "getting away with not being punished" but a different form of sanction, and one with distinctive aims. Whether that kind of pluralism will be respected and accepted is not a certainty. "Restorative approaches to sentencing might be a significant, deserved, proportionate and just alternative to such [i.e., very short] prison sentences."[84] However, whether they will be regarded that way is by no means a sure thing. Many members of the public might feel that while pluralism is an important dimension of the social world and political culture it should not extend to introducing new forms into jurisprudence and criminal justice. It would not have very good prospects if it is widely regarded as nothing other than a type of special, non-punitive option for certain groups.

Defenders of restorative justice are correct when they point out that it is not an altogether novel form of proceeding but in fact has roots deep in the traditions of many indigenous peoples and minorities even if they are not indigenous. In some respects, restorative justice is a retrieval of traditions rather than an innovation. Or, rather, it is an innovation in common law jurisprudence but many of the indigenous traditions have lengthy histories of their own. The pluralism of contemporary society might seem to offer a setting in which restorative justice can be pursued in a variety of contexts. Given that society and the state seem more willing (in at least some respects) to tolerate and condone diverse perspectives, attitudes, and practices restorative justice conferences could offer considerable potential for knitting together social ties that just would not be brought about otherwise. However, progress regarding many of the most serious issues of criminal justice might not be likely without developments in social and economic policy, education, and public health. Those issues are almost surely to remain more prominent than the attempt to broaden the appeal of restorative justice as a significant alternative to conventional criminal justice. It will appeal to some, and it might win numerous new adherents. But it is likely to remain an accessory to conventional criminal justice.

Greater consensus on various views of the moral issues, on the wisdom of the law, on the aims and justification of sanction, and on the legitimacy of practices of law enforcement might help enlarge the appeal of restorative justice. But it does not seem an approach that can carry the main burden of criminal justice for at least the following reasons. One is that many people are likely (and not without reason) to be skeptical of the appropriateness of restorative justice. They might regard it as having some worthwhile aims but doubt whether restoration as understood by its proponents should be the primary concern. They see the guiding, basic norms of criminal justice as appropriately having priority over the aims of restorative justice. A second reason is that societies might be falling short regarding the extent to which the various aspects of justice in a just social order need to be in place for restoration to seem a plausible option. The success of restorative justice might depend on other aspects of justice. Its defenders could argue that those other aspects are indeed sought by restorative justice; it could be an important instrument in bringing about some of the needed reforms. Still, the main work required for restorative justice to have the needed solidity of a basis cannot come from processes of restorative justice. To be sure, even if one endorses a conventional, retributivist conception of sanction the justice of such sanctions will depend in part on the justice or injustice of other aspects of the relevant socio-political world. But restorative justice seems to depend in an especially significant way on other features of the society and the ways that people conceptualize the society and the rule of law.

There are several critiques of contemporary criminal justice and many are motivated by claims about the ways that criminal justice should be related to other aspects of justice. That might seem to create an opening for a much more extensive employment of restorative justice. However, that would reflect not just a change in policy but a change—or significant openness to change—in norms. Criminal justice might have principles and procedures of its own but it is not a fully stand-alone form of justice.[85] There does seem to be growing recognition that significant reform of criminal justice needs to be part of a more complex, multi-aspect set of reforms that also speak to other aspects of justice, especially distributive justice and the political implications of persons lacking an audible political voice and the opportunity and ability to participate effectively in the political process. That is increasingly recognized as a betrayal of some of the fundamental values and principles of liberal democracy. That will result in (or it has resulted in) two-tier criminal justice, with considerable differences in the ability of persons to effectively exercise their rights and protect their interests. Though it is quite clear that the normative aspects of criminal justice can only be adequately understood through their connections with other aspects of social, political, and moral normativity it is also widely held that criminal justice involves certain principles and norms distinctive to it and to its integrity. Much fuller debate is needed regarding the question of whether restorative justice is adequately responsive to those or perhaps they should be revised.

At least in the U.S. and U.K. it is probably safe to say that the prospects for restorative justice are modest and the reform of other aspects of justice has priority both in terms of prevailing public sentiment and in terms of the depth and urgency of the issues. Actualizing more satisfactory versions of the multiple layers of normativity involved in criminal justice is a plausible aim if the basic principles and values of those layers are defensible. There are many people who believe that they are not defensible. However, careful consideration of them might put them in a much better light if we find that the most serious defects are due to distortions and corruptions of them and impediments to them rather than being intrinsic to them and any socio-political world striving to realize them.

Notes

1 J. Braithwaite and P. Pettit, *Not Just Deserts: A Republican Theory of Criminal Justice*, Oxford: Clarendon Press, 1990, p. 83.
2 Nicola Lacey, *State Punishment*, p. 151.
3 Ibid.
4 Ibid., pp. 198–199.
5 Many of the rights and liberties often taken for granted—freedom of expression, of association, of conscience, and the liberty to move about and travel as one wishes—are achievements of liberalism. It has been a lengthy historical process, and for various groups progress has been agonizingly slow and uneven. But much of what Westerners would now regard as beyond question in regard to political values has been brought about through commitment to liberal principles.
6 Nicola Lacey, "Socializing the Subject of Criminal Law? Criminal Responsibility and the Purposes of Criminalization," *Marquette Law Review* 99 (3): Spring 2016, pp. 541–557, p. 542.
7 Ibid., p. 543.
8 Ibid., p. 544.
9 Ibid., p. 557.
10 Ibid., p. 552.
11 Ibid., p. 553.
12 Ibid., p. 548.
13 Alice Ristroph, "Responsibility for the Criminal Law," in *Philosophical Foundations of Criminal Law*, eds. R. A. Duff and S. Green, New York: Oxford University Press, 2011, pp. 107–124, p. 109.
14 Ibid., p. 113.
15 Ibid., p. 118.
16 See, for example, Duff, *Punishment, Communication, and Community* for his view on how to understand the notion of common law. See also, his "Responsibility, Ctizenship, and Criminal Law," pp. 125–148.
17 Duff, "Responsibility, Citizenship, and Criminal Law," pp. 125–148, p. 131.
18 Ristroph, "Responsibility for the Criminal Law," p. 107.
19 Ibid., p. 108.
20 Ibid.

21 Lacey, *State Punishment*, p. 557.
22 Schinkel, *Being Imprisoned*, p. 11.
23 Ibid.
24 See Grace O'Brien. "Racial Profiling, Surveillance and Over-Policing: The Over-Incarceration of Young First Nations Males in Australia," *Social Sciences* 10: p. 68, https://doi.org/10.3390/socsci10020068.
25 Ibid.
26 http://www.prisonreformtrust.org.uk/WhatWeDo/Projectsresearch/Race.
27 Ibid.
28 William Stuntz, *The Collapse of American Criminal Law*, Cambridge, MA: The Belknap Press of Harvard University Press, 2011, p. 49.
29 Ibid., p. 48.
30 O'Brien, "Racial Profiling, Surveillance and Over-Policing," p. 7.
31 Ibid., p. 3.
32 Lucia Zedner, "Security Against Arbitrary Government in Criminal Justice," in *Criminal Law and the Authority of the State*, eds. Antje du Bois-Pedain, Magnus Uluang, and Petter Asp, Oxford: Hart Publishing, 2017, pp. 89–110, p. 98.
33 Ibid., p. 100.
34 Ibid., p. 103.
35 Ibid.
36 Ibid., p. 105.
37 Braithwaite and Pettit, *Not Just Deserts*, p. 56.
38 Ibid., p. 60.
39 Ibid., p. 68.
40 Ibid. pp. 64–65.
41 Ibid., p. 69.
42 John Braithwaite, "Principles of Restorative Justice," in *Restorative Justice & Criminal Justice: Competing or Reconcilable Paradigms?* eds. A. von Hirsch, J. Roberts, A. Bottoms, K. Roach, and M. Schiff, Oxford: Hart Publishing, 2003, pp. 1–20, p. 1.
43 Ibid., p. 1.
44 Ibid., p. 5.
45 Ibid., p. 6. Italics in original
46 Ibid., p. 7.
47 Ibid., p. 12.
48 Allen Buchanan, *Ethics, Efficiency, and the Market*, Totowa: Rowman & Littlefield Publishers, Inc., 1988, p. 101.
49 Ibid.
50 Peter Singer, quoted on p. 102 of Buchanan. Buchanan is referring here to Peter Singer's "Altruism and Commerce: A Defense of Titmuss Against Arrow," *Philosophy & Public Affairs* 2 (3): 1972, pp. 312–317.
51 See the National Philanthropic Trust site: https://www.nptrust.org/philanthropic-resources/charitable-giving-statistics/ There is data on who gives, how much they give, and where the contributions are directed.
52 Buchanan, *Ethics, Efficiency, and the Market*, pp. 102–103.
53 Braithwaite and Pettit, *Not Just Deserts*, p. 60.
54 Ibid., p. 63.
55 Ibid., p. 60.
56 Ibid., p. 203.
57 Ibid., p. 63.
58 Ibid.
59 Braithwaite, "Principles of Restorative Justice," p. 9.
60 Ibid., p. 10.

61 Ibid.
62 Braithwaite and Pettit, *Not Just Deserts*, p. 93.
63 Lode Walgrave, "Imposing Restoration Instead of Inflicting Pain," in *Restorative & Criminal Justice: Competing or Reconcilable Paradigms*, eds. A. Von Hirsch, J. Roberts, A. Bottoms, K. Roach, and M. Schiff, Oxford: Hart Publishing, 2003, pp. 6–78, p .65.
64 Ibid., p. 76.
65 Ibid., p. 73.
66 Ibid., p. 72.
67 Joanna Shapland, "Restorative Justice and Criminal Justice: Just Responses to Crime?" in *Restorative & Criminal Justice: Competing or Reconcilable Paradigms*, eds. A. Von Hirsch, J. Roberts, A. Bottoms, K. Roach, and M. Schiff, Oxford: Hart Publishing, 2003, pp. 195–217, p. 208.
68 Ibid., p. 209.
69 Ibid., p. 206.
70 Anthony Bottoms, "Some Sociological Reflections on Restorative Justice," *RJ & CJ: Competing or Reconcilable Paradigms*, pp. 79–110, p. 110.
71 Lode Walgrave, "Restorative Justice and the Republican Theory of Criminal Justice: An Exercise in Normative Theorising on Restorative Justice," in *Restorative Justice: Philosophy to Practice*, eds. H. Strang and J. Braithwaite, Aldershot: Ashgate Publishing, 2000, pp. 165–184, p. 177.
72 Ibid., p. 178.
73 Ibid., p. 179.
74 Joanna Shapland et al., "Situating Restorative Justice Within Criminal Justice," *Theoretical Criminology* 10 (4): 2006, pp. 505–532, p. 507.
75 Ibid., p. 507.
76 Ibid.
77 "The issue of indigenous underrepresentation in Canadian criminal juries" American Psychology-Law Society, AP-LS News June 2017 https://www.apadivisions.org/division-41/publications/newsletters/news/2017/06/, p. 3.
78 Ibid., p. 2. Sapers, H. (2015). Annual report of the office of The correctional investigator, 2014-2015. The Correctional Investigator Canada. Ottawa, Ontario. Retrieved from: http://www.ocibec.gc.ca/cnt/rpt/pdf/annrpt/annrpt20142015-eng.pdf.
79 Ibid., p. 4.
80 Ibid., p. 5.
81 Julian V. Roberts and Kent Roach, "Restorative Justice in Canada: From Sentencing Circles to Sentencing Principles," in *RJ&CJ: Competing or Reconcilable Paradigms?* eds. A. Von Hirsch, J. Roberts, and A. Bottoms, Oxford: Hart Publishing, 2003, pp. 237–256, p. 247.
82 abs.gov.au.
83 New Zealand Department of Corrections, 2019.
84 Roberts and Roach, "Restorative Justice in Canada," p. 251.
85 I discuss this issue at some length in *The Liberal State and Criminal Sanction: Seeking Justice and Civility*, New York: Oxford University Press, 2020, especially in Chapters Two and Three.

Conclusion

The points made by Duff, Lacey, and Ristroph as well as others make it clear that normative aspects of responsibility need to be thought through very carefully in conjunction with the empirical situation regarding different levels and aspects of responsibility in the criminal justice sphere. We tend to focus on those who violate the law but the understanding of crime and its normative significance requires a more textured, multi-dimensional treatment. Decisions about what to criminalize, how to punish, and how to actually apply the law in ways that reflect a concern with the justice of who is arrested and charged, prosecutorial discretion, plea-bargaining, and sentence-bargaining are all aspects of taking responsibility for the rule of law. The rule of law is not just an abstract notion of legality; in its actualization it involves practices and decisions, and real impacts on people's lives.

It is not as though the approaches taken to law enforcement are an altogether separate matter.

> In a democratic polity, politics (rather than markets, or bureaucratic authority, or the judgment of the wise, or force of the strongest) is the arena for deciding between competing resource claims and distributing basic social goods (and bads). It is also a space for mediating claims for recognition, for determining who belongs, who 'we' are and the terms we set for our coexistence.[1]

Even if one is a robust proponent of the market—and for more than purely economic reasons—it is still true that in a democracy politics shapes the market in having a decisive role in shaping arrangements for the allocation of distributive shares. That is the case even if the market is given a fundamental role in regard to allocation of capital, which skills and expertise are rewarded, and the distribution of income. That it has that role is a political decision even if there was not a specific moment at which that was decided. In a democracy it is crucial that citizens have an informed, realistic appreciation of the issues they need to address and of the principles and values most fundamental to the rule of law and political order in which they live. Advocates of democracy

DOI: 10.4324/9781003037323-8

rightly emphasize the role of the people and the voice of the people in shaping politics; they should also emphasize the responsibility that people have in that role. There is normative depth to democratic political participation as well as the opportunity to assert one's preferences and promote one's interests.

There is normative depth to criminology, as well. It is not just the study of aspects of crime, law enforcement, and sanction. The phenomena it studies are saturated with normative significance and there is need for careful articulation of the forms of normativity involved. Political theory, historical understanding, and various social sciences are needed in the project of articulating a strongly supportable conception of criminal law, responsibility, and criminal sanction. There clearly is the need for a healthier democratic politics than the currently predominant highly antagonistic and uncompromising approach so often taken.

Loader and Sparks refer to what they call "democratic under-labouring" and they say it

> can bring to bear on public debate a disposition one might hope to find in politics but which often in fact breaks the rules of the political game and exists only at its margins. It is a disposition that refuses to take the social world for granted or accept received political "imperatives," that aims to provoke and unsettle, and poses questions about our responses to crime that insecurity fuelled and ideology-lite political cultures have forgotten how to ask.[2]

They add that among what is needed are

> proposals for remaking and re-imagining the institutional arrangements for fostering security and delivering justice that connect with, and seek to creatively reconstruct, the meanings of current social practices and beliefs in ways that take us beyond the mental and institutional structures of the present (see also Unger 1987).[3]

And they say explicitly, "a democratic under-labourer criminology also has a clear normative dimension."[4] The view they characterize does not sacrifice methodological rigor.

> What we propose instead is best described as a sensibility or disposition, a way of being in and relating to public life, together with a cluster of issues and questions that we think those who research crime and justice, as criminologists or under some preferred but allied banner, might usefully devote more time to thinking about and folding into their work than they have generally tended to do hitherto.[5]

They are accepting the fact that criminological studies can have a great deal of normative significance, and they are not trying to distance themselves from that significance by claiming that engagement with it would be unscientific. Of course there are irresponsible—intellectually and morally irresponsible—ways to connect criminological studies with politics and public opinion. Also, I am not suggesting that the *only* responsible way to pursue criminological studies is with a view to direct practical engagement. But the view that I have sketched out in this book maintains that the scientific credibility of criminological investigations should not deny that those studies can have normative significance. There are enormously complicated issues concerning how expert knowledge most appropriately figures in policy-making and the administration of institutions in a liberal democracy. Questions concerning the intersection of law and morality, and concerning the role of expertise in democratic politics are not themselves going to be conclusively resolved by the social sciences though the latter might have plenty of relevant results. The main issues concerning how criminological explanation is made practical are ultimately political matters, and political in certain specific senses appropriate to liberal democracy. Loader and Sparks's *Public Criminology?* explores this very helpfully.

Locke had described his contribution in *An Essay Concerning Human Understanding* as that of an under-laborer "in clearing ground a little, and removing some of the rubbish that lies in the way to knowledge."[6] A couple of centuries later Peter Winch was critical of the idea of philosophy as only an under-laborer, "for according to it philosophy cannot contribute any positive understanding of the world on its own account: it has the purely negative role of removing impediments to the advance of our understanding."[7] Winch thought that philosophy has a much more substantive role to play in regard to enlarging and deepening our understanding of the world, and that recognizing the relations between language, thought, and the world would bring that into view. If Loader and Sparks's view can indeed contribute to "a better politics of crime and its regulation"[8] in the ways they suggest that would be a very robust and effective version of under-laboring, and that would be in large measure because of the ways that many of the relevant normative considerations are shown to be empirically grounded.

I have argued that the relations between explanatory and normative explanation, analysis, and theorizing regarding criminal justice should be much closer, and that letting go of a certain view of the relation between facts and values is a crucial first step. This is not to say that every empirical criminologist should also undertake philosophical explication of concepts and values, as though criminology without explicit discussion of normative issues cannot be excellent criminology. There is plenty for each discipline to undertake just in its own terms. However, positivism as a characteristic of a great deal of social science, sometimes has been an impediment to approaches that could be especially illuminating in regard to the normative significance of what is explained. One way to put this is to observe that positivism actually disqualifies much *less* than it claims to; the social sciences *can* contribute knowledge with normative significance. There are norms that are not limited to being expressive prescriptions. We need in-depth knowledge of the forms of normativity and how acting in accord with various norms shapes important features of our lives both as individuals and as a society.

Suppose a criminologist—one with a positivist disposition—asks, "All right; what is it I am supposed to do? How are normative considerations to figure in my research and in the explanations I offer? How am I to remake my work?" One plausible reply would be: "You needn't do anything differently. There aren't directives coming down about how normativity is to be included in what you do. The chief point concerns the defensibility of positivism, the implications of positivist doctrine and whether in fact, they are what they are widely taken to be." The point I have tried to make here is that the normative and moral significance of what is studied is, so to speak, *already there*. It is not something that is added on. However, that does not mean that the normative aspects are obvious or evident to anyone who pays attention.

Moral judgment always involves *thought* and is not simply a mode of perception or some felt item of sensibility. But neither should normative significance be denied or be excluded from study on the grounds of positivist methodology. My concern has not been to dismiss positivist social science but to explain why it is just one element of the theoretical and explanatory story and it does not have the "master" methodological status sometimes claimed for it. (It does not have that in the philosophy of science or in epistemology. Why should it nevertheless have it in the social sciences?) The methodological and, in the broad sense, practical issue is "What sort of attention is to be paid to normative and moral significance?"

Logical Positivism in philosophy claimed that philosophy can make no substantive claims. All such claims are scientific, if in accord with what positivism says is cognitively meaningful. In addition, the criteria for that rule out all but a thinly expressive interpretation of moral discourse. That is a crucial source of the so-called fact/value distinction. If the critique of positivism offered here is basically sound we can see that positivist philosophy errs by claiming that nothing substantive remains to be explained after positivist analysis has done its work. Accordingly, in the context of the social sciences nothing substantive remains to be thought or said regarding values once positivist social science has done its work. That bit of epistemic hubris is not sustainable. Positivist social science can undertake its explanatory projects in ways that are important and illuminating though a more circumspect, qualified, and less restrictive positivist position regarding what can be achieved by other approaches is in order. The notion that there is no genuine role for empirically informed and analytically rigorous moral thought is actually quite remarkable. Granted, there are plenty of difficulties and challenges regarding what constitute sound moral understanding and moral judgment but there is little prospect for improving them if we insist that there are no such things; just the pretense of them. This is not just a matter of what we would like to believe. The positivist dissolution of moral thought and moral judgment has itself come undone. Even Hume was prepared to carry on moral theorizing because he saw that his critique of moral realism and moral rationalism took down a number of theories but not morality itself.

Whether criminologists (or anybody, for that matter) exercise careful, informed consideration of their moral views is a matter for individuals to address themselves. But there are good reasons to believe that there is not a clean break between facts and values in a way that constitutes an impediment to fact-based moral judgment. Moral judgment involves its own distinctive conceptions and perspective. A great deal of hard thought and explanatory refinement might be required to get at the moral significance of the facts and to disclose that significance.

In the Introduction to *A Reader on Punishment* Duff and Garland write:

> But most penology takes the existing institutions for granted, and situates itself within them, so that more radical questions about alternative ways of responding to crime or administering punishment tend not to be part of its research agenda (see Garland 1990: ch.1; Garland and Young 1983:ch.1).
>
> The sociology of punishment, in contrast, is less closely tied to the existing institutions and more willing to raise basic questions about the ways in which society organizes and deploys its power to punish.[9]

The sociological focus on the relation between punishment and society and its willingness to imagine alternatives to current institutions and practices is very welcome. There would be additional gains from careful, empirically informed and philosophically fluent analysis regarding the various levels and aspects of normativity relevant to the phenomena studied. Speaking of how philosophical conceptions of agency and responsibility are expressed in criminal law and criminal justice Lacey remarked:

> But to understand how and why they do so, we need to turn our attention to both history, which illuminates the development of ideas over time, and the social sciences, which shed light on the role of criminal law and criminalization in the broader project of governance and in the production of social order. And this in turn implies that our analysis of criminal responsibility must be located firmly within an account of the rationale for the social practice of criminalization within a broadly liberal polity. The subject of criminal law is, inevitably, socialized; so, therefore, must be our criminal law scholarship.[10]

The handling of topics in the present book suggests that issues concerning criminal justice have conceptual, empirical, and normative aspects and the issues are best understood through recognizing the ways those aspects are related. Of course, one can undertake a project of conceptual analysis, or of empirical inquiry, or moral evaluation, for example, without also undertaking explorations of other aspects of the issues. It would be a mistake to argue that there is no value to investigations or analyses that remain focused on just one type of aspect, rigorously following one distinctive methodology. But there is fuller significance in seeing the phenomena in relation to other aspects and that is because the reality of the phenomena is not neatly carved up into different, stand-alone aspects.

Appreciating the significance of that fact can take some effort since inquiries and analyses are often methodologically self-conscious in ways that are meant to highlight the integrity of focusing on just one aspect. It is helpful to remind ourselves that the fact that some phenomenon can be described in the idiom of one specific level of description or the idiom of a particular theory does not mean that the phenomenon is thereby fully and exhaustively described in that way, certainly not in ways that preclude other descriptions. Something can be *fully* described in the idiom of a particular theory without that implying that the idiom *exclusively* describes it. One can make a case for a specific methodology having virtues without also insisting that no other methodology could be illuminating. Positivism happens to be an approach that is often accompanied by such exclusivist claims.

I realize that some (perhaps many) readers might react to this entire discussion with a sense of annoyance and frustration that though it is about the understanding of normativity and moral value it has a basically conservative character and does not directly raise the issue of whether the liberal-democratic political order at a fundamental level needs to be changed. The discussion seems not to extend to deep or systemic social criticism and it seems to take the Anglo-American political order for granted as *the way things are*, without aggressively raising the issue of how they ought to be. If there are any important is-ought relations that would certainly seem to be one. With the exception of some discussion of possible significant reform in Chapter 6 there has not been consideration of that issue.

In the Introduction we mentioned some of Steinmetz's interpretation of the history and character of positivism and his view is helpful here in the Conclusion. He wrote, "[e]arlier critiques of positivism were usually a subordinate part of wider political programs."[11] And

> There have been at least three periods in which positivism became an explicit target of critique: around the turn of the twentieth century, in response to the doctrines of Mach, Pearson. Poincare, and other influential positivists; during the 1930s, when logical positivism was criticized by such writers as Parsons...and Sellars...and again in the 1960s and 1970s, which saw antipositivist movements that were closely tied to other cultural and political rebellions."[12]

The present is a time during which there is a resurgence of social criticism, explicit contest of ideologies, and rival claims regarding which views have the moral and political legitimacy to shape our social institutions and governing norms. I have not said much directly about that in this book. One reason is that formulating and addressing the question of whether morality can be a proper object of empirical social science seemed to me enough of an anchoring concern for the book. Another is that I believe that the main values and principles of liberal democracy in the common law tradition are worthy of endorsement.

There currently are several political, social, and economic issues crying out for attention and remedy in the Anglophone countries, perhaps especially the United States. There is an emerging public debate over whether the basic constitutional elements of the political order and the fundamental economic arrangement have failed to be just, and whether they should be more or less radically revised. Elsewhere I have argued for the view that significant reform is urgently needed but not reform that would fundamentally alter the constitutional arrangement—whether written or unwritten. I believe that most of the more radical proposals are not strongly supported by empirical considerations (though there are always facts that can be employed as paradigmatically illustrating failure) nor are they based on conceptual and normative considerations that fare well under careful, critical scrutiny. There is a great deal in favor of the rights, values, and principles characteristic of liberal democracy and its notion of the rule of law. Liberal democracy is an achievement, and in order for it to be sustained people—politicians and citizens generally—need to be willing to work at it in responsible, informed, reasonable ways.

Unfortunately, in the U.S. and perhaps other Anglophone nations as well, politics has been deteriorating into a strident, ideologically brittle, and carelessly unsubtle character. There seems to be little careful informed discussion of civics, and instead, it is politics—and a vulgar version of it—all the way down. Politicians have led the descent and not nearly enough citizens are registering dismay with that fact. They are following the politicians down to an even lower, more vulgar mode of addressing the issues. By "civics" I mean basic matters concerning the principles, norms, and ideals appropriate to the political order in contrast to the actual political bargaining and competition for the levers of power. Civics concerns the normativity of politics. There is a great deal to value in liberal democracy but it becomes more and more obscure as we become less and less fluent with the normative concepts of politics. It seems as though what passes for education in recent decades has rendered a great many people inarticulate and uninformed, without a sense of owing others coherent, fact-supported reasons for their views. And large numbers of people—on the left and on the right—are completely comfortable with being that way. Whatever else that is, it is a failure of education. I do not mean that everyone should be trained in philosophy and the social sciences or that a certain view of moral issues should be part of education. Perhaps the chief failure is that so few people seem bothered by the fact that they seem to have little genuine commitment to intellectual responsibility. A broad, informal but important concern with being intellectually responsible can be crucial to a citizen's grasp of civics. It is needed for making reasoned, intelligible claims about norms, their assumptions, implications, and relations to institutions, practices, values, and facts.

The relation between facts and values has been the main concern of this book. Whether we are moral realists or antirealists morality is as present in the empirical world as anything else. I am not presupposing a realist interpretation of morality, only that moral considerations have a place in the way we lead our lives and they are to be understood in relation to facts rather than wholly independent of them. Excluding moral considerations from the explanatory project is not a way of preserving the purity or proper focus of that project. Of course, if one's project does not concern morality at all, there may be no place for moral considerations. But that is *never* because there just are no such considerations and they could not have a role in explaining social scientific phenomena. The moral aspects of people's lives figure with no less genuineness than other aspects.

In Chapter 1 I argued that normativity is pervasive in the human world and that it is neither a romantic illusion nor a metaphysical excess, something that cannot have a legitimate place in our best understanding of the world and ourselves. Normativity is not an attempt at re-enchanting the natural world. It is a feature of numerous forms of coherence, intelligibility, and significance. Positivism's dualism of analyticity and verifiability leaves us with wholly inadequate resources for account for the relation between facts and values. This is not because we should assume Platonism regarding norms and values. If that sort of realist overreach is one form of distinctively philosophical error, another is to legislate *a priori* and exhaustively with regard to what the relations between facts and values could be.

I have not presented an argument in favor of a realist interpretation of moral value. And I have suggested a way of understanding Hume that fully acknowledges his rejection of both moral realism and moral rationalism while also acknowledging his own recognition of the genuineness of morality. It is almost as if he saw that there is no dispensing with normativity, even on the basis of the very austere view of epistemological legitimacy he elaborated. He appealed to a form of naturalism meant to comport with that austere view of epistemology while accommodating the various aspects of normativity we find indispensable and ineliminable.

Hume saw that morality is not something separated off from, unconnected with the empirical realities of our lives and society. Even if we settle on an antirealist metaethics, there remain ways in which moral considerations have empirically significant roles in our lives. The issue is not whether they have any explanatory significance; of course they do. The moral features of people's actions and practices and the moral features of institutions are not "there" *only* when someone else is morally evaluating them. Emotivists were right to emphasize the practical significance of moral judgment, that it has to do with motivation and can influence behavior. But that is not the only significance of moral judgments and it is not as though they are without significance apart from a prescriptive purpose. It is not as though, when we are talking about or explaining human action, there is no moral reality present because moral reality is *purely* practical.

Positivism did tend to claim a monopoly on epistemic validity and as the grip of positivism on the social sciences loosened criminological studies exhibited an increasingly broad range of approaches. With regard to methodology we should recognize the difference between relativism and pluralism just as we do in other contexts. In some cases the integration of theories might serve us best and we should be willing to pursue that sort of integration. It need not be regarded as spoiling the "purity" of this or that theory. The aim is a more adequate and clearer explanation, and if we make our way there via bringing together elements of different theories we should not assume there is something exotic about the phenomena or about the explanation. Our elaboration of theories might always be partial to some extent and in need of refinement and development. And genuine integration cannot be achieved by taking some from here, some from there, and simply asserting that a synthesis of them provides the best explanation. Actual integration must include conceptual articulation, clear formulation of explanatory idiom, and showing how the elements of the view actually achieve a more adequate, coherent, empirically supported account. There are, of course, some theories or hypotheses that are very implausible or are plainly inconsistent with other things we have very good reasons to accept. And any number of hypotheses have been disconfirmed. Not every theory or hypothesis merits equal standing and they are not all innocent until proven guilty. There are crazy ones that are guilty from the start. Of those that do merit careful examination their merit needs to be shown by what they explain and how they illuminate matters, and that cannot be ascertained *a priori*.

Criminology is an especially rich source of interrelations between empirical, conceptual, and normative issues, and many of the issues it explores have real, and often urgent practical significance. For that reason (among others) it is crucial to explicate the relation between facts and values. That cannot be shunted aside as a mere accessory to the *real* work of explanation. The real work includes more than more than a descriptive, normatively neutral account of the responses and attitudes people have, and facts about how they understand responsibility, obligations, and the authority of law and the aims of criminal justice. Moral considerations have a substantive role in explaining many phenomena of interest to criminologists—and the rest of us. That is a large part of what is meant in saying that there is more to morality than people's moral beliefs, opinions, and responses. There is also the issue of how plausible, how sound and defensible those are, and of how we should understand the moral significance of facts, acts, and institutions so that we are able to evaluate policies and actions in a way that goes deeper than just emotive expression. That is a way of taking responsibility for the moral significance of how we formulate and address issues of criminal justice.

Notes

1 Loader and Sparks, *Public Criminology?* p. 122.
2 Ibid., p. 130.
3 Ibid., p. 131.
4 Ibid., p. 126.
5 Ibid., pp. 116–117.
6 John Locke, Epistle to the Reader, *An Essay Concerning Human Understanding*, ed. A. D. Woozley, New York: Penguin Books, 1964, p. 58.
7 Peter Winch, *The Idea of a Social Science and Its Relation to Philosophy*, 2nd ed., Atlantic Highlands: Humanities Press International, 1990, p. 4.
8 Loader and Sparks, *Public Criminology?* p. 117.
9 Duff and Garland, Introduction, *A Reader on Punishment*, p. 22.
10 Lacey, *State Punishment*, p. 557.
11 Steinmetz, "Positivism and Its Others in the Social Sciences," p. 43.
12 Ibid., p. 41.

Appendix I

While I have tried to maintain neutrality with regard to endorsing a specific approach to moral theory I will say a little about the approach to ethics that seems to me most promising. This involves indicating a few key points regarding the merit of a virtue-centered approach to morality. In part, this is meant as a gesture of full disclosure in case the issue is of interest to readers. In addition, a few of the points in the main body of the book are influenced by the view I'll discuss in this Appendix though I managed to keep specifics of the view largely out of the treatment of topics. By "most promising" I mean that the best case can be made for a virtue-centered approach to ethics on grounds of metaethics, normative ethics, and moral psychology. That amounts to a lot of grounds. Presenting an overall case regarding such matters—even just *sketching* an overall case—would be a very considerable undertaking, one I will not attempt. However, it will be helpful to say a bit about the differences between normative ethics, moral psychology, and metaethics.

By *normative ethics* I mean claims about what is morally right, morally required, and what is morally prohibited and why. Normative ethics concerns what is often referred to as "first-order" substantive ethical claims and judgments. Many of the most influential ethical theories include significant normative claims, and normative ethics often takes the form of a theory of right action or a theory of ethical virtue, and so forth. Kant's conception of moral requirements involving a distinctively categorical imperative concerns normative ethics. Mill's claim that actions are morally right (or not) on the basis of how much net utility they bring about impartially is a claim in normative ethics. *Moral psychology* concerns attitudes, aspects of sensibility, forms of regard for oneself and others, and matters such as resentment, gratitude, respect, and the acquisition and role of states of character, the relation between virtue and happiness, and features of moral experience and moral motivation. Several important issues of moral experience and moral agency are matters of moral psychology. The relation between happiness and ethical virtue is such an issue and so too is the issue of whether persons are capable of altruism without any admixture of self-interest. *Metaethics* concerns the epistemology, metaphysics, and semantics of moral value. Issues concerning the objectivity or subjectivity of moral value are metaethical issues. Questions concerning the meaning of moral discourse are metaethical questions. The debate about the relation between descriptive meaning and prescriptive meaning—or whether that is even a valid distinction—is a metaethical debate, as is the debate about whether moral value is to be interpreted in naturalistic terms, and what that means.

Often, discussion of a moral topic will involve considerations of different types, some metaethical and some normative, for example. Or an issue clearly straddles moral psychology and normative ethics. That is the case, for example, regarding the relation between happiness and the good. In many cases that is fine and not problematic. But there are also cases and contexts in which being clear about what type of consideration is being discussed can be very important. Logical Positivists were insistent that philosophy has nothing substantive to contribute to ethics; its entire role is a matter of analyzing and clarifying the meaning of moral discourse. Thus, its 'official,' philosophically distinctive role concerns metaethics. Philosophers can comment on all manner of ethical issues. But the role of philosophy as such is clearly—they argued—limited.

By a "virtue-centered" approach I mean a broadly Aristotelian conception though that does not mean treating Aristotle's thought as doctrine, as though all we need to do is learn the doctrine and maybe make a few updating revisions.[1] Instead, what I mean is that his philosophy includes resources for the most successful handling of the issues of metaethics, normative ethics, and moral psychology, and the ways they are related. In his philosophy cognition, sensibility, desire, and motivation are connected in ways that are especially illuminating in regard to ethical judgment, ethical motivation, and agency.[2] Agency concerns issues such as the way that voluntariness is understood, the role of states of character in explaining moral reasoning and choice, how states of character are acquired, the conception of practical reasoning, and the role in ethics of self-conceptions, guiding valuative conceptions, ideals, and commitments. Among the Aristotelian resonances in the view I would defend are (i) the notion that habituation by others shapes our dispositions while young but individuals are responsible (to an extent) for the states of character they settle into as adults—we habituate ourselves as well as being habituated by others; (ii) the states of character we acquire reflect what we value, dispositions of desire and emotion, and patterns of practical reasoning; (iii) virtues are dispositions that enable a person to act well and realize objective goods in their actions; (iv) that presupposes that there are objective goods for human beings, and the metaethics connected with the view makes a case for that objectivity; (v) there isn't a fundamental principle or criterion for right action (there is no counterpart to the Categorical Imperative or the Principle of Utility) and in a great many cases the virtuous agent recognizes that multiple values are involved and need to be considered in an integrative judgment; (vi) the virtuous agent finds it pleasing or gratifying to act well—pleasure is not what right action aims at, but a person with a sound conception of good appreciates the worth and desirability of acting well; (vii) it is difficult, but not impossible, to change one's mature states of character (apart from the ways we change just as a result of aging). To make such changes requires sustained effort and resolve.

Some of the discussion of rules and norms in Chapter 1 borrowed from John McDowell's "Virtue and Reason" and that paper has influenced the conception of virtue I would defend, especially with regard to the role of rationality.[3] In that conception ethics is not a system of principles on the basis of which a codification of requirements and prohibitions can be constructed. In a widely shared understanding of ethics it has that sort of structure. While I certainly recognize that there are numerous, important ethical principles I would argue that there is not a fundamental or "master" criterion or principle of right action permitting (at least, to a significant extent) a codification of ethical requirements. That is one of the chief considerations *in favor* of a virtue-centered rather than principles-based ethics.

Moral life and moral experience present many features that are obstacles to a codification of ethics even though they are not impediments to objectively justified judgment. A virtuous agent has acquired a form of attention through which that person recognizes the ethically significant features of actions, situations, practices, and persons.[4] That attention involves recognition and responsiveness. Someone can know that courage involves managing fear and the willingness to act even in the face of danger or risk without having the virtue courage. But in lacking the virtue the agent will not reliably recognize when courage is required *and* respond by acting in the way the circumstances require of the agent. There are numerous plausible ethical generalizations. For instance, justice has to do with seeing to it that each receives in accord with what each is due or that each person's rights are respected. But of course, the real work of the virtues concerns judging what each is due and striving to see that realized. Someone could know that generalization about justice but still be a poor judge of such things. Such a person would know something about virtue but would not be a just person. Similarly for a great many other virtues. Again, knowing what courage is does not ensure knowing what courage *requires in this set of circumstances*, and does not ensure that the agent then acts accordingly.

The disposition I call "attention" is a significant element of virtue and it has been discussed much less than it merits. A person who does not possess discriminating attention might not even recognize that there are ethically significant features of the situation or might discern only some of them. By attention I mean a developed capacity for awareness and discrimination of ethically relevant aspects of situations, actions, and persons. Through attention an agent is receptive to forms of ethical significance and is able to be responsive to the particulars of the situation. One of the suspect aspects of a fundamental-principle approach to ethics is that it often treats ethically relevant features individually, in isolation, as though only one feature (e.g., what would be involved in maximizing utility) is ethically significant. There is an important relation between the acquisition of fluency with ethical concepts on the one hand, and attention on the other. One cannot acquire such fluency without a corresponding development of attention. If one person thinks that, in the situation, compassionate empathy is what is required but someone else sees that fairness, courage, and considerateness (say, consideration of a person's privacy) are also required in that situation the latter person has more alert, receptive ethical attention. That is developed along with an increasingly textured and discerning grasp of ethically relevant features and the concepts through which we show understanding of them. Thus, we can characterize the possession of virtue as *a disposition of attention including fluency with a repertoire of concepts through which one understands ethically relevant features, and such understanding is reliably action-guiding*.

To possess a virtue is to possess an action-guiding understanding concerning human good. Thus, motivational dispositions are integral to virtue. If someone has an articulate grasp of the ethically relevant aspects of a situation, yet is utterly unmoved by that grasp then there is something incomplete in that person's virtue. Granted, there are plenty of situations in which judgment without also acting is appropriate; the agent might be discussing a situation that concerns only other people. But failure to act rightly when action is required is indicative of incomplete virtue. Suppose a person lacks courage in some respects. In situations requiring courage that agent will not do what is required at least sometimes, and because moral values do not typically obtain one at a time that person, through lack of courage, could also fail to be generous and honest in the way the situation requires. Lack of a virtue can impact the realization of other virtues. Granted, the lack might be excusable, and in any case, no one's virtue is perfectly developed, leaving no scope for a more complete, more fully integrated, more fluent grasp of what matters ethically. But it is important to see that virtue includes being motivated to act in the manner one understands to be right. It would be unfair and unreasonable to expect anyone to have perfect, complete virtue. Our grasp of what is ethically significant, and our fluency with the relevant concepts, is always capable of more complete elaboration and more coherent integration.

This suggests another important aspect of a virtue-centered approach, namely, that in a given situation, for agent A to do what is required might involve different challenges than those faced by agent B in similar circumstances. Let's suppose X is a quite determinate specification of what is the right thing to do in the circumstances. For A to do X might involve overcoming an inclination to indulge one's selfishness a bit too often, while for B to do X, that person will have to manage fear successfully. They are both trying to do the same thing but doing it is a somewhat different project for each of them on account of their states of character, their dispositions and propensities.[5] Agent A might be thinking, "I really would like to get most of the credit for this but that would involve overstating my actual contribution to its success." B might be thinking, "this is exactly the sort of thing I hate having to do. I would like to just wish it away, but I see that I simply have to face it." It is true that if someone has well developed virtues they will generally not encounter inner obstacles to acting rightly. That is part of what it means to possess a virtue; namely, the agent does not struggle with inner conflict over whether to do what is right. But few persons have virtues developed so fully that there are no situations in which they feel some contrary-to-virtue inclination or some weakening of resolve.

The virtue-centered view includes commitment to objective goods. That is not the same as commitment to a single *telos* for all human beings. Thus, the view I would defend does not include a commitment to there being a single best way of life for human beings or a fixed, universal set of states of character exhibited similarly by every virtuous agent.[6] There are virtues that any virtuous agent will have—any virtuous agent possesses wisdom, courage, and honesty, for example—but the diversity of human situations and the variety of challenges people encounter are strong bases for thinking that virtuous persons will not all have exactly the same character. They will have a grasp of important aspects and elements of human good but there are any number of ways for those goods to be realized and the differences in circumstances can make for differences in what is ethically required. The practical wisdom possessed by virtuous agents is action-guiding understanding of human good. "Human good" refers to a potentially complex and multi-aspect conception that can be realized in diverse ways in diverse circumstances, but without involving relativism.

People in very different settings, whether they are different socio-cultural settings or very different settings within a common socio-cultural world, can encounter very different circumstances but that does not mean that human good is radically different. It means that the ways that human good is realized can differ. The practical wisdom that is appropriate to a particular cultural context will be intelligible to persons with practical wisdom acquired in a different context. We should not expect it to be obvious, evident without requiring reflection and careful consideration but neither will it be so strange, so foreign that it is mystifying how it could be practical wisdom.

In addition, in many cases what is ethically required is not derived in a manner analogous to theorems being derived from axioms in geometry. Often, the relation between a conception of good and an ethical requirement is more like what Aquinas called "determination" (when he was explicating the relation between natural law and the determination of specific ethical requirements). Aquinas wrote,

> But it must be noted that something may be derived from the natural law in two ways; first, as a conclusion from principles; secondly, by way of determination of certain common notions. The first way is like that by which, in the sciences, demonstrated conclusions are drawn from the

> principles; while the second is likened to that whereby, in the arts, common forms are determined to some particular. Thus, the craftsman needs to determine the common form of a house to the shape of this or that particular house.[7]

Suppose an architect/builder is asked to build a house for a particular client. The architect/builder needs to know how large the group is, what sort of budget is available, what is the desired timeline for progress, whether certain types of materials (brick instead of wood, or wood instead of stone, and so forth) are desired, whether it is important to have space indoors for animals during winter, whether the ground in the specific location tends to be wet, and so on. There are various general rules and principles of design that the architect/builder will follow, and there will be specific determinations of them for the relevant climate and conditions. Working from those general rules and principles in conjunction with the specifications indicated by the purchaser the builder will arrive at determinations of various characteristics for this particular house and the house will be the physical realization of those determinations.

If the prospective buyer says that it is crucial that the structure should be a floating structure and that it should be made of stone exclusively the builder will decline the job; there is no realizable determination of such a house. There are all sorts of possible styles of architecture, different construction materials, and different designs and, accordingly, a large variety of different determinations of design and materials but it is not a matter of *anything goes*. There are objective limits and within those there are reasonable, prudent, safe limits. A person *could* live in a single room atop a tripod of telephone poles, the living space reachable only by a rope ladder. But apart from novelty it is difficult to see what makes that a rationally desirable design.

In her discussion of the difference between *the circumstances of a life* and *leading a life* Julia Annas emphasizes how, in the latter the commitment to good is crucial. We should not confuse pluralism, the fact there are multiple sources of ethical value, with pluralism in a sense that indicates fragmentation, the notion that there is no integrative conception of virtuous activity through which good is realized in the exercise of practical reason. That one can have a durable, integrated conception of good does not mean that every virtuous agent's conception of it will be exactly the same. But each virtuous agent's practical reasoning and valuative judgment will be guided by a conception of good, which can be refined, elaborated, and corrected. On the view that she defends,

> although in exercising different virtues the virtuous person is directed towards different values, the different virtues can, and should in a good life, be unified by the person's living their life in accordance with a unified conception of goodness, one to be discovered and exercised by the

> person's practical reasoning, which unifies the acquisition and expression of the virtues. The virtues are, then, unified into an integrated commitment to goodness and are exercised in the living of a good, flourishing life.[8]

There are pluralists who deny the point (Nietzsche, for example) and to them she argues that virtue "involves a commitment to goodness *because* it is goodness."[9] She notes that, "we should not expect all commitments to goodness to have the same form."[10] This does not limit virtuous persons to one, narrow way of leading a life. Not even Aristotle's view made such a (dubious) commitment. When he argued that there are certain states of character virtuous persons need he did not also mean that all virtuous persons will be just like each other, leading the same kind of life. That is immensely implausible. A diversity of virtues and a diversity of conceptions of good can be accommodated without denying that virtuous persons have a distinctive commitment, exhibited regularly in the person's practical reasoning, to an overall, integrated conception of good. We can distinguish between (i) a unified life in which a variety of ends, interests, and concerns are integrated by practical reason and (ii) being committed to a pluralism of values such that there is no reason to believe they can be integratively realized through an overall commitment to good. In the latter, ethical judgment and ethical life are in a problematic predicament concerning coherence and integrity. An agent's commitment to good can be recognized as such even though good is realizable in many ways and in many contexts allows for a high degree of individuality and cultural difference. Those differences and the fact that virtue-centered theory (at least the version for which I would argue) is pluralistic regarding value (there are numerous goods) are not reasons for thinking the view is relativistic. Virtue has a concern with integrity of commitment but that is compatible with a pluralism of values and virtues needing to be exercised differently in different circumstances.

What might this mean for the social scientific study of morality? Regarding this issue I will make only a couple of observations. There is a difference between explicating the morality of people one is studying and morally evaluating the people one is studying. There need not be anything ethnocentric or morally imperialistic about either project. It seems perfectly in order to judge the Pol Pot regime as morally horrific, South Africa's formerly apartheid regime, and the disappearances of people during the Pinochet regime as morally very bad. On a much smaller scale if the fence you put up (entirely on your own property) between your driveway and the neighbor's driveway does not meet with your neighbor's approval, and he then shoots and kills your cat and your dog and tears up your vegetable garden, it is very difficult to find anything morally redeemable in that. Contrariwise, if everyone who lives in the building makes a donation of time and effort to help clean up after fire ruined apartments in the next building, and people prepare meals to take to those whose kitchens have been wrecked by the fire that would seem commendable in an unproblematic sense. There is a great deal that can be morally judged without much dispute even if people have different background experiences and are accustomed to different sorts of situations. Of course there is plenty that is disputable but it is easy to overlook a very broad expanse of moral agreement.

Is virtue-centered ethics an effective approach to the study of other societies' moralities? Suppose the other society's culture is such that it is not clear that they recognize a distinction between law and morality, or between religion and civil society in the way such distinctions are recognized in liberal democracies. Suppose there is not even a clean break between private life and public life in the community. It might be a very traditional society in which religion, morality, and politics are deeply interwoven. Yet, it could still be the case that investigators can ascertain the guiding conceptions of good, worth, and meaning that are important to the society, and the ways they respond to failures to respect those values and departures from the guiding norms. Even if the specific values and norms of the society seem very much unlike one's own it should be possible to recognize what ends are served by various practices and the ways that evaluations of acts and judgments of responsibility—even if they take a very unfamiliar form—have weight.

It would almost certainly be inappropriate and not especially illuminating to try to formulate the society's values along the lines of, say, Kant's categorical imperative. The notion that *a priori* rational considerations are the basis for their most important principles might just be utterly irrelevant. There might be ways in which there are helpful comparisons and counterparts but the key to understanding their ethics needs to be their values and how they take them to be realized. It should be possible to ascertain how merit and demerit, or praise and blame, or encouragement and discouragement are distributed and what people are meant to strive for in what they do and how they do it. It would be very surprising if there just are no recognizable patterns of activity and judgment concerning the realization or actualization of important ends or values.

Suppose it is not a deeply religious, tradition-shaped society but still quite different from one's own. Again, it should be possible to detect some of the main ways that members of the society negotiate the space of reasons and what sort of ends and achievements they regard as especially worthwhile. Also, if the patterns of affect and dispositions of sensibility seem very unlike those of the investigator's society those aspects of their lives should not be inscrutable, altogether inaccessible. This is because we and they act for reasons and are intelligible to each other even if this requires considerable effort. One way in which virtue-centered morality could be helpful is that it does not highlight a fundamental principle or a small number of fundamental principles; it is alert to a more textured conception of value and it recognizes how a basic value, justice, for example, is realized in different ways in different contexts. The forms of attention that are integral to virtue-centered ethics can help us appreciate or at least discern the intelligibility of values that are quite different from our own. In any case, being accustomed to ethical thought in the forms it takes in virtue-centered ethics can help an investigator avoid the error of supposing that there is some single, master principle that is to be identified. It could be that a society has such a principle. Still, it would seem likely that actually acting on it requires judgment of how it applies in the circumstances and it would be very odd for there to be just one way to act rightly in all circumstances, for example, always praising and rewarding the tallest person.

A virtue-centered approach includes a focus on the kind of attention with which people become aware of, and responsive to ethically relevant considerations. What sorts of things do people find ethically relevant; what ethically matters to them? Do they focus on what they regard as matters of justice, or on whether people are generous, or compassionate? Are they chiefly concerned with people fulfilling certain well-defined, static social roles and responsibilities? Are there differences in status that determine one's obligations? Is there scope for individuals to deliberate or are ethical requirements generally fully fixed? Is there a "master" value, something to which other values and considerations are related, and which is claimed to always be the valuative "center of gravity"? The main point here is the importance of ascertaining the form of attention and the repertoire of concepts employed by the persons studied. It is crucial to have a grasp of what sorts of discriminations they regard as most important, and how those figure in their judgments, decisions, and actions. Each of the considerations mentioned here is part of what is involved in getting a sense of how the people studied map and negotiate the space of reasons. Their reasons might be quite unfamiliar or they might be connected with religious or other considerations in ways that are unfamiliar to the investigator. It might be more illuminating to try to explicate the values that appear to matter most to the people studied and to ask, "What are their values?" than to start with the question, "What are the elements of their ethical code?" as though any society's ethical views must take the form of codification. Noticing that certain actions are required in a distinctive way or that certain rules seem to be especially important can be a step on the way to attaining a better understanding of what they *value*. That is crucial to getting a grip on their morality.

One way to approach this is to ask what sorts of answers members of the society give to the question, "what sorts of 'have to' are recognized?" That is a way of ascertaining the kinds of practical necessity to which people respond. These are different forms of practical necessity. There is the "have to" of legal requirement, the "have to" of strong desire, the "have to" of self-interest, the "have to" of religious practice, the "have to" of etiquette, the "have to" of cultural custom, and perhaps some others as well. Is there a "have to" of ethical requirement (or prohibition) in the society's view of practical necessity? Perhaps the ethical "have to" is best understood as an intersection of some of the others. Perhaps it has its own distinct character. In any case, distinguishing forms of practical necessity can be a way of focusing on a society's conception of ethical reasons and requirements. The intelligibility of their actions depends on the intelligibility of the reasons for them. Their social life and their actions are intelligible through the norms that inform their activity and the kinds of explanations and justifications they give. That is not to say that their actions will of course be satisfactorily justified. However, it is crucial to grasp what they take to be reasons and the different weights they assign to different reasons. That is a way to begin to recognize the layers of normativity informing their actions, practices, and institutions.

Notes

1 There are numerous different forms of Aristotelian ethical theories because there are so many resources in Aristotle's thought. However, the notion that there is such a thing as practical wisdom, that there are goods for human beings based on fundamental features of our nature, and that virtuous agents find it pleasing to act virtuously seem to me especially important borrowings from Aristotle. There is nothing about them that somehow confines them to ancient Athenian society or to a pre-modern biology or metaphysics. Such claims are often indicative of a shallow grasp of Aristotle's thought and a shallow grasp of ethical thought generally.

2 Agency is a much-disputed notion and many discussions of it involve aspects of the debate about freedom of the will. I think it is possible to employ the notion of agency in a way that is conceptually plausible and clear without first (somehow) resolving the free will vs determinism debate or showing that the debate is itself somehow ill-formulated. There is much that could be added here to explicate the notion of agency but for present purposes I hope that the characterization of it given is sufficient.

3 See McDowell, "Virtue and Reason," pp. 331–350.

4 I began to appreciate the importance of attention as a result of reading Iris Murdoch's *The Sovereignty of Good*, in which she employs the notion as a centrally important aspect of moral life and experience. Murdoch's use of the notion drew on insights of Simone Weil. Murdoch wrote, "I have used the word 'attention,' which I borrow from Simone Weil, to express the idea of a just and loving gaze directed upon an individual reality. I believe this to be the characteristic and proper mark of the moral agent." My use of the notion is slightly different from Murdoch's but they overlap and are mutually compatible.

5 The combination of the fact that many ethical judgments are integrative and concern more than one value, with the fact that, in facing similar circumstances different persons might find them challenging and difficult in different ways (though the same thing is the right thing for each to do) merits more attention than it receives.

6 Aristotle himself wrestled with a kind of pluralism regarding the best life for a human being. In Book X of *Nicomachean Ethics* he seems to go back and forth between the active, practical life of virtue and the life of intellectual virtue as the best kind of life. Moreover, whatever his view of that question, he certainly did not think that all virtuous persons will have exactly similar characters. The notion that a virtuous society would be one of boringly homogeneous characters finds no support in his philosophy.

7 S. T. Aquinas, "Q. 95, Art. 2," in *Introduction to St. Thomas Aquinas*, ed. Anton C. Pegis, New York: Modern Library, 1948, p. 649.

8 J. Annas, *Intelligent Virtue*, New York: Oxford University Press, 2011, p. 115.

9 Ibid., p. 111.

10 Ibid.

Index

Made in the USA
Monee, IL
12 November 2026

f713e845-c91f-42cf-9ce0-2de062e20527R01

Psychological Insights for Understanding COVID-19 and Media and Technology

In the *Psychological Insights for Understanding COVID*-19 series, international experts introduce important themes in psychological science that engage with people's unprecedented experience of the pandemic, drawing together chapters as they originally appeared before COVID-19 descended on the world.

This book explores how COVID-19 has impacted our relationship with media and technology, and chapters examine a range of topics including fake news, social media, conspiracy theories, belonging, online emotional lives and relationship formation and identity. It shows the benefits media and technology can have in relation to coping with crises and navigating challenging situations, whilst also examining the potential pitfalls that emerge due to our increasing reliance on them. In a world where the cyberpsychological space is constantly developing, this volume exposes the complexities surrounding the interaction of human psychology with media and technology, and reflects on what this might look like in the future.

Featuring theory and research on key topics germane to the global pandemic, the *Psychological Insights for Understanding COVID-19* series offers thought-provoking reading for professionals, students, academics and policy makers concerned with the psychological consequences of COVID-19 for individuals, families and society.

Ciarán Mc Mahon, Ph.D., is a director of the Institute of Cyber Security, author of *The Psychology of Social Media*, and co-author of *Cyber Security ABCs: Delivering Awareness, Behaviours and Culture Change.*

Psychological Insights for Understanding COVID-19

The *Psychological Insights for Understanding COVID-19* series aims to highlight important themes in psychological science that engage with people's unprecedented experience of the COVID-19 pandemic. These short, accessible volumes draw together chapters as they originally appeared before COVID-19 descended on the world but demonstrate how researchers and professionals in psychological science had developed theory and research on key topics germane to the global pandemic. Each volume includes a specially commissioned, expert introduction that contextualises the chapters in relation to the crisis, reflects on the relevance of psychological research during this significant global event, and proposes future research and vital interventions that elucidate understanding and coping with COVID-19. With individual volumes exploring society, health, family, work and media, the *Psychological Insights for Understanding COVID-19* series offers thought-provoking reading for professionals, students, academics and policy makers concerned with psychological consequences of the pandemic for individuals, families and society.

Titles in the series:

Psychological Insights for Understanding COVID-19 and Families, Parents, and Children
Edited by Marc H. Bornstein

Psychological Insights for Understanding COVID-19 and Media and Technology
Edited by Ciarán Mc Mahon

Psychological Insights for Understanding COVID-19 and Society
Edited by S. Alexander Haslam

Psychological Insights for Understanding COVID-19 and Work
Edited by Cary L. Cooper

Psychological Insights for Understanding COVID-19 and Health
Edited by Dominika Kwasnicka and Robbert Sanderman

For more information about this series, please visit: www.routledge.com/Psychological-Insights-for-Understanding-COVID-19/book-series/COVID

Psychological Insights for Understanding COVID-19 and Media and Technology

Edited by Ciarán Mc Mahon

Routledge
Taylor & Francis Group
LONDON AND NEW YORK

First published 2021
by Routledge
2 Park Square, Milton Park, Abingdon, Oxon OX14 4RN

and by Routledge
52 Vanderbilt Avenue, New York, NY 10017

Routledge is an imprint of the Taylor & Francis Group, an informa business

British Library Cataloguing-in-Publication Data
A catalogue record for this book is available from the British Library

Library of Congress Cataloging-in-Publication Data
A catalog record for this book has been requested

ISBN: 978-0-367-64007-1 (hbk)
ISBN: 978-0-367-64006-4 (pbk)
ISBN: 978-1-003-12175-6 (ebk)

Typeset in Times New Roman
by Apex CoVantage, LLC

Selected chapters are taken from the following original Routledge publications

The Psychology of Fake News: Accepting, Sharing, and Correcting Misinformation
Rainer Greifeneder, Mariela Jaffe, Eryn Newman, Norbert Schwarz
ISBN: 978-0-367-27181-7 (hbk) ISBN: 978-0-367-27183-1 (pbk) ISBN: 978-0-429-29537-9 (ebk)

The Psychology of Social Media
Ciarán Mc Mahon
ISBN: 978-1-138-04774-7 (hbk) ISBN: 978-1-138-04775-4 (pbk) ISBN: 978-1-315-17061-9 (ebk)

The Psychology of Conspiracy Theories
Jan-Willem van Prooijen
ISBN: 978-1-138-69609-9 (hbk) ISBN: 978-1-138-69610-5 (pbk) ISBN: 978-1-315-52541-9 (ebk)

An Introduction to Cyberpsychology
Irene Connolly, Marion Palmer, Hannah Barton, Gráinne Kirwan
ISBN: 978-1-138-82378-5 (hbk) ISBN: 978-1-138-82379-2 (pbk) ISBN: 978-1-315-74189-5 (ebk)

The Psychology of Belonging
Kelly-Ann Allen
ISBN: 978-0-367-34753-6 (hbk) ISBN: 978-0-367-34752-9 (pbk) ISBN: 978-0-429-32768-1 (ebk)

Applications of Social Psychology: How Social Psychology Can Contribute to the Solution of Real-World Problems
Joseph P. Forgas, William D. Crano, Klaus Fiedler
ISBN: 978-0-367-41832-8 (hbk) ISBN: 978-0-367-41833-5 (pbk) ISBN: 978-0-367-81640-7 (ebk)

Wired Youth: The Online Social World of Adolescence, Second Edition
Ilan Talmud, Gustavo Mesch
ISBN: 978-0-8153-7883-9 (hbk) ISBN: 978-0-8153-7884-6 (pbk) ISBN: 978-1-351-22774-2 (ebk)

Emergent Identities: New Sexualities, Genders and Relationships in a Digital Era
Rob Cover
ISBN: 978-1-138-09858-9 (hbk) ISBN: 978-1-138-09861-9 (pbk) ISBN: 978-1-315-10434-8 (ebk)

Contents

Contributors

Kelly-Ann Allen, School of Education, Monash University, Australia, drkellyallen@gmail.com

Susannah Chandhok, Graduate Student, Department of Psychology, University of Michigan, susac@umich.edu

Rob Cover, Media and Communication Studies, University of Western Australia, Australia, rob.cover@uwa.edu.au

Olivia Hurley, Institute of Art, Design + Technology (IADT), Ireland, Olivia.Hurley@iadt.ie

Madeline Jalbert, Graduate Student, Department of Psychology, University of Southern California, Los Angeles, USA, mcjalber@usc.edu

Ethan Kross, Department of Psychology, University of Michigan, USA, ekross@umich.edu

Gustavo Mesch, Department of Sociology, University of Haifa, Israel, gustavo@soc.haifa.ac.il

Norbert Schwarz, Department of Psychology, University of Southern California, Los Angeles, USA, norberts@usc.edu

Ilan Talmud, Department of Sociology, University of Haifa, Israel talmud@soc.haifa.ac.il

Jan-Willem van Prooijen, Department of Experimental and Applied Psychology, VU Amsterdam, Netherlands, j.w.van.prooijen@vu.nl

Introduction

Ciarán Mc Mahon

I hope this finds you well

'In these extraordinary times' seems like a trite understatement, but it has become a common phrase in emails in 2020. Conventional language seems redundant given the horror of the COVID-19 pandemic. Similarly, it can feel peculiar to be still writing and reading about such abstract things as media psychology. But our way of life must somehow continue, as soon as we have completed the more fundamental task of surviving.

In a generally prescient study of the psychology of pandemics, Taylor (2019, p. 108) writes, "If the next pandemic is like some past pandemics in which children and young adults were most susceptible, then there will be many parents grieving for their lost children." Thankfully this has not come to pass, as children do not appear to be especially susceptible to this virus. But I suspect that many parents of school-goers are currently experiencing something akin to grief – grief for their offspring's childhood – friendships disrupted, habits broken, learning interrupted. A vast unexpected experiment in home-schooling and working-from-home has been dropped on a large portion of the population, and most of us do not quite know what has hit us – perhaps we should instead be talking about living at school, or homing at work. This new normal has driven a coach-and-four into lots of social concepts – from work/life balance to screen time and presumably many more besides.

In whatever future we had been imagining, a chasm of vantablack has appeared. Nothing like this has happened in living memory – we are in utterly unchartered territory. This is true in almost every human or social science direction we care to gaze, but perhaps exceptionally so when we think of the cyberpsychological space – the complicated interaction of human psychology with our various forms of media and technology. In itself, this is a new and exciting field of scholarly activity. For researchers in this area, almost everything is still 'to be decided'. There are few settled questions, and novel controversies emerge practically with each passing week.

Yet at the same time, there is no way out of this pandemic without an increasingly complicated and mediated future. Throughout society a 'data feeding frenzy' has begun – even into our beloved pubs (Walsh, 2020) as patrons record their personal details for contact tracing purposes. A boom in workplace surveillance is happening as employers roll out temperature checks and try to predict employees' risk of infection (Chyi, 2020). As more people work from home, bosses are 'panic-buying' surveillance software, snapping screenshots of their remote employees (Mosendz & Melin, 2020). Many of these workers are also parents, whose home schooling experience has been repeatedly described as 'hell' (Cassidy, 2020; Krishan, 2020; Sellgren, 2020). In an excruciating example of a deepening digital divide, the BBC (2020) reported one family attempting to home-school six children on a single phone – and they are surely not alone.

And when those of us who do have the luxury of our own personal devices do finally get a chance to relax of an evening, we may realise that our favourite content creators are also feeling the pinch. Online advertising revenues are falling due to a collapsing economy, while competition for viewers increases as everyone from TV celebrities to the average Joe films their daily experience of the pandemic (Lorenz, 2020). As hard as it is to imagine, the internet is now even more awash with content than it was before.

It feels appropriate to quote Marshall McLuhan (1967, p. 94): "These are difficult times because we are witnessing a clash of cataclysmic proportions between two great technologies. We approach the new with the psychological conditioning and sensory responses of the old." It is the natural instinct of a researcher, when encountering a new problem, to see how previous comparable problems were cracked. Unhelpfully, we seem to know little about the wider societal impact of the last global pandemic, namely the so-called Spanish Flu. Perhaps this is because it occurred during a wartime era, with strict controls on publicity and little budget for reflexive scholarship. Or maybe people wanted to forget about it? Perhaps we will want to forget about this one, but I doubt we will be able to.

Crucially, I suspect we will be studying the technological aspects of this moment for quite some time. This is because that context was already within a cultural moment of significant angst, beginning with the Snowden revelations in 2013, right through the Cambridge Analytica controversy of 2018 and several other scandals in between. Furthermore, this period's woes will now be crystallised in our 'technologies of memory' like Wikipedia (Betuel, 2020). Whether we would like to forget it or not, all aspects of the COVID-19 pandemic will be recorded digitally, and how those records are managed and updated will affect in turn how we psychologically remember this pandemic.

However, this unrest is much more in evidence with regard to profit-generating tech services than non-profits like Wikipedia. It is something of an understatement to say that over the last five to ten years, the global community has been unnerved by the increasing power of the major tech corporations – in spite of their extraordinary abilities to create technologies that so many of us seem to love using every day. Consequently, this pandemic moment has presented an acute challenge to the likes of Apple, Google and Microsoft.

Some commentators have opined that while a moment of redemption may have presented itself for such companies, it seems to have passed. At the beginning of the crisis, "screens were no longer an addictive distraction from real life, but the locus of real life itself" (Oremus, 2020). But that moment passed when a host of regulatory and political concerns reared their head once more. For example, a trust deficit (Fung, 2020) has emerged for Facebook, with large numbers of advertisers departing its services due to its handling of misinformation and hate speech issues. Furthermore, at the beginning of the crisis, social media users all across the world noticed something strange happening to their newsfeeds. Favourite accounts suddenly disappeared, and innocuous content was unexplainably marked as spam and removed. As Facebook, Twitter and YouTube sent human content moderators home (Matsakis & Martineau, 2020), the algorithms were left in control, and the result was not pretty.

The irony is that we are now being asked to place our trust in technology to at least partially get us out of this mess. As I mentioned in *The Psychology of Social Media* (Mc Mahon, 2019) an essential truth about social media services is that they encourage users to commodify themselves – their personal information, their emotions, their sociality – and put it online. This is a reality that most of us feel uncomfortable about on the rare occasion when we pause to examine it. But now in 2020, we are being asked to share our location and interaction history with contact tracing apps, where the personal information is gathered for the purpose of saving lives. Will this feel less unpleasant, because we're not generating private profit but attempting to help the greater good? Or will it feel more like the consolidation of this unease, a normalisation of this model of commodification and surveillance?

Despite the fact that "tech-based solutions being pursued and deployed are far from ideal and have a number of issues that suggest they may not be fit-for-purpose" (Kitchin, 2020, p. 7), such smartphone applications are being pushed out by governments all across the world in an attempt to halt the spread of the coronavirus. In that light, the failure of many advanced nations, including the United Kingdom, to build such an app without the involvement help of Google and Apple (Sabbagh & Hern, 2020) is remarkable. What does that say about state capacity to protect its citizens in the technology sphere? As one scholar has queried, even if these tech giants get everything right about the privacy aspects of these apps, is there still something fundamentally wrong (Sharon, 2020)? We are now at a point where tech corporations' involvement in modern life has moved from the useful to the essential: it is difficult to see how societies can now function without them.

Treatments

In this volume, we have put together a selection of scholarship which, while not explicitly about this crisis, is as close to that intellectual neighbourhood as one could hope to be. It is hoped that the enormity of this crisis can be better understood by reflecting on the individual's experience of it – how we try to navigate and make sense of this world with the technologies around us.

Chapter 1, titled "When (Fake) News Feels True: Intuitions of Truth and the Acceptance and Correction of Misinformation," comes from Norbert Schwarz and Madeline Jalbert (2021) and could not be a more apposite example of this. The pandemic has spawned an explosion of news coverage as scared citizens search for accurate information about this new and unknown threat. However, this crisis is spawning an equally vast explosion of untruths. Research has observed that major producers of disinformation tend to produce less content than professional media organisations, but they can attract as much as 10 times the level of online engagement with their content (Howard, 2020). In Schwarz and Jalbert's chapter we understand why this is concerning. Essentially, the conditions necessary for correcting misconceptions, such as interested recipients, with time to consider the counter-messaging and with some incentives too, contrast signficantly with the reality of public information campaigns, where social media users are continually bombarded with all kinds of conflicting information and enticements. Policy makers attempting to counteract the COVID-19 infodemic would do well to consider this chapter in detail.

Our second chapter, "Connections," comes from my own *The Psychology of Social Media* (2019). Here I discuss the benefits and drawbacks which we experience on social media from being able to connect with lots of people in a single space. For example, research has shown that users of Facebook and Snapchat benefit differently from either site. That is, knowing that some social media sites can help users develop bridging social capital, while others help more with bonding social capital, can help researchers better understand how social media users may be coping during the pandemic. For example, has physical distancing affected what users want from their social media services? Has that contributed to the increased popularity of TikTok?

I also discuss Dunbar's numbers within social media studies, and in particular the lesser-known ones, namely the sympathy group and the support clique. This treatment may be useful with regard to, for example, the mutual aid groups which have sprung up in many locations (Butler, 2020). Another concept discussed here is that of FOMO – or the fear of missing out. How has this phenomenon evolved during the pandemic? Media outlets are reporting conflicting experiences, with some saying that the lockdown has "cured their FOMO" (Burleigh, 2020) while others admit that while they feel bad about it, they are still experiencing fear of missing out (Tait, 2020).

In Chapter 3, we come to "When Do People Believe Conspiracy Theories?" by Jan-Willem van Prooijen (2018). He quickly dismisses the idea that our modern internet is somehow more conducive to belief in conspiracies. On the contrary, van Prooijen shows that it is in fact societal crisis situations, not any particular aspect of the media landscape, which give rise to this kind of thinking – an apt illustration in these times.

Startlingly, this chapter contains a very prescient section, asking the reader to imagine what would happen if a head of government fell ill or died with a flu virus. Would the public believe that their illness was indeed caused by a medical condition, or would they prefer a conspiracy theory of some kind? In fact, as we have seen, when Prime Minister Johnson fell ill with COVID-19 (and thankfully recovered unlike in van Prooijen's example), conspiracy theories immediately flourished. Not only did a Downing Street spokesperson have to deny disinformation claims that he was going to be put on a ventilator (McGuinness, 2020), but reports also circulated that not only was Johnson not really sick, but that staff at the hospital where he was being treated had to sign the Official Secrets Act to that effect (Milne, 2020). All of which is false, and all of which only further serves to illustrate van Prooijen's point in this chapter: that conspiracy theories are basically natural reactions to social situations of fear and uncertainty. I suspect that this is something that many of us know but have not paused to admit: for the last few months, we have been living in dread, with none of the normal confidence about the future. Consequently, it is inevitable that conspiracy theories would spring up at this time. As van Prooijen explains: "Sense making thus is essential in the psychology of conspiracy theories."

The fourth chapter in this volume is Olivia Hurley's "The Dynamics of Groups Online" (2016). In the 'before times', this would have been an interesting chapter. Today, as vast amounts of our socialising have been forced online, it becomes an essential read. I note, for example, Hurley's sketching of the most common reasons for joining online groups, including 'alleviating loneliness' – "whether that is temporary, such as moving to a new city, or chronic, such as being housebound for long periods of time". When researchers come to examine online sociality during the lockdown, will they find that we have joined lots more online groups than usual? Similarly, the pandemic has brought a variety of new online organising tools for communities (Brechter, 2020), so researchers and practitioners will be eager to apply concepts from this chapter, such as online group cohesion, social loafing and groupthink to their contexts. Has the lockdown exacerbated – or intensified? – these phenomena?

The meme 'Congratulations, you survived a meeting that could have been an email' leads off our fifth chapter, Kelly-Ann Allen's "Belonging in an Age of Technology" (2021). This came to life for many people working remotely over the last few months as lots of meetings did in fact become emails. The point Allen makes is not a trivial one though – in the 21st century we have lots of ways of connecting with each other, but is this technology helping or hindering our sense of belonging?

In exploring how communication technology has become the 'bricks and mortar of our daily existence', Allen gives us a useful treatment of the concept of 'screen time', which has surely taken a battering over the last few months. As many of us have worked and schooled from home recently, our patterns of technology use have surely drastically altered, but also our sense of belonging. A relatively new practice which has exploded during the lockdown period in many countries is the phenomenon of the watchparty (Wallenstein, 2020) – where people in separate locations can chat together online while watching the same TV show or movie. Can we be alone together, via Netflix? As Allen carefully explains, this depends not only how we define belonging, but also how we manage the process of technological change.

Next we come to Ethan Kross and Susannah Chandhok's chapter, "How Do Online Social Networks Influence People's Emotional Lives?" (2020). This piece confronts perhaps the most essential debate in media psychology. How come, on the one hand, many studies reveal negative associations between emotional well-being and social media usage, whereas on the other, many reveal positive associations? This they term *The Puzzle* – a conceptual and methodological challenge which will likely intensify in the post-pandemic world.

Helpfully, Kross and Chandhok address questions such as 'Why do people continue to use social media if doing so consistently leads them to feel worse?' and 'Are there ways of harnessing social media to improve well-being?' We can see aspects of this during this lockdown. For many of us logging on to social media in 2020 may have been quite a deflating, if not depressing, experience, with wave after wave of terrible news. Yet at the same time, through hashtags and memes such as #inthis-together, 'flattening the curve' and 'stay home save lives', perhaps we found ways to influence our own emotions on social media by attempting to help each other.

In our seventh chapter, we move to online relationship formation in young people, by Ilan Talmud and Gustavo Mesch (2020). This piece contains pressing analysis for those working with teens and young people. Their focus here is on the similarities, differences and overlap between online and offline social relationships in adolescents.

A recent viewpoint in *The Lancet* makes the point that the physical distancing measures put in place to prevent the spread of COVID-19 will have removed face-to-face contact from social connection, thereby disrupting the peer-to-peer interaction at the heart of adolescent well-being (Orben, Tomova, & Blakemore, 2020). The authors suggest that use of digital technologies may mitigate this disruption and that further research is urgently necessary.

In their chapter, Talmud and Mesch give us some clues as to how this mitigation may occur and what researchers should look out for. They note that while research shows that online friendships are regularly perceived to be lower in quality than offline friendships, the quality of online friendships improves significantly more so than do offline relationships. Perhaps social distancing may in fact produce stronger online friendships for teens? Crucially however, Talmud and Mesch argue that the very concept of 'online relationship' itself requires clarification, which is something researchers must address in the post-pandemic context.

During the last few months, along with everything else we have gone through, many of us will have gained new aspects to our psychological identities. Some of us will have become 'cocooners', 'shielders' or 'compromised' – and preliminary research warns of potential divides between 'distancers' and 'non-distancers' (Prosser, Judge, Bolderdijk, Blackwood, & Kurz, 2020). Strikingly, in the United States the very act of wearing a mask has become endowed with political symbolism (Hess, 2020).

As such, it is very useful to conclude this volume with "Identity Citizenship" by Rob Cover (2019). While this chapter is largely concerned with sexual and gender identities, we can also see how this work is acutely relevant in the post-pandemic context. In particular, Cover begins by showing while new ways of thinking about sexuality and gender first appear online, it is not really useful to think of digital media as causing these new ideas to emerge. Rather, he argues we should consider the cultural conditions which give rise to such ideas. Of the cultural factors he incorporates into this analysis, the 'cult of authenticity' and the 'role of populism' strike me as of being highly relevant in how we come to understand ourselves in the new normal.

To conclude, all has changed, changed utterly, a terrible beauty has once again been born. At time of writing (July 2020) it is far from clear what new future will emerge from this crisis, nor how much of the past will survive. I hope in this Introduction I have adequately shown, however, that our new lives will most certainly be mediated by the complicated interaction of human psychology and information technology – moreover, that the chapters which follow will be useful in understanding that context. It is understanding the issues which are covered in subsequent pages – from fake news and conspiracy theories, to our identities and emotions, our sense of belonging and online groups, connections and relationships – which will be crucial to how we survive within an increasingly mediated post-COVID-19 world.

References

Allen, K.-A. (2021). *The psychology of belonging*. London: Routledge.

BBC News. (2020, May 19). Homeschooling six children with just one phone. *BBC News*. Retrieved from https://www.bbc.com/news/av/education-52717519/coronavirus-homeschooling-six-children-with-just-one-phone

Betuel, E. (2020, June 23). How the internet will change our coronavirus memories. *Inverse*. Retrieved from https://www.inverse.com/mind-body/COVID19-memory-history

Brechter, H. A. (2020, April 8). In coronavirus pandemic, groups use online tools to fight isolation. *USA Today*. Retrieved from https://eu.usatoday.com/story/opinion/2020/04/07/coronavirus-pandemic-groups-use-online-tools-fight-isolation-column/5090452002/

Burleigh, N. (2020, May 3). Fomo haunted me for years – but the coronavirus pandemic cured me. *The Guardian*. Retrieved from https://www.theguardian.com/commentisfree/2020/may/03/coronavirus-pandemic-fomo-vanity

Butler, P. (2020, March 16). COVID-19 Mutual Aid: how to help vulnerable people near you. *The Guardian*. Retrieved from https://www.theguardian.com/world/2020/mar/16/COVID-19-mutual-aid-how-to-help-the-vulnerable-near-you

Cassidy, A. (2020, April 28). Homeschooling hell: "I'm under so much pressure and it's from the mums" WhatsApp groups'. *Image*. Retrieved from https://www.image.ie/life/homeschooling-hell-im-much-pressure-mums-whatsapp-groups-187142

Chyi, N. (2020, May 12). The workplace-surveillance technology boom. *Slate*. Retrieved from https://slate.com/technology/2020/05/workplace-surveillance-apps-coronavirus.html

Cover, R. (2019). *Emergent identities*. London: Routledge.

Fung, B. (2020). Facebook exec admits there is a "trust deficit" as advertiser boycott accelerates. *CNN Business*. Retrieved from https://edition.cnn.com/2020/06/24/tech/facebook-trust-deficit/index.html

Hess, A. (2020, June 2). The Medical Mask Becomes a Protest Symbol. *The New York Times*. Retrieved from https://www.nytimes.com/2020/06/02/arts/virus-mask-trump.html

Howard, P. N. (2020). Bending the Curve of Fake Pandemic News. *Project Syndicate*. Retrieved from https://www.project-syndicate.org/commentary/much-COVID19-disinformation-traceable-to-authoritarian-regimes-by-philip-n-howard-2020–06

Hurley, O. (2016). The dynamics of groups online. In I. Connolly, M. Palmer, H. Barton, & G. Kirwan (Eds.), *An Introduction to Cyberpsychology* (pp. 98–110). Oxford: Routledge. https://doi.org/10.4324/9781315741895-18

Kitchin, R. (2020). Civil liberties or public health, or civil liberties and public health? Using surveillance technologies to tackle the spread of COVID-19. *Space and Polity*, *0*(0), 1–20. https://doi.org/10.1080/13562576.2020.1770587

Krishan, P. (2020, May 26). The reality of homeschooling has been an experience from hell - and it's affected my son too. *INews*. Retrieved from https://inews.co.uk/opinion/the-reality-of-homeschooling-has-been-an-experience-from-hell-and-its-affecting-my-son-too-431220

Kross, E., & Chandhok, S. (2020). *Applications of social psychology*. London: Routledge. https://doi.org/10.4324/9780367816407-13

Lorenz, T. (2020). Influencing? In This Economy? It's Only Gotten More Competitive. Retrieved June 25, 2020, from https://www.nytimes.com/2020/04/23/style/creator-coach-influencers-coronavirus.html

Matsakis, L., & Martineau, P. (2020, March 18). Coronavirus Disrupts Social Media's First Line of Defense. *Wired*. Retrieved from https://www.wired.com/story/coronavirus-social-media-automated-content-moderation/

Mc Mahon, C. (2019). *The psychology of social media*. London: Routledge. https://doi.org/10.4324/9781315170619

McGuinness, A. (2020, April 6). Coronavirus: Downing Street slams Russian "disinformation" over Boris Johnson ventilator claim. *Sky News*. Retrieved from https://news.sky.com/story/coronavirus-downing-street-slams-russian-disinformation-over-boris-johnson-ventilator-claim-11969398

McLuhan, M. (1967). *The medium is the massage*. London: Penguin.

Milne, C. (2020, April 15). False posts that suggest Boris Johnson didn't have COVID-19 are based on a blog post now labelled as satire. *Full Fact*. Retrieved from https://fullfact.org/online/false-post-boris-johnson-hospital-official-secrets/

Mosendz, P., & Melin, A. (2020). Bosses Panic-Buy Spy Software to Keep Tabs on Remote Workers. *Bloomberg*. Retrieved from https://www.bloomberg.com/news/features/2020-03-27/bosses-panic-buy-spy-software-to-keep-tabs-on-remote-workers

Orben, A., Tomova, L., & Blakemore, S. J. (2020). The effects of social deprivation on adolescent development and mental health. *The Lancet Child and Adolescent Health*, *4*(8), 634–640. https://doi.org/10.1016/S2352-4642(20)30186-3

Oremus, W. (2020). Will Tech's Monopolies Survive 2020? *OneZero*. Retrieved from https://onezero.medium.com/will-techs-monopolies-survive-2020-90a8ea05b6c3

Prosser, A. M. B., Judge, M., Bolderdijk, J. W., Blackwood, L., & Kurz, T. (2020). 'Distancers' and 'non-distancers'? The potential social psychological impact of moralizing COVID-19 mitigating practices on sustained behaviour change. *British Journal of Social Psychology*, *59*, 653–662. https://doi.org/10.1111/bjso.12399

Sabbagh, D., & Hern, A. (2020, June 18). UK abandons contact-tracing app for Apple and Google model. *The Guardian*. Retrieved from https://www.theguardian.com/world/2020/jun/18/uk-poised-to-abandon-coronavirus-app-in-favour-of-apple-and-google-models

Schwarz, N., & Jalbert, M. (2021). When (Fake) News Feels True: Intutions of Truth and the Acceptance and Correction of Misinformation. In R. Greifeneder, M. Jaffe, E. Newman, & N. Schwarz (Eds.), *The Psychology of Fake News*. London: Routledge.

Sellgren, K. (2020, July 8). Coronavirus: Home-schooling has been hell, say parents. *BBC News*. Retrieved from https://www.bbc.com/news/education-53319615

Sharon, T. (2020). When Google and Apple get privacy right, is there still something wrong? Retrieved June 25, 2020, from https://medium.com/@TamarSharon/when-google-and-apple-get-privacy-right-is-there-still-something-wrong-a7be4166c295

Tait, A. (2020, April 16). Is everyone partying on Zoom without me? *PaperMag*. Retrieved from https://www.papermag.com/quarantine-fomo-zoom-parties-2645734658.html

Talmud, I., & Mesch, G. (2020). *Wired youth: The online social world of adolescence* (2nd ed.). London: Routledge.

Taylor, S. (2019). *The psychology of pandemics*. Cambridge: Cambridge Scholars Publishing.

van Prooijen, J.-W. (2018). *The psychology of conspiracy theories*. London: Routledge.

Wallenstein, A. (2020, June 24). "Watch Party" Trend Sweeping the Video World Amid Lockdown. *Variety*. Retrieved from https://variety.com/2020/digital/news/watch-party-video-trend-coronavirus-1234643586/

Walsh, R. (2020). Details at the pub door: COVID is becoming a data feeding frenzy. Retrieved June 25, 2020, from https://www.politics.co.uk/comment-analysis/2020/06/25/details-at-the-pub-door-covid-is-becoming-a-data-feeding-fre

1

WHEN (FAKE) NEWS FEELS TRUE

Intuitions of truth and the acceptance and correction of misinformation

Norbert Schwarz and Madeline Jalbert

An analysis of 2.8 million episodes of news sharing on Twitter found that 59% of the news items were shared without having been opened (Gabielkov, Ramachandran, Chaintreau, & Legout, 2016). Apparently, six out of ten readers found the headline compelling enough to share the piece without reading it. In this chapter, we review what makes a message "feel" true, even before we have considered its content in any detail. We first discuss the basic psychological processes involved in assessing the truth of a message and illustrate them with select experiments. Subsequently, we address the implications of these processes for information sharing on social media and the correction of misinformation.

Evaluating truth

While retweeting something without reading it may strike many readers as surprising and irresponsible, it is not distinctly different from how we communicate in everyday life. In daily conversations, we proceed on the tacit assumption that the speaker is a cooperative communicator whose contributions are relevant to the ongoing conversation, truthful, informative, and clear (Grice, 1975; Sperber & Wilson, 1986). Unless we have reason to doubt that the speaker observes these tacit rules of conversational conduct, we accept the content of the utterance without much questioning and treat it as part of the common ground of the conversation. These conversational processes contribute to many errors in human judgment (for reviews, see Schwarz, 1994, 1996). Some research even suggests that comprehension of a statement requires at least temporary acceptance of its truth (Gilbert, 1991) before it can be checked against relevant evidence.

While suspension of belief is possible (Hasson, Simmons, & Todorov, 2005; Schul, Mayo, & Burnstein, 2008), it requires implausibility of the message or distrust at the time it is received. Hence, the deck is usually stacked in favor of accepting information rather than rejecting it, provided there are no salient markers that call the speaker's cooperativeness into question. Going beyond the default of information acceptance requires motivation and cognitive resources, which we are most likely to invest when the topic is important to us and there are few competing demands and distractions. In the absence of these conditions, information is likely to be accepted – and sometimes passed on – without much scrutiny.

When people do evaluate whether information is likely to be true, they typically consider some (but rarely all) of the five criteria shown in Table 5.1 (Schwarz, 2015). Is the claim compatible with other things they know? Is it internally consistent and coherent? Does it come from a trustworthy source? Do other people agree with it? Is there much evidence to support it? Each of these criteria is sensible and does, indeed, bear on the likely truth of a message. These criteria can be assessed by considering relevant knowledge, which is a relatively slow and effortful process and may require extensive information search. The same criteria can also be assessed by relying on one's intuitive response, which is faster and less taxing. When the initial intuitive response suggests that something may be wrong, people are likely to turn to the more effortful analysis, provided time and circumstances allow for it. This makes initial intuitive assessments of truth a key gatekeeper for whether people will further engage with the message using a critical eye or just nod along in agreement. These assumptions are compatible with a long history of research in social (e.g., Petty & Cacioppo, 1986) and cognitive (e.g., Kahneman, 2011; Stanovich, 1999) psychology, where the slow and effortful strategy is often referred to as "analytic", "systematic", or "system 2"

TABLE 5.1 Truth criteria

Criterion	*Analytic evaluation*	*Intuitive evaluation*
Compatibility: Is it compatible with other things I know?	Is this compatible with knowledge retrieved from memory or obtained from trusted sources?	Does this make me stumble or does it flow smoothly?
Coherence: Is it internally coherent?	Do the elements fit together in a logical way? Do the conclusions follow from what is presented?	Does this make me stumble or does it flow smoothly?
Credibility: Does it come from a credible source?	Does the source have the relevant expertise? Does the source have a vested interest? Is the source trustworthy?	Does the source feel familiar and trustworthy?
Consensus: Do other people believe it?	What do my friends say? What do the opinion polls say?	Does it feel familiar?
Evidence: Is there supporting evidence?	Is there supportive evidence in peer-reviewed scientific articles or credible news reports? Do I remember relevant evidence?	Does some evidence easily come to mind?

processing and the fast and intuitive strategy as "intuitive", "heuristic", or "system 1" processing.

Key to intuitive assessments of truth is the ease with which the message can be processed. For example, when something is incompatible with other things we know or the story we are told is incoherent, we stumble and backtrack to make sure we understood it correctly (Johnson-Laird, 2012; Winkielman, Huber, Kavanagh, & Schwarz, 2012). This makes the subjective experience of ease of processing, often referred to as processing fluency, a (fallible) indicator of whether the message may have a problem that needs closer attention. Similar considerations apply to the other truth criteria, as discussed later in the chapter. Throughout, difficult processing marks the message for closer scrutiny, whereas easy processing favors message acceptance.

If ease or difficulty of processing was solely determined by attributes substantively associated with whether a message is likely to be true, relying on one's processing experience would not pose a major problem. However, messages can be easy or difficult to process for many reasons – reading may be slow because the message is incoherent (a relevant criterion) or because the print font is hard to read (which is unrelated to truth). Because people are more sensitive to their subjective experiences than to the source of those experiences (Schwarz, 2012), many incidental influences that have no bearing on the substance of the message can influence its perceived truth. We discuss these incidental influences and their role in media consumption after reviewing the five dominant truth criteria. As will become apparent, when thoughts flow smoothly, people are likely to agree without much critical analysis (see also Oyserman & Dawson, this volume).

The "big five" of truth judgment: analytic and intuitive processes

A claim is more likely to be accepted as true when it is *compatible* with other things one knows than when it is at odds with other knowledge. Compatibility can be assessed analytically by checking the information against one's knowledge, which requires motivation and time (Petty & Cacioppo, 1986). A less demanding indicator is provided by one's metacognitive experiences and affective responses. When something is inconsistent with existing beliefs, people tend to stumble – they take longer to read it, and have trouble processing it (e.g., Taber & Lodge, 2006; Winkielman et al., 2012). Moreover, information that is inconsistent with one's beliefs produces a negative affective response, as shown in research on cognitive consistency (Festinger, 1957; Gawronski & Strack, 2012). Accordingly, one's processing experiences and affective responses can serve as (fallible) indicators of whether a proposition is consistent with other things one believes.

A given claim is also more likely to be accepted as true when it fits a broader story that lends *coherence* to its individual elements, as observed in research on mental models (for a review, see Johnson-Laird, 2012) and analyses of jury decision making (Pennington & Hastie, 1993). Coherence can be determined through a systematic analysis of the relationships between different pieces of declarative information. Alternatively, it can be assessed by attending to one's processing experience: coherent stories are easier to process than stories with internal contradictions (Johnson-Laird, 2012), which makes ease of processing a (fallible) indicator of coherence. Indeed, people draw on their fluency experience when they evaluate how well things "go together" (Topolinski, 2012), as observed in judgments of semantic coherence (Topolinski & Strack, 2008, 2009) and syllogistic reasoning (Morsanyi & Handley, 2012).

Information is also more likely to be accepted as true when it comes from a credible and trustworthy source. As decades of persuasion research illustrates, evaluations of *source credibility* can be based on declarative information that bears, for example, on the communicator's expertise, education, achievement, or institutional affiliation and the presence or absence of conflicting interests (for reviews, see Eagly & Chaiken, 1993; Petty & Cacioppo, 1986). However, credibility judgments can also be based on feelings of familiarity. In daily life, people trust familiar others more than strangers (Luhmann, 1979), from personal interactions to e-commerce (Gefen, 2000). Familiarity resulting from previous encounters or even just repeatedly seeing pictures of a face is sufficient to increase perceptions of honesty and sincerity as well as agreement with what the person says (Brown, Brown, & Zoccoli, 2002; Weisbuch & Mackie, 2009). Similarly, the mere repetition of a name can make an unknown name seem familiar, making its bearer "famous overnight" (Jacoby, Woloshyn, & Kelley, 1989), which may also increase perceived expertise. Familiar people are also easier to recognize and remember, and their names become easier to pronounce with repeated encounters. Variables that influence the ease with which source information can be processed can therefore enhance the perceived credibility of the source. Indeed, a given claim is more likely to be judged true when the name of its source is easy to pronounce (Newman et al., 2014).

To assess the likely truth of a claim, people also consider whether others believe it – if many people agree, there's probably something to it. This *social consensus* (Festinger, 1954) criterion is central to many social influence processes and is sometimes referred to as the principle of "social proof" (Cialdini, 2009). As numerous studies indicated, people are more confident in their beliefs if they are shared by others (Newcomb, 1943; Visser & Mirabile, 2004), more likely to endorse a message if many others have done so as well (Cialdini, 2009), and place more trust in what they remember if others remember it similarly (Harris & Hahn, 2009; Ross, Buehler, & Karr, 1998). Conversely, perceiving dissent reliably undermines message acceptance, which makes reports on real or fabricated controversies an efficient strategy for swaying public opinion (Lewandowsky, Ecker, Seifert, Schwarz, & Cook, 2012; Lewandowsky, Gignac, & Vaughan, 2013). To assess the extent of consensus, people may consult public opinion polls or ask their friends. Alternatively, they may rely on how "familiar" the belief feels – after all, one should have encountered popular beliefs, shared by many, more frequently than unpopular beliefs, held by few. Empirically, familiar information is easier to read, understand, and remember than unfamiliar information, which makes ease of processing a (fallible) indicator of familiarity and popularity. Accordingly, incidental changes in ease of processing can influence perceived consensus.

Finally, people's confidence in a belief increases with the *amount of supporting evidence*. Support can be assessed through an external search, as in a scientific literature review or through recall of pertinent information from memory; in either case, confidence increases with the amount of supportive information. Alternatively, support can be gauged from how easy it is to find supportive evidence – the more evidence there is, the easier it should be to find some (in memory or in the literature). This lay theory is at the heart of Tversky and Kahneman's (1973) availability heuristic. Unfortunately, this heuristic can be misleading. If the only supportive piece of information comes to mind easily because it has been endlessly repeated or is very vivid and memorable, we may erroneously conclude that support is strong. Moreover, attention to *what* comes to mind and attention to the *ease* with which it does so will often lead to different conclusions. On the one hand, reliance on the substantive arguments brought to mind results in higher confidence the more arguments one retrieves or generates. On the other hand, reliance on ease of recall results in lower confidence the more arguments one tries to come up with because finding many arguments is difficult, which suggests that there probably aren't many (Haddock, Rothman, Reber, & Schwarz, 1999; for reviews, see Schwarz, 1998; Schwarz & Vaughn, 2002).

Regardless of which truth criteria people draw on, easily processed information enjoys an advantage over information that is difficult to process: it feels more familiar, more compatible with one's beliefs, more internally consistent, more widely held, better supported, and more likely to have come from a credible source. These inferences reflect that familiar, frequently encountered information and information that is coherent and compatible with one's knowledge is indeed easier to process than information that is not. Hence, ease of processing provides heuristically useful – but fallible – information for assessing how well a claim meets major truth criteria.

Making claims "feel" true

So far, our discussion highlighted that ease or difficulty of processing can result both from variables that are meaningfully related to key criteria of truth or from incidental influences. This is important for two reasons. From a research perspective, it allows researchers to manipulate processing fluency in ways that are independent of substantive characteristics of a message and its source. From an applied perspective, it highlights that claims can "feel" true merely because they are easy to process, which provides many opportunities for manipulation. Next, we review some of the most important variables that influence the ease or difficulty of message processing.

Repetition

Demagogues have known for millennia that truth can be created through frequent repetition of a lie – as Hitler put it, "Propaganda must confine itself to a few points and repeat them over and over again" (cited in Toland, 1976, p. 221). Empirical research supports demagogues' intuition. Studying wartime rumors, Allport and Lepkin (1945) found that the best predictor of whether people believed a rumor was the number of times they were exposed to it. Testing this observation in the laboratory, Hasher, Goldstein, and Toppino (1977) asked participants to rate their confidence that each of 60 statements was true. Some statements were factually correct (e.g., "Lithium is the lightest of all metals"), whereas others were not (e.g., "The People's Republic of China was founded in 1947"). Participants provided their ratings on three occasions, each two weeks apart. Across these sessions, some statements were repeated once or twice, whereas others were not, resulting in one, two, or three exposures. As expected, participants were more confident that a given statement was true the more often they had seen it, independent of whether it was factually true or false. Numerous follow-up studies confirmed the power of repetition across many content domains, from trivia statements (e.g., Bacon, 1979) to marketing claims (e.g., Hawkins & Hoch, 1992) and political beliefs (e.g., Arkes, Hackett, & Boehm, 1989), with the time delay between exposure and judgment ranging from minutes (e.g., Begg & Armour, 1991) to months (Brown & Nix, 1996). Dechêne, Stahl, Hansen, and Wänke (2010) provide a comprehensive meta-analysis of this "illusory truth" effect.

The influence of repetition is most pronounced for claims that people feel uncertain about, but is also observed when more diagnostic information about the claims is available (Fazio, Rand, & Pennycook, 2019; Unkelbach & Greifeneder, 2018). Worse, repetition even increases agreement among people who actually know that the claim is false – if only they thought about it (Fazio, Brashier, Payne, & Marsh, 2015). For example, repeating the statement "The Atlantic Ocean is the largest ocean on Earth" increased its acceptance even among people who knew that the Pacific is larger. When the repeated statement felt familiar, they nodded along without checking it against their knowledge. Even warning people that some of the claims they will be shown are false does not eliminate the effect, although it attenuates its size. More importantly, warnings only attenuate the influence of repetition when they *precede* exposure to the claims – warning people *after* they have seen the claims has no discernable influence (Jalbert, Newman, & Schwarz, 2019).

Repetition also increases perceived social consensus, that is, the perception that a belief is shared by many others. Weaver, Garcia, Schwarz, and Miller (2007) had participants read opinion statements purportedly taken from a group discussion in which a given opinion was presented once or thrice. Each opinion statement was attributed to a group member. Not surprisingly, participants assumed that more people shared the opinion when they read it three times from three different group members (72%) than when they read it only once (57%). However, reading the opinion three times from the *same* group member was almost as influential, resulting in a consensus estimate of 67% – apparently, the single repetitive source sounded like a chorus. Later studies showed that people trust an eyewitness report more the more often it is repeated, even when all repetitions come from the same single witness (Foster, Huthwaite, Yesberg, Garry, & Loftus, 2012). Similarly, newspaper readers are more confident in the accuracy of a report when the same message is presented in several newspapers, even if all newspapers solely rely on the same single interview with the same speaker (Yousif, Aboody, & Keil, 2019). Such findings suggest that frequent repetition of the same soundbite in TV news can give the message a familiarity that increases its perceived popularity and truth. This concern also applies to social media, where the same message keeps showing up as friends and friends of friends like it and repost it, resulting in many exposures within a network.

Beyond repetition

Despite its popularity with past and present demagogues, repetition is just one of many variables that can facilitate easy processing of a statement, making the statement appear more popular, credible, and true. Next, we review some of these other variables.

Reber and Schwarz (1999) manipulated the ease of reading through the *color contrast* of the print font. Depending on condition, some statements (e.g., 'Orsono is a city in Chile') were easy to read due to high color contrast (e.g., dark blue print on a white background), whereas others were difficult to read due to low color contrast (e.g., light blue print on a white background). As predicted, the same statement was more likely to be judged true when it was easy rather than difficult to read. Similarly, the readability of *print fonts* can influence intuitive assessments of truthfulness and the extent to which we closely scrutinize a message. For example, when asked, "How many animals of each kind did Moses take on the Ark?" most people answer "two" even though they know that the biblical actor was Noah, not Moses. Song and Schwarz (2008) presented this Moses question (taken from Erickson & Mattson, 1981) in one of the fonts shown in Figure 5.1. They warned participants that some of the questions may be misleading, in which case they should answer "Can't say". When the Moses question was presented in the easy to read black Arial font, 88% failed to notice a problem and answered "two", whereas only 53% did so when the question was presented in the more difficult to read gray Brush font.

Other variables that influence ease of processing have similar effects. For example, handwritten essays are more compelling when the *handwriting* is easy to read (Greifeneder et al., 2010) and so are spoken messages when the speaker's *accent* is easy to understand (Levy-Ari & Keysar, 2010). Similarly, the same conference talk is less impressive when its video recording has low *audio quality*, and a

Print font	% answering without noticing error
How many animals of each kind did Moses take on the Ark?	88%
How many animals of each kind did Moses take on the Ark?	53%

FIGURE 5.1 Print font and the detection of misleading information

Source: Adapted from Song and Schwarz (2008), Experiment 1.

poor phone connection during a researcher's radio interview can impair listeners' impression of the quality of her research program (Newman & Schwarz, 2018). People also find a statement to be more true when presented with a version of it that *rhymes* rather than one that doesn't, even when the two versions are substantively equivalent (McGlone & Tofighbakhsh, 2000). Even a *photo* without any probative value can increase acceptance of a statement, provided the photo makes it easier to imagine what the statement is about (for a review, see Newman & Zhang, this volume).

Merely having a name that is easy to *pronounce* is sufficient to endow the person with higher credibility and trustworthiness. For example, consumers trust an online seller more when the seller's eBay username is easy to pronounce – they are more likely to believe that the product will live up to the seller's promises and that the seller will honor the advertised return policy (Silva, Chrobot, Newman, Schwarz, & Topolinski, 2017). Similarly, the same claim is more likely to be accepted as true when the name of its source is easy to pronounce (Newman et al., 2014).

As this selective review indicates, any variable that can influence ease of processing can also influence judgments of truth. This is the case because people are very sensitive to their processing experience but insensitive to where this experience comes from. When their attention is directed to the incidental source of their experience, the informational value of the experienced ease or difficulty is undermined and its influence attenuated or eliminated, as predicted by feelings-as-information theory (for reviews, see Schwarz, 2012, 2018).

Analytic versus intuitive processing

As in other domains of judgment, people are more likely to invest the time and effort needed for careful information processing when they are sufficiently motivated and have the time and opportunity to do so (for reviews, see Greifeneder, Bless, & Pham, 2011; Greifeneder & Schwarz, 2014). One may hope that this favors careful processing whenever the issue is important. However, this optimism may not be warranted. In the course of everyday life, messages about issues we consider personally important may reach us when we have other things on our minds and lack the opportunity to engage with them. Over repeated encounters, such messages may become familiar and fluent enough to escape closer scrutiny even when the situation would allow us to engage with them. As reviewed previously, telling recipients that some of the information shown to them is false is only protective when the warning precedes the first exposure; later warnings show little effect (Jalbert et al., 2019). Similarly, the motivation and opportunity to examine a message critically may exert only a limited influence once the message has been encoded (for a review, see Lewandowsky et al., 2012).

Implications for social media

The dynamics of truth judgment have important implications for the acceptance and correction of false information in the real world. Beginning with the proliferation of cable TV and talk radio, citizens in democracies enjoyed ever more opportunities to selectively expose themselves to media that fit their worldview. The advent of social media is the latest step in this development and, in many ways, one might think that social media were designed to make questionable messages seem true. To begin with, most social media messages are short, written in simple language, and presented in optics that are easy to read, which satisfies many of the technical prerequisites for easy processing. These fluent messages are posted by one's friends, a credible source. The content they post is usually compatible with one's own beliefs, given the similarity of opinions and values in friendship networks (for a review of network homophily, see McPherson, Smith-Lovin, & Cook, 2001). Posted messages are liked by other friends, thus confirming social consensus, and reposted, thus ensuring multiple repeated exposures. With each exposure, processing becomes easier and perceptions of social consensus, coherence, and compatibility increase. Comments and related posts provide additional supporting evidence and further enhance familiarity. At the same time, the accumulating likes and reposts ensure that the filtering mechanism of the feed makes exposure to opposing information less and less likely. The *Wall Street Journal*'s "Blue Feed/Red Feed" site illustrates how Facebook's filtering mechanism resulted in profoundly different news feeds for liberals and conservatives during the 2016 elections in the United States, and a growing body of research traces how opinion homophily within networks contributes to controversies between networks (Del Vicario et al., 2016; Gargiulo & Gandica, 2017). The observed narrowing of recipients' information diet on social media is enhanced through the personalization of internet offerings outside of social media, where internet providers and search engines track users' interests to tailor information delivery (Pariser, 2011).

These processes not only increase the acceptance of claims that feel increasingly familiar and compatible with what else one knows but also foster a high sense of expertise and confidence. After all, much of what one sees in one's feed is familiar, which suggests that one knows most of what there is to know about the topic. It has also been seen without much opposing evidence, suggesting that the arguments are undisputed. This enhances what Ross and Ward (1996) described as "naïve realism" – the belief that the world is the way I see it and whoever disagrees is either ill-informed (which motivates persuasion efforts) or ill-intentioned (if persuasion fails). These beliefs further contribute to polarization and the mutual attribution of malevolence.

Implications for the correction of misinformation

That people can arrive at judgments of truth by relying more on analytic or more on intuitive strategies poses a major challenge for public information campaigns aimed at correcting false beliefs. Extensive research in education shows that students' misconceptions can be corrected by confronting them with correct information, showing students step by step why one idea is wrong and another one right, preferably repeating this process multiple times (for reviews, see Vosniadou, 2008). This works best when the recipient wants to acquire the correct information and is sufficiently motivated to pay attention, think through the issues, and remember the new insights (for a review, see Sinatra & Pintrich, 2003). Public information campaigns often follow these procedures by confronting the "myths" with "facts", consistent with content-focused theories of message learning (McQuail, 2000; Rice & Atkin, 2001). While this works in the classroom, with motivated recipients, sufficient time, and the benefit of incentives, the reality of public information campaigns is starkly different. For any given topic, only a small segment of the population will care enough to engage with the details; most are likely to notice the message only in passing, if at all, and will process it superficially while doing something else. Even if they remember the corrective message as intended when tested immediately, it may fade quickly from memory.

Under such conditions, repeating false information in order to correct it may mostly succeed in spreading the false information to disinterested recipients who may otherwise never have encountered it. Not having processed the message in detail, they may now find the false claims a bit more familiar and easier to process when they hear or see them again. This way, the attempt to correct the erroneous beliefs of a few may prepare numerous others to accept those beliefs through repeated exposure (for a review, see Schwarz, Sanna, Skurnik, & Yoon, 2007). For example, Skurnik, Yoon, Park, and Schwarz (2005) exposed older and younger adults once or thrice to product statements like "Shark cartilage is good for your arthritis", and these statements were explicitly marked as "true" or "false". When tested immediately, the corrections seemed successful – all participants were less likely to accept a statement as true the more often they were told that it is false. This is the hoped-for success and most studies stop at this point. But after a three-day delay, repeated warnings backfired and older adults were now more likely to consider a statement "true", the more often they had been explicitly told that it is false. Presumably, the recipients could no longer recall whether the statement had been originally marked as true or false, but still experienced repeated statements as easier to process and more familiar, which made the statements "feel" true.

Even exposing people to only true information can make it more likely that they accept a false version of that information as time passes. Garcia-Marques, Silva, Reber, and Unkelbach (2015) presented participants with ambiguous statements (e.g., "crocodiles sleep with their eyes closed") and later asked them to rate the truth of statements that were either identical to those previously seen or that directly contradicted them (e.g., "crocodiles sleep with their eyes open"). When participants made these judgments immediately, they rated repeated identical statements as more true, and contradicting statements as less true, than novel statements, which they had not seen before. One week later, however, identical as well as contradicting statements seemed more true than novel statements. Put simply, as long as the delay is short enough, people can recall the exact information they just saw and reject the opposite. As time passes, however, the details get lost and contradicting information feels more familiar than information one has never heard of – yes, there was something about crocodiles and their eyes, so that's probably what it was.

As time passes, people may even infer the credibility of the initial source from the confidence with which they hold the belief. For example, Fragale and Heath (2004) exposed participants two or five times to statements like "The wax used to line Cup-o-Noodles cups has been shown to cause cancer in rats". Next, participants learned that some statements were taken from the *National Enquirer* (a low credibility source) and some from *Consumer Reports* (a high credibility source) and had to assign the statements to their likely sources. The more often participants had heard a statement, the more likely they were to attribute it to *Consumer Reports* rather than the *National Enquirer*. In short, frequent exposure not only increases the apparent truth of a statement, it also increases the belief that the statement came from a trustworthy source. Similarly, well-intentioned efforts by the Centers for Disease Control and the *Los Angeles Times* to debunk a rumor about "flesh-eating bananas" morphed into the belief that the *Los Angeles Times* had warned people not to eat those dangerous bananas, thus reinforcing the rumor (Emery, 2000). Such errors in source attribution increase the likelihood that people convey the information to others, who themselves are more likely to accept (and spread) it, given its alleged credible source (Rosnow & Fine, 1976).

Such findings illustrate that attempts to correct misinformation can backfire when they focus solely on message content at the expense of the message's impact on recipients' later processing experience. Even when a corrective message succeeds in changing the beliefs of recipients who deeply care about the topic and process the message with sufficient attention, it may spread the false information to many others who don't care about the topic. Unfortunately, the latter are likely to outnumber the former. In those cases, the successful correction of a few false believers may come at the cost of misleading many bystanders. To avoid such backfire effects, it will usually be safer to refrain from any reiteration of false information and to focus solely on the facts. The more the facts become familiar and fluent, the more likely it is that they will be accepted as true and serve as the basis of judgments and decisions (Lewandowsky et al., 2012; Schwarz et al., 2007, 2016).

Unfortunately, the truth is usually more complicated than false stories, which often involve considerable simplification. This puts the truth at a disadvantage because it is harder to process, understand, and remember. It is therefore important to present true information in ways that facilitate its fluent processing. This requires clear step-by-step exposition and the avoidance of jargon. It also helps to pay close attention to incidental influences on ease of processing. Making the font easy to read and the speaker's pronunciation easy to understand, adding photos and repeating key points are all techniques that should not be left to those who want to mislead – they can also give truth a helping hand and should be used.

Finally, at the individual level, the best protection against the influence of misinformation is skepticism at the time the information is first encountered (for a review, see Lewandowsky et al., 2012). Once people have processed the false information, warnings exert little influence. In addition to explicit warnings, general feelings of suspicion and distrust increase message scrutiny and decrease message acceptance (for reviews, see Mayo, 2017; Schwarz & Lee, 2019). Explicit warnings as well as suspicion and distrust entail that the communicator may not adhere to the norms of cooperative conversational conduct (Grice, 1975), thus flagging the message for closer scrutiny. Unfortunately, in a polarized public opinion climate, merely realizing that a message supports the "other" side is itself likely to elicit suspicion and distrust, further impairing correction attempts in polarized contexts.

Acknowledgments

Preparation of this chapter was supported by the Linnie and Michael Katz Endowed Research Fellowship Fund through a fellowship to the second author and funds of the USC Dornsife Mind and Society Center to the first author.

References

Allport, F. H., & Lepkin, M. (1945). Wartime rumors of waste and special privilege: Why some people believe them. *Journal of Abnormal and Social Psychology, 40*, 3–36.

Arkes, H. R., Hackett, C., & Boehm, L. (1989). The generality of the relation between familiarity and judged validity. *Journal of Behavioral Decision Making, 2*, 81–94.

Bacon, F. T. (1979). Credibility of repeated statements: Memory for trivia. *Journal of Experimental Psychology: Human Learning and Memory, 5*, 241–252.

Begg, I., & Armour, V. (1991). Repetition and the ring of truth: Biasing comments. *Canadian Journal of Behavioural Science, 23*, 195–213.

Brown, A. S., Brown, L. A., & Zoccoli, S. L. (2002). Repetition-based credibility enhancement of unfamiliar faces. *The American Journal of Psychology, 115*, 199–2009.

Brown, A. S., & Nix, L. A. (1996). Turning lies into truths: Referential validation of falsehoods. *Journal of Experimental Psychology: Learning, Memory, and Cognition, 22*, 1088–1100.

Cialdini, R. B. (2009). *Influence: Science and practice*. Boston: Pearson Education.

Dechêne, A., Stahl, C., Hansen, J., & Wänke, M. (2010). The truth about the truth: A meta-analytic review of the truth effect. *Personality and Social Psychology Review, 14*, 238–257.

Del Vicario, M., Bessi, A., Zollo, F., Petroni, F., Scala, A., Caldarelli, G., . . . Quattrociocchi, W. (2016). The spreading of misinformation online. *Proceedings of the National Academy of Sciences, 113*(3), 554–559.

Eagly, A. H., & Chaiken, S. (1993). *The psychology of attitudes*. Fort Worth, TX: Harcourt Brace.

Emery, D. (2000, February 23). The great banana scare of 2000. Retrieved May 24, 2002, from http://urbanlegends.about.com/library/weekly/aa022302a.htm

Erickson, T. D., & Mattson, M. E. (1981). From words to meaning: A semantic illusion. *Journal of Verbal Learning & Verbal Behavior, 20*, 540–551.

Fazio, L. K., Brashier, N. M., Payne, B. K., & Marsh, E. J. (2015). Knowledge does not protect against illusory truth. *Journal of Experimental Psychology: General, 144*(5), 993–1002.

Fazio, L. K., Rand, D. G., & Pennycook, G. (2019). Repetition increases perceived truth equally for plausible and implausible statements. *Psychonomic Bulletin & Review, 26*(5), 1705–1710.

Festinger, L. (1954). A theory of social comparison processes. *Human Relations, 7*, 123–146.

Festinger, L. (1957). *A theory of cognitive dissonance*. Evanston, IL: Row, Peterson.

Foster, J. L., Huthwaite, T., Yesberg, J. A., Garry, M., & Loftus, E. (2012). Repetition, not number of sources, increases both susceptibility to misinformation and confidence in the accuracy of eyewitnesses. *Acta Psychologica, 139*, 320–326.

Fragale, A. R., & Heath, C. (2004). Evolving information credentials: The (mis)attribution of believable facts to credible sources. *Personality and Social Psychology Bulletin, 30*, 225–236.

Gabielkov, M., Ramachandran, A., Chaintreau, A., & Legout, A. (2016). Social clicks: What and who gets read on Twitter? *ACM SIGMETRICS Performance Evaluation Review, 44*, 179–192. http://dx.doi.org/10.1145/2896377.2901462

Garcia-Marques, T., Silva, R. R., Reber, R., & Unkelbach, C. (2015). Hearing a statement now and believing the opposite later. *Journal of Experimental Social Psychology, 56*, 126–129.

Gargiulo, F., & Gandica, Y. (2017). The role of homophily in the emergence of opinion controversies. *Journal of Artificial Societies and Social Simulation, 20*(3), 8. doi: 10.18564/jasss.3448. Retrieved from http://jasss.soc.surrey.ac.uk/20/3/8.htm

Gawronski, B., & Strack, F. (Eds.). (2012). *Cognitive consistency: A fundamental principle in social cognition*. New York: Guilford Press.

Gefen, D. (2000). E-commerce: The role of familiarity and trust. *Omega, 28*, 725–737.

Gilbert, D. T. (1991). How mental systems believe. *American Psychologist, 46*, 107–119.

Greifeneder, R., Alt, A., Bottenberg, K., Seele, T., Zelt, S., & Wagener, D. (2010). On writing legibly: Processing fluency systematically biases evaluations of handwritten material. *Social Psychological and Personality Science, 1*, 230–237.

Greifeneder, R., Bless, H., & Pham, M. T. (2011). When do people rely on cognitive and affective feelings in judgment? A review. *Personality and Social Psychology Review, 15*, 107–141.

Greifeneder, R., & Schwarz, N. (2014). Metacognitive processes and subjective experience. In J. W. Sherman, B. Gawronski, & Y. Trope (Eds.), *Dual-process theories of the social mind* (pp. 314–327). New York, NY: Guilford Press.

Grice, H. P. (1975). Logic and conversation. In P. Cole & J. L. Morgan (Eds.), *Syntax and semantics, vol. 3: Speech acts* (pp. 41–58). New York: Academic Press.

Haddock, G., Rothman, A. J., Reber, R., & Schwarz, N. (1999). Forming judgments of attitude certainty, importance, and intensity: The role of subjective experiences. *Personality and Social Psychology Bulletin, 25*, 771–782.

Harris, A. J. L., & Hahn, U. (2009). Bayesian rationality in evaluating multiple testimonies: Incorporating the role of coherence. *Journal of Experimental Psychology: Learning, Memory, and Cognition, 35*, 1366–1372.

Hasher, L., Goldstein, D., & Toppino, T. (1977). Frequency and the conference of referential validity. *Journal of Verbal Learning & Verbal Behavior, 16*, 107–112.

Hasson, U., Simmons, J. P., & Todorov, A. (2005). Believe it or not: On the possibility of suspending belief. *Psychological Science, 16*, 566–571.

Hawkins, S. A., & Hoch, S. J. (1992). Low-involvement learning: Memory without evaluation. *Journal of Consumer Research, 19*, 212–225.

Jacoby, L. L., Woloshyn, V., & Kelley, C. M. (1989). Becoming famous without being recognized: Unconscious influences of memory produced by dividing attention. *Journal of Experimental Psychology: General, 118*, 115–125.

Jalbert, M., Newman, E. J., & Schwarz, N. (2019). *Only half of what I tell you is true: How experimental procedures lead to an underestimation of the truth effect.* Manuscript under review.

Johnson-Laird, P. N. (2012). Mental models and consistency. In B. Gawronski & F. Strack (Eds.), *Cognitive consistency: A fundamental principle in social cognition* (pp. 225–243). New York: Guilford Press.

Kahneman, D. (2011). *Thinking, fast and slow.* New York: Macmillan.

Levy-Ari, S., & Keysar, B. (2010). Why don't we believe non-native speakers? The influence of accent on credibility. *Journal of Experimental Social Psychology, 46*, 1093–1096.

Lewandowsky, S., Ecker, U. K. H., Seifert, C., Schwarz, N., & Cook, J. (2012). Misinformation and its correction: Continued influence and successful debiasing. *Psychological Science in the Public Interest, 13*, 106–131.

Lewandowsky, S., Gignac, G. E., & Vaughan, S. (2013). The pivotal role of perceived scientific consensus in acceptance of science. *Nature Climate Change, 3*, 399–404.

Luhmann, N. (1979). *Trust and power.* Chichester, UK: Wiley.

Mayo, R. (2017). Cognition is a matter of trust: Distrust tunes cognitive processes. *European Review of Social Psychology, 26*, 283–327.

McGlone, M. S., & Tofighbakhsh, J. (2000). Birds of a feather flock conjointly (?): Rhyme as reason in aphorisms. *Psychological Science, 11*, 424–428.

McPherson, M., Smith-Lovin, L., & Cook. J. M. (2001). Birds of a feather: Homophily in social networks. *Annual Review of Sociology, 27*, 415–444.

McQuail, D. (2000). *McQuail's mass communication theory.* Newbury Park, CA: Sage Publications.

Morsanyi, K., & Handley, S. J. (2012). Logic feels so good: I like it! Evidence for intuitive detection of logicality in syllogistic reasoning. *Journal of Experimental Psychology: Learning, Memory, and Cognition, 38*, 596–616.

Newcomb, T. M. (1943). *Personality and social change.* New York: Holt, Rinehart, & Winston.

Newman, E. J., Sanson, M., Miller, E. K., Quigley-McBride, A., Foster, J. L., Bernstein, D. M., & Garry, M. (2014). People with easier to pronounce names promote truthiness of claims. *PLoS One, 9*(2). doi: 10.1371/journal.pone.0088671

Newman, E. J., & Schwarz, N. (2018). Good sound, good research: How audio quality influences perceptions of the researcher and research. *Science Communication, 40*(2), 246–257.

Newman, E. J., & Zhang, L. (2020). Truthiness: How nonprobative photos shape beliefs. In R. Greifeneder, M. Jaffé, E. J. Newman, & N. Schwarz (Eds.), *The psychology of fake news: Accepting, sharing, and correcting misinformation* (pp. 90–114). London, UK: Routledge.

Oyserman, D., & Dawson, A. (2020). Your fake news, our fakes: Identity-based motivation shapes what we believe, share, and accept. In R. Greifeneder, M. Jaffé, E. J. Newman, & N. Schwarz (Eds.), *The psychology of fake news: Accepting, sharing, and correcting misinformation* (pp. 173–195). London, UK: Routledge.

Pariser, E. (2011). *The filter bubble: How the new personalized web is changing what we read and how the think*. New York: Penguin Books.

Pennington, N., & Hastie, R. (1993). The story model for juror decision making. In R. Hastie (Ed.), *Inside the juror* (pp. 192–223). New York: Cambridge University Press.

Petty, R. E., & Cacioppo, J. T. (1986). The elaboration likelihood model of persuasion. *Advances in Experimental Social Psychology, 19*, 123–205.

Reber, R., & Schwarz, N. (1999). Effects of perceptual fluency on judgments of truth. *Consciousness and Cognition, 8*, 338–342.

Rice, R., & Atkin, C. (Eds.). (2001). *Public communication campaigns* (3rd ed.). Newbury Park, CA: Sage Publications.

Rosnow, R. L., & Fine, G. A. (1976). *Rumor and gossip: The social psychology of hearsay*. New York: Elsevier.

Ross, L., & Ward, A. (1996). Naive realism in everyday life: Implications for social conflict and misunderstanding. In E. S. Reed, E. Turiel, & T. Brown (Eds.), *Values and knowledge* (pp. 103–135). Hillsdale, NJ: Lawrence Erlbaum.

Ross, M., Buehler, R., & Karr, J. W. (1998). Assessing the accuracy of conflicting autobiographical memories. *Memory and Cognition, 26*, 1233–1244.

Schul, Y., Mayo, R., & Burnstein, E. (2008). The value of distrust. *Journal of Experimental Social Psychology, 44*, 1293–1302.

Schwarz, N. (1994). Judgment in a social context: Biases, shortcomings, and the logic of conversation. *Advances in Experimental Social Psychology, 26*, 123–162.

Schwarz, N. (1996). *Cognition and communication: Judgmental biases, research methods, and the logic of conversation*. Hillsdale, NJ: Erlbaum.

Schwarz, N. (1998). Accessible content and accessibility experiences: The interplay of declarative and experiential information in judgment. *Personality and Social Psychology Review, 2*, 87–99.

Schwarz, N. (2012). Feelings-as-information theory. In P. A. Van Lange, A. W. Kruglanski, & E. Higgins (Eds.), *Handbook of theories of social psychology* (pp. 289–308). Thousand Oaks, CA: Sage Publications.

Schwarz, N. (2015). Metacognition. In M. Mikulincer, P. R. Shaver, E. Borgida, & J. A. Bargh (Eds.), *APA handbook of personality and social psychology: Attitudes and social cognition* (pp. 203–229). Washington, DC: APA.

Schwarz, N. (2018). Of fluency, beauty, and truth: Inferences from metacognitive experiences. In J. Proust & M. Fortier (Eds.), *Metacognitive diversity: An interdisciplinary approach* (pp. 25–46). New York: Oxford University Press.

Schwarz, N., & Lee, S. W. S. (2019). The smell of suspicion: How the nose curbs gullibility. In J. P. Forgas & R. F. Baumeister (Eds.), *The social psychology of gullibility: Fake news, conspiracy theories, and irrational beliefs* (pp. 234–252). New York: Routledge and Psychology Press.

Schwarz, N., Newman, E., & Leach, W. (2016). Making the truth stick and the myths fade: Lessons from cognitive psychology. *Behavioral Science & Policy, 2*(1), 85–95.

Schwarz, N., Sanna, L. J., Skurnik, I., & Yoon, C. (2007). Metacognitive experiences and the intricacies of setting people straight: Implications for debiasing and public information campaigns. *Advances in Experimental Social Psychology, 39*, 127–161.

Schwarz, N., & Vaughn, L. A. (2002). The availability heuristic revisited: Ease of recall and content of recall as distinct sources of information. In T. Gilovich, D. Griffin, & D. Kahneman (Eds.), *Heuristics and biases: The psychology of intuitive judgment* (pp. 103–119). Cambridge: Cambridge University Press.

Silva, R. R., Chrobot, N., Newman, E., Schwarz, N., & Topolinski, S. (2017). Make it short and easy: Username complexity determines trustworthiness above and beyond objective reputation. *Frontiers in Psychology, 8*, 2200.

Sinatra, G. M., & Pintrich, P. (2003). The role of intentions in conceptual change learning. In G. M. Sinatra & P. R. Pintrich (Eds.), *Intentional conceptual change*. Mahwah, NJ: Lawrence Erlbaum Associates.

Skurnik, I., Yoon, C., Park, D. C., & Schwarz, N. (2005). How warnings about false claims become recommendations. *Journal of Consumer Research, 31*, 713–724.

Song, H., & Schwarz, N. (2008). Fluency and the detection of misleading questions: Low processing fluency attenuates the Moses illusion. *Social Cognition, 26*, 791–799.

Sperber, D., & Wilson, D. (1986). *Relevance: Communication and cognition*. Cambridge, MA: Harvard University Press.

Stanovich, K. E. (1999). *Who is rational? Studies of individual differences in reasoning*. Mahwah: Erlbaum.

Taber, C. S., & Lodge, M. (2006). Motivated skepticism in the evaluation of political beliefs. *American Journal of Political Science, 50*(3), 755–769.

Toland, J. (1976). *Adolf Hitler*. Garden City, NY: Doubleday.

Topolinski, S. (2012). Nonpropositional consistency. In B. Gawronski & F. Strack (Eds.), *Cognitive consistency: A fundamental principle in social cognition* (pp. 112–131). New York: Guilford Press.

Topolinski, S., & Strack, F. (2008). Where there's a will: There's no intuition: The unintentional basis of semantic coherence judgments. *Journal of Memory and Language, 58*, 1032–1048.

Topolinski, S., & Strack, F. (2009). The architecture of intuition: Fluency and affect determine intuitive judgments of semantic and visual coherence and judgments of grammaticality in artificial grammar learning. *Journal of Experimental Psychology: General, 138*, 39–63.

Tversky, A., & Kahneman, D. (1973). Availability: A heuristic for judging frequency and probability. *Cognitive Psychology, 5*, 207–232.

Unkelbach, C., & Greifeneder, R. (2018). Experiential fluency and declarative advice jointly inform judgments of truth. *Journal of Experimental Social Psychology, 79*, 78–86.

Visser, P. S., & Mirabile, R. R. (2004). Attitudes in the social context: The impact of social network composition on individual-level attitude strength. *Journal of Personality and Social Psychology, 87*, 779–795.

Vosniadou, S. (Ed.). (2008). *International handbook of research on conceptual change*. New York, NY: Routledge.

Weaver, K., Garcia, S. M., Schwarz, N., & Miller, D. T. (2007). Inferring the popularity of an opinion from its familiarity: A repetitive voice can sound like a chorus. *Journal of Personality and Social Psychology, 92*, 821–833.

Weisbuch, M., & Mackie, D. (2009). False fame, perceptual clarity, or persuasion? Flexible fluency attribution in spokesperson familiarity effects. *Journal of Consumer Psychology, 19*(1), 62–72.

Winkielman, P., Huber, D. E., Kavanagh, L., & Schwarz, N. (2012). Fluency of consistency: When thoughts fit nicely and flow smoothly. In B. Gawronski & F. Strack (Eds.), *Cognitive consistency: A fundamental principle in social cognition* (pp. 89–111). New York: Guilford Press.

Yousif, S. R., Aboody, R., & Keil, F. C. (2019). The illusion of consensus: A failure to distinguish between true and false consensus. *Psychological Science, 30*(8), 1195–1204.

2

CONNECTIONS

Ciarán Mc Mahon

After setting up their profile, users' second task after creating a social media account is probably connecting with other users. From friends to followers, social media is, for many people, largely about publicly connecting with each other.

It gives ordinary people access to potentially huge audiences –for free and at the click of few buttons. But is it all really that easy? And how real are our audiences? How much work do we have to put into building our connections – and what price do we pay to access them? The critical point is to weigh up the benefits and drawbacks of being able to connect to so many different people in one particular place.

CASE STUDY: THE ICE BUCKET CHALLENGE

The 'ice bucket challenge' is often described as one of social media's greatest successes. It began with a silly prank, but it raised a serious amount of money for a worthy cause. While it is genuinely difficult to carry out accurate historical research on social media services,[1] it seems that an ice bucket challenge existed on Facebook for some time before it became so very popular.[2] The format was there from the start – a video posted to Facebook of someone stating that they have accepted the challenge, and then getting a bucket of ice poured over their head. After some shrieking, the victim calls on some of their social media connections to do the same within 24 hours or donate to a particular charity as a forfeit.

It only became associated with the disease known as Amyotrophic Lateral Sclerosis (also known as Lou Gehrig's Disease) when Chris Kennedy, from Sarasota, Florida, was given the challenge by a friend.[3] He selected the Amyotrophic Lateral Sclerosis Association as his charity of choice and nominated a relative of his, whose partner was suffering from the disease, to take the challenge. From there it spread through his extended family and friends, but also through supporters of the ALS Association, many of whom put in a huge effort to spread the challenge through their personal networks. The Association itself reportedly began seeing an unusual surge in donations by the end of July, and before long the challenge was being issued to all manner of celebrities, including Mark Zuckerberg.

While some analysts have argued that not everyone who made a video donated, I think this misses the point. The logic of the challenges is that the people 'called out' in the video must dunk themselves within 24 hours or donate as a forfeit. If you're too busy to make a video, or afraid of ice-cold water, you can get out of it by simply opening your wallet. That's the premise of the challenge. So really, if you actually did pour a bucket of ice over yourself, you shouldn't have to donate. But, of course, that isn't what happened.

It seems that the 'feel-good' quality of videos spreading through social media connections meant that the logic of the forfeit was forgotten as the phenomenon took off. People who dunked themselves donated money, and, more than likely, lots of people who weren't challenged at all donated money too.

By the beginning of September 2014, over 17 million videos related to the ice bucket challenge had been posted to Facebook, which had apparently been viewed by more than 440 million people.[4] Of course, as the summer drew to an end, and the idea of soaking oneself in ice-cold water became less appealing, this dropped off drastically. However, the phenomenon resulted in the Amyotrophic Lateral Sclerosis Association receiving over $100 million in additional funding, which was put towards research which ultimately found a breakthrough[5] in the study of the disease. This does not include many other charities who also raised significant amounts of money. As a result, the ice bucket challenge became the blueprint for countless more 'challenges', where many other charities and causes would also seek to harness the power of social media connections.

BONDING AND BRIDGING

But outside of such cultural phenomena, what do we gain from adding people on social media, some of whom we probably don't know very well? The answer to these questions means talking about resources and support.

One of social media's most highly cited research papers was published at Michigan State University in 2007. In this study,[6] Ellison, Steinfield and Lampe were interested in how using Facebook might interact with users' psychological well-being, specifically in a concept called 'social capital'. This refers to the observation that as we know more or less people, we gain or lose valuable information and opportunities. Social scientists generally work on the basis of there being two types of social capital: bonding and bridging. The former refers to the type of resources one gains from close relationships, such as family and best friends: people who would do literally anything for you. And the latter refers to the type of things gained from casual acquaintances: people who might give you information, but probably not emotional support. As such, while bonding social capital is much more valuable than bridging, generally speaking we have fewer connections that produce the former than the latter.

The researchers asked participants several questions regarding their Facebook behaviours, such as how many Facebook friends they had and how many minutes they thought they had spent on Facebook in the last month. But they were also asked whether or not they agreed with attitude statements like 'I am proud to tell people I'm on Facebook', 'I feel out of touch when I haven't logged onto Facebook for a while' and 'I would be sorry if Facebook shut down'. Collated together, participants' responses to all these items were used as a measure of the 'intensity' of their Facebook usage.

What Ellison and colleagues found was that this 'Facebook usage intensity' was strongly associated with both creating and maintaining bridging social capital. However, it was only weakly associated with bonding social capital. So, for example, you might have met someone once a few years ago and added them on Facebook but have no real desire to ever meet them again. Then one day, they post a social media update with job advertisement you're interested in. This is the kind of resource that you wouldn't have if you didn't have that Facebook connection. But, on the other hand, with regards to creating deeper, more meaningful relationships, this paper doesn't show that being connected on Facebook is much use.

So, to go back to the ice bucket challenge – you probably won't call out someone with whom you only have a bridging social capital kind of relationship. You might like their video, and they might like yours, but you will probably reserve your nominations for the sort of people with whom you have a bonding social capital kind of relationship.

Interestingly, these associations were only found with regards to Facebook usage intensity – they were not found with regards to internet use. You have to be interacting with people online – for example, on social media like Facebook – to accumulate social capital. As such, it is pretty easy to see how Facebook is very useful to the type of person that Ellison and her team were surveying. It allows college students to cheaply maintain friendships with their high school friends back home, and it also allows them to connect with new classmates – all in all, a very neat psychological tool.

But is it always this simple? And have things changed since 2007? A more recent paper[7] by researchers at the University of the West of England is revealing in this regard. These researchers were also interested in social capital, but in relation to the newer social media service, Snapchat. Like Ellison and her team in 2007, in 2016 Piwek and Joinson carried out a survey of users. However, they noted that the 'transient nature' of Snapchat presents certain methodological difficulties. Bear in mind that the whole point of Snapchat is that its images are supposed to vanish once viewed by the intended recipient. So how do you study that?

Consequently, unlike in the study mentioned earlier, where participants were asked about their overall Facebook usage, in this study participants were asked to focus on the most recent Snap that they had received. In other respects, Piwek and Joinson carried out a similar study to Ellison and co-workers. It also used a college student population, and they adapted the 'Facebook intensity scale' to measure the intensity of Snapchat usage, using largely identical questions. This adaptation of measures across studies is useful as it allows us to validly compare their results.

Strikingly, in direct contrast to Ellison's Facebook study, Piwek and Johnson found that Snapchat usage was associated with bonding social capital, but less so with bridging social capital. In other words, Snapchat seems to be most useful in the context of deep and meaningful relationships, rather than casual acquaintances. The authors suggest that this is due to a number of factors. For one thing, they note that their participants reported using Snapchat to communicate with a small number of friends – certainly a far smaller number than one would expect on Facebook. For another, Piwek and Joinson also suggest that Snapchat offers a more intimate and more private conversational setting than does Facebook. Hence, once again, we can see that different social media services can offer different psychological experiences to their users in how they connect with each other.

As an aside, this study was carried out before the Snapchat 'Snapstreak' feature became popular. In the new version of Snapchat launched in March 2016,[8] if users sent each other Snaps every day, they were rewarded with a fire symbol beside their friend's name, and a number representing the amount of days they kept this interaction going. Consequently, with this sort of 'gamification' of its social media service, Snapchat encouraged the development of close friendships that would create this kind of bonding social capital. But how many people can you actually keep this level of interaction up with? Let me tell you a curious tale about groups of gorillas and the size of their skulls.

CLIQUES AND CONTEXTS

The quantity of people we connect with on social media brings us to one of the more famous concepts in evolutionary psychology. In 1992, anthropologist Robin Dunbar wrote an influential paper[9] on brain sizes in humanity's nearest relatives. The purpose of this study was to examine the possibility of a correlation between the size of primates' neocortexes and the size of their social groups. Remarkably, Dunbar showed that, indeed, primates like lemurs do have both smaller brains and smaller social groups than, for example, gorillas, who have both bigger brains and bigger social groups. This is known as the 'social brain hypothesis' and while it is not a watertight law – it isn't accurate for orangutans, for example, who seem to live in smaller groups than their brain size would imply – it stands to reason that one might extrapolate from this trend to ourselves. How big should human social groups be, given the size of our brains? According to Dunbar, the answer seems to be around 150. Admittedly this is an average, for what he termed our 'egocentric social network', but it did become henceforth known as 'Dunbar's number'.

The idea of natural human social group sizes is an interesting finding for psychology generally, but even more so for social media research, which became very interested in the 150 number. However, in later work, Dunbar showed how human networks also include a 'sympathy group' of about 15 individuals, as well as a 'support clique' of five individuals. The larger group is defined as the sort of people you would describe as close friends, who you would contact at least once a month, whereas the smaller group are those who you would rely on for emotional support. So it is a simplification to talk about 'Dunbar's number' on social media connections, as if there is only one – there are two more that we should be looking for too.

The core issue here is how our apparent neurological limits are improved by the affordances of social media. Does social media allow us to be more time-efficient with our connections? Recently, Dunbar has tackled this issue head on in a 2016 paper with two surveys of several thousand UK adults.[10]

Dunbar did indeed find that most of his participant's personal social networks contained roughly 150 individuals, and, within that, many did indeed have a sympathy group of about 15 individuals, as well as a support clique of about five. But what is rather striking is that these numbers were largely unaffected by how many social media connections participants had. In other words, connecting with lots of people did not help social media users gain more close friendships – the sympathy groups and support cliques stayed roughly the same size.

As such, Dunbar shows that, despite the fact that social media makes it easier to connect with lots of people, that doesn't mean we can therefore gain more emotional support. Meaningfully connecting with people still takes time.

Notably, while there doesn't seem to be much research combining the 'social capital' concept mentioned previously with Dunbar's numbers, these findings do seem to make sense together: social media may help you increase the quantity of your connections, but not necessarily the quality. One last thing that Dunbar points out is worth noting here. Social media services allow us to gather our connections in the one place, but they don't generally let us organise them into a hierarchy of importance of the kind he is interested in.

But perhaps we might not want to do that publicly. In bygone days on Myspace, users agonised over which of their connections to put in their 'Top 8' group of people they wanted to visibly list on their profile as friends. That leads us to another aspect of connecting with lots of people on social media. Psychology is not only interested in how we cope with this *neurologically*, but also how we manage it *socially*.

A potential drawback of social media is that users might want to segment their connections into different groups. For example, you may not have any problem with being connected to your boss on LinkedIn but might feel differently if they sent you a Facebook Friend request. Keeping walls between our social media connections like this is a fairly normal desire, but it is a pretty difficult one to achieve. In practice, these walls don't hold, because, as Marwick and boyd say, 'context collapse' occurs between them.[11]

Their 2010 paper involved an interesting methodology: asking Twitter users, on Twitter, about who their tweets were written for. That's a critical problem with communicating on social media: despite having lots of connections, we don't really have much certainty about who is paying attention to us at any given time. As such, Marwick and boyd use the concept of the *imagined audience*. Even in everyday conversations, we cannot be exactly sure of how our message will be relayed, or who is listening in on us, but this issue is intensified on social media. When you think about how many of your Twitter followers might be online, who they might retweet to, and under what searches you might appear in, you really have difficulty in imagining who is actually reading your tweets.

Marwick and boyd's survey participants gave some interesting answers to questions about who they were tweeting for. Harking back to Chapter 2 and our talk about identities, it is interesting that several participants stated that their tweets were written for an audience that you might not have considered: they said they were writing for themselves. As Marwick and boyd put it, "consciously speaking to an audience is perceived as inauthentic". Perhaps this was more of a feature of Twitter in 2010, but it is still curious that the first person some social media users trying to connect with is themselves.

Other Twitter users, especially those with large numbers of followers, thought about their audience in terms of fans, as a community, as broadcasting or as consistent political messaging. But even in those contexts, and also users with fewer followers, a common theme emerged: not being able to segment audiences and hence having to aim for a 'lowest common denominator' sort of message – safe, bland and inoffensive.

Marwick and boyd interpreted their survey responses as reflecting either one of two tactics to negotiate these problems. On one hand, some Twitter users simply avoided discussing certain topics altogether – they self-censored for fear of possibly insulting some of their followers. And on the other hand, some Twitter users try to balance their more professional tweets with updates with more personal information. In other words, Twitter users try to avoid annoying their imagined audiences by appearing more human and more relatable. This latter tactic is interesting as it harks back, yet again, to the ongoing difficulty we have on social media in trying to appear authentic. Hence, what Marwick and boyd's paper shows is that while we know that social media services, such as Twitter, create many new opportunities for connection, they also create new tensions and indeed, conflicts.

CONNECTIONS AND CONFLICT

Reflecting on our social media connections as a whole, it is interesting to think about the inter-relationships between them. Besides being our own friends, some of our connections may be connected to each other, some may harass us and some may stay quiet altogether. What do we know about the psychology of them?

For example, when talking about social media in the context of children and parenting, a common fear is the risk of cyberbullying. While previous research focussed on individual and psychological factors associated with this type of aggression, few have examined more social and structural factors. In other words, can we explain why someone is a cyberbully entirely because of their personality, age or gender, or should we also examine their position within the cliques and friendship groups of their school? In that light, a study[12] on how aggressive schoolchildren have unique positions within their social networks is worth teasing out. This paper is noteworthy as it demonstrates the importance of a distinction made in Chapter 1. Because they were interested in social networks *per se*, and in actual fact did not explicitly treat any online services, you could argue that I should not include it in a book on social media at all! But it is very revealing of how little we understand of the psychology of social media connections.

In this study, Festl and Quandt carried out what might be termed a fairly standard social science methodology in an educational context – they gave German high school students a questionnaire to fill in. Like many such research projects, they asked participants questions about their individual characteristics, such as their age, gender, personality traits, how much they used computers and whether or not they were involved in cyberbullying. More unusually, they also asked structural questions, such as asking students to list their best friends. This information allowed the researchers to understand the social network of the school, revealing cliques of friendships, relative levels of popularity and reciprocal relationships. In other words, some students were on a lot more best friends lists than others were.

More crucially, this structural data revealed many interesting findings with regard to cyberbullying. Beyond the individual factors, such as female adolescents being more likely to be the victims of cyberbullying than males, the structural factors revealed some unexpected findings. While both perpetrators and victims of cyberbullying were found to be, in general, less popular than their fellow classmates, this did not hold true for another important category. Those students who had experienced both being the perpetrator and as well as the victim of cyberbullying were highly popular among their classmates. In other words, children who had been a cyberbully, but had also suffered cyberbullying themselves, were more popular than children who had only been cyberbullies, or only been victims.

Fascinatingly, Festl and Quandt also say that, while not statistically significant, it seems that these 'perpetrator/victims' showed a curious pattern of connection within the social network as a whole. A visual representation of the participants' structural relationships revealed that perpetrator/victims were often found to be links between different cliques, rather than central to any clique. This position seems to give them a certain amount of influence over distinct groups, but also vulnerable to being attacked by either. As such, when we examined how aggression like cyberbullying occurs online, it seems that we have a lot yet to learn about the psychology of social media connections. Festl and Quandt conclude rather bluntly that, without taking these kinds of structural factors into account, explanations for online aggression like cyberbullying will remain insufficient.

However, this is in reference to social connections where there is some level of actual interaction. You would be forgiven for thinking that there is nothing interesting happening in our social media connections where there are is no interaction at all. But there is, and the research here is quite revealing of the psychology of these services: welcome to the wonderful world of FOMO. An early paper on this topic by Przybylski and colleagues continues to set the agenda here, as it developed a questionnaire to measure 'fear of missing out', and tested it over three studies.[13] The final version of this scale included such items as "When I go on vacation, I continue to keep tabs on what my friends are doing". Przybylski and colleagues were interested in understanding how fear of missing out correlated with other psychological issues, namely its motivational, emotional and behavioural associations. What they found was that FOMO is primarily experienced by young people, and by young men more than young women. It is also associated with not being psychologically satisfied in a number of areas, including personal autonomy, relatedness and competence. In other words, if you feel like you lack independence, closeness to other people and general capability, you are probably at risk of experiencing FOMO when you go on social media. Again, doesn't this strike you as being similar to the deeper challenge of social media: the struggle to be authentic?

Hence, it would probably be a good idea to think twice before we post content on social media – even if it is positive or jolly, we have no idea how it may make our connections feel. In particular, those people who are struggling to find their place in the world may find our apparently perfect lives difficult to stomach. But we will be talking more about updates in the next chapter.

SUMMARY

In this chapter we saw how social media connections can be valuable, though not in the most straightforward manner. While the ice bucket challenge supports the core social media value that connecting with people is a good thing, in personal circumstances, things are more complex. We saw that Facebook helped college students create and maintain connections with acquaintances – but wasn't much help for closer relationships. Yet the opposite was true with Snapchat, which is better for maintaining close friendships than associates. You have to pick your social media service to suit your relationships.

Regarding our connections as a whole, we discussed 'Dunbar's number', which suggested a neurological limit to the size of our social groups. Not only was it reflected in our social media connections, but so were the sympathy group and the support clique – indicating that we are only able to emotionally connect with a certain number of people, whether online or not.

Furthermore, we have the issue of context collapse – not wanting everyone to see every update we post, but having no idea who is paying attention. So we only share updates that won't offend anyone, or balance with personal revelations, in order to appear more relatable to our 'imagined audience'.

We also considered the friction that can occur between our connections. Notably, perpetrators and victims of cyberbullying do not seem to be popular within their schoolyard social networks, but perpetrator/victims seem to be particularly socially influential. Finally, we muse about that quiet spot in our social media connections, those people who do not interact, and how we might try to avoid giving them the 'fear of missing out', by being careful about what we put in our updates.

NOTES

1 Levin, J. (2014, August 22). Who invented the ice bucket challenge? *Slate*. Retrieved from www.slate.com/articles/technology/technology/2014/08/who_invented_the_ice_bucket_challenge_a_slate_investigation.single.html
2 Sifferlin, A. (2014, August 18). Here's how the ALS ice bucket challenge actually started. *TIME*. Retrieved from http://time.com/3136507/als-ice-bucket-challenge-started/
3 van Ogtrop, K. (n.d.). Ever wonder how the whole "Ice Bucket Challenge" started? *Real Simple*. Retrieved from www.realsimple.com/magazine-more/jeanette-senerchia-ice-bucket
4 Facebook. (2014, August 18). The ice bucket challenge on Facebook. *Facebook Newsroom*. Retrieved from https://newsroom.fb.com/news/2014/08/the-ice-bucket-challenge-on-facebook/

5 Woolf, N. (2016, July 27). Remember the ice bucket challenge? It just funded an ALS breakthrough. *The Guardian*. Retrieved from www.theguardian.com/society/2016/jul/26/ice-bucket-challenge-als-charity-gene-discovery
6 Ellison, N. B., Steinfield, C., & Lampe, C. (2007). The benefits of Facebook "Friends": Social capital and college students' use of online social network sites. *Journal of Computer-Mediated Communication*, *12*(4), 1143–1168. https://doi.org/10.1111/j.1083-6101.2007.00367.x
7 Piwek, L., & Joinson, A. (2016). "What do they snapchat about?" Patterns of use in time-limited instant messaging service. *Computers in Human Behavior*, *54*, 358–367. https://doi.org/10.1016/j.chb.2015.08.026
8 Foley, M. (2016, May 24). What is a Snapchat streak? Here's everything you need to know about Snapstreaks. *Bustle*. Retrieved from www.bustle.com/articles/162803-what-is-a-snapchat-streak-heres-everything-you-need-to-know-about-snapstreaks
9 Dunbar, R. I. M. (1992). Neocortex size as a constraint on group size in primates. *Journal of Human Evolution*, *22*(6), 469–493. https://doi.org/10.1016/0047-2484(92)90081-J
10 Dunbar, R. I. M. (2016). Do online social media cut through the constraints that limit the size of offline social networks? *Royal Society Open Science*, *3*(1), 1–9. https://doi.org/10.1098/rsos.150292
11 Marwick, A. E., & boyd, danah. (2010). I tweet honestly, I tweet passionately: Twitter users, context collapse, and the imagined audience. *New Media & Society*, *13*(1), 114–133. https://doi.org/10.1177/1461444810365313
12 Festl, R., & Quandt, T. (2013). Social relations and cyberbullying: The influence of individual and structural attributes on victimization and perpetration via the internet. *Human Communication Research*, 39(1), 101–126. https://doi.org/10.1111/j.1468-2958.2012.01442.x
13 Przybylski, A. K., Murayama, K., Dehaan, C. R., & Gladwell, V. (2013). Motivational, emotional, and behavioral correlates of fear of missing out. *Computers in Human Behavior*, 29(4), 1841–1848. https://doi.org/10.1016/j.chb.2013.02.014

FURTHER READING

Beer, D. (2016). *Metric power*. London: Palgrave Macmillan.
boyd, danah. (2014). *It's complicated: The social lives of networked teens*. New Haven, CT: Yale University Press.
Danziger, K. (1997). *Naming the mind: How psychology found its language*. London: Sage.
De Vos, J. (2013). *Psychologization and the subject of late modernity*. London: Palgrave Macmillan.
Howard, P., & Wooley, S. (eds.) (2018). *Computational propaganda: Political parties, politicians, and political manipulation on social media*. Oxford: Oxford University Press.

Hughes, B. (2018). *Psychology in crisis*. London: Red Globe Press.
Livingstone, S., & Blum-Ross, A. (forthcoming). *Parenting for a digital future*. Oxford: Oxford University Press.
Marwick, A. E. (2013). *Status update: Celebrity, publicity and branding in the social media age*. New Haven, CT: Yale University Press.
Rainie, L., & Wellman, B. (2012). *Networked: The new social operating system*. Cambridge, MA: MIT Press.
Rose, N. (1989). *Governing the soul*. London: Free Association Books.
Suler, J. R. (2015). *Psychology of the digital age: Humans become electric*. Cambridge: Cambridge University Press.
Taylor, C. (1989). *Sources of the self: The making of modern identity*. Cambridge, MA: Harvard University Press.
Vaidhyanathan, S. (2018). *Antisocial media: How Facebook disconnects us and undermines democracy*. Oxford: Oxford University Press.
van Dijck, J. (2013). *The culture of connectivity: A critical history of social media*. Oxford: Oxford University Press.

3

WHEN DO PEOPLE BELIEVE CONSPIRACY THEORIES?

JAN-WILLEM VAN PROOIJEN

"How do you explain the fact that conspiracy theories are on the rise nowadays?" This is a question that I get exceptionally often – from students, from members of an audience after giving a talk, or from journalists who are writing a newspaper article on conspiracy theories. The answer often surprises people: I don't think that conspiracy theories are on the rise. Surely there is some waxing and waning of conspiracy theories throughout the decades. In that respect I am perfectly open to the possibility that in 2016 – with Donald Trump spreading conspiracy theories during the entire US election and the UK voting in favor of a "Brexit" – conspiracy theories have received more attention than in, say, 2006. But I dispute the assertion that there is a stable trend towards more conspiracy theories in the long run. On average, the current population is not more or less conspiratorial than 30, or even 100, years ago. Scientific evidence offers little support for the idea that people have become more conspiratorial over time.

In what I regard as one of the most important, and certainly one of the most labor-intensive, studies on conspiracy theories that has been conducted so far, two political scientists from the University of Miami (helped by a team of trained research assistants) analyzed published letters that US citizens had sent to the *Chicago Tribune* and the *New York Times*.[1] The letters spanned a time period of 120 years, ranging from

1890 to 2010. Each year was about equally represented in the sample of letters, and the letters to be analyzed were randomly selected out of all the letters that were published during this period. Of primary interest to the researchers was the extent to which these letters contained conspiracy theories. In the end, these researchers read, and coded for conspiratorial content, a total of 104,803 published letters.

As might be expected, there is variation across the years in the extent to which the letters contain conspiratorial content; furthermore, in different time periods people wrote about different conspiracy theories. But over time, there was no trend upwards in the proportion of letters that contained conspiracy theories. In fact, there were two time periods that seemed to stand out in frequency of conspiratorial content, but both were not in the new millennium. The first time period when there was evidence for increased conspiratorial content was around the year 1900, during the peak of the Second Industrial Revolution. The second time period when there was evidence for increased conspiratorial content was in the late 1940s–early 1950s: at the start of the Cold War. These data clearly speak against assertions that conspiracy theories are on the rise.

Necessarily there are minor imperfections of this study that people could seize on to discredit its importance. For instance, one might reason that the letters that were actually published in these newspapers were selected by an editor and hence were not random. Some editors may have been more likely to publish conspiratorial letters than others. These are unavoidable limitations of a project like this. But we should also be realistic: This is an enormous number of letters, published in two different newspapers, selected by many different editors, over a range of a full 120 years. If there is any merit to the statement that conspiracy theories are on the rise in our modern age, there should be some trace of this visible in these data. For instance, if digital communication technologies make citizens more susceptible to conspiracy theories, the letters should show an increase in conspiratorial content starting somewhere in the early '90s and gradually increasing until the last year of measurement (2010). The data show none of this.

Also other data contradict the idea that people nowadays are more suspicious of power holders than they were about 30 years go. One study looked at the extent to which people trust and are satisfied with politicians in various EU countries over time using yearly data of the Eurobarometer.[2] Particularly the data on satisfaction are of interest, as they range from well before regular citizens had Internet, social media, and smartphones (1974) until a time when these technologies were a normal part of everyday life (2012) (the data on trust are less telling, as these ranged from 1997 to 2012 – although it is worth noting that also in these data no trend emerged suggesting a decline in trust over time). Although admittedly dissatisfaction with politicians is not the same as believing in a political conspiracy theory, one is highly likely to be diagnostic for the other: People are dissatisfied with politicians if they believe that these politicians are conspiring (and vice versa). Again, the results revealed fluctuation in the extent to which citizens were satisfied or dissatisfied with politicians, but there was no trend suggesting a drop in satisfaction levels as time progressed. Furthermore, throughout the years the average satisfaction level that citizens expressed about politicians was quite low. It would thus be a mistake to think that citizens nowadays are less satisfied with politicians than ever before. Back in the 1970s, citizens were also very much dissatisfied with politicians and, apparently, to about an equal extent as nowadays.

All of this may seem counterintuitive. After all, conspiracy theories are everywhere on the Internet and on Social Media, and these modern tools are primary means through which people learn about conspiracy theories or get into contact with other conspiracy theorists. Note that I am not saying that modern information technologies have no impact. But there is a difference between speed of dissemination and the proportion of citizens who believe conspiracy theories. My prediction would be that these modern communication technologies increase the speed through which people learn about conspiracy theories but do not increase the proportion of citizens who believe them. In a time when citizens did not have Internet or social media at their disposal, conspiracy theories were likely to spread through different, slower communication channels (e.g., word of mouth), but major conspiracy theories would spread nevertheless and ultimately reach most people anyway.

Certainly conspiracy theories spread fast nowadays. On 2 December 2015 the San Bernardino (California) shootings took place in the late morning. A married couple killed 14 people and injured another 22 with semi-automatic rifles. After the shooting, a manhunt ensued which lasted for about four hours, after which both perpetrators were killed. As the event unfolded it was evening in Amsterdam, where I was watching live coverage of this event on TV together with my wife. About two hours after the start of the shooting (and hence, two hours *before* the perpetrators were killed) I could not resist the temptation and Googled something like "San Bernardino conspiracy". Instantly various conspiracy theories came up suggesting that the shooting was a false-flag operation. We could read conspiracy theories about this terrorist attack while it was still unfolding! Without modern communication technology, however, these conspiracy theories may have reached us too, eventually – or alternatively, in Amsterdam we might not have heard about the San Bernardino shooting in the first place, and we would instead have focused more on local distressing events (leading to local conspiracy theories). Modern information technologies play a role in conspiracy theories, but when we seek answers to the question why people believe or disbelieve them, these technologies are only a piece in a much bigger puzzle.

Instead of seeking an explanation in "zeitgeist" or technology, a better and more comprehensive explanation for conspiracy beliefs can be found in psychology. I propose that conspiracy theories are rooted in a subjective psychological state that has been inherent to the human condition since the start of humanity: Conspiracy theories are a natural reaction to social situations that elicit feelings of fear and uncertainty. Specifically, the more strongly people experience such aversive emotions, the more likely it is that they assign blame for distressing events to different groups. As a consequence, we can expect conspiracy theories particularly in the wake of distressing societal events.

CONSPIRACY THEORIES AND SOCIETAL CRISIS SITUATIONS

People regularly are confronted with societal crisis situations – rapid changes in society that could potentially threaten their well-being, their way of life, or even their existence. Examples of such crisis situations are terrorist attacks, natural disasters, wars, revolutions, economic and financial crises, disease epidemics, and the like. Such crisis situations almost invariably lead to conspiracy theories. Two key examples of sudden, unexpected crises in modern history that inspired widespread conspiracy theories are the 9/11 terrorist strikes and the assassination of John F. Kennedy. Both were events that shocked society, that installed strong feelings of fear and uncertainty in people, and that gave people the feeling that the world would never be the same again. Many people have "flashbulb memories" about these events, as they still vividly recall what they were doing when they first heard the news. Both events also initiated conspiracy theories that are still being endorsed today by large groups of citizens and that many people by now have internalized as historical "facts".

The two spikes that emerged in conspiratorial content within the letters sent to the *New York Times* and *Chicago Tribune* can also be regarded as crisis situations that formed the basis of feelings of uncertainty and fear. The first spike with increased conspiracy beliefs was during the Second Industrial Revolution. During this time period major companies started to emerge, and power structures within society changed dramatically. It was a time of rapid technological progress, quick development of new infrastructure, and the efficient mass-production of a wide range of goods. Although life conditions improved for many citizens, regular laborers who were working in factories had reason for concern: There was a continuous threat of unemployment, as many jobs became obsolete after being replaced by machines. It is quite likely that these workers – who constituted a large portion of the population – experienced substantial uncertainty about their future, producing a range of conspiracy theories. The second spike with increased conspiracy beliefs was at the start of the Cold War. Shortly after the Second World War many citizens feared the prospect of a new major war, and the threat of communism was looming. As a consequence, many citizens were wary of the possibility that specific people, institutions, or groups were somehow connected to communism. This "McCarthyism" – named after senator Joseph McCarthy who was a significant figure in fueling fear of communism – was hence characterized by many (often unfounded) allegations of communist conspiracies within society. These communist conspiracy theories caused reputation damage, unemployment, and sometimes even imprisonment of people who were accused of communist sympathies.

But we do not need to restrict ourselves to the past century in order to find a connection between crisis situations and conspiracy theories. Also in the Middle Ages, examples abound of crisis situations that initiated widespread belief in conspiracy theories. Medical science was not as advanced as our current generation is used to, and it was common for young children to die of a range of dangerous diseases that nowadays are easily prevented with vaccines. Furthermore, there was no understanding of viruses or bacteria (or the importance of personal hygiene for that matter), and antibiotics were yet to be discovered. As a consequence, disease epidemics were frequent and would kill many people, but people were unable to fully understand how these diseases originated. People therefore often blamed these epidemics on people or groups in society, and such scapegoating regularly took the form of conspiracy theories. One common belief was that many young women were actually witches who conspired with the Devil to impose harm on the population such as epidemics or failed harvests. As a result of these beliefs – which are both superstitious and conspiratorial – many innocent women were burnt alive. Also the Jewish community was a frequent target of conspiracy theories suggesting that they had a causal role in crisis situations such as disease epidemics or setbacks during the Crusades, stimulating widespread persecution of Jews in Medieval Europe.[3]

These are just examples of a more general principle: In challenging times that elicit fear and uncertainty among large groups of people, conspiracy theories flourish. People start blaming people or groups that they felt uncomfortable about to begin with and come up with theories that explain the harm they experience through a malevolent conspiracy. As a result, conspiracy theories will increase in the population once there is widespread concern about a high-profile terrorist attack, a natural disaster, an economic or financial crisis, a war, a revolution, and so on. Events that pose no direct threat to peoples' own lives also can stimulate conspiracy theories, as long as it captures the attention of a large audience and causes feelings of distress among many citizens (e.g., the unexpected death of a celebrity).

In fact, even imaginary crisis situations can cause conspiracy beliefs. A case in point is the conspiracy theory that the 1969 moon landings were filmed in a TV studio. One might reason that these conspiracy theories were not a reaction to an "objective" crisis situation – it was a reaction to a positive event where humanity and science reached a new level of accomplishment. But someone who believes that the government continuously and willfully deceives the nation subjectively experiences the nation as being in crisis. Put differently, many people hold general conspiratorial beliefs about the government, and these beliefs are distressing in and of themselves, which causes further conspiracy theorizing. This is a general insight that I will return to in other chapters: Belief in one conspiracy theory stimulates belief in other conspiracy theories. In this case, citizens who hold conspiracy theories about the government are likely to approach any action of that government – including a monument to scientific accomplishment like the moon landings – with skepticism, and with additional conspiracy theories.

THE ROLE OF FEAR AND UNCERTAINTY

In order to understand why feelings of uncertainty and fear are associated with conspiracy theories, we need to establish how people cope with these negative emotions. The most common response to fear and uncertainty is to become vigilant: People start paying close attention to their environment, they start to ruminate, and they try to establish the causes of their negative feelings. Fear and uncertainty thus lead people to try to make sense of their physical and social environment.[4] Such increased sense making is an automatic response that in all likelihood is rooted in an instinct for self-preservation. Feelings of fear and uncertainty signal that there are imminent threats in the environment. Paying close attention to this environment therefore increases the chances of the organism to effectively cope with these threats and survive.

As part of this self-preservation instinct, evolutionary psychologists have noted that people tend to be risk-averse in the face of uncertain and possibly threatening situations.[5] Imagine seeing a long object in the grass, and it is unclear whether the object is a stick or a snake. In such cases, it is a natural response for people to be cautious and assume the object to be a snake. Mistakes do not have equal consequences in this situation: Someone who picks up the object assuming it to be a stick may die if it turns out to be a venomous snake. But for someone who assumes the object to be a snake and hence acts cautiously, it does not matter whether that judgment is correct or not. If one is mistaken and the snake is in fact a stick, one may take an unnecessary detour, but for the rest no real harm is done.

Feelings of uncertainty lead people to make sense of the situation that they find themselves in, and during this mental sense making it is natural for them to assume the worst. This also pertains to how people perceive others. One common finding in psychology is the "myth of self-interest". Just for clarification, this term does not mean that self-interest is a myth; of course people can be selfish from time to time. Instead, this term means that people *overestimate* the extent to which the behavior of *others* is driven by self-interest. People can be selfish sometimes, but they can also be genuinely altruistic and caring – but when trying to explain the behavior of others, people more often assume selfishness and less often assume truly benevolent motivations than is actually justified. (When Mark Zuckerberg decided to donate 99% of his Facebook shares to charity, I was astonished to read one blog after the other of people who believed him to do this out of self-interest.)

Interestingly, this myth of self-interest increases when people feel uncertain. In an experiment, participants were informed that a second participant would allocate valuable recourses between the two of them. To a varying extent, however, participants experienced uncertainty in the form of lacking information: They were not fully informed about how the allocator distributed the resources. Results showed that this informational uncertainty led participants to overestimate the valuable resources that the allocators had given to themselves and to underestimate the valuable resources that the allocators had given to the participants. People expected the allocators to be more selfish than they actually were, and this effect increased to the extent that people had less information about the distributions. As the authors conclude, when people lack information they "fill in the blanks" with assumptions of selfishness.[6]

This myth of self-interest is about how negatively people view other individuals, but through a similar process, feelings of fear and uncertainty also influence how negatively people view other groups in society. When making sense of the societal and political events that people encounter in their daily life, people have a tendency to assume the worst of groups that are powerful (and that could hence cause real harm), that they perceive as "different", and that they feel uncomfortable with – such as governmental institutions, major companies, or distrusted minority groups. As a result, people come up with conspiracy theories about the malpractice of these groups, which answers many unresolved questions that people have about the societal events that they try to comprehend. Feelings of uncertainty and fear put people in a suspicious, information-seeking state-of-mind, leading them to perceive malevolent conspiracies as responsible for a range of societal events.

Much psychological research has examined the relationship between fearful, uncertain feelings and people's tendency to believe conspiracy theories. One study was conducted in the last three months of 1999. During those months, many citizens around the world feared a major shutdown of computer systems due to the "millennium bug". This was a major issue at the time. The possibility of a millennium bug received continuous news coverage, and people feared major fallout of for instance power plants, banking systems, water supplies, and the like. If these fears had been justified and the millennium bug had become a reality, it would have had serious consequences for the economy, health care, and many other domains that directly influence the life and well-being of citizens: Anything that was run by computers would shut down. (In the end, the year 2000 started without unusual problems.) Against this background, over 1,200 US citizens responded to a questionnaire that not only asked how afraid they were for the millennium bug but also to what extent they believed in a range of common conspiracy theories. As it turned out, people who feared the millennium bug by the end of 1999 were also more likely to believe that President Kennedy was killed by a conspiracy; that the Air Force was hiding evidence that the US has been visited by UFOs; that the US government deliberately had put drugs in inner city communities; and that the Japanese were conspiring to destroy the US economy. Fear for the millennium bug was associated with belief in a range of conspiracy theories, including theories that are conceptually unconnected with the millennium bug.[7]

While these findings support the idea that feelings of fear are related with belief in conspiracy theories, they do not establish causality: We do not know whether fear of the millennium bug increased conspiracy beliefs or, instead, people who happened to believe these conspiracy theories were more likely to fear the millennium bug. In order to test for the causal order that fear and uncertainty lead to conspiracy theories, it is necessary to conduct a psychological experiment in which part of the research participants experience these distressing feelings and part of the research participants do not – and then examine whether belief in conspiracy theories is stronger among the distressed participants. Various studies tried to install these distressing feelings in participants by reminding them of situations in which they experienced a lack of control. Specifically, people have a need to feel that they are in control of whatever they do, ranging from simple movements to more complex actions such as driving a car. If people experience a lack of control they feel helpless and therefore start feeling uncertain. In a typical experiment, some of the research participants are asked to write down a specific incident in their lives where they had no control over the situation; other research participants are asked to write down a specific incident in their lives where they were in full control of the situation. After that, they are asked how plausible they find certain conspiracy theories.

Various researchers have conducted experiments along these lines, and these studies typically show that people believe in conspiracy theories more strongly when they feel distressed (e.g., because they were reminded of a situation where they lacked control) than when they do not feel distressed (e.g., because they were reminded of a situation where they had control).[8] Together with psychologist Michele Acker and a group of research assistants, we also conducted such an experiment in Amsterdam. The experiment took place against the background of the construction of a new and controversial metro line that would connect the northern and southern part of the city. Although such a metro line is likely to have many benefits once completed, it encountered severe objections among Amsterdam residents, as it would imply major construction works for years, right through the historical center. In fact, a majority of residents had voted against this project in a referendum, but the city council moved forward with it anyway. Furthermore, the construction itself ran into many problems, including being overbudget and behind schedule. Public hostility against this project reached its peak in 2009, when the construction caused unforeseen problems that posed direct harm to city residents: The underground construction had damaged the foundations of several old houses, which then had to be evacuated, as the houses literally were sinking into the ground.

When the "sinking houses" made continuous news headlines, our team of research assistants went to university cafeterias in

Amsterdam with short questionnaires and asked residents to participate in a short study in exchange for a candy bar. Participants were asked to describe either a situation from their lives where they lacked control or one where they had full control. A third group of participants were asked to describe a neutral situation from their lives, unrelated to feelings of fear or uncertainty. Then we asked participants about their conspiracy theories of the North-South Metro line: For instance, participants indicated whether they believed that members of the city council were bribed by the construction companies, whether they deliberately withheld information about the project from the public to avoid hampering its construction, and so on. In keeping with many other findings, results revealed that participants who felt fearful and uncertain (after describing a situation where they lacked control) believed these conspiracy theories more strongly than participants who felt confident (after describing a situation where they had control).[9]

In sum, feelings of fear and uncertainty fuel belief in conspiracy theories. Yet there are two complications to these effects that deserve to be noted. A first complication is that these aversive emotions do not lead to conspiracy theories among everyone and in every circumstance: Sometimes fear and uncertainty can actually *increase* support for authorities. So far we have discussed the conspiracy theories that emerged after 9/11, but we should also recognize the opposite: In the months directly after 9/11, George W. Bush was among the most positively endorsed presidents in history in terms of public approval ratings. Apparently, 9/11 not only elicited widespread conspiracy theories about the Bush administration; it also elicited massive support for the Bush administration. How can we reconcile this discrepancy with the present arguments?

The key here is that fear and uncertainty lead to conspiracy theories, but only if these theories involve powerful groups or institutions that people distrusted to begin with. Fear and uncertainty may actually increase support for powerful groups or institutions that people do trust. One study investigated whether or not the perception of leaders being moral or immoral influences belief in conspiracy theories. Naturally, people believe conspiracy theories more strongly about leaders that they find immoral than about leaders that they find moral. When people experience uncertainty, however, these effects of morality on belief in conspiracy theories become more impactful. Put differently, uncertainty makes people endorse conspiracy theories more strongly for leaders that they find immoral but less strongly for leaders that they find moral.[10] Fear and uncertainty hence do not lead to indiscriminate conspiracy theorizing; they lead people to place blame on authorities, institutions, or groups that they felt uncomfortable with from the start.

The second complication is that, often, also the "official" explanation of a crisis event entails a conspiracy. The official reading of the 9/11 strikes is that there was a conspiracy of 19 Al Qaeda suicide terrorists. Why did many citizens disbelieve this official reading and instead perceived a different conspiracy of a malevolent government performing a false-flag operation? Two interrelated issues may answer this question. First, as noted previously, when people experience fear and uncertainty, it is their natural response to be cautious and assume the worst possible explanation. In that sense, believing that 9/11 was a governmental conspiracy (and not an Al Qaeda conspiracy) is a risk-averse response: It is a lot more disturbing, frightening, and dangerous to assume that one's own government would be behind a major terrorist act, as compared to a known foreign terrorist group that is being closely monitored by secret service agencies. Second, and relatedly, a governmental conspiracy is a more grandiose explanation for 9/11 than an Al Qaeda terrorist cell: It would for instance mean that more people were involved, the level of deception would be bigger, and the scheme that was carried out would be more ingenious, and in general a government has more power than a terrorist cell. The 9/11 terrorist strikes constituted a major event in modern history, and a governmental conspiracy would be a major explanation for it. The tendency to believe a grandiose conspiracy theory may be influenced by a basic heuristic of the human mind called the proportionality bias: People have a tendency to assume that a big consequence must have had a big cause.

BIG CONSEQUENCES, BIG CAUSES?

A president is a human being, and is therefore fragile enough to die from accidents or sudden illnesses. It is perfectly possible for an otherwise healthy president to die from a tiny flu virus, just like everyone else. Now, imagine for a moment that this would actually happen to a sitting US president or a UK prime minister. Would many citizens believe that this event indeed was caused by a simple virus, or would they believe a conspiracy theory? Although certainly the opinions would differ among the public, and a lot would depend upon specific details of the case, in general I am quite confident that many citizens would come up with major conspiracy theories asserting that the president was murdered (or was kidnapped, or staged his/her own death). The explanation of an event as big as the death of a president through a cause as small as a flu virus is just hard to swallow for many people: It cannot possibly be this simple, there must be more to such an impactful, world-changing event than that. This is the essence of the proportionality bias: the assumption that a big consequence must have had a big cause.

Naturally, the unexpected death of a president would elicit strong feelings of fear and uncertainty among the population. But the proportionality bias is also broader than regulating these aversive feelings: It is a simple mental heuristic that can be seen across judgment domains, also in areas unrelated to conspiracy theories that do not elicit fear and uncertainty. Imagine two comparable students that both experience a computer crash right before having to hand in an important paper. For the first student, the consequences are disastrous: The professor fails the student for the class and does not grant an extension for the paper; this leads the student to not graduate in time and to therefore lose an attractive job offer. For the second student, the consequences are relatively small: The professor allows the student an extension to hand in the paper. As a result the student does graduate in time and can start with the attractive job. What may have caused the computer crash for the first and second student?

In a research study, half of the participants read a hypothetical scenario of the first student, and the other half read a scenario of the second student. They then selected what they thought was the most likely cause of the crash: a widespread computer virus (big cause) or a malfunctioning computer cooling fan (small cause). Research participants massively recognized a widespread computer virus as a bigger computer problem than a malfunctioning fan. But more importantly, when the consequences were big for the student, research participants were more likely to believe that the computer crash had a big cause – that is, a computer virus. These findings are unlikely to be explained by fear and uncertainty: After all, these were hypothetical scenarios of an unknown student. Instead, the proportionality bias was at work here: Participants assumed a big cause for a big consequence – in this case, a computer virus if the crash caused the student to fail his studies.[11]

The proportionality bias similarly has been shown to influence people's tendency to believe conspiracy theories. Imagine that a president of a small country gets assassinated. In one case, this assassination instigates an unforeseen chain of events ultimately leading to a war. In the other case, the assassination may still be tragic, but does not lead to a war. Put differently, the assassination has a big consequence (a war) or not. Who assassinated the president – was it a lone gunman, or was it a governmental conspiracy? A study revealed that participants considered a conspiracy more likely if the assassination led to a war than if it did not lead to a war. Again, people assumed a big cause for a big consequence, which in this case fueled a conspiracy theory. Various other studies suggest a similar principle: The more impactful and harmful a societal event is (including hypothetical ones), the more likely it is that people come up with a conspiracy theory to explain it.

Besides fear and uncertainty, the proportionality bias constitutes an additional explanation for the observation that we particularly can expect conspiracy theories in the wake of impactful, harmful societal events. Note that both the emotional explanation (fear and uncertainty) as well as the cognitive explanation (the proportionality bias) are rooted in people's desire to understand and make sense of the harmful events that they perceive in society. Sense making thus is essential in the psychology of conspiracy theories. In the following chapter, I will more precisely uncover the mental processes that are at work when people make sense of societal events – and how these may lead to conspiracy theories.

NOTES

1 Uscinksi & Parent, 2014
2 Andeweg, 2014
3 Pipes, 1997
4 Park, 2010
5 Neuberg, Kenrick, & Schaller, 2011
6 Vuolevi & Van Lange, 2010
7 Van Prooijen & Acker, 2015
8 Sullivan et al., 2010; Van Harreveld et al., 2014; Whitson & Galinsky, 2008
9 Van Prooijen & Acker, 2015
10 Van Prooijen & Jostmann, 2013
11 Leboeuf & Norton, 2012

REFERENCES

Andeweg, R. B. (2014). A growing confidence gap in politics? Data versus discourse. In J.-W. van Prooijen & P. A. M. van Lange (Eds.), *Power, politics, and paranoia: Why people are suspicious of their leaders* (pp. 176–198). Cambridge, UK: Cambridge University Press.

LeBoeuf, R. A., & Norton, M. I. (2012). Consequence-cause matching: Looking to the consequences of events to infer their causes. *Journal of Consumer Research*, 39, 128–141.

Neuberg, S. L., Kenrick, D. T., & Schaller, M. (2011). Human threat management systems: Self-protection and disease avoidance. *Neuroscience and Biobehavioral Reviews*, 35, 1042–1051.

Park, C. L. (2010). Making sense of the meaning literature: An integrative review of meaning making and its effects on adjustment to stressful life events. *Psychological Bulletin*, 136, 257–301.

Pipes, D. (1997). *Conspiracy: How the paranoid style flourishes and where it comes from.* New York, NY: Simon & Schuster.

Sullivan, D., Landau, M. J., & Rothschild, Z. K. (2010). An existential function of enemyship: Evidence that people attribute influence to personal and political enemies to compensate for threats to control. *Journal of Personality and Social Psychology*, 98, 434–449.

Uscinski, J. E., & Parent, J. M. (2014). *American conspiracy theories.* New York, NY: Oxford University Press.

Van Harreveld, F., Rutjens, B. T., Schneider, I. K., Nohlen, H. U., & Keskinis, K. (2014). In doubt and disorderly: Ambivalence promotes compensatory perceptions of order. *Journal of Experimental Psychology: General*, 143, 1666–1676.

Van Prooijen, J.-W., & Acker, M. (2015). The influence of control on belief in conspiracy theories: Conceptual and applied extensions. *Applied Cognitive Psychology*, 29, 753–761.

Van Prooijen, J.-W., & Jostmann, N. B. (2013). Belief in conspiracy theories: The influence of uncertainty and perceived morality. *European Journal of Social Psychology*, 43, 109–115.

Vuolevi, J. H. K., & Van Lange, P. A. M. (2010). Beyond the information given: The power of a belief in self-interest. *European Journal of Social Psychology*, 40, 26–34.

Whitson, J. A., & Galinsky, A. D. (2008). Lacking control increases illusory pattern perception. *Science*, 322, 115–117.

FURTHER READING

Books about conspiracy theories

- For an interesting popular science book about conspiracy theories, read *Suspicious minds: Why we believe conspiracy theories* by Rob Brotheron (2015; New York, NY: Bloomsbury Sigma).
- For a US political science perspective, read *American conspiracy theories* by Joseph E. Uscinski and Joseph M. Parent (2014; New York, NY: Oxford University Press). This book also contains the study that analyzes more than 100,000 letters over a time period of 120 years, described in Chapter 2 .
- For a historical perspective on conspiracy theories, read *Conspiracy: How the paranoid style fl ourishes and where it comes from* by Daniel Pipes (1997; New York, NY: Simon & Schuster).
- Also of interest is the political-historical approach of *Political paranoia: The psychopolitics of hatred* by Robert S. Robins and Jerrold M. Post (1997; New Haven, CT: Yale University Press).
- For a volume on conspiracy theories in which multiple authors offer their view, read *The psychology of conspiracy* edited by Michal Bilewicz, Aleksandra Cichocka, and Wiktor Soral (2015; Oxon, UK: Routledge).
- For a volume in which various authors address not only conspiracy theories but also the question whether power really does corrupt, read *Power, politics, and paranoia: Why people are suspicious of their leaders* edited by Jan-Willem van Prooijen and Paul A. M. van Lange (2014; Cambridge, UK: Cambridge University Press).

Books about belief in general

- For an excellent popular science book about the ideas in Chapter 3 on the architecture of beliefs, read *The believing brain: From ghosts and*

gods to politics and conspiracies – How we construct beliefs and reinforce them as truths by Michael Shermer (2011; New York, NY: Henry Holt).
- Another good popular science book on the psychology of belief is " *The belief instinct: The psychology of souls, destiny, and the meaning of life* " by Jesse Bering (2011; New York, NY: W.W. Norton & Co).

Books about populism/extremism and conspiracy theories

- For a good introduction to populism, read *What is populism?* by Jan-Werner Müller (2016; Philadelphia, PA: University of Pennsylvania Press). The book also addresses the role of conspiracy theories in populist movements.
- For the qualitative study on extremist fringe groups and conspiracy theories, read *The power of unreason: Conspiracy theories, extremism and counter-terrorism* by Jamie Bartlett, J. and Carl Miller (2010; London, UK: Demos).

Books about belief versus reality

- Do some of the pseudo-scientifi c "9/11 for truth" conspiracy theories appear plausible to you? Then defi nitely read *Debunking 9/11 myths: Why conspiracy theories can't stand up to the facts* by David Dunbar and Brad Reagan (2011; New York, NY: Hearst Books). In it, you will learn what scientists and witnesses actually have to say about the conspiracy theories associated with this event.
- Do you feel that there may be a grain of truth in some paranormal phenomena? Please learn about the scientifi c evidence in *Paranormality: The science of the supernatural* by Richard Wiseman (2011; London, UK: Pan Books).

Other

- Watch how a blacksmith refutes the 9/11 "melted steel" conspiracy theory described in Chapter 6: www.youtube.com/watch?v=FzF1KySHmUA
- See the TV interview in which Prince talks about chemtrails, described in Chapter 1: http://youtu.be/3zEiAQdyAGk
- Read an interview with the author, about the psychology of conspiracy theories: www.vox.com/science-and-health/2017/4/25/15408610/conspiracy-theories-psychologist-explained

4 The dynamics of groups online

Olivia Hurley

CHAPTER OVERVIEW

This chapter outlines how online groups form and regulate themselves. It examines the dynamics of online groups compared to their offline counterparts, focusing on why online group membership is an attractive option for many people, especially in today's digital age. Specifically, the chapter addresses topics such as how roles, norms and group identity are expressed in online groups. Other recent research areas, such as the impact of an over-reliance on online social networks on individuals' mental well-being, and the phenomenon of groupthink related to online groups, are also presented.

KEY TERMS

Collective identity describes how people are similar to each other, when the psychological connection between the individual self and the social group the individual is a member of is considered. **Groupthink** refers to 'the tendency for cohesive groups to become so concerned about group consolidation that they fail to critically and realistically evaluate their decisions and antecedent assumptions' (Park, 1990, p. 229). **Group norms** are the rules individuals are expected to obey as members of a particular group, while **group roles** are the parts that individuals play within a group, or the positions they fill within a group, both formal and informal. **Social loafing** describes the reduction in effort exerted by some individuals when performing a task as part of a group, compared to completing the task alone.

INTRODUCTION

This chapter outlines how online groups form and regulate themselves. Some key questions one might be interested in posing when considering this topic of groups online could include: What is the psychological impact of being a member of an online group, such as a Facebook group, a Twitter group, or being a LinkedIn member, compared with being a member of an offline group – for example, in a physical work setting or a sports club setting? Are people more likely to join groups online than they would be to join a similar group offline? Are online groups more or less homogeneous – that is, do individuals in online groups share more common characteristics with other group members, when compared to similar offline groups? Are shy people really 'bolder' or 'braver' online? In order to answer such questions, one must first understand what a group is, how it is formed and why such groups form.

What is a group? How and why do groups form?

A group is any collection of people in a particular location or setting. Most people are considered members of many groups during their lifetime, such as their class group, their work group, or, more common in today's digital age, a member of an online group, such as an online social networking group (Kirwan & Power, 2014). The question of how and why groups form has been investigated for decades, perhaps most frequently by social psychologists, such as Maslow (1943), who, in his paper 'The theory of human motivation', described how human beings have 'needs', which are prioritised, with physical needs and safety needs positioned at the bottom levels of a hypothetical pyramid that he had suggested, followed by love and belonging needs. These love and belonging needs refer to the human 'need' to be cared for, to form social bonds, and to seek out contact with other human beings. Such needs are considered fundamental to what it means to be human. So, human beings are considered social creatures with a need to 'belong', to be accepted by their peers, to be valued, yet unique individuals, with common goals and interests compared to other group members (Baumeister & Leary, 1995). This social need to 'belong' appears to be a strong motivating factor for why many people join groups, including groups in the online world (Chiu *et al.*, 2008). However, online group membership is determined by more than just social factors. It is also determined by users' access to the necessary technology to enable them to join and interact in such groups, and their usability skills for such technology (Daneback *et al.*, 2012). So, having addressed some of the issues surrounding what groups are, and what motivates individuals to join groups, the reasons why individuals join online groups specifically, and group behaviours online will now be discussed.

Why do individuals join online groups?

According to researchers such as Code and Zaparyniuk (2009), and Kirwan and Power (2014), some of most common reasons for joining online groups include, first, the *need to alleviate loneliness* (whether that is temporary, such as moving to a new city, or chronic, such as being housebound for long periods of time due to ill health, for example), and second, the attraction of the *relative anonymity* that such online groups provide, which may be especially appealing for shy individuals, such as those struggling with social anxiety disorders (Kirwan & Power, 2014), or those who wish to control the *amount and type of self-disclosures* they provide to other members of their social groups. People with social anxiety disorders, for example, who find it difficult to interact in groups in everyday real life, may find the online community a more attractive option for them in which to interact with others because they may feel safer, and more at ease expressing themselves online as they are not required to be physically present for such interactions to take place. Similarly, individuals' anxieties regarding the reactions of others in their offline world, to *their 'different' or 'special' interests*, could result in such individuals being, or feeling, ostracised and isolated from their offline, real world, peer groups, thus accounting perhaps for their, and a third motivation, to seek out like-minded individuals online to converse with instead (Bargh & McKenna, 2004; Kirwan & Power, 2014; Walther, 2007).

A fourth attraction to joining online groups is their ability to allow individuals to *communicate remotely* with other members of a group they share perhaps a common predicament or problem with, or when time to meet in person is not possible due to time constraints, work/family commitments, or location difficulties – i.e. living in a remote place with little public transport services. There is no need to be in the same location or face to face with group members in order to communicate online in such situations. However, many visual cues – for example, body language – are often lost in such online interactions (i.e. those that are type-based communications, via email or message boards). Such non-verbal cues in face-to-face exchanges are considered to add to the richness of the discourse taking place between the group members (Riva, 2002). The loss of visual contact between online group members can mean a loss of understanding of the discourse, in its meaning and context, by individuals who only have written words, and perhaps emoticons, on which to base their interpretations of what is being communicated. However, such typed responses also afford group members the luxury of re-reading their responses before sending them on to other group members, meaning that such responses may be 'toned down' or rephrased in a way that is not truly reflective of what would be said if the group members were engaged in a face to face exchange (Murgado-Armenteros *et al.*, 2012).

Despite the above cited limitation, of typed online group interactions losing their non-verbal cues, such online social communities continue to grow in number and popularity (Kuss & Griffiths, 2011; Facebook, 2012; Van Belleghem *et al.*, 2012). Indeed, the growth of such online communities has resulted in researchers debating the previously held views of how social and psychological dynamics contribute to human relationships, communication and community formation. For example, some early research supported the view that the relative anonymity of Internet communication encourages self-expression and facilitates the formation of relationships outside of what might be considered 'normal' socially mediated communication (Wallace, 1999).

A fifth attraction of online group membership is that the Internet offers a way for individuals to *present a 'version' of themselves* to their group. Identities online are, therefore, sometimes described as 'fluid' or dynamic in nature – that is, they are subject to change, depending on the demands of the online group membership. Indeed, Code and Zaparyniuk (2009) described how individuals often join online groups because this affords them the capacity to experiment and develop their identities in their online groups. Such 'impression management' continues to be extensively researched by cyberpsychologists (Kirwan & Power, 2014).

A sixth attraction of online group membership is perhaps the possibility of forming *multinational groups* as again, cited above, physical contact is not needed to form such online relationships. This ability to communicate with individuals from other countries and cultures opens up a world of interesting exchanges between online group members. However, it is often the case that group members are less spontaneous and more guarded in what they communicate in such multicultural group settings online, as there is perhaps greater uncertainty about the way an exchange in such an environment might be interpreted (Murgado-Armenteros *et al.*, 2012).

The online environment also removes environmental variables, such as room temperature, seating types and arrangements, noise levels – that is, the physical personal space, from the interaction, which may be a favourable feature of online group interactions for individuals who like to control such variables as much as possible. The offline world often places great emphasis on the physical appearance of individuals also, which is removed from interactions in many online settings. This can result in individuals forming bonds with other individuals they share common views and goals with, rather than being related to physical attractiveness, for example. Such relationships may then have greater opportunities to grow in the online world, which could greatly benefit the social bonds of the individuals concerned. Indeed, some early research by Parks and Floyd (1995) reported that people felt the personal relationships they formed via the Internet were close, meaningful and rewarding. This view was supported by McKenna *et al.* (2002) in their two-year longitudinal study of randomly selected Internet newsgroup participants. McKenna *et al.* reported that 84 per cent of their participants claimed that their Internet relationships were as important and 'real' to them as were their non-Internet relationships.

OVER-RELIANCE ON ONLINE GROUP MEMBERSHIP

There are, however, implications for group members who display an over-reliance on their online social groups, such as their 'friends' on social media websites like Facebook, or their 'followers' on Twitter, for example. Melville (2010) reported that individuals may suffer symptoms of depression if they feel rejected by their online 'friends'. Such individuals then risked alienating themselves from their online groups, in a similar fashion to that which may occur with members of groups in their offline world. Also, Kalpidou *et al.* (2011) reported the longer such individuals spend with their online groups in the online world, the lower their self-esteem levels appeared to become offline. However, Kim *et al.* (2009) reported that individuals who scored low on their ability to function in offline social settings declared the beneficial use of online social groups in meeting their unfulfilled social offline group needs. These group members perceived their online groups existed in a 'safer' environment for them. Kim *et al.* did also comment, however, that the difficulties individuals reported having in their offline social interactions, and how they felt about them, were not enhanced, or solved, by participating in online social groups. Therefore, reliance on the online world for social support may result in individuals becoming more socially withdrawn from the offline world, thus facilitating their social anxiety to a greater degree.

Some researchers have specifically tested the psychological impact of denying individuals time to interact on their social networking websites. For example, in their study, Sheldon *et al.* (2011) denied students access to their Facebook accounts for a 48-hour period. These students actually displayed lower levels of aggression and procrastination, while also reporting greater levels of life-satisfaction, for the period they were denied access to their Facebook accounts. They did, however, display a rebound effect in their extended use of Facebook following their 48-hour period of absence from their sites in order, it would appear, to 'make up' for their reported feelings of being 'disconnected' from this online world during the 48-hour period of abstinence imposed during the study.

Gentzler *et al.* (2011) also reported that group members who spent more time interacting with their parents through social media groups displayed higher levels of loneliness and anxious attachment with their parents compared to those who interacted more with their parents in the offline world. The individuals who reported spending more time with their parents in an offline environment stated that their relationships with their parents were more intimate, supportive and satisfying for them, compared to the individuals who interacted more with their parents online.

As previously cited, the Internet and online social networks may provide socially shy individuals with a comfortable environment in which to communicate with others, while avoiding face-to-face interactions (Ebeling-Witte *et al.*, 2007). However, is it true that such individuals are more confident and less self-conscious online? Brunet and Schmidt (2008) attempted to answer this question. They reported that the behaviour and confidence exhibited by shy individuals, who reported being more self-conscious in social settings, was context dependent when they communicated online. For example, when there was a webcam operating, the self-conscious individuals provided less self-disclosure information compared to their less shy counterparts.

To conclude this section, perhaps online groups can provide a peer-supportive forum and a positive environment in which to interact, for some group members, such as those who are shy or self-conscious, or who have special interests. However, some online groups can also be a negative source of social support, especially if they result in feelings of 'disconnectedness', or if they lead to anxious attachments to significant others, such as family and friends in the real world. They can also be damaging, if their online groups encourage, and foster, negative health-related behaviours, such as disordered eating (Tierney, 2006). Such groups can also have a contagion-like effect on vulnerable group members (Lewis & Arbuthnott, 2012).

Having addressed some of the reasons why individuals are motivated to join online groups, and some key advantages and disadvantages of such online group memberships for individuals, the issues of how people behave in groups online, compared to offline, and how such online groups maintain their membership numbers will now be discussed, considering issues such as group identity, roles, norms and social loafing in online groups.

HOW DO PEOPLE BEHAVE IN ONLINE GROUPS?

So, how does group behaviour online differ from group behaviour offline, if indeed any differences do exist? In order to answer such a question, the term 'group dynamics' should first be explained. According to Moran (2012), group dynamics is a term used to describe the way individuals act in groups, the factors thought to influence group behaviour and the processes thought to change group behaviour. But first, what constitutes examples of online groups? In the online world, environments which constitute groups include social networks, such as Facebook, Twitter and Instagram, chat-rooms, email lists, discussion boards, bulletin boards, news and discussion groups, list servers, as well as Massively Multiple Online Role Playing Games (MMORPG; such large groups will be discussed in detail in Chapter 19). The main objective of such online groups is to provide members with a common cyberspace in which to share their experiences, to seek advice, and to communicate with others (Castelnuovo *et al.*, 2003). There are many similarities between such online groups and their offline equivalents (e.g. clubs, societies, gym groups, political groups), such as the need of members for social connections and social support, as outlined earlier in this chapter. However, there are also some key differences between such groups online, compared to similar offline groups (Howard, 2014). So, do online groups serve a different purpose in a person's life, compared to their offline groups? Do individuals fulfil different roles in online groups, when compared to their offline roles in their real-world lives? According to Chmiel *et al.* (2011), Internet communication patterns do appear to differ when compared to those displayed in traditional, face-to-face settings. Therefore, the influence of cohesion, roles and norms on online group functioning, the types of leadership structures that exist online, and some of the negative features of online group behaviour, such as groupthink and social loafing, will now be discussed.

Online group cohesion

Similar to the concept of team cohesion in sporting and work-related environments (Moran, 2012), group survival in the online world relies on groups sharing some form of task and social cohesion. This means that a group must help an individual to fulfil some objectives or goals (i.e. tasks), while also meeting some interpersonal (or social) needs of the individual, if that individual is to remain a member of the group. The extent to which the task, or social, element of this 'bond' between the group and its members remains a topic of interest for researchers, and similar to the sport, and organisational, psychology literature, the cyberpsychology literature seems to suggest that task needs are somewhat more important in maintaining the online group environment, than are social requirements. For example, Ren *et al.* (2012) specifically examined the impact of enhancing members' attachment to their online communities, by manipulating levels of group identity or interpersonal bonds. The results of their study revealed that increasing group identity was a more effective way to enhance members' attachment to their online communities, compared to increasing the interpersonal bonds between the members. This implies that members of groups seem to feel a stronger attachment to groups they can relate to more in terms of group objectives and characteristics, rather than those in which they have specifically close-knit social, or attraction-based bonds with other members of the group. Therefore, group identity in online groups appears to fulfil an important function in online group growth and development.

Group and collective identity, roles and norms

The term 'group identity' is a term used to describe the common characteristics and common goals, similar beliefs and standards that often exist between group members (Chen & Li, 2009). 'Collective identity' is a related term which refers to how people are similar to each other within a group, when the psychological connection between the individual self and the social group is considered (Abrams & Hogg, 2001). As with many groups, roles and norms emerge within online groups to allow them to function effectively. A role within any group refers to the 'position' a person may fill within that group, such as a 'leadership' role, similar to a 'captain's role' within a team perhaps. Roles within groups can, therefore, be described as formal or informal. An example of a formal role would be a managerial role or a captaincy role. Such roles are explicitly stated and clearly identified. An informal role could include the 'joker' role, or indeed, the 'peacemaker' role within the group. Norms differ from roles in groups as they typically refer to the rules a group puts in place in order to regulate the behaviour of the group members. Groups often develop their norms by observing the 'normal' or 'accepted' behaviours of other groups (Borsari & Carey, 2003). For example, a norm within a work setting might be that all employees are expected to arrive to work on time, with only special exceptions to this rule being tolerated. Penalties are often put in place to punish members of groups when they 'break' the rules, in order to motivate the members to conform to the group norms, and so that the group can exist in a harmonious way (Kirwan & Power, 2014).

'Depersonalisation' is a specific term within group dynamics used to describe the phenomenon where people conform to a group prototype and behave according to group norms (Code & Zaparyniuk, 2009). At times, in such groups, individuals relinquish their individual views, beliefs or needs, in order to accept the group's views. When individuals find themselves being influenced in such a way by the opinions of other group members, the term 'groupthink' may be used to describe the phenomenon.

Groupthink

As cited above, sometimes a kind of 'groupthink' can emerge in groups. Groupthink refers to changes in the cognitions of individuals in groups, especially when they are in contact with, or interacting with, other group members. The reasons why groupthink occurs has been examined extensively by many social psychologists (Bandura, 1986). Among young people who are likely to join online groups, peer pressure may be one reason why groupthink occurs. In 2008, boyd completed a qualitative study on American teenagers who joined online social networks. boyd reported that strong and direct peer pressure was placed on American teenagers to join online social networks, such as Facebook and Bebo. The teenagers interviewed in boyd's study reported that, in addition to pressure from peers to join these groups, they also experienced feelings of isolation and being 'left out' if they did not join such online communities.

Perhaps different types of online groups are also more, or less, susceptible to features such as groupthink? Researchers have attempted to characterise and generalise online group topographies (Bargh & McKenna, 2004). A limitation of this research has emerged, namely, whether different online groups communicate and interact in similar ways that makes them comparable, or is it possible that they differ significantly in the way they function? Howard (2014) attempted to address this limitation of some of the previous research examining online group formation and function (Bargh & McKenna, 2004), which had, overall, failed to examine the generalisability of online group features identified, such as group identity and social support issues. Howard (2014) specifically examined some of the overlapping qualities of online groups previously identified by researchers such as McKenna and colleagues (see Bargh & McKenna, 2004), qualities such as group identity, social support, self-presentation and well-being. Howard compared three types of online groups, namely a cancer support group (representing an online 'support group'), a Harry Potter fan group (representing an online 'avocation group') and a Lesbian Gay Bisexual Transgender (LGBT) group (representing a 'stigmatised group'). All three groups selected represented forum online groups only. The decision to include such groups alone was made in an attempt to maintain consistency in the comparisons made between the three types of online groups examined. Howard's results indicated that online groups do indeed appear to differ in their properties, especially in relation to their group members' group identity, social support and well-being features. Howard suggested that future research might attempt to uncover *why* group members vary in their characteristics across different types of online groups. Perhaps such research could also shed some light on the reasons why features, such as groupthink, emerge among some online groups more than others.

Of course, group formation and function is influenced by many other factors. One such factor could be the leadership structure within groups, which will now be discussed in relation to online groups.

Leadership roles in online groups

Formal leadership roles have often been examined in the offline world (Moran, 2012). Based on the social identity theory of leadership (Hogg & Reid, 2001), individuals who exhibit more prototypical characteristics of a group typically emerge as the group's leaders. Such individuals often exhibit a high degree of overlap between their own characteristics and the characteristics of the other group members (especially in relation to their goals, values and attitudes). While such incidences apply in the offline world, they could apply more strongly on the Internet where other influential factors for leadership are not as apparent, such as physical appearance and the degree of interpersonal dominance potential leaders might have over other group members (Hogg & Reid, 2001). Regarding specific leadership research in online groups, the question of who governs online chat-rooms, for example, has been examined (Bowker & Liu, 2001). However, overall, this area does not appear to have been researched in great depth in the past ten years and could now be considered in need of examination by current researchers.

Social loafing

Of course, some negative group interactions also exist in online groups, in the same way as they are present in offline groups, such as social loafing. This term refers to individuals' decreased efforts when they are working together as part of a group, compared to working alone on the task. In the offline world, such behaviour can have a significant negative effect on performance, especially within sporting, and work-based, groups (Moran, 2012). Online, social loafing in groups has been linked to variables such as increased group size (Blair *et al.*, 2005), a finding also reported as groups increased in size in the offline environment (Moran, 2012). Ways to minimise the occurrence of such behaviour while maximising the contributions of group members remains a challenge for online groups, as it does for their offline counterparts.

Having discussed matters related to online group cohesion, group identity and negative aspects of group behaviour, such as groupthink and social loafing, the debate surrounding the ability of the Internet either to strengthen the bonds of groups or diminish face-to-face interactions will now be considered.

There was some concern that online communication platforms would dilute traditional human relations (Arora, 2011). However, research findings from the early 2000s suggested that, rather than weakening social bonds between groups and communities, online communities have the ability to add to the offline relationships enjoyed by members of groups (see Wellman *et al.*, 2002). Such online networks may add new layers of activities to offline groups and can, therefore, enhance their positive group interactions. Later research has also shown that some individuals do prefer and form stronger social bonds with online support group members than they do with offline social group members, especially if they are left unsatisfied with the support they have or are receiving within their offline groups – for example, individuals not happy with health, or medically related, concerns or conditions (Eun Chung, 2013).

FUTURE DIRECTIONS FOR RESEARCH IN ONLINE GROUPS

Having reviewed some key issues related to online groups, their behaviours and advantages for group members, a number of exciting areas for future research have emerged. For example, more research on the characteristics of members attracted to different types of online groups is a potential area for future research, as advocated by Howard (2014). More specific research examining the characteristics of online leaders is also warranted, to follow up on research by the likes of Bowker and Liu (2001). Such research could help to increase the number of female leaders in the offline world also – for example, where female representation in power positions remains low, compared to their male counterparts (United Nations (UN) Women, 2014).

CONCLUSION

To conclude, this chapter has given an overview of groups online, what they are, why and how they exist, what their strengths and weaknesses are for group members, and how their continued study may contribute to the overall understanding of group dynamics, both in the online and offline world.

ACTIVITY

Create an online social support network group (on Facebook or Twitter) for young adolescents, focusing on a topical issue, such as cyberbullying or mental health issues (e.g. suicide prevention). Document in a final report all activity on the site, such as the material posted, the membership numbers, the volume of traffic to the site and an analysis of the comments posted on the site.

DISCUSSION QUESTIONS

1. Compare and contrast the behaviours of groups in online and offline environments.
2. Discuss the increasing use of the Internet as a source of social support for group members.
3. Outline the dangers of an over-reliance on social networks, such as Facebook, Twitter and chat-rooms, for primary social support.
4. Discuss the impact of individuals experimenting with their social identity online, both for the individual and the group as a whole.

RECOMMENDED READING LIST

Lina Eklund's study examined the link between online/offline group interactions, using social online gaming. The findings of the study demonstrate how on-and offline interactions are closely linked.

Eklund, L. (2014). Bridging the online/offline divide: The example of digital gaming. *Computers in Human Behaviour.* DOI: 10.1016/j.chb.2014.06.018.

Howard's study set out to examine the dynamics of three different online groups: a cancer support group, an LGBT forum and a Harry Potter fan forum. The results indicate that such groups do differ in their properties, such as their group members' group identity.

Howard, M.C. (2014). An epidemiological assessment of online groups and a test of a typology: What are the (dis)similarities of the online group types? *Computers in Human Behavior, 31*, 123–133.

This textbook is a comprehensive source of information on social aspects of the Internet. It provides detail on both the positive and negative influences of the online world.

Amichai-Hamburger, Y. (2013). *The Social Net: Understanding Our Online Behaviour.* (2nd edn). Oxford: Oxford University Press.

GLOSSARY

Collective identity Describes how people are similar to each other, when the psychological connection between the individual self and the social group the individual is a member of is considered.

Groupthink 'The tendency for cohesive groups to become so concerned about group consolidation that they fail to critically and realistically evaluate their decisions and antecedent assumptions' (Park, 1990, p. 229).

Group norms The rules individuals are expected to obey as members of a particular group.

Group roles The parts that individuals play within a group, or the positions they fill within a group (formal or informal).

Social loafing Describes the reduction in effort exerted by some individuals when they are performing as part of groups.

REFERENCES

Abrams, D. & Hogg, M.A. (2001). Collective identity: Group membership and self-conception. In M.A. Hogg & S. Tinsdale (eds), *Blackwell Handbook of Social Psychology: Group Processes* (pp. 425–460). Malden, MA: Blackwell.

Arora, P. (2011). Online social sites as virtual parks: An investigation into leisure online and offline. *The Information Society*, *27*, 113–120.

Bandura, A. (1986). *Social Foundations of Thought and Action*. Englewoods Cliffs, NJ: Prentice-Hall.

Bargh, J.A. & McKenna, K.Y.A. (2004). The Internet and social life. *Annual Review of Psychology*, *55*, 573–590.

Baumeister, R.F. & Leary, M.R. (1995). The need to belong: Desire for interpersonal attachments as a fundamental human motivation. *Psychological Bulletin*, *117*(3), 497–529.

Blair, C.A., Thompson, L.F. & Wuensch, K.L. (2005). Electronic helping behaviour: The virtual presence of others makes a difference. *Basic and Applied Social Psychology*, *27*, 171–178.

Borsari, B. & Carey, K.B. (2003). Descriptive and injunctive norms in college drinking: A meta-analytic integration. *Journal of Studies on Alcohol and Drugs*, *64*(3), 331–341.

Bowker, N.I. & Liu, J.L. (2001). Are women occupying positions of power online? Demographics of chat room operators. *CyberPsychology and Behavior*, *4*(5), 631–644.

boyd, d. (2008). Taken out of context: American teen sociality in networked publics. Ph.D. dissertation. University of California-Berkeley, School of Information.

Brunet, P.M. & Schmidt, L.A. (2008). Are shy adults really bolder online? It depends on the context. *CyberPsychology & Behavior*, *11*(6), 707–709.

Castelnuovo, G., Gaggioli, A., Mantovani, F. & Riva, G. (2003). From therapy to e-therapy: The integration of traditional techniques and new communication tools in clinical settings. *CyberPsychology & Behavior*, *6*(4), 375–382.

Chen, Y. & Li, X. (2009). Group identity and social preferences. *American Economic Review*, *99*(1), 431–457.

Chiu, P.Y., Cheung, C.M.K. & Lee, M.K.O. (2008). Online social networks: why do 'we' use Facebook? *Communications in Computer and Information Science*, *19*, 67–74.

Chmiel, A., Sienkiewicz, J., Thelwall, M., Paltoglou, G., Buckley, K., Kappas, A. & Holyst, J.A. (2011). Collective emotions online and their influence on community life. *PLoSONE*, *6*(7), e22207.DOI: 10.1371/journal.pone.0022207.

Code, J.R. & Zaparyniuk, N. (2009). Social identities, group formation, and the analysis of online communities. In S. Hatzipanagos & S. Warburton (eds), *Handbook of Research on Social Software and Developing Communities Ontologies* (pp. 86–101). Hershey, PA: Ideal Group.

Daneback, K., Månsson, S. & Ross, M.W. (2012). Technological advancements and Internet sexuality: Does private access to the Internet influence online sexual behaviour? *CyberPsychology, Behavior & Social Networking*, *15*(8), 386–390.

Ebeling-Witte, S., Frank, M.L. & Lester, D. (2007). Shyness, Internet use, and personality. *CyberPsychology and Behavior*, *10*(5), 713–716.

Eklund, L. (2014). Bridging the online/offline divide: The example of digital gaming. *Computers in Human Behaviour*. DOI: 10.1016/j.chb.2014.06.018.

Eun Chung, J. (2013). Social interaction in online support groups: Preference for online social interaction over offline social interaction. *Computers in Human Behaviour*, *29*, 1408–1414.

Facebook. (2012). One billion people on Facebook. Retrieved from: http://newsroom.fb.com/News/One-Billion-People-on-Facebook-1c9.aspx.

Gentzler, A.L., Oberhauser, A.M., Westerman, D. & Nadorff, D.K. (2011). College students' use of electronic communication with parents: Links to loneliness, attachment, and relationship quality. *CyberPsychology, Behavior, and Social Networking*, *14*(1–2), 71–74.

Hogg, M.A. & Reid, S.A. (2001). Social identity, leadership, and power. In A.Y. Lee-Chai & J.A. Bargh (eds), *The Use and Abuse of Power: Multiple Perspectives on the Causes of Corruption* (pp. 159–180). Philadelphia, PA: Psychology Press.

Howard, M.C. (2014). An epidemiological assessment of online groups and typology: What are the (dis)similarities of the online group types? *Computers in Human Behavior*, *31*, 123–133.

Kalpidou, M., Costin, D. & Morris, J. (2011). The relationship between Facebook and the wellbeing of undergraduate college students. *CyberPsychology, Behavior, and Social Networking*, *14*(4), 183–189.

Kim, J., LaRose, R. & Peng, W. (2009). Loneliness as the cause and the effect of problematic Internet use: The relationship between Internet use and psychological well-being. *CyberPsychology and Behavior*, *12*, 451–455.

Kirwan, G. & Power, A. (2014). What is cyberpsychology? In A. Power & G. Kirwan (eds), *Cyberpsychology and New Media: A Thematic Reader* (pp. 3–14). Hove: Psychology Press.

Kuss, D.J. & Griffiths, M.D. (2011). Online social networking and addiction – a review of the psychological literature. *International Journal of Environmental Research & Public Health*, *8*, 3528–3552.

Lewis, S.P. & Arbuthnott, A.E. (2012). Searching for thinspiration: The nature of Internet searches for pro-eating disorder website. *Cyberpsychology, Behavior and Social Networking*, *15*(4), 200–204.

Maslow, A.M. (1943). A theory of motivation. *Psychological Review*, *50*, 370–396.

McKenna, K.Y.A., Green, A.S. & Gleason, M.E.J. (2002). Relationship formation on the Internet: What's the big attraction? *Journal of Social Issues*, *58*, 9–31.

Melville, K. (2010). Facebook use associated with depression. Retrieved from: www.scienceagogo.com/news/20100102231 1001data_trunc_sys.shtml.

Moran, A.P. (2012). *Sport and Exercise Psychology: A Critical Introduction*. Hove: Routledge.

Murgado-Armenteros, E.M., Torres-Ruiz, F.J. & Vega-Zamora, M. (2012). Differences between online and face to face focus groups, viewed through two approaches. *Journal of Journal of Theoretical and Applied Electronic Commerce Research*, 7, 73–86. DOI: 10.4067/S0718–18762012000200008

Park, W. (1990). A review of research on groupthink. *Journal of Behavioral Decision Making*, *3*(3), 229–245.

Parks, M.R. & Floyd, K. (1995 May). Friends in cyberspace: Exploring personal relationships formed through the Internet. Paper presented at the annual meeting of the International Communication Association, Albuquerque, NM.

Ren, Y., Harper, F.M., Drenner, S., Terveen, L., Kiesler, S., Riedl, J. & Kraut, R.E. (2012). Building member attachment in online communities: Applying theories of group identity and interpersonal bonds. *MIS Quarterly*, *36*(3), 841–864.

Riva, G. (2002). The sociocognitive psychology of computer-mediated communication: The present and future of technology-based interactions. *CyberPsychology and Behaviour*, *5*(6), 581–598.

Sheldon, K.M., Abad, N. & Hinsch, C. (2011). A two-process view of Facebook use and relatedness need-satisfaction: Disconnection drives use and connection rewards it. *Journal of Personality and Social Psychology*, *100*(4), 766–775. DOI:10.1037/a0022407.

Tierney, S. (2006). The dangers and draw of online communication: Pro-anorexia websites and their implications for users, practitioners, and researchers. *Eating Disorders*, *14*, 181–190.

United Nations (UN) Women. (2014). Progress for women in politics, but the glass ceiling remains firm. Retrieved from: www.unwomen.org/en/news/stories/2014/3/progress-for-women-in-politics-but-glass-ceiling-remains-firm.

Van Belleghem, S., Thys, D. & De Ruyck, T. (2012). Social media around the world 2012. Retrieved from: www.slideshare.net/InSitesConsulting/social-media-around-the-world-2012-by-insitesconsulting.

Wallace, P.M. (1999). *The Psychology of the Internet*. New York: Cambridge University Press.

Walther, J.B. (2007). Selective self-presentation in Computer Mediated communication: Hyperpersonal dimensions of technology, language and cognition. *Computers in Human Behaviour*, *23*, 2538–2557.

Wellman, B., Boase, J. & Chen, W. (2002). The networked nature of community: Online and offline. *IT & Society*, *1*(1), 151–165.

5

BELONGING IN AN AGE OF TECHNOLOGY

Kelly-Ann Allen

As a society, while many of us have the ability to connect to more and more people in an increasing variety of ways, the decline in face-to-face communication also means that fewer social opportunities are available for some of those who rely on more traditional forms of interactions (Drago, 2015). Are these changes affecting our social satisfaction and leading to increases in the number of people feeling lonely? Are our social skills suffering as a result? Less-direct exposure to other people and fewer opportunities to experience and observe them at first hand could have a particularly large impact on young people (Goodman-Deane et al., 2016). The connections we have today with family, friends and neighbours are unavoidably shaped by rapid developments in technology. But is technology helping or hampering our sense of belonging? This chapter engages with this question and discusses new research into how rapid changes in technology are influencing our social interactions and sense of belonging.

WHEN TECHNOLOGY DIVIDES

On the 14 March 2019, a 28-year-old shooter opened fire on worshipers at two mosques in Christchurch, New Zealand, leaving 50 people dead and scores of others injured. Technology played a central role in these horrifying events. Not only did the shooter livestream the shootings via Facebook, but he also used other social media sites, including Instagram and Twitter, to post videos, articles and Internet memes that pedalled a toxic far-right agenda of social exclusion and hatred. A manifesto for his actions, criticising racial integration and migration, also circulated online. One of the most disturbing outcomes was the amplification of his message by news and media outlets who broadcast the video stream in the wake of the event, giving his views and actions a global reach that they would have otherwise lacked.

Technology is no longer just an extension of our lives, like a porch built onto a house. It now forms the bricks and mortar of our daily existence. Technology is integrated with all manner of typical behaviours and is used as part of our everyday habits. It intersects our relationships and has an inevitable impact on human development. Children now grow up in environments in which their parents spend far more time in front of screens than did previous generations. Work and domestic labours have always drawn the attention of parents away from their children, but modern technology poses a host of new challenges. Not only does it encourage an "always-on" attitude towards working practices, bringing the workplace home into more households than ever before, but the feed of alerts, texts, message group responses, social media updates, news stories and so on being constantly fed directly into the hands of adults provides additional distractions.

This new environment throws up a range of important questions. What is the impact on children of parents checking their work emails while their child plays alone? How does additional parental screen time affect the social development of children? Are effects compounded if the children are also watching a screen at the same time? Tempting as it is to respond to these questions based on intuitions about negative consequences, it is important to let the research speak for itself. In fact, there do seem to be at least some positive outcomes for parent–child relationships from the increasing prevalence of technology, especially with respect to flexibility with work for some, which may mean more time spent at home. Nevertheless, it seems that parental screen time may indeed have an influence on the amount of time that children spend on their screens, with some studies finding a correlation between parents who spend a lot of time on screen media and children who do likewise (Lauricella et al., 2015).

Screen time also appears to be connected to socioeconomic status. Children from more affluent backgrounds are reportedly using screens less, while children from lower-income families are spending more time on screens (Tandon et al., 2012). This raises the troubling question of whether the excessive use of technology might become responsible for creating yet another disadvantage for those from less affluent backgrounds.

HOW MUCH SCREEN TIME DO PARENTS HAVE OUTSIDE WORK ON AVERAGE?

Parents report as spending as many as nine to 11 hours on screen media each day, with over 80% of that time related to personal use. While this number may seem extremely high, it becomes easier to comprehend when we consider the extent to which we are surrounded by screens in our everyday lives. Not only do most of us carry smartphones, but almost everywhere we go there are also tablets, computers and televisions within easy reach. We do not just use these devices when we are sitting still either – they are constant companions on the go as well, and we have come to rely on them for everything from mapping a journey in our car to summoning up a recipe in the kitchen. We text partners and friends as we walk, and we use email to let people know when we are running late. We may not all be using our devices constantly for nine or more hours each day, but many of us are using them much more than we might first think.

You do not need to look too far afield to find research that raises concerns about the heavy use of electronic devices and the consequent high number of hours of screen time. Studies have identified issues related to a range of negative outcomes for children, such as increases in attention-seeking behaviour, sleep disturbances, language delays, and physical inactivity and impediments to executive functioning, social skill development and school readiness (Richards et al., 2010; Parent et al., 2016; Duch et al., 2013; Christofaro et al., 2016). Technology effects the way we socialise, and this influences how we bond with others and develop a sense of belonging.

WHAT EFFECT CAN SCREEN TIME HAVE ON CHILDREN'S SENSE OF BELONGING WITH THEIR PARENTS?

On the one hand, technology affords us a range of benefits, such as the ability to work remotely or from home, which hold out the possibility of more family-friendly lives. But these potential benefits also come with consequences. While it may please some to work at home surrounded by their family, many others feel additional burdens from increased expectations and demands associated with the assumption that they are available 24/7, and there are in turn inevitable distractions from family and home life. For some, at least, being able to spend more time at home does not equate with having more time for family life. In addition to work burdens, distractions caused by digital media, and particularly smartphones, can often interrupt moments that have the potential for allowing genuine connections between parents and children (Kushlev & Dunn, 2018).

Studies have demonstrated that parents feel less connected to their children the more that parents use their smartphones (Kushlev & Dunn, 2018). Other research has shown that a sense of connection can be interrupted during parent–child learning experiences, with negative consequences for learning outcomes. Indeed, it is easy to see why incidental learning opportunities could easily be hampered by the parent's attention being divided between their child and their smartphone. Unsurprisingly, some children have reported feeling that they actually have to compete against a smartphone for their parents' attention (McDaniel & Radesky, 2018). This issue can be particularly challenging for parents who juggle multiple roles.

ARE THERE ANY POSITIVE EFFECTS OF PARENTAL SCREEN TIME?

At the most basic level, when electronic devices and screen time are used as tools to improve work efficiency and thus free up time to connect and foster relationships with their children, they have a clear, indirect positive effect. But there are also more direct contexts in which benefits can be detected.

CHILD-CENTRED PROGRAMMES

Significant positive effects can also emerge from screen media, and these can make it hard to offer straightforward guidelines about appropriate levels of screen time. For example, there is evidence to suggest that from around two years of age, age-appropriate television programmes that are conscientiously constructed can have educational benefits and provide increased learning opportunities (Mares & Pan, 2013). This has been found to be especially true for programmes that encourage imaginative/pretend play.

VIEWING TOGETHER

Some benefits also derive from parental guidance during a child's interaction with screen media (e.g. when parents view and interact with screen media together with their child). In the case of appropriately guided interactions, research has found some degree of benefit for the promotion of early literacy skills (Strouse et al., 2013). There is also an emerging body of literature that supports the value of certain wellbeing apps on smartphones and tablets, which can help teach children a range of skills related to coping and emotional regulation (Morris et al., 2010; Bakker & Rickard, 2018). However, how these benefits relate specifically to a sense of belonging to family relationships is a question that requires further research.

Other examples of the use of electronic devices can also create moments of meaningful connection, especially when the screen is shared and/or used as a relationship-building tool. A parent's talking and reminiscing with their child over baby photos on a smartphone is just one example of the productive and positive use of screen media. In many cases, context is key to whether an interaction will be an opportunity to build belonging or whether it will distract from belonging.

ADOLESCENTS AND TECHNOLOGY

Once upon a time, not that long ago, adolescents would sit glued to fixed-line telephones, to the great frustration of their parents and anyone trying to call. These days, however, it seems that written communication is preferred over verbal communication. Some analysis of modern communications suggests that written communications are going through a process of rapid change and condensation. In the context of a text, email or instant message, brevity is often key; whole sentences are sometimes reduced to a few consonants and vowels, and words are often done away with entirely in favour of an acronym, symbol or emoji. And while this way of communicating is efficient, we have to wonder whether this style of communicating for young people is allowing them to build the connections they need to fulfil their need to belong and equip them with the necessary skills to build relationships with others in the future.

The effects of technology on adolescent wellbeing may not be as severe as the media frequently leads us to believe (Orben & Przybylski, 2018). However, caution is necessary here: the research is still catching up with contemporary habits, and we do not yet have the kind of data that will allow us to understand the true implications of technology on our sense of belonging to others and to groups. There is already a broad intuitive awareness among the public that the effects of technology can be profound, and this has led more and more people to experiment with the idea of the "digital detox". Increasing numbers of apps are now available to block or limit the use of social media sites, while other tools, such as greyscale filters, can be used to make screen time less appealing. More direct measures can also be taken, with some schools going as far as to enact complete bans on the use of mobile phones on their grounds.

We know that excessive screen time or the compulsion to check our phones for updates can disrupt our ability to connect with others. However, the long-term implications for adolescents on their changing behavioural patterns have not yet been determined. But it is not all doom and gloom. While some of the consequences of modern technology may have concerning implications for the average teenager, even the dangers have the potential to make us more aware of how young people connect with others. For instance, simply reflecting on what we risk losing can lead us to focus more consciously on vital elements of a relationship – especially between parent/caregiver and a young person or the relationships between teenagers.

Another concern that has been raised about the effects of digital technology on young people is the potential of technology to reduce opportunities for the attainment and development of social skills. Turkle (2011) suggests that connecting with people through technological rather than physical means may result in a loss of the types of social skills required for face-to-face interaction. It is reasonable to expect that children who spend large amounts of time on electronic devices could have more social difficulties during later adolescence.

In the absence of research on the topic, many schools have banned the use of mobile phones during class and break times, and some have banned their use on school grounds altogether. These decisions have polarised the academic community, some of whom believe that in the absence of electronic devices, young people will not learn the necessary skills to use them appropriately. School leaders and teachers have anecdotally reported that students are spending less time looking at their devices and more time interacting with peers. What happens beyond the school gates, however, is not under the direct control of schools.

THE BROADER ISSUE

In *Bowling Alone: The Collapse and Revival of American Community*, Robert D. Putnam (2000) writes that the connections we have with family, friends and neighbours are shaped by rapid developments in technology. Putman notes a decline in *social capital* – that is, the value of social networks that arise from social intercourse with other individuals and families. Putman acknowledges that the Internet is a useful tool for connecting *physically distant* people. However, he also asks whether access to technology might challenge the possibility of forming genuine relationships and building communities: "is virtual social capital itself a contradiction of terms?" (p. 170). And he asks whether technology has contributed to a trend in deteriorating social connectedness. These questions were prescient when he wrote his book 20 years ago and have become ever more urgent in the years since. While there is a consensus that feeling a sense of belonging has a positive impact on physical health and wellbeing, further investigation is needed to help us understand the factors which influence belonging itself, particularly with respect to technology.

A MODERN SENSE OF COMMUNITY

A sense of community in the modern world need not be limited by physical contact or geography. Some relational communities are not linked to a locality but are based instead on a shared interest or purpose. McMillan and Chavis (1986) describe a psychological sense of community as a "feeling that members have of belonging, a feeling that members matter to one another and to the group, and a shared faith that members' needs will be met through their commitment to be together" (p. 9).

Research into the structures and the processes underlying online communities and groups is growing. Social media enables individuals to find a smaller subset of the broader community which they identify with and to which they feel they belong. Examples can be found in the formation of online groups around a particular hobby or support groups that enable people to come together around a common issue, adversity or diagnosis. However, few researchers have studied whether online communities create *the same type* of belonging that we feel when we connect to groups in the physical world. The qualities and actions of online groups appear to be like those of offline communities, but although social networks share some features of offline communities (e.g. exchanging resources and social support), more research is needed to investigate the full benefits of belonging towards an *online* community group. It may be that online social networks can serve different functions. For example, casual membership in a social networking site to "keep in contact with friends" might provoke different forms of cognition and different effects than would membership in an online support group or forum designed for individuals with cancer.

In late 2017, Katie Gilchrist (@mysenseoftumour), a senior consultant, was diagnosed with an acoustic neuroma brain tumour. In 2019, she underwent surgery and struggled to find the right social support networks online, so she built her own on Instagram. The following is Katie's story:

> When I was first diagnosed, I went looking online for support networks and information others with the same condition had shared. To my surprise, what I found was a web of negativity. As a way of coping (and also to share my story with others) I created an Instagram account and a blog where I have documented my story from day one. Now with a bit of a following, I have created a community of support for not only myself but others with the same condition.

You can read Katie's blog at https://mysenseoftumour.com.

One explanation for Katie's experience may be that different platforms provide different benefits. Pittman and Reich (2016) found that image-based visual platforms such as Instagram and Snapchat have users with less self-reported loneliness and increased happiness than users of more *text-based* platforms. It may be possible that when we view other photos of people, we are more likely to have the feeling that another person, a friend, is really there.

PERCEPTION OF FRIENDSHIP

Turkle (2011) has suggested that the difference between online communities and offline communities may be rooted in the fact that connecting with people over the Internet gives us only the perception of friendship; we are in contact but we remain physically alone. Jones (1997) suggests that some online groups are *virtual communities*, whereas others are *virtual settlements*, with frequent changes in members and consequently less emotional connection. Researchers have also noted that "heavy Internet use" can alienate people and reduce social contact (e.g. Beard, 2002; Erdoğan, 2008; Weiser, 2001), thereby hindering face-to-face relationships, regardless of the possible value of online communities.

Other scholars have used cross-cultural perspectives to examine perceptions of friendships. Sheldon and colleagues (2017) compared Croatian users and American users of Instagram, finding that Croatian participants reported greater gratification from social media use than did the American participants in the study. The researchers speculated that Croatians were more "we"-focused and Americans more "me"-focused, drawing from individualism vs collectivism thoughts; however, it was also suggested that the Croatian participants perceived their "followers" as friends, whereas American participants were more likely to consider them as "fans".

LONELINESS AND TECHNOLOGY

A major concern that has been raised with the increasing prevalence of technology is its negative association with loneliness. Stepanikova and colleagues (2010) examined digital tools and found that people who spent increased time on the Internet – using chat rooms, messaging groups and newsgroups, for example – felt lonelier than those who spent less time or no time at all. Email neither increased nor decreased wellbeing. While certain studies have shown that the Internet increases loneliness (e.g. Erdoğan, 2008), not all studies have drawn the same conclusion, particularly when investigating certain groups of people. For example, the Internet has actually been shown to decrease feelings of loneliness in people who identify themselves as lonely or shy. Bonetti and colleagues (2010) found that Internet use allowed people who were shy to interact in ways they would not have done in "real life" due to feeling too intimidated. Online groups may, then, provide communities in which shy people can feel emotionally safe.

Studies have also found that people who report feeling lonely may benefit from Internet use, with the research suggesting that increased Internet use can decrease feelings of loneliness and increase social support in real life. Studies have arrived at similar findings when examining Internet use in older and isolated populations (e.g. Khosravi et al., 2016), and people who are considered introverts (Kircaburun & Griffiths, 2018). Kuss and Griffiths (2011) found that extraverts use online platforms to consolidate friendships that already exist, whereas introverts use online networks to create meaningful relationships. There have been further speculations about why social media use may decrease loneliness. Yang (2016) suggests that not all social media use is as passive as it may first appear. In fact, people may use social media as a prelude to social contact. Moreover, social media networks might also remind people about how big their social networks are, even if they are not interacting with them daily.

FINAL THOUGHTS

Given the prevalence of technology in our daily lives, it has never been more important to study its capacity to foster belonging. Research so far has suggested that whether technology detracts from or strengthens our ability to belong is dependent on the context, use and the individual. New technologies change the way we share and consume knowledge but also influence how we socially interact. To really grasp the ongoing effects this kind of technological change has on individuals and society, new research is needed to study not only how the technology itself influences our social interactions and how, in turn, we define belonging, community and advancement but also how we manage and process the speed of the change, the rapid turnover of technologies and the social and cultural change it brings.

REFERENCES

Bakker, D., & Rickard, N. (2018). Engagement in mobile phone app for self-monitoring of emotional wellbeing predicts changes in mental health: MoodPrism. *Journal of Affective Disorders*, 227, 432–442.

Beard, K. W. (2002). Internet addiction: Current status and implications for employees. *Journal of Employment Counseling*, 39(1), 2–11.

Bonetti, L., Campbell, M. A., & Gilmore, L. (2010). The relationship of loneliness and social anxiety with children's and adolescents' online communication. *Cyberpsychology, Behavior, and Social Networking*, 13(3), 279–285.

Christofaro, D. G. D., De Andrade, S. M., Mesas, A. E., Fernandes, R. A., & Farias Junior, J. C. (2016). Higher screen time is associated with overweight, poor dietary habits and physical inactivity in Brazilian adolescents, mainly among girls. *European Journal of Sport Science*, 16(4), 498–506.

Drago, E. (2015). The effect of technology on face-to-face communication. *Elon Journal of Undergraduate Research in Communications*, 6(1), 13–19.

Duch, H., Fisher, E. M., Ensari, I., Font, M., Harrington, A., Taromino, C., Yip, J., & Rodriguez, C. (2013). Association of screen time use and language development in Hispanic toddlers: A cross-sectional and longitudinal study. *Clinical Pediatrics*, 52(9), 857–865.

Erdoğan, Y. (2008). Exploring the relationships among internet usage, internet attitudes and loneliness of Turkish adolescents. *Cyberpsychology: Journal of Psychosocial Research on Cyberspace*, 2(2), article 4.

Goodman-Deane, J., Mieczakowski, A., Johnson, D., Goldhaber, T., & Clarkson, P. J. (2016). The impact of communication technologies on life and relationship satisfaction. *Computers in Human Behavior*, 57, 219–229.

Jones, Q. (1997). Virtual-communities, virtual settlements & cyber-archaeology: A theoretical outline. *Journal of Computer-Mediated Communication*, 3(3), JCMC331.

Khosravi, P., Rezvani, A., & Wiewiora, A. (2016). The impact of technology on older adults' social isolation. *Computers in Human Behavior*, 63, 594–603. Retrieved from: https://doi.org/10.1016/j.chb.2016.05.092; https://www.sciencedirect.com/science/article/pii/S0747563216304289

Kircaburun, K., & Griffiths, M. D. (2018). Instagram addiction and the Big Five of personality: The mediating role of self-liking. *Journal of Behavioral Addictions*, 7(1), 158–170.

Kushlev, K., & Dunn, E. W. (2019). Smartphones distract parents from cultivating feelings of connection when spending time with their children. *Journal of Social and Personal Relationships*, 36(6), 1619–1639.

Kuss, D. J., & Griffiths, M. D. (2011). Online social networking and addiction – A review of the psychological literature. *International Journal of Environmental Research and Public Health*, 8(9), 3528–3552.

Lauricella, A. R., Wartella, E., & Rideout, V. J. (2015). Young children's screen time: The complex role of parent and child factors. *Journal of Applied Developmental Psychology*, 36, 11–17.

Mares, M. L., & Pan, Z. (2013). Effects of sesame street: A meta-analysis of children's learning in 15 countries. *Journal of Applied Developmental Psychology*, 34(3), 140–151.

McDaniel, B. T., & Radesky, J. S. (2018). Technoference: Longitudinal associations between parent technology use, parenting stress, and child behavior problems. *Pediatric Research*, 84(2), 210–218.

McMillan, D. W., & Chavis, D. M. (1986). Sense of community: A definition and theory. *Journal of Community Psychology*, 14(1), 6–23.

Morris, M. E., Kathawala, Q., Leen, T. K., Gorenstein, E. E., Guilak, F., DeLeeuw, W., & Labhard, M. (2010). Mobile therapy: Case study evaluations of a cell phone application for emotional self-awareness. *Journal of Medical Internet Research*, 12(2), e10.

Orben, A., & Baukney-Przybylski, A. K. (2018). Screens, teens and psychological well-being: Evidence from three time-use diary studies. *Psychological Science*, 30(5), 682–696.

Parent, J., Sanders, W., & Forehand, R. (2016). Youth screen time and behavioral health problems: The role of sleep duration and disturbances. *Journal of Developmental and Behavioral Pediatrics: JDBP*, 37(4), 277–284.

Pittman, M., & Reich, B. (2016). Social media and loneliness: Why an Instagram picture may be worth more than a thousand Twitter words. *Computers in Human Behavior*, 62, 155–167.

Putnam, R. D. (2000). *Bowling alone: The collapse and revival of American community*. New York, NY: Simon and Schuster.

Richards, R., McGee, R., Williams, S. M., Welch, D., & Hancox, R. J. (2010). Adolescent screen time and attachment to parents and peers. *Archives of Pediatrics & Adolescent Medicine*, 164(3), 258–262.

Sheldon, P., Rauschnabel, P. A., Antony, M. G., & Car, S. (2017). A cross-cultural comparison of Croatian and American social network sites: Exploring cultural differences in motives for Instagram use. *Computers in Human Behavior*, 75, 643–651.

Stepanikova, I., Nie, N. H., & He, X. (2010). Time on the Internet at home, loneliness, and life satisfaction: Evidence from panel time-diary data. *Computers in Human Behavior*, 26(3), 329–338.

Strouse, G. A., O'Doherty, K., & Troseth, G. L. (2013). Effective coviewing: Preschoolers' learning from video after a dialogic questioning intervention. *Developmental Psychology*, 49(12), 2368–2382.

Tandon, P. S., Zhou, C., Sallis, J. F., Cain, K. L., Frank, L. D., & Saelens, B. E. (2012). Home environment relationships with children's physical activity, sedentary time, and screen time by socioeconomic status. *International Journal of Behavioral Nutrition and Physical Activity*, 9(1), 88.

Turkle, S. (2011). *Alone together: Why we expect more from technology and less from each other.* New York, NY: Basic Books.

Weiser, E. B. (2001). The functions of internet use and their social and psychological consequences. *Cyberpsychology & Behavior*, 4(6), 723–743.

Yang, C. C. (2016). Instagram use, loneliness, and social comparison orientation: Interact and browse on social media, but don't compare. *Cyberpsychology, Behavior, and Social Networking*, 19(12), 703–708.

6

HOW DO ONLINE SOCIAL NETWORKS INFLUENCE PEOPLE'S EMOTIONAL LIVES?

Ethan Kross and Susannah Chandhok

The advent of online social networking sites like Facebook have rapidly altered the way human beings interact. With a gentle tap of one's finger, people can share their inner thoughts and feelings with untold numbers of people. A gentle swipe down on one's smartphone reveals a compilation of updates on other people's lives from an endlessly populated newsfeed.

These features of social media aren't restricted to an exclusive set of technophiles; they have been widely embraced by humanity. Indeed, at the time of our writing this chapter, close to 2.8 billion people use social media, a number that is predicted to keep rising (Statista, 2019). Moreover, the average user spends approximately 50 minutes per day on Facebook, Instagram, and Facebook Messenger (Stewart, 2016).

But what consequence—if any—does engaging with these online social networks have on how people feel? When we and our colleagues became curious about this issue in the late 2000s, we did what most researchers do when we become interested in a new topic: we performed a literature review. That's when we came across what we now call *The Puzzle*.

On the one hand, several studies revealed negative cross-sectional associations between self-reported Facebook usage and emotional well-being (Farahani, Kazemi, Aghamohamadi, Bakhtiarvand, & Ansari, 2011; Labrague, 2014; Pantic et al., 2012). But other studies revealed the opposite (Datu, Valdez, & Datu, 2012; Ellison, Steinfield, & Lampe, 2007; Nabi, Prestin, & So, 2013; Valenzuela, Park, & Kee, 2009). Still other work suggested that the relationships between Facebook usage and well-being was more nuanced; it depended on additional factors like individual differences in loneliness (Kim, LaRose, & Peng, 2009) or the number of Facebook friends people had (Manago, Taylor, & Greenfield, 2012). At the end of the literature review, we were left with more questions than answers.

In this chapter, we will review the work that we and others have performed to systematically address this puzzle over the past decade. We begin by providing a brief overview of research on online social network usage and well-being, highlighting the conceptual and methodological challenges that prevented early work from drawing strong inferences about the links between these variables. We will then describe a program of research designed to address these concerns by focusing on the mechanisms underlying how two different types of online social network usage—active versus passive usage—shape the emotional outcomes people experience inside and outside of the laboratory. In addressing these issues, we will focus our discussion predominantly on Facebook, the world's largest online social network, because it has been the focus of the majority of empirical attention. We conclude by discussing (a) how researchers can draw inferences about emotion from "big data" and (b) whether online social networks can be strategically harnessed to promote well-being.

Facebook Use & Well-being: Early Research

Does using Facebook influence people's well-being? Our review of early research that focused on this question revealed two issues that made it difficult to answer. First, nearly all of the studies that had been performed on this issue involved asking participants to self-report how much they used Facebook and how they felt in general. While there is clear value to using trait self-report measures to address certain kinds of questions, concerns about using them to measure people's moment-to-moment behaviors and emotions are well-established (for discussion see Kahneman & Deaton, 2010; Kahneman, Krueger, Schkade, Schwarz, & Stone, 2004). Second, the majority of the studies on this topic had utilized cross-sectional, correlational designs that made it impossible to draw inferences about the causal or likely causal relationship between Facebook use and well-being.

As a first step toward overcoming these limitations, we used experience sampling, a methodology that is widely considered the "gold standard" for assessing in vivo behavior and psychological experiences over time and drawing inferences about the *likely* causal sequence of events between variables (Bolger, Davis, & Rafaeli, 2003; Larson & Csikszentmihalyi, 2014). Specifically, over the course of several months, we text messaged 82 participants five times per day between 10 a.m. and midnight for 14 consecutive days, resulting in a data set consisting of 4,589 observations. Each time we texted participants, we asked them to rate how positive and negative they felt. We also asked them to rate how much they had used Facebook since the last time we texted them. We then examined whether the amount of time participants spent using Facebook systematically predicted changes in how they felt from the start of that period to its end.

Our results indicated that the more participants reported using Facebook during one chunk of time, for example, between 9 a.m. and 11 a.m., the more their positive mood declined over the course of that time period. We also found that the reverse pattern of results was not true—i.e., feeling bad at one moment in time did not predict increases in subsequent usage. It was likewise not moderated by any of the individual differences we assessed—e.g., number of Facebook friends, motivation for using Facebook, perceptions of their Facebook network, gender, self-esteem, loneliness, or depressive symptoms.

Importantly, each time we text messaged participants, we also asked them to rate how much they had interacted with other people directly—i.e., face-to-face or via phone—since the last time we text messaged them, to rule out the possibility that any results we observed might be attributed to general social interaction. In fact, our analyses indicated that interacting with other people directly predicted the exact opposite set of results—the more people reported interacting with other people directly during one time period, the more their positive mood rose from the beginning of that time period to its end (Kross et al., 2013).

The paper reporting these results triggered a number of commentaries (e.g., Bohannon, 2013; Konnikova, 2013). In the exchanges that followed, a key question arose: How does Facebook use undermine subjective well-being? To address this question, we turned our attention to the different ways that people interact with Facebook and how it might differentially influence the way they feel.

Prior research had distinguished between two broad categories of Facebook usage: passive and active usage (Burke, Marlow, & Lento, 2010; Deters & Mehl, 2013; Krasnova, Wenninger, Widjaja, & Buxmann, 2013). Passive usage refers to voyeuristically consuming information on a social media site—e.g., scrolling through one's news feed to peer in on the lives of others without generating information. Active usage, on the other hand, involves producing information on the site and engaging in direct exchanges with others—e.g., chatting, uploading posts and pictures. Going into the next phase of the work, we predicted that passively using Facebook in particular might account for its harmful emotional outcomes.

We based this prediction on the idea that social media allows people to curate the way they present themselves to others to a degree that is not possible in daily life. We human beings, of course, always curate how we present ourselves to others to varying degrees (Goffman, 1956, 1963, 1967. Indeed, across multiple seminal works in sociology, Goffman (1956, 1963, 1967) argued that human beings are driven to present themselves in flattering terms. For example, most people think strategically about what clothing they should wear based on who they are going to interact with later on that day. An important meeting may warrant dress attire, whereas a casual get-together with one's friends calls for more relaxed garb. But on social media, the ability to manage the way we present ourselves to others takes on a new form. It allows us to curate the way we appear to others to a degree that is not possible in daily life. We can add filters to our photos, carefully edit our posts, or even send them to friends for review before sharing. Indeed, one study found that a key reason people use Facebook is to serve self-presentational needs (Nadkarni & Hofmann, 2012).

But what might the emotional consequences of scrolling through a world populated by the most glamorized portraits of other people's lives be? Classic research on social comparisons (Festinger, 1954; Goethals, 1986; Wood, 1996) provides a clear answer to this question: When we are exposed to the unobtainable glorified lives of other people, we engage in upward social comparisons that promote envy and lead us to feel worse (Salovey & Rodin, 1984). As argued by Blanton, Burrows and Regan (this volume) in their chapter on health messages in video games, even exaggerated or "unreal" experience with technology can influence real-world behavior. Thus, even if people are aware that a social media profile is augmented beyond something obtainable in reality, such experiences can still have significant consequences on well-being.

We tested these assumptions over the course of two studies (Verduyn et al., 2015). In the first study, we brought participants into the laboratory and randomly assigned them to use Facebook actively or passively for ten minutes. We then assessed how people felt both immediately after the manipulation and at the end of the day (via an email survey).

Immediately after the active versus passive Facebook use manipulations, participants in the two groups did not differ on how they felt. But by the end of the day, participants in the passive Facebook usage group displayed a significant positive emotion decline compared to both their baseline levels of emotion and the levels of end of the day affect that characterized the active Facebook users. The active Facebook usage condition, in contrast, did not display any changes in how they felt over the course of the three assessments.

But were the emotional well-being declines experienced by the passive Facebook users driven by envy? And would these findings be replicated in a more ecologically valid context? We shifted back to experience sampling to address these questions. Specifically, we repeated the experience sampling protocol that we had used in our initial study (Kross et al., 2013), but this time asked people to rate how much they had used Facebook actively and passively since the last time we text messaged them. We also asked them to rate how envious they felt of others each time we texted them.

Our findings indicated that most of the time that people were using Facebook, they were using it passively. In fact, participants used Facebook passively 50 percent more than they did actively. In retrospect, this finding explained why we observed emotional well-being declines linked with overall Facebook usage in our first study (Kross et al. 2013)—i.e., most of the time people were on Facebook, they were likely using it the harmful way. Critically, longitudinal mediation analyses indicated that passive Facebook usage predicted emotional well-being declines, and it did so by promoting feelings of envy. Conceptually replicating the laboratory results, active Facebook usage once again had no impact on people's emotions.

Together, the results from these initial studies began to paint a portrait that described how using Facebook influenced people's emotional lives; an image suggesting that the majority of the times people use Facebook, they do so passively, which in turn leads people to feel envious and predicts declines in their positive mood over time.

Does Counting Emotion Words Provide a Window into Emotion?

An early challenge to these findings came in 2014 when a group of researchers published a controversial experiment in which they manipulated the percentage of positive and negative emotional words contained in 689,003 Facebook users' news feeds for one week (Kramer, Guillory, & Hancock, 2014).[1] The researchers leading the study were interested in examining emotional contagion on social media—i.e., the idea that emotions could spread across social networks just like diseases are transmitted between people who come into physical contact with each other. They predicted that consuming different amounts of positive (or negative) information on social media should lead people to experience more positive or negative emotions in their own lives. They furthermore suggested that they could index people's emotional states by counting the number of emotion words contained in their Facebook posts.

Kramer and colleagues (2014) tested their prediction by manipulating the amount of positive and negative words contained in participants' Facebook news feeds for one week. As predicted, they observed a statistically significant effect of their manipulation. Participants who were exposed to news feeds that contained more (or less) positive (or negative) words ended up using more (or less) positive (or negative) words in their own news feed. They interpreted these findings in support of their predictions noting, "these results indicate that emotions expressed by others on Facebook influence our own emotions, constituting experimental evidence for massive-scale contagion via social networks" (Kramer et al., 2014).

At first blush, these findings directly contradicted the findings that had accumulated up to that point (Kross et al., 2013; Turkle, 2011; Verduyn et al., 2015; Vogel, Rose, Okdie, Eckles, & Franz, 2015). The results of our studies suggested that consuming positive information in other people's news feeds instigates a social comparison process that leaves people feeling worse, not an emotional contagion process that enhances how good people feel.

However, there was an important difference when characterizing these two lines of work. In prior studies on Facebook and well-being, emotional well-being was indexed by asking participants directly how they felt. Concerns about self-report measures notwithstanding, asking people how they feel remains the standard tool for indexing subjective experiences (Kahneman et al., 2004;

Kahneman & Riis, 2005). In the aforementioned study, however, the authors assumed that counting the number of emotion words contained in participants' online social network posts would provide an equally valid tool for drawing inferences about people's emotional experience. But was this a reasonable assumption? Shortly following the publication of the Kramer study, we noted that there were three reasons to question it.

First, word counting methods fail to take context into account. Consider, for example, the following two statements: "I am feeling so great" and "I am not feeling great." A word-counting algorithm that counts the percentage of positive words contained in each of these statements would produce the same result—20 percent (one out of five words in each statement contains a positive emotion word)—even though the two statements convey opposite meaning.

Second, it is well documented that people tend to self-present on social media in ways that may not be accurate or authentic (Nadkarni & Hofmann, 2012; Walther, Van Der Heide, Ramirez, Burgoon, & Peña, 2015). For example, in response to learning that a colleague received a job promotion, a person might write, "That's great news," but not really feel happy for their colleague. They might also simply try to mimic the person they are interacting with to enhance rapport, a common technique in face-to-face interactions (Chartrand & Bargh, 1999; Chartrand & Jefferis, 2003). Thus, we suggested that it was also possible that a person might say something online that on the surface conveyed positive (or negative) emotion, but didn't correlate with how they actually felt.

Finally, compounding these conceptual concerns was the fact that no validation evidence existed to support the idea that counting emotion words on online social networks does in fact track how people feel. Some studies had looked at the correlation between online social network emotional word usage and judges' ratings of the emotionality of participants' posts. But if participants' posts don't honestly convey how they feel, then there's no reason to expect judges to be able to accurately categorize participants' posts (for additional validation concerns see Kross et al., 2018).

So, do people's usage of emotion words in their posts actually reflect how they feel? To address this question, we collapsed four experience sampling data sets that contained two types of information: (a) participants' self-reports of how they felt throughout the day and (b) their Facebook wall posts corresponding to the same time period that they rated their emotions (Kross et al., 2018). For each participant, we computed the percentage of positive and negative words contained in their posts and then examined whether they correlated with how participants reported feeling around the same time that they made each post. Regardless of how we analyzed the data, our results did not reveal any significant associations between participants' usage of emotion words in their Facebook posts and their self-reports of how they felt—a set of findings that cast doubt on researchers' ability to draw inferences about people's emotional states by counting the number of emotion words contained in their online social network posts (for conceptual replication, see Sun, Schwartz, Son, Kern, & Vazire, in press).

The Broader Landscape

Between 2004 and 2012, 412 studies on Facebook were published. Yet, not a single one of those papers examined the relationship between Facebook usage and changes in people's well-being over time. Since that time, the literature on this topic has grown substantially. In 2017, we reviewed this literature, focusing specifically on longitudinal and experimental studies that had examined the relationship between Facebook usage and well-being up to that point (Verduyn, Ybarra, Résibois, Jonides, & Kross, 2017). We concluded that passive Facebook usage robustly predicts emotional well-being declines whereas the relationship between active Facebook usage and well-being was more tenuous. While some relationships revealed positive links between active Facebook usage and well-being improvements, many studies did not.

Since our 2017 review, several additional large-scale studies have been performed which broadly align with these conclusions. For example, Tromholt (2016) randomly assigned over a thousand Danish participants to either use Facebook as usual, or stop using it altogether. Results indicated that Facebook abstention led to an increase in both cognitive and affective well-being (also see Mosquera, Odunowo, McNamara, Guo, & Petrie, 2018; and Allcott, Braghieri, Eichmeyer, & Gentzkow, 2019).

In 2018, researchers at the University of Pennsylvania adopted a slightly different approach to experimentally examine the effects of online social network usage on emotionality (Hunt, Marx, Lipson, & Young, 2018). Rather than use a deprivation paradigm that cut off participants' Facebook usage entirely, they randomly assigned 143 participants to either keep using social media as usual or to limit social media use to ten minutes per day for three weeks. Their results indicated that the limited social media use group showed significant reductions in loneliness and depression over the course of the study period. However, there were no significant effects on social support, self-esteem, or psychological well-being—a pattern of differential results that points to the need for future research to examine how the nature and length of Facebook interventions may systematically impact different variables (Hunt et al., 2018).

Finally, in one particularly persuasive study, Shakya and Christakis (2017) used Facebook log data in conjunction with three waves of nationally representative data to examine the longitudinal relationship between Facebook usage and changes in well-being over time in a sample of 5,208 participants. Their prospective findings indicated that Facebook use predicted decreases in well-being over time (Shakya & Christakis, 2017). Interestingly, the authors found that the more often participants engaged in active usage behaviors like updating one's status or liking another post, the more likely they were to have lower self-reported well-being—a finding that further speaks to the potentially nuanced nature of the relationship between active social media usage and well-being.

Frequently Asked Questions

Given the prevalence of social media, and the somewhat counterintuitive nature of the findings suggesting that a technology built to connect people frequently ends up undermining rather than elevating their positive mood, it is perhaps not surprising that people often have several questions about the aforementioned findings. Here we address two common questions that often arise.

FAQ #1: Why do people continue to use social media if doing so consistently leads them to feel worse? It is well established that people are motivated to approach pleasure and avoid pain (e.g., Freud, 1920; Higgins, 1997). Given this feature of the human condition, why do people continue to engage in a behavior that undermines their positive mood? Although a definitive answer to this question has yet to emerge, here we suggest three possibilities.

First, human behavior is multiply determined; there are several goals activated at any moment. In the context of social media, for example, we may be motivated to engage in a behavior that improves the way we feel. But we may also be motivated by social goals that motivate us to stay abreast of how our social networks are functioning. In this vein, one study found that 88 percent of people report using social media to maintain social relationships (Whiting & Williams, 2013). Thus, it is possible that people use social media despite its negative emotional effects because doing so allows people to stay informed of what is happening in their social networks.

Second, it is well established that people engage in behaviors that they are addicted to even when they reap negative consequences—a phenomenon that neuroscience research has illuminated by highlighting the fact that different brain systems are involved in *wanting* and *liking* (Robinson & Berridge, 2001). These findings are noteworthy in the current context because a growing amount of evidence suggests that social media has addictive properties (Alter, 2017; Andreassen, 2015; Ryan, Chester, Reece, & Xenos, 2014). Further research could examine the role of desire and motivated behavior in social media use (for more details about real-world applications of this cognitive theory, see Papies, this volume).

Finally, some research suggests that people mispredict how using Facebook will make them feel. For example, one study found that participants predicted they would feel better after using Facebook for 20 minutes. In fact, they felt worse after doing so (Sagioglou & Greitemeyer, 2014). This misprediction might be captured by an evolutionary mismatch between how our brains evolved to seek social connections, and the negative consequences they yield on social media (see van Vugt et al., this volume, for a discussion about the concept of evolutionary mismatches).

Taken together, these different findings begin to explain why people may continue to engage in a behavior that leads to emotional well-being declines. However, future research is needed to examine the role that each of these and other factors play in isolation and interactively in predicting types of social media usage.

FAQ #2: Are there ways of harnessing social media to improve well-being? There are many attempts underway to address this important question. One route that we have pursued to examine this issue involves focusing on people suffering from depression. A large literature stretching back to the 1980s indicates that people with depression are characterized by impoverished social support networks (Fiore, Becker, & Coppel, 1983; Rook, 1984). One of the explanations that research has provided for why individuals with depression are characterized by low social support is because they talk frequently about their negative feelings (Blumberg & Hokanson, 1983; Kuiper & McCabe, 1985) in ways that end up pushing away those that care about them (Teichman & Teichman, 1990). In other words, there may be poor interpersonal synchrony between individuals with depression and others (for more details about interpersonal synchrony, please see Koole et al., this volume).

Park and colleagues (2016) were interested in whether these findings would generalize to social media. Given the psychological distance that social media provides people with, they wondered whether the social networks of depressed individuals might be more responsive in the online versus offline world. They addressed this question across two studies (Park et al., 2016).

In Study 1, they focused on an unselected sample of participants with varying levels of depressive symptoms; in Study 2 they recruited psychiatrically diagnosed individuals with Major Depressive Disorder and their age-matched control participants. Across both studies, the experimenters had judges code how supportive the posts of participants' Facebook friends were in response to any negative experiences described by participants on their Facebook accounts over the course of a month. They then compared the amount of support that depressed versus non-depressed participants received, controlling for the number of negative expressions that participants made during the month-long period. As expected, participants with depression self-disclosed negative information more and positive information less to their Facebook networks. However, in direct contrast to prior research examining the links between offline social support and depression, participants with depression received *more* social support from their Facebook friends.

These findings illustrate how social media may provide a platform for providing social support to individuals that may otherwise have difficulty acquiring it, highlighting the need for future research to extend these findings to other vulnerable populations. In particular, one application of social psychology to this line of research would be in testing which aspects of a social media platform could be manipulated to provide better social support for its members.

Concluding Comment

> The Internet does not, contrary to current popular opinion, have by itself the power or ability to control people, to turn them into addicted zombies, or make them dispositionally sad or lonely … the Internet is one of several social domains in which an individual can live his or her life, and attempt to fulfill his or her needs and goals, whatever they happen to be.
>
> *McKenna & Bargh, 2000*

At the turn of the millennium, McKenna and Bargh concluded that the overall sentiment toward the internet was negative, if not "apocalyptic" (McKenna & Bargh, 2000). Over the course of the next few years, they documented the beneficial aspects of internet use, highlighting how it can foster social relationships and provide people with meaningful routes to express themselves authentically (Bargh, McKenna, & Fitzsimons, 2002; Bargh & McKenna, 2004).

Their work was notably published before the birth of Facebook in 2004. Since that time, the tide of research has drawn away from focusing on internet use to examining the links between social media and well-being instead. Yet, we see a similar pattern emerging. Some have voiced a concern that digital technology is destroying society (Twenge, 2017). Other have suggested that social networking addiction should be a clinically diagnosable disorder and have developed a Facebook Addiction Scale (Andreassen et al., 2012; Karaiskos et al., 2010; Ryan et al., 2014; also see Alter, 2017).

The goal of this chapter is not to paint a picture one way or the other about social media being good or bad. The social media world is multifaceted. Much like the offline terrestrial world, social media allows people to experience an infinite number of healthy and harmful emotional experiences. A critical challenge for future research is to illuminate the mechanisms that systematically predict these different kinds of emotional experiences. Doing so has the potential to enrich our understanding of how a ubiquitous technology can be harnessed to promote rather than undermine well-being.

Note

1 The controversy was a function of the fact that Facebook users were unaware that they were participating in this experiment (Kosinski, Matz, Gosling, Popov, & Stillwell, 2015; Puschmann & Bozdag, 2014; Shaw, 2016).

References

Allcott, H., Braghieri, L., Eichmeyer, S., & Gentzkow, M. (2019). *The welfare effects of social media*. 116.

Alter, A. (2017). *Irresistible: The rise of addictive technology and the business of keeping us hooked*. New York, NY: Penguin Press.

Andreassen, C. S. (2015). Online social network site addiction: A comprehensive review. *Current Addiction Reports*, *2*(2), 175–184. doi.org/10.1007/s40429-015-0056-9

Andreassen, C. S., Torsheim, T., Brunborg, G. S., & Pallesen, S. (2012). Development of a Facebook addiction scale. *Psychological Reports*, *110*(2), 501–517.

Bargh, J. A., & McKenna, K. Y. (2004). The Internet and social life. *Annual Review of Psychology*, *55*, 573–590.

Bargh, J. A., McKenna, K. Y., & Fitzsimons, G. M. (2002). Can you see the real me? Activation and expression of the "true self" on the Internet. *Journal of Social Issues*, *58*(1), 33–48.

Blumberg, S. R., & Hokanson, J. E. (1983). The effects of another person's response style on interpersonal behavior in depression. *Journal of Abnormal Psychology*, *92*(2), 196–209. doi.org/10.1037/0021-843X.92.2.196

Bohannon, J. (2013, August 14). ScienceShot: Facebook is making you sad. *Science Magazine*. Retrieved from www.sciencemag.org/news/2013/08/scienceshot-facebook-making-you-sad.

Bolger, N., Davis, A., & Rafaeli, E. (2003). Diary methods: Capturing life as it is lived. *Annual Review of Psychology*, *54*(1), 579–616. doi.org/10.1146/annurev.psych.54.101601.145030

Burke, M., Marlow, C., & Lento, T. (2010, April). Social network activity and social well-being. In *Proceedings of the SIGCHI conference on human factors in computing systems* (pp. 1909–1912). ACM.

Chartrand, T. L., & Bargh, J. A. (1999). The chameleon effect: The perception-behavior link and social interaction. *Journal of Personality & Social Psychology*, *76*(6), 893–9101.

Chartrand, T. L., & Jefferis, V. E. (2003). Consequences of automatic goal pursuit and the case of nonconscious mimicry. In J. P. Forgas & K. D. Williams (Eds.), *Social judgments: Implicit and explicit processes* (pp. 290–305). New York: Cambridge University Press.

Datu, J. A. D., Valdez, J. P., & Datu, N. (2012). Does Facebooking make us sad? Hunting relationship between Facebook use and depression among Filipino adolescents. *International Journal of Research Studies in Educational Technology*, *1*(2). doi.org/10.5861/ijrset.2012.202

Deters, F. große, & Mehl, M. R. (2013). Does posting Facebook status updates increase or decrease loneliness? An online social networking experiment. *Social Psychological and Personality Science*, *4*(5), 579–586. doi.org/10.1177/1948550612469233

Ellison, N. B., Steinfield, C., & Lampe, C. (2007). The benefits of Facebook "friends:" Social capital and college students' use of online social network sites. *Journal of Computer-Mediated Communication*, *12*(4), 1143–1168. doi.org/10.1111/j.1083-6101.2007.00367.x

Farahani, H. A., Kazemi, Z., Aghamohamadi, S., Bakhtiarvand, F., & Ansari, M. (2011). Examining mental health indices in students using Facebook in Iran. *Procedia – Social and Behavioral Sciences*, *28*, 811–814. doi.org/10.1016/j.sbspro.2011.11.148

Festinger, L. (1954). A theory of social comparison processes. *Human Relations*, 7(2), 117–140. doi.org/10.1177/001872675400700202

Fiore, J., Becker, J., & Coppel, D. B. (1983). Social network interactions: A buffer or a stress. *American Journal of Community Psychology; New York, 11*(4), 423–439.

Freud, S. (1920). Beyond the pleasure principle. In J. Strachey, A. Freud, A. Strachey, & A. Tyson (Trans.), *Beyond the pleasure principle, group psychology and other works (1925-1926)* (pp. 1–64).

Goethals, G. R. (1986). Social comparison theory: Psychology from the lost and found. *Personality and Social Psychology Bulletin, 12*, 261–278. doi.org/10.1177/0146167286123001

Goffman, E. (1956). *The presentation of self in everyday life*. New York, NY: Anchor Books.

Goffman, E. (1963). *Behavior in public places*. New York: Free Press.

Goffman, E. (1967). *Interaction ritual*. New York: Pantheon.

Higgins, E. T. (1997). Beyond pleasure and pain. *American Psychologist, 52*(12), 1280–1300. doi.org/10.1037/0003-066X.52.12.1280

Hunt, M. G., Marx, R., Lipson, C., & Young, J. (2018). No more FOMO: Limiting social media decreases loneliness and depression. *Journal of Social and Clinical Psychology, 37*(10), 751–768. doi.org/10.1521/jscp.2018.37.10.751

Karaiskos, D., Tzavellas, E., Balta, G., & Paparrigopoulos, T. (2010). Social network addiction: A new clinical disorder? *European Psychiatry, 25*, 855.

Kahneman, D., & Deaton, A. (2010). High income improves evaluation of life but not emotional well-being. *Proceedings of the National Academy of Sciences, 107*(38), 16489–16493. doi.org/10.1073/pnas.1011492107

Kahneman, D., & Krueger, A. B., Schkade, D. A., Schwarz, N., & Stone, A. A. (2004). A survey method for characterizing daily life experience: The day reconstruction method. *Science, 306*(5702), 1776–1780. doi.org/10.1126/science.1103572

Kahneman, D., & Riis, J. (2005). Living, and thinking about it: Two perspectives on life. In F. A. Huppert, N. Baylis, & B. Keverne (Eds.), *The science of well-being* (pp. 284–305). doi.org/10.1093/acprof:oso/9780198567523.003.0011

Kim J., LaRose R., Peng, W. (2009). Loneliness as the cause and the effect of problematic Internet use: The relationship between Internet use and psychological well-being. *Cyberpsychology & Behavior: The Impact of the Internet, Multimedia and Virtual Reality on Behavior and Society,* 12, 451–455.

Konnikova, M. (2013, September 10). How Facebook makes us unhappy. *The New Yorker*. Retrieved from www.newyorker.com/tech/annals-of-technology/how-facebook-makes-us-unhappy

Kosinski, M., Matz, S. C., Gosling, S. D., Popov, V., & Stillwell, D. (2015). Facebook as a research tool for the social sciences: Opportunities, challenges, ethical considerations, and practical guidelines. *American Psychologist, 70*(6), 543–556. doi.org/10.1037/a0039210

Kramer, A. D. I., Guillory, J. E., & Hancock, J. T. (2014). Experimental evidence of massive-scale emotional contagion through social networks. *Proceedings of the National Academy of Sciences, 111*(24), 8788–8790. doi.org/10.1073/pnas.1320040111

Krasnova, H., Wenninger, H., Widjaja, T., & Buxmann, P. (2013). *Envy on Facebook: A hidden threat to users' life satisfaction?* 11th International Conference on Wirtchaftsinformatik (WI).

Kross, E., Verduyn, P., Boyer, M., Drake, B., Gainsburg, I., Vickers, B., … Jonides, J. (2018). Does counting emotion words on online social networks provide a window into people's subjective experience of emotion? A case study on Facebook. *Emotion, 19*, 97–107. doi.org/10.1037/emo0000416

Kross, E., Verduyn, P., Demiralp, E., Park, J., Lee, D. S., Lin, N., ... Ybarra, O. (2013). Facebook use predicts declines in subjective well-being in young adults. *PLoS One, 8*(8), e69841. doi.org/10.1371/journal.pone.0069841

Kuiper, N. A., & McCabe, S. B. (1985). The appropriateness of social topics: Effects of depression and cognitive vulnerability on self and other judgments. *Cognitive Therapy and Research, 9*(4), 371–379. doi.org/10.1007/BF01173087

Labrague, L. J. (2014). Facebook use and adolescents' emotional states of depression, anxiety, and stress. *Health Science Journal, 8*(1), 80–89.

Larson, R., & Csikszentmihalyi, M. (2014). The experience sampling method. In M. Csikszentmihalyi, *Flow and the foundations of positive psychology* (pp. 21–34). doi.org/10.1007/978-94-017-9088-8_2

Manago, A. M., Taylor, T., & Greenfield, P. M. (2012). Me and my 400 friends: The anatomy of college students' Facebook networks, their communication patterns, and well-being. *Developmental Psychology, 48*(2), 369–380.

McKenna, K. Y., & Bargh, J. A. (2000). Plan 9 from cyberspace: The implications of the Internet for personality and social psychology. *Personality and Social Psychology Review, 4*(1), 57–75.

Mosquera, R., Odunowo, M., McNamara, T., Guo, X., & Petrie, R. (2018). The economic effects of Facebook. *SSRN Electronic Journal*. doi.org/10.2139/ssrn.3312462

Nabi, R. L., Prestin, A., & So, J. (2013). Facebook friends with (health) benefits? Exploring social network site use and perceptions of social support, stress, and well-being. *Cyberpsychology, Behavior, and Social Networking, 16*(10), 721–727. doi.org/10.1089/cyber.2012.0521

Nadkarni, A., & Hofmann, S. G. (2012). Why do people use Facebook? *Personality and Individual Differences, 52*(3), 243–249. doi.org/10.1016/j.paid.2011.11.007

Pantic, I., Damjanovic, A., Todorovic, J., Topalovic, D., Bojovic-Jovic, D., Ristic, S., & Pantic, S. (2012). Association between online social networking and depression in high school students: Behavioral physiology viewpoint. *Psychiatria Danubina, 24*(1), 90–93.

Park, J., Lee, D. S., Shablack, H., Verduyn, P., Deldin, P., Ybarra, O., ... Kross, E. (2016). When perceptions defy reality: The relationships between depression and actual and perceived Facebook social support. *Journal of Affective Disorders, 200*, 37–44. doi.org/10.1016/j.jad.2016.01.048

Puschmann, C., & Bozdag, E. (2014). Staking out the unclear ethical terrain of online social experiments. *Internet Policy Review*. Retrieved from https://policyreview.info/articles/analysis/staking-out-unclear-ethical-terrain-online-social-experiments

Robinson, T. E., & Berridge, K. C. (2001). Incentive-sensitization and addiction. *Addiction, 96*(1), 103–114. doi.org/10.1046/j.1360-0443.2001.9611038.x

Rook, K. S. (1984). The negative side of social interaction: Impact on psychological well-being. *Journal of Personality and Social Psychology, 46*(5), 1097–1108. doi.org/10.1037/0022-3514.46.5.1097

Ryan, T., Chester, A., Reece, J., & Xenos, S. (2014). The uses and abuses of Facebook: A review of Facebook addiction. *Journal of Behavioral Addictions, 3*(3), 133–148. doi.org/10.1556/JBA.3.2014.016

Sagioglou, C., & Greitemeyer, T. (2014). Facebook's emotional consequences: Why Facebook causes a decrease in mood and why people still use it. *Computers in Human Behavior, 35*, 359–363. doi.org/10.1016/j.chb.2014.03.003

Salovey, P., & Rodin, J. (1984). Some antecedents and consequences of social-comparison jealousy. *Journal of Personality and Social Psychology, 47*(4), 780–792. doi.org/10.1037/0022-3514.47.4.780

Shakya, H. B., & Christakis, N. A. (2017). Association of Facebook use with compromised well-being: A longitudinal study. *American Journal of Epidemiology*. doi.org/10.1093/aje/kww189

Shaw, D. (2016). Facebook's flawed emotion experiment: Antisocial research on social network users. *Research Ethics*, *12*(1), 29–34. doi.org/10.1177/1747016115579535

Statista. (2019). Number of social media users worldwide from 2010 to 2021 (in billions). Retrieved May 6, 2019 from www.statista.com/statistics/278414/number-of-worldwide-social-network-users/

Stewart, J. B. (2016). Facebook has 50 minutes of your time each day. It wants more. *The New York Times*. Retrieved from http://www.nytimes.com/2016/05/06/business/facebook-bends-the-rules-ofaudience-engagement-to-its-advantage.html. Retrieved October 12, 2016.

Sun, J., Schwartz, H. A., Son, Y., Kern, M. L., & Vazire, S. (in press). The language of well-being: Tracking fluctuations in emotion experience through everyday speech. *Journal of Personality and Social Psychology*.

Teichman, Y., & Teichman, M. (1990). Interpersonal view of depression: Review and integration. *Journal of Family Psychology*, *3*(4), 349–367. doi.org/10.1037/h0080549

Tromholt, M. (2016). The Facebook experiment: Quitting Facebook leads to higher levels of well-being. *Cyberpsychology, Behavior, and Social Networking*, *19*(11), 661-666.

Turkle, S. (2011). *Alone together: Why we expect more from technology and less from each other*. New York, NY: Basic Books.

Twenge, J. M. (2017, September). Have smartphones destroyed a generation? *The Atlantic*. Retrieved from www.theatlantic.com/magazine/archive/2017/09/ has-the-smartphone-destroyed-a-generation/534198/

Valenzuela, S., Park, N., & Kee, K. F. (2009). Is there social capital in a social network site? Facebook use and college students' life satisfaction, trust, and participation. *Journal of Computer-Mediated Communication*, *14*(4), 875–901. doi.org/10.1111/j.1083-6101.2009.01474.x

Verduyn, P., Lee, D. S., Park, J., Shablack, H., Orvell, A., Bayer, J., … Kross, E. (2015). Passive Facebook usage undermines affective well-being: Experimental and longitudinal evidence. *Journal of Experimental Psychology: General*, *144*(2), 480–488. doi.org/10.1037/xge0000057

Verduyn, P., Ybarra, O., Résibois, M., Jonides, J., & Kross, E. (2017). Do social network sites enhance or undermine subjective well-being? A critical review. *Social Issues and Policy Review*, *11*(1), 274–302. doi.org/10.1111/sipr.12033

Vogel, E. A., Rose, J. P., Okdie, B. M., Eckles, K., & Franz, B. (2015). Who compares and despairs? The effect of social comparison orientation on social media use and its outcomes. *Personality and Individual Differences*, *86*, 249–256. doi.org/10.1016/j.paid.2015.06.026

Walther, J. B., Van Der Heide, B., Ramirez, A., Burgoon, J. K., & Peña, J. (2015). Interpersonal and hyperpersonal dimensions of computer-mediated communication. In S. S. Sundar (Ed.), *The handbook of the psychology of communication technology* (pp. 1–22). doi.org/10.1002/9781118426456.ch1

Whiting, A., & Williams, D. (2013). Why people use social media: A uses and gratifications approach. *Qualitative Market Research: An International Journal*, *16*(4), 362–369. doi.org/10.1108/QMR-06-2013-0041

Wood, J. V. (1996). What is social comparison and how should we study it? *Personality and Social Psychology Bulletin*, 22, 520–537. doi.org/10.1177/0146167296225009

7 Online relationship formation

Ilan Talmud and Gustavo Mesch

Introduction

As stated in Chapter 3, online sociability is an integral part of young people's digital literacy and cultural consumption of technological artefacts. The ability of the Internet to facilitate online contact, especially with geographically remote people, has caught the popular imagination and the empirical attention of researchers studying online relationship formation. The main consequence of adolescents' online engagement is the expansion of their social ties. However, this expansion is random. It is confined by social regularities governing the ways in which humans interact, online or offline, thus making the formation patterns of online social ties predictable by social analysts.

Studies on the use of ICT by youth apprise us of the active role that youth play in online activity, and that the parents' and the adolescents' views regarding ICT do not always converge. Parents indicate that the computer is bought and connected to the Internet, reflecting their willingness to provide a tool to improve their children's academic performance, to provide access to information needed for school work, to adapt to the school requirement of typed assignments, and to link the teens to the information society. By contrast, teens experience the Internet as a tool for social purpose and play (Lenhart et al., 2001; Livingstone and Bober, 2004; Cohen, Lamish, and Schejter, 2008). Boase and Wellman (2006) argue that in contrast to the popular image of the Internet as a trigger and facilitator of new relationships, "only a relatively small proportion of internet users have ever met someone new online."

Adolescents play an active role in their communicative conduct. Consequently, their primary uses of the Internet do not always match their parents' expectations and wishes. Adolescents are most likely to use the Internet to communicate with others for social and gaming purposes, and in some cases to reach out and communicate with others not of their proximate or immediate social circle at school or in their neighborhood. Moreover, adolescents learn to utilize computer-mediated communication as an additional form of social environment, developing digital literacy, and making new contacts over the Internet. Online relationships nowadays appear to be an integral part of youth culture (Helsper, 2008a). The technological features of ICT smooth barriers of communication, yet they cannot completely remove the effects of social constraints on social interaction. The odds of forming new relations are higher among those socially similar, geographically close, and having at least one friend in common ("transitive relations") (Kadushin, 2004). Forming online relationships might be one of the most appealing aspects of Internet use to young people, given that forming relationships is an important developmental task of adolescence, and in this task youth are limited in their choices by geographical constraints.

Understanding the process involves studying motivations impelling youth to form relationships online, their choice of communication channels and content, the effect of online ties on young people's existing ties and social life, and the quality of online associations. In this chapter, we tackle these topics.

The notion of online relationship formation requires conceptual clarification. Most research has not clearly defined what is meant by online ties. It was largely conducted to elucidate the effects of channel characteristics on interpersonal communication, emphasizing the lack of social presence, lack of richness, and lack of clues in Internet communication (Sproul and Kissler, 1986), and it sought the conditions under which this communication is non-personal or becomes hyper-personal (Walther, 1996). Another direction has been research to understand channel choice across distances and to inquire whether one online communication supplements or replaces the use of other channels of communication among kin and friends. These studies show that Internet use is associated with more and not less communication, and that the more individuals contact by phone and face-to-face, the more they contact using email (Chen et al., 2002); it is suggested that connectivity increases local and long-distance communication (Hampton and Wellman, 2002). Most of this research reflects the conduct of online communication but makes no major attempt to define the nature of the online relationship. Lack of conceptual clarity may lead to contradictory findings.

Prior to the information age, adolescents' social choices were severely restricted by time and place. Their lack of geographical mobility and their belonging to an age group expected to go to school structurally reduced their social circle to friends who were in the neighborhood, at school, and at extracurricular activities. Proximity was a central social constraint for relationship formation. Living in the same neighborhood and attending the same school entailed a high level of social similarity.

Internet and mobile access and communication have produced a number of changes in social communication patterns. Relationship formation has been expanded from geographical spaces of interaction (the neighborhood, the school) to digital spaces (social networks applications). Friendships that in the past were based on social groups with clear boundaries and social expectations of mutual interaction changed to personalized peer-diverse and dispersed personalized peer networks that lack clear boundaries and norms of social behavior. Channels of interpersonal communication are multiplex, including in addition to face-to-face and phone, mobile applications and diverse platforms of social media.

As a result, the limits of interpersonal communication have been blurred and include:

- perpetual contact with the social network anywhere and anytime;
- communication is personalized, relying on ego-networks rather than social groups;
- contents are not exclusive and can be forwarded without the owner's knowledge;
- activities are coordinated through social media.

These major changes in the patterns, frequency, content, and quality in interpersonal friendship formation, maintenance, and communication have been noted by a large number of studies that focus on different aspects of this major social change. In this chapter we focus on one important aspect, namely, the similarities, differences, and overlaps between online and offline social relationships.

With the growing popularity and ubiquity of social media, the public and, to some extent, also research were concerned with the increasing growth of online relationships and the concern that these are replacing more high quality offline relationships. Studies conducted in the early 1990s found that adolescents in western countries were reporting that they meet individuals and maintained interpersonal communication with others whom they had met online at the same time as they met with friends face-to-face. Online/offline relationships were at that time defined according to the space of interaction that the respondents indicated was where they meet their friends. Online relationships were the ones that were formed in forums, chat rooms, gaming, and messenger. Offline relationships were usually defined as the ones that were initiated in the neighborhood, school, or any other face-to-face space of social interaction.

It is important to recognize that a comparison between the two kinds of relationships designated as online and offline may imply either that they are mutually exclusive or opposed to each other. Yet over time is clear that interpersonal relationships are created, developed, and sustained through integrated online and offline interaction. The entire range of offline relationships, from family through school and work to social relations in the wider neighborhood, may also be present online in a manner that is rarely separated out from one's offline life. The popular perception of online relationships as relationships that can be contrasted with a "real world"—inhabited by one's real or more authentic offline relationships—seems therefore simplistic and misleading. This corresponds to an earlier critique of the concept of the "virtual," a term prominent during the early years of Internet use. In short, our study treats social media in much the same way that everyone treats the landline telephone, never described today as a separate "online/on-phone" facet of life. It is, however, essential for us as researchers to recognize that whatever misgivings we may feel as academics about this dualistic terminology, it remains a primary mode by which people around the world understand and experience digital media.

Because of this perception that online life can be contrasted to offline life, we start this chapter with a summary of the perspectives that explain online relationships formation.

"The rich get richer hypothesis" proposes that individuals with higher extroversion, who are more more comfortable in social situations or have already social resources would be more likely to use social media for online relationship formation, extending their social networks and enhancing the quality of their friendships (Kraut et al., 2002). According to this hypothesis, individuals who are extroverted and already have strong social skills would do better in sharing their views and asking for help online, thereby attaining additional social support and higher life satisfaction through cyberspace (Khan et al., 2016).

Conversely, "the poor get poorer hypothesis" argues that individuals who are introverted have higher levels of social anxiety, and have poorer social skills and confidence would be more likely to use the Internet to escape from and avoid problems in real life, and this could lead to negative outcomes.

Studies present some interesting evidence on the association of personality characteristics and online relationship formation. The first HomeNet study was a longitudinal investigation of 93 non-representative families in the Pittsburgh area. They were provided with computers and an Internet connection free of charge for three years. The study found extroversion was negatively related to frequency of Internet use; introverts were more likely to be frequent Internet users (Kraut et al., 1998). Internet effects proved to differ according to personality characteristics, in particular, extroversion/introversion. The authors found support for "the rich get richer hypothesis": extroverts reported more Internet use and creating more online relationships. Introverts who used the Internet extensively reported less social involvement. In sum, Internet use was associated with better outcomes for extroverts and worse outcomes for introverts. In particular, extroverts who used the Internet more reported increased well-being, including low levels of loneliness. In contrast, introverts who were heavy Internet users showed a decline in their well-being (Kraut et al., 2002). The HomeNet study was based on the dystopian assumption (see Preface) that the Internet exerts negative effects on the individual's well-being, partly because of another assumption that time invested in the Internet is non-social time, diverted from other sources of sociability.

Others who subscribe to these perspectives have investigated the link between personal attributes and online activities, such as sensation-seeking and Internet dependence (Lin and Tsai, 2002). The social needs outlook has found much corroboration in social psychology. A study in Holland with a sample of 687 adolescents investigated personality characteristics and the perception of online communication. Socially anxious and lonely adolescents were found to value online communication more strongly. Youngsters with these personality characteristics perceived the Internet as providing them with more opportunities to reflect and control the messages they sent, and they perceived online communication as deeper and more reciprocal than face-to-face communication (Peter and Valkenburg, 2006). Similarly, in Germany, Wolfradt and Doll (2001) investigated the relation between extroversion/introversion and three Internet uses (information, entertainment, and interpersonal communication) among 122 adolescent Internet users. The social needs hypothesis was mainly supported by specific personality traits, such as neuroticism, which was proved to be positively associated with the entertainment motive and with the interpersonal communication motive; extroversion was positively associated with the communication motive only. Wolfradt and Doll (2001) argued accordingly that personality traits predict corresponding types of Internet activities. All in all, existing knowledge indicates that personality characteristics are influential in the use and choice of this medium for relationship formation. Online communication is an important means for socially anxious, introverted, and lonely adolescents to overcome their inhibitions in face-to-face settings. The Internet not only offers such young people a new venue to fulfill the need for association and involvement in a social circle, it also compensates for their lack of social skills and ultimately may help them to gain self-confidence, to be enjoyed later in face-to-face interactions.

The association between online communication and relational closeness is particularly interesting. Using a large sample of Dutch youth aged 12–17 years, Valkenburg and Peter (2007a) investigated whether online communication stimulated or reduced closeness to friends, and whether intimate disclosure of personal information online affected their closeness to online ties. These authors found that only 30 percent of the adolescents perceived online communication as effective in disclosing personal information. Furthermore, online communication with others whom they met online proved to have a negative effect on the perceived closeness to friends (Valkenburg and Peter, 2007a).

The social compensation hypothesis

On the contrary, the social compensation hypothesis proposes that individuals with higher levels of social anxiety or lower levels of social support, use social media to create online relationships to compensate for their lack of social ties, as social anxiety is a barrier for the creation of offline relationships (Van Ingen and Wright, 2016). According to this hypothesis, the relative anonymity of social media and the process of self-disclosure online provide individuals with a more comfortable social situation due to a perceived lower risk for self-disclosure because of the lack of nonverbal cues (Schouten et al., 2007). Furthermore, the Internet may provide more opportunities for some people to gain social support, explore their self-identities and social identities, and improve their social skills, as well as a greater opportunity to use online coping resources (Van Ingen and Wright, 2016). Additionally, Ellison et al. (2007) proposed that online activities were beneficial for individuals to form weak ties in social networking, which would be very useful for those with lower self-esteem to improve their social capital but would be harmful for those with higher self-esteem since it would reduce their opportunities to maintain their strong offline ties. In other words, "the poor get richer" and "the rich get poorer."

Social diversification

As discussed, most of the previous perspectives focus on personality characteristics as motivations for online relationship formation. The social diversification perspective relies on social network and social capital assumptions to explain variations in these motivation for disadvantaged groups in society.

The social diversification hypothesis deals specifically with differences in the use of communication and information technologies among racial and ethnic minorities (Mesch and Talmud, 2010; Gonzales, McCrory, Calarco, and Lynch, 2018). Relying on the literature demonstrating the stratification of multicultural societies along ethnic and social class lines, the social diversification hypothesis argues that network-based social closure affects the ability to obtain social capital and is more likely to benefit the dominant group's members (Mesch et al., 2012). According to this perspective, social media platforms might support the expansion of social relationships, including improving access to information, knowledge, and skills that are unavailable locally, and provide opportunities for the diversification of social relationships (Mesch and Talmud, 2010). As Mazur and Kozarian (2010) found in their study of older adolescents, despite the partial overlap of online and offline ties, online communication tends to diversify the structure of peer networks and expose youngsters to others who share their interests, regardless of their age, gender, or location. In that sense, the social diversification hypothesis argues that social media provides a platform for overcoming the existing segregation in society. Therefore, this perspective maintains that disadvantaged groups will have greater incentives to use Facebook to expand their social circle and overcome existing physical and social barriers to information and association. At the same time, majority groups will use the Internet to keep their existing relationships and maintain the closure of the network. In addition, they will be less likely than disadvantaged minorities to use Facebook to expand their social ties.

The social diversification perspective emphasizes the potential of social media platforms for empowering disadvantaged groups through affiliation with weak ties (Mazur and Kozarian, 2010). Indeed, a study of the online practices of young adolescents in a large rural area in California, planning for their vocational future, determined that the youngsters relied on computer-mediated communication and the establishment of contacts with weak ties to access information unavailable to them locally (Robinson, 2011). Similarly, the use of social media has been associated with the diversification of core networks of discussion (Hampton, Sessions, and Her, 2011). A study of a large sample of college students established that access to the Internet was still higher among White students than among Latinos and African Americans. However, when it comes to the use of social media platforms for content creation (blogs, video clips), a social capital-enhancing activity, Blacks and Hispanics reported a higher average of online content creation than Whites, even after controlling for socio-economic status, gender, and age, as well as Internet experience and psychological predictors (Correa and Jeong, 2011).

For young adolescents, SNSs may provide an opportunity to expand the size and composition of their social networks. Indeed, a study of

Internet use in a representative sample of Greek and Turkish youth in Cyprus suggests the existence of a reverse digital divide, as the more disadvantaged community engaged more often in Internet use for self-expression and association with weak ties (Milioni, Doudaki, and Demertzis, 2014). Mesch (2018a) conducted a test of this hypothesis and investigated the role of race and ethnicity in the self-reported strength of the social ties of young adolescents on Facebook. Based on the social diversification hypothesis, which argues that in multicultural societies, race and ethnicity are key factors that shape the nature of associations, we investigated whether there are ethnic and racial differences in the size and strength of the ties of adolescent Facebook users and the role of the strength of these ties in several positive outcomes. Using data from the US Teens' Social Media and Privacy Survey conducted by the Pew Research Center's Internet and American Life Project among 802 teens aged 12–17, we found no differences in the total number of ties that adolescents from different ethnic and racial groups reported. However, African Americans reported a significantly higher number of online weak ties, while White Americans had a significantly higher number of online strong ties. The results are consistent with the social diversification hypothesis.

Online ties and the structure of youth social networks

A prominent theme in the public discourse regarding social networks, reflected in the tone of many scholastic studies, is the claim that creating online social ties reduces the number of offline friends. Studies have warned that excessive Internet use may isolate adolescents from their friends. Available data indicate that the size of a social network is not affected by online relationship formation. A temporary decrease may be expected as more energy and time are invested in the creation of online ties; but over time, as online associations become integrated, the size of the network even slightly increases as new associations are added and old ones kept (Valkenburg and Peter, 2007b). In that sense, the effect of online relationship formation seems not to differ from the effect of cell phones. Igarashi, Takai, and Yoshida (2005), analyzing text messages over cell phones in Japan, found general support for the claim that mobile phones can change social networks among young people by increasing the number of possible contacts and promoting selective relationship formation. Mobile phones increase the frequency of communication, and allow opportunities for expanding interpersonal relationships.

The effect of expansion of social networks seem more pronounced on extroverts than on introverts, and varies according to attachment style, but overall, online relationship formation enlarges the social network for the majority of adolescents who choose to become involved in this activity (Mesch and Talmud, 2010).

Associating with similar people is another social network dimension influenced by online relationship formation. One of the most significant and consistent findings reported in the literature is that social relationships are characterized by social similarity, or homophily. Studies on the formation of close social relationships have emphasized the importance of social similarity in friendship and attraction in intimate social relationships. Similarity molds network ties, resulting in relatively homogeneous social networks in terms of socio-demographic, behavioral, and interpersonal characteristics. This tendency of individuals to associate with others who are similar to them has important social consequences. For example, similar individuals exchange information that suits their personal characteristics, preferences, and social style. Contacting similar individuals, however, limits personal social horizons, thus restricting the exposure to different others, thereby reproducing social stereotypes.

Studies found that adolescents who created online social ties also reported a higher heterogeneity of their social network by age, gender, and location. In an early study, Mesch and Talmud compared youngsters with online friends and with face-to-face friends for the respective average age difference between those friends and themselves (Mesch and Talmud, 2010). The former reported that their online friends were on average older than themselves; the latter did not report this. The difference was small, online friends being on average one year and a half older. Accordingly, to a certain extent, online friendship formation breaks through the barriers of age-grade segregation which is imposed by the social structure of schools.

An important dimension to consider is the perceived closeness of youth to their online ties, and its possible effect on their perceived closeness to their face-to-face ties. Online relationship formation is a dynamic process, and accordingly calls for longitudinal studies. The perception of being less close to online friends seems to depend on the developmental stage of the relationship. Online ties are relatively newer than face-to-face ties, and are based on narrower shared interests. Furthermore, it takes time to develop relationships. Hence, more investigation is required to examine the process of changing the perceived online ties' strength. Still, there is no evidence that youth are exchanging close offline friendships for distant and narrower ones. Online ties, then, do not seem to replace but to supplement face-to-face connections.

Studies comparing the percentage of friends of the opposite sex, as reported by youth with and without online friends, found less sex segregation for the former than for the latter (Mesch and Talmud, 2006a,

2006b). More to the point, adolescents whose friends were similar in age, ethnic background, and place of residence were more likely to report forming friendships online (Mesch and Talmud, 2006a, 2006b).

Another component of the shared opportunity for mutual exposure is residential proximity. Proximity facilitates the likelihood of friendship formation and communication by increasing the probability that individuals will meet and interact. Proximity is of particular importance for adolescents limited in their geographic mobility as they must rely on public transport, which is not always reliable. For adolescents who are restricted in their physical mobility, and for whom the main arenas of social interaction are the school, the neighborhood, and extracurricular activities, the Internet represents a new focus of common activities. Adolescents connect to the Internet, chat, and exchange emails with friends, with friends of friends, and with unknown individuals. In these activities they encounter a new space that facilitates joint activities and social interaction. For adults, as well as for a large majority of adolescents, the Internet is an innovative place for social interaction, different from the phone and television.

Quality of offline and online ties

One of the key features of friendships is their quality. The quality of friendships refers to the experienced closeness, trust, and understanding between friends. Several studies have investigated and compared the quality of online versus offline friendships (Mesch and Talmud, 2006a, 2006b). These studies have consistently demonstrated that online friendships are perceived to be lower in quality than offline friendships (Mesch and Talmud, 2006a). Furthermore, although the quality of both online and offline friendships increased over time, the quality of online friendships improved significantly more than offline relationships. Specifically, they discovered when online friendships lasted for more than a year, their quality became comparable to offline friendships.

The association between online communication and relational closeness is particularly interesting. Using a large sample of Dutch youth aged 12–17 years, Valkenburg and Peter (2007a) investigated whether online communication stimulated or reduced closeness to friends, and whether intimate disclosure of personal information online affected their closeness to online ties. These authors found that only 30 percent of the adolescents perceived online communication as effective in disclosing personal information. Furthermore, online communication with others whom they met online proved to have a negative effect on the perceived closeness to friends (Valkenburg and Peter, 2007a). A possible explanation for the perception of relational closeness of online ties is provided by an Israeli study with a large representative sample of adolescents, in which this perception was found to result from the length of communication. In fact, online ties are acquainted for less time than face-to-face ties, so they are still at the phase of relationship development and are therefore perceived to be of lesser depth and breadth (Mesch and Talmud, 2006b). Yet as time goes by, and as the topics of conversation expand from a small number of shared interests to a wider range, the perceived distance to online contacts is assumed to decrease.

Recent research

In the early days of ICT, the main distinction made was between online and offline ties. The definition of these ties was based on the origin of the relationship that often shaped the communication channels and the communication content. With the increase in Internet access, the proliferation of online platforms of communication (including social network sites, Instant Messaging, WhatsApp), the distinction became more difficult and today it is more reasonable to capture the social world of young and adults as being composed of online, offline, and mixed mode friendships. By mixed mode friendships, we mean the integration of online and offline ties and their interaction in our lives. Thus mixed mode friendships are the ones that originate online and extend to offline settings.

The notion of online relationship formation requires conceptual clarification. Most research has not clearly defined what is meant by online ties. It was largely conducted to elucidate the effects of channel characteristics on interpersonal communication, emphasizing the lack of social presence, lack of richness, and lack of clues in Internet communication and it sought the conditions under which this communication is non-personal or becomes hyper-personal (Walther, 1996). By contrast, in our view, the definition of online and face-to-face ties has to do more with the origin of the relationship and not with the mode of communication. This is a more pertinent perspective as social media has undergone significant convergence and has changed the domestication of ICT and youth sociability via digital social media (see Chapter 3). Youth communicate with close school friends using Instant Messaging, email, social networks sites, and school forums. In this case, someone can have friends whom one meets every day at school, yet conducts most of their communication online. Our interest lies mainly in the differences between online and face-to-face ties origination, so that our definition is that online ties refer to individuals who were first met online by means of applications, such as email, Instant Messaging, SNSs, chat rooms, or online game groups. According to our definition, then, a face-to-face friend is someone whom one met in person, in a setting such as school, the neighborhood, or other extracurricular activity (Mesch and Talmud, 2010).

How do online, offline, and mixed-mode friendships differ? Antheunis, Valkenburg and Peter (2012) conducted a study in which they compared the quality of online, offline, and mixed-mode friendships and the relative contribution of proximity, perceived similarity to the quality of friendship. The study was based on data gathered from a large sample of members of a Dutch social networking site (n = 2,188). An important finding is that differences in quality between online and offline friendships were found and remained significant over time, but those between mixed-mode and offline friendships disappeared. As already mentioned in the literature, the migration of a connection from being a person met online to one met face-to-face and voice-phone is an important step that increases the closeness between them. For that reason, mixed mode relationships tend to be more similar over time than solely face-to-face and only online ties.

The first question is the extent to which proximity and perceived similarity differ among online, mixed-mode, and offline friendships. The study found significant differences in the level of proximity between the types of friendship, the actual distance between offline friends is the lowest, followed by mixed-mode and online friends. As to perceived similarity between online, mixed-mode, and offline friendships. there is a significant difference in perceived similarity between the online and mixed-mode friendships, and between online and offline friendships. Perceived similarity was the highest in mixed-mode friendships and offline friendships, and lowest in online friendships (Antheunis et al., 2012).

In accordance with earlier studies, they found that respondents perceived offline friendships to be of higher quality than online friendships. However, the study also found that mixed-mode friendships, which are also formed online but then also migrate to offline communication modalities (i.e., telephone, face-to-face communication), were rated similar in quality as offline friendships. Thus, it is not important whether a friendship is formed online or offline, but rather, it is more important that newly formed friendships also migrate to cue-richer communication modalities, such as telephone and face-to-face contact friendships (Antheunis et al., 2012).

The study found that the quality of all three types of friendship improved as the friendship developed over time. The quality of online friendships remained significantly lower than that of offline friendships, even after two years. According to those authors:

- *Proximity*. They in fact found that offline friends lived closer to each other than mixed-mode and online friends. This suggests that in online and mixed-mode friendships, actual geographic proximity is less important to becoming friends.
- *Similarity*. they found that the level of perceived similarity was lower in online friendships compared to mixed-mode and offline friendships. They did find, however, that the effect of similarity on the quality of friendship was higher for online friendships than for mixed-mode and offline friendships. These results indicate that though the level of similarity is low in online friendships, similarity is a more important determinant of friendship quality in online friendships than in the other two categories of friendships (Antheunis et al., 2012).

Virtual interactions and online spaces are, in fact, additional sites of interaction in which youth can explore their identities, belonging, and sense of themselves (Stern, 2004). As they get older, their Internet literacy as well as their tendency to share personal information seem to grow, though with limited understanding of the risks involved (Livingstone, 2008). Still, perceptions regarding the risk involved in online relations have been modified: while in 2003 distrust in online ties was associated with geographical proximity between persons, the link between mistrust of the Internet to geographical proximity had disappeared between 2003 to 2006 (Dutton and Shepherd, 2003; Helsper, 2008b). Additionally, young people report a growing dependency on the Internet for activities ranging from managing their daily lives to building and maintaining online social interaction. The embeddedness of ICT in social structure creates a dual nature of communicative space, where both adolescents' offline and online domains serve as facilitators of communicative action in key life experiences (McMillan and Morrison, 2006). Over time, enthusiasm for meeting strangers on the Internet wanes, and reports of boredom surface, even among children (Livingstone and Bober, 2004).

In the context of the "fear of strangers," it is important to note the process of movement from online to face-to-face relationships. After the young people became acquainted online, and discovered common interests and topics of discussion, sometimes they would exchange emails, often using IM, then they communicate by phone, and finally in few cases they arranged to meet face-to-face in a public place. This is cautious progress, moving from online meeting as strangers, followed by a rise in the frequency of communication and in the number of its channels. The goal of these successive moves is the establishment of trust, resulting from progressive disclosure of personal information (Mesch and Talmud, 2007a).

Furthermore, the concept of the stranger is not always adequate to describe relationship formation online. Frequently, online communication and mobile communication are a way to introduce mutual friends to each other (Wolack et al., 2003). This happens when a new friend is introduced to an existing group or when an adolescent suggests to another friend that he or she meet a new person who has the same interests or the same personal problems.

Interpersonal lives and the computer and mobile activities of early adolescents reflexively amplify each other. Contemporary moral development is less about mastering distinctly right and wrong answers, and more about negotiating different social contexts. Additionally, even in a CMC environment, interpersonal and even intimate clues can be possible (Walther, 1996). There is evidence that the number of personal relationships occurring via the Internet is increasing as more people gain access to it (Underwood and Findlay, 2004; Lawson and Leck, 2006). What adolescents do after school hours, through the windows of their computer screens, has become an integral and important part of their individual and social identity formation and of their moral development (Bradley, 2005).

Valentine and Holloway (2002) found a rich variety of adolescents' strategies to reconfigure their personal activities between offline and online spaces. The study found four ways in which adolescents, aged 11–16, incorporated their offline worlds and their online spaces: (1) by direct (re)presentations of their offline identities and activities; (2) by the production of alternative identities also contingent on their offline identities; (3) by the reproduction online of offline class and gender divides; and (4) by reducing the ways in which everyday material realities limit the scope of their online activities. These authors also identified three different processes whereby adolescents incorporate online space into their offline worlds: (1) online activities maintain and develop both distant and local offline relationships; (2) information gathered online is incorporated into offline activities; and (3) online friendships are incorporated into or reconfigure offline social networks and position within networks (Valentine and Holloway, 2002).[1]

Notwithstanding important, adolescents' conduct offline seems similar to their conduct online. Their ways of social coping online and offline are markedly associated. Seepersad (2004) found a strong relationship between avoidant coping strategies offline and Internet use for entertainment. Moreover, adolescents who considered communication the most important use of the Internet also contended with loneliness through expression of emotion and social coping. Results suggest that online and offline coping behaviors are strongly related, especially if they are avoidant

(Seepersad, 2004). Many positive and negative developmental behaviors, such as dating, smoking, formation of musical tastes and frictional violence, are transferred via adolescents' peer social networks (Neal, 2007).

Adolescent friendships, networked individuals, and the information society

For some young users, the Internet is becoming another location to meet and socialize, and relations created there tend to migrate to other settings too (Wolak et al., 2003; Mesch and Levanon, 2003). As young people become less controlled by traditional social authorities, they can overstep their geographical limits and their local groups' boundaries, using electronic communication technologies (Wellman, 2001).

The Internet is typically used by adolescents as an additional space of activity and social interaction, which often complements rather than replaces offline spaces of social communication, activity, and gathering. Networked publics provide an additional virtual context for youth to develop social norms in negotiation with their peers, forming social ties, maintaining friendship networks, and accruing information and entertainment items and devices from remote environments. The adolescent is a sophisticated "networked individual," who negotiates a wider range of messages and identities using multiple means of computer-mediated, mobile, and face-to-face channels of communication.

Adolescents' online activity and subculture are unique. This distinctiveness stems from both an age effect and a generational effect. The age effect refers to the influence of life-stage characteristics on adolescents' social conduct and network structure. The generational (or cohort) effect refers to the cultural change adolescents are exposed to in their formative years. Nowadays computer and Internet literacy, online communication, smartphone and hyper-textual literacy are skillfully mastered. Social networks sites are unique artefacts that allow early adolescents to share and discuss ideas and feelings, ask and answer each other's questions, or showcase projects, all of which promote a pro-social attitude. If in the past the formation of the youth culture was limited to neighborhood hangouts, now spaces and channels of interaction are expanded, allowing individuals to find peers to share interests, hobbies, and feelings conditional upon having access and skills.

Expansion of weak ties via online social networks compensates, in particular, youth with deprived life outcomes. A study of social networks sites has suggested a close association between the use of Facebook and social capital, the firmest relationship being with "bridging" social capital. In addition, Facebook usage was found to interact with measures of psychological well-being, suggesting that it might provide greater benefits for users experiencing low self-esteem and low life satisfaction (Ellison, Steinfield, and Lampe, 2007).

Typically, adolescents' offline networks are denser and much more age- and sex-homogeneous than those of adults. Typically, adults also have more options to form new social ties, drawn from more diversified social foci of activity, than adolescents. Peer-group pressure on adolescents is more likely to encourage dense social ties, comprising of closely knit, transitive relations (in which a person's friends know his or her third parties as well), which tend to be geographically proximate as well.

In our view, the digital communication space reflects the social structure, its access and use are dependent on the social stratification process. Individuals bring to their online participation the diverse social status that they occupy and their social norms of behavior. Yet, at the same time online communication exerts some transformative effects on adolescents' behavior and friendship formation. Conceptualizing the Internet as foci of activity, we argue that technology is embedded in social structure. Digital platforms are another sphere of social interaction and action, where social agents play digital games, and exchange information, give and gain social support, and other instrumental and expressive resources. Thus, digital platforms are conceived as a social arena of shared and integrated activities. Hence, the social context molds relationship formation, not merely individual motivations and preferences. Technological features impact the use of digital platforms as well, by reducing costs, proximity considerations, and scope of choice among various channels of synchronous and asynchronous communication devices. Digital social interaction embeds certain properties from adolescents' offline social networks as well as from the digital environment; these act as social contextual facilitators, relevant to online sociability. These properties are in fact social affordance devices, bringing individuals together for purposes that create opportunities for social interaction, and introducing individuals to one another.

A comprehensive survey of 1,303 adolescents in Seoul, Singapore, and Taipei found that the Internet users among them differed in their Internet connectedness patterns in the nature of their social environments, in their family social status, and in other environmental factors (Jung, Lin, and Cheong, 2005). Most notably, the rate of Internet adoption by peers was an important factor explaining social media use. As the proportion of friends using the Internet increased, the more likely was the user to find technical support and to broaden and intensify online communication, thus increasing the likelihood of connecting through digital spaces. Considering that online activities are more likely to be shared among peers, the high rate of participation in these activities suggests a strong effect of peer groups in the likelihood of conducting communication is digital spaces (Jung, Lin and Cheong, 2005).

Effects of online relationship formation on social networks

The last part of this chapter is dedicated to understanding some of the potential effects of online relationship formation on young people's social circle. Table 4.1 presents the different perspectives on online relationship formation.

An important dimension of social networks, and one at the center of many studies, is the extent that its use reduces, enlarges, or does not change the number of friends. Studies have warned that excessive use of digital spaces may isolate adolescents from their friends. As we saw in Chapter 3, the available data indicate that the size of a social network is not negatively affected by online relationship formation. A temporary decrease may be expected as more energy and time are invested in

Table 4.1 Perspectives on online relationship formation

Disciplinary origin	*Perspective*	*Implications*
Psychology	Motivation theory	Correlation between personality traits and communication needs and gratification
	Social needs	Either the expansion of social ties, or the compensation for face-to-face relationship scarcity
	Sensation seeking Intimacy theory	Compensation for anxiety, isolation, or stimuli
Social structural	Dual embeddedness	Reconfiguration of communication strategies; coping in virtual space is similar to offline life
	Social affordance	Information spreads rapidly in CMC, but neither universally nor homogeneously
	Social network analysis	Homophily and transitivity drive relationship formation, but online relations are larger in size, weaker, and more sparse

the creation of online ties; but over time, as online associations become integrated, the size of the network even slightly increases as new associations are added and old ones kept (Mesch and Talmud, 2006a; Valkenburg and Peter, 2007b). In that sense, the effect of online relationship formation seems not to differ from the effect of cell phones. Igarashi, Takai, and Yoshida (2005), analyzing text messages over cellular phones in Japan, found general support for the claim that mobile phones can change social networks among young people by increasing the number of possible contacts and promoting selective relationship formation. Mobile phones increase the frequency of communication, and allow opportunities for expanding interpersonal relationships.

The effect of expansion of social networks seem more pronounced on extroverts than on introverts, and varies according to attachment style, but, overall, online relationship formation enlarges the social network for the majority of adolescents who choose to become involved in this activity (Buote et al., 2009; Hamburger and Ben-Artzi, 2000).

Associating with similar people is another social network dimension influenced by online relationship formation. One of the most significant and consistent findings reported in the literature is that social relationships are characterized by social similarity, or homophily. Studies on the formation of close social relationships have emphasized the importance of social similarity in friendship and attraction in intimate social relationships. Similarity molds network ties and results in homogeneous social networks in terms of socio-demographic, behavioral, and interpersonal characteristics. This tendency of individuals to associate with others who are similar to them has important social consequences. For example, similar individuals exchange information that suits their personal characteristics and social style. By mutual influence or by association, they reject social links and information coming from others who differ from them in social attributes, attitudes, or values. Contact with similar individuals limits one's personal social horizons, restricting exposure to different others, thereby reproducing social stereotypes.

Perceiving oneself as being less close to online friends seems to depend on the developmental stage of the relationship. Online ties are relatively newer than face-to-face ties, and are based on narrow shared interests. Relationships take time to develop and the process of moving from being perceived as less close requires more investigation. Regarding their effect on existing ties, there is no evidence that youth are exchanging close friendships for distant and narrow ones. Online ties, then, seem not to replace but to supplement face-to-face connections.

A highly consistent finding in the literature is that school years are characterized by gender-based segregation. There is evidence that the extent of segregation decreases over the years, in particular from middle school to high school, but it remains relatively high even at the end of high school (Shrum, Cheek, and Hunter, 1988). Studies have shown that in adolescence there is a "sex cleavage" in friendship relations (Cotterell, 1996). In our study, we compared the percentage of friends of the opposite sex as reported by youth with and without online friends. We found less sex segregation for the former than for the latter (Mesch and Talmud, 2006a). Adolescents whose friends were similar in age, ethnic background, and place of residence were more likely to report forming friendships online (Mesch and Talmud, 2006a).

Summary

In this chapter we have discussed how online spaces are used in the context of relationship formation and the creation of friendship ties by means of ICT. We have emphasized the role of online communication as providing an alternative and also a complementary space for relationship formation, given the specific restrictions that youth face. These constraints are mainly geographic, constituting a contextual barrier that motivates some adolescents to turn to the Internet in seeking others who share their specific interests or differ in their racial/ethnic background and social characteristics. Heterogeneity in adolescents' social networks, occurring more often when the origin of the friendship is online, has developmental implications that require further investigation. For example, Stanton-Salazar and Spina (2005) found that non-romantic, cross-gender online relationships between adolescents proved an important source of social support. They afforded emotional support, particularly for the males. If the Internet reduces friendship gender segregation for young adolescents, this in the future may have an impact on the process of dating and first-time sexual relationships. Another potential effect is in the early exposure to individuals of diverse ethnic and racial groups and of varying political views. If this is confirmed in future research, digital spaces are very likely to become a central agent of socialization, which has to be integrated into our understanding of youth socialization.

The existing division in research between the "virtual" and the "real" does not of course accurately capture the lived social experiences and identity negotiations of adolescents in their socialization process, nor their belonging to peer groups, nor does it encompass the complexity in which offline and online spaces are mutually embedded.

The emergence of ICT into adolescents' identity management, personal communities, and friendship formation seems to have changed the character of "private" and "public" spaces, constituted by adolescents' activities on and around the screen. In Chapter 5, we connect elements of offline and online interactions regarding the maintenance and expansion of social ties, and the diversification of social networks through ICT.

Note

1 For a general theory considering the reconfiguration of ICT communication, see Walther (1996).

Bibliography

Antheunis, M.L., Valkenburg, P.M., and Peter, J. (2012) The quality of online, offline, and mixed-mode friendships among users of a social networking site, *Cyberpsychology: Journal of Psychosocial Research on Cyberspace*, 6(3), Article 6. https://doi.org/10.5817/CP2012-3-6.

Boase, J. and Wellman, B. (2006) Personal relationships: on and off the internet, in D. Perlman and A.L. Vangelistihe (Eds.), *Handbook of Personal Relations*, Cambridge: Cambridge University Press.

Bradley, K. (2005) Internet lives: social context and moral domain in adolescent development, *New Directions for Youth Development*, 108, 57–76.

Buote, V.M., Wood, E. and Pratt, M. (2009) Exploring similarities and differences between online and offline friendships: the role of attachment style, *Computers in Human Behavior*, 25, 560–567.

Chen, W., Boase, J., and Wellman, B. (2002) The global villagers, in B. Wellman and C. Haythornthwaite (Eds.), *The Internet in Everyday Life*, Oxford: Blackwell, pp. 74–113.

Cohen, A.A., Lamish, D., and Schejter, A.M. (2008) The wonder phone in the land of miracles: mobile telephony in Israel, *New Media: Policy and Social Research Issues*, Cresskill, NJ: Hampton Press.

Correa, T. and Jeong, S.H. (2011) Race and online content creation: why minorities are actively participating in the Web, *Information, Communication and Society*, *14*(5), 638–659.

Cotterell, J. (1996) *Social Networks and Social Influences in Adolescence*, London: Routledge.

Dutton, W.H. and Shepherd, A. (2003) Trust in the Internet: the social dynamics of an experience technology. Research Report No. 3, Oxford: Oxford Internet Institute.

Ellison, N.B., Steinfeld, C., and Lampe, C. (2007) The benefits of Facebook "friends:" social capital and college students' use of online social network sites, *Journal of Computer Mediated Communication*, 12, 1143–1168.

Gonzales, A., McCrory Calarco, J., and Lynch, T. (2018) Technology problems and student achievement gaps: a validation and extension of the technology maintenance construct, *Communication Research*. https://doi.org/10.1177/0093650218796366.

Hamburger, Y.A. and Ben-Artzi, E. (2000) The relationship between extraversion and neuroticism and the different uses of the Internet, *Computers in Human Behavior*, 16, 441–449.

Hampton, K.N., Sessions, L.F., Her, E.J., and Rainie, L. 2009. *Social Isolation and New Technology*, Washington, DC: Pew Internet and American Life Project.

Hampton, K.N. and Wellman, B. (2002) The not so global village of Netville, in B. Wellman and C. Haythornthwaite (Eds.), *The Internet in Everyday Life*, Oxford: Blackwell, pp. 345–372.

Helsper, E.J. (2008a) Gendered internet use across generations and life stages in the UK. Paper presented at AOIR Conference, Copenhagen, October.

Helsper, E.J. (2008b) Perceptions of security and risks on the internet: experience and learned levels of trust. Presentation slides from IT Security in Practice Conference, Aarhus University, January 24.

Igarashi, T., Takai, J., and Yoshida, T. (2005) Gender differences in social network development via mobile phone text messages: a longitudinal study, *Journal of Social and Personal Relationships*, 22(5), 691–713.

Jung, J.Y., Kim, Y.C., Lin, W.Y., and Cheong, P.H. (2005) The influence of social environment on internet, connectedness of adolescents in Seoul, Singapore and Taipei, *New Media and Society*, 7(1), 64–88.

Kadushin, C. (2004) *Understanding Social Networks: Theories, Concepts, and Findings*. Oxford: Oxford University Press.

Khan, S., Gagné, M., Yang, L., and Shapka, J. (2016) Exploring the relationship between adolescents' self-concept and their offline and online social worlds, *Computers in Human Behavior*, 55, 940–945.

Kraut, R., Kiesler, S., Boneva, B., Cummings, J., Helgeson, V., and Crawford, A. (2002) Internet paradox revisited, *Journal of Social Issues*, 58, 49–74. https://doi.org/10.1111/1540-4560.00248.

Kraut, R., Patterson, M., Lundmark, V., Kiesler, S., Mukopadhyay, T., and Scherlis, W. (1998) Internet paradox: a social technology that reduces social involvement and psychological well-being?, *American Psychologist*, 53, 1011–1031.

Lawson, H. and Leck, K. (2006) Dynamics of internet dating, *Social Science Computer Review*, 24(2), 189–208.

Lenhart, A. (2009) It's personal: similarities and differences in online social network use between teens and adults. Available at: www.pewinternet.org/Presentations/2009/19-Similarities-and-Differences-in-Online-Social-Network-Use.aspx.

Lin, S.S.J. and Tsai, C.C. (2002) Sensation seeking and internet dependence of Taiwanese high school adolescents, *Computers in Human Behavior*, 18(4), 411–426.

Livingstone, S. (2008) Taking risky opportunities in youthful content creation: teenagers' use of social networking sites for intimacy, privacy and self expression, *New Media and Society*, 10(3), 393–411.

Livingstone, S. and Bober, M. (2004) *U.K. Children Go Online*, London: London School of Economics.

Mazur, E. and Kozarian, L. (2010) Self-presentation and interaction in blogs of adolescents and young emerging adults, *Journal of Adolescent Research*, 25(1), 124–144. https://doi.org/10.1177/0743558409350498.

McMillan, S.J. and Morrison, M. (2006) Coming of age with the internet: a qualitative exploration of how the internet has become an integral part of young people's lives, *New Media and Society*, 8(1), 73–95.

Mesch G.S. (2018a) Race, ethnicity and the strength of Facebook ties, *Journal of Youth Studies* 21(5), 575–589.

Mesch, G.S. and Levanon, Y. (2003) Community networking and locally based social ties in two suburban localities, *City and Community*, 2, 335–351.

Mesch G.S. and Talmud, I. (2006a) Online friendship formation, communication channels, and social closeness, *International Journal of Internet Sciences*, 1(1), 29–44.

Mesch, G.S. and Talmud, I. (2006b) The quality of online and offline relationships, the role of multiplexity and duration, *The Information Society*, 22(3), 137–148.

Mesch, G.S. and Talmud, I. (2007a) Similarity and the quality of online and offline social relationships among adolescents in Israel, *Journal of Research in Adolescence*, 17(2), 455–465.

Mesch, G.S. and Talmud, I. (2010) Internet connectivity, community participation, and place attachment: a longitudinal study, *American Behavioral Scientist*, 53(8), 1095–1110.

Mesch, G.S. Quase-Han, A., and Talmud, I. (2012) IM social networks: individual, relational and cultural characteristics, *Journal of Personal and Social Relationships*, 29(6), 736–759.

Milioni, D.L., Doudaki, V., and Demertzis, N. (2014) Youth, ethnicity, and a 'reverse digital divide': a study of internet use in a divided country, *Convergence*, 20, 316–336.

Neal, J.W. (2007) Why social networks matter: a structural approach to the study of relational aggression in middle childhood and adolescence, *Child and Youth Care Forum*, 36, 195–211.

Peter, J. and Valkenburg, P.M. (2006) Research note: individual differences in perception of internet communication, *European Journal of Communication*, 21(2), 213–226.

Robinson, L. (2011) Information-channel preferences and information-opportunity structures, *Information, Communication and Society*, 14(4), 472–494.

Shrum, W., Cheek Jr, N.H., and Hunter S. (1988) Friendship in school: gender and racial homophily, *Sociology of Education*, 61, 227–239.

Sproull, L. and Kiesler, S. (1986) Reducing social context cues: electronic email in organizational communications, *Management Science*, 32, 1492–1512.

Stanton-Salazar, R.D. and Spina, S.U. (2005) Adolescent peer networks as a context for social and emotional support, *Youth and Society*, 36(4), 379–417.

Stern, S.R. (2004) Expressions of identity online: prominent features and gender differences in adolescents' world wide web home pages, *Journal of Broadcasting and Electronic Media*, 48(2), 218–243.

Underwood, H. and Findlay, B. (2004) Internet relationships and their impact on primary relationships, *Behaviour Change*, 21(2), 127–140.

Valentine, G. and Holloway, S.L. (2002) Cyberkids? Exploring children's identities and social networks in on-line and off-line worlds, *Annals of the Association of American Geographers*, 92(2), 302–319.

Valkenburg, P.M. and Peter, J. (2007a) Preadolescents' and adolescents' online communication and their closeness to friends, *Developmental Psychology*, 43(2), 267–277.

Valkenburg, P.M. and Peter, J. (2007b) Online communication and adolescent wellbeing: testing the stimulation versus the displacement hypothesis, *Journal of Computer-Mediated Communication*, 12, 1169–1182.

Van Ingen, E., and Wright, K.B. (2016) Predictors of mobilizing online coping versus offline coping resources after negative life events, *Computers in Human Behavior*, 59, 431–439.

Walther, J.B. (1996) Computer-mediated communication: impersonal, interpersonal and hyperpersonal interaction, *Communication Research*, 23(1), 3–43.

Wellman, B. (2001) Computer networks as social networks, *Science*, 293, 2031–2034.

Wolak, J., Mitchell, K.J., and Finkelhor, D. (2003) Escaping or connecting? Characteristics of youth who form close online relationships, *Journal of Adolescence*, 26, 105–119.

Wolfradt, U. and Doll, J. (2001) Motives of adolescents to use the internet as a function of personality traits, personal and social factors, *Educational Computing Research*, 24(1), 13–27.

8

IDENTITY CITIZENSHIP

Authenticity, intersectionality and a new populism

Rob Cover

Introduction: the cultural production of a new taxonomy online

Over the past chapters I have been presenting and analysing the recent emergence of a new taxonomy of gender and sexuality comprised of new identity labels, developments in the range of attraction types (beyond romantic and sexual), and new languages for addressing and representing gender (cisgender, transgender and non-binary gender). These have significant implications for contemporary culture in that they challenge the dominant understandings of identity that have remained relatively stable across the twentieth and early twenty-first centuries. An important point that I have referred to several times is the fact that these new ways of thinking about sexuality, gender and relationships first appear in online settings, principally social networking sites that have become popular places for discussing social justice causes, such as Tumblr, as well as dating sites and in more 'mainstream' online practices such as the use of Facebook. These have been significant in facilitating the kinds of conversations that can bring to light a new discursive arrangement – the networking of the excluded, the disenfranchised and the marginalised can make new identities possible, and these identities can be constituted in a sense of virtual community that sees itself as oppositional to the dominant or empowered.

While digital media has thus afforded the production of a broad new taxonomy of (continuously proliferating) labels, categories and classifications of sexuality and gender, it is likewise not necessarily helpful to understand digital media as the *source* or *cause* of this emergence. Rather, it is important to ask instead what might be the cultural conditions that prompt the contemporary emergence of new sexual subjectivities, since these arise by neither accident nor deliberate design but, as with all cultural shifts, through positionings and tensions between historical continuities and ruptures. In that context, I would like to begin this chapter by giving an overview of the specific role of digital media in affording the emergence of the new taxonomy of gender/sexual subjecthood through its capacity to foster and host interactivity, identity performativity online, and networked facilitation of political engagement. In showing that digital media facilitates the setting for emergence but does not cause it, I would like to use this chapter to discuss five factors which may be considered to be among the cultural structures, norms, disciplinary and biopolitical circumstances that foster the development of the new taxonomy.

These five factors are as follows: (1) the framework of *sexual citizenship* as a way of making sense of sexual and gender identities; (2) what I refer to as the *cult of authenticity* that demands subjects are answerable always 'as subjects', whereby categories – no matter how many or how proliferate – are the most efficient mechanism by which to measure the legitimacy of subjecthood; (3) the *demands of inclusivity* which provide an impetus for ensuring that subjects can find a grounding in a categorised gender and sexuality; (4) the *anti-fluidity backlash* that, in several ways, has sponsored the cultural desire or demand for more discrete, sensible and organised classifications of identity upon which diverse behaviours, desires, attractions and experiences can be mapped; and, finally (5) the role of *populism* as a particular cultural practice of anti-institutionalism and anti-expertise, differing somewhat from earlier decades of avant-garde artistic, political and liberatory practice. Together, these five cultural phenomena are implicated in the conditions that shape the need, desire or demand for an alternative framework of sexuality and gender identity. I will discuss each of these after pointing to some of the ways in which digital media enables them to produce forms of contemporary emergence.

The affordances of digital identity for a new taxonomy

Digital interactivity, and the co-creativity it proscribes, has been one of the most powerful settings making possible emergent re-conceptualisations of language, identity, subjectivity, gender and sexuality. Digital media, as I have previously argued, operate as a most efficient and most effective tool for individual and community identity construction, performance, recognition, reflection and self-articulation (Cover 2016). Helen Kennedy (2006) pointed out more than a decade ago that webpages, which are one among many forms of digital communication, are a media type marked by being never entirely quite finished, just as identity composition itself is a continuous process: both are constantly "under construction" (p. 869). In the same way, more recent, interactive forms of digital community-focused and network-building communication such as social networking pages, YouTube content, commentary and responses across forums and image-hosting databases and so on are the sites at which identity becomes most pointed and notable. This partly results from the debates around identity authenticity operating in those spaces, but also party because the sites themselves are geared to encourage a particular kind of identitarian reflectiveness as a central part of their process (Cover 2014). Unlike both face-to-face communication and early Web 1.0 communication, interactive social networking has encouraged the practice of articulating self-labels for sexual and gender identity in ways which have helped challenge the strictures of more simplistic binary-based hetero/homo-sexualities and masculine/feminine exclusive genders.

To put this another way, contemporary digital media culture enables the *intelligibility* of the cultural practices of gender and sexuality identity formation to be channelled differently via a range of mechanisms that relate to the *relationship between communication, form, engagement and – especially – identity as constituted in discourse.* It is helpful to think through the ways in which new practices emerge as a result of new ways of thinking that are produced through digital, networked engagement, that which Daniel Miller and Jolynna Sinanan (2014) have referred to as 'attainment'. Attainment here accepts and understands digital technologies as aspects of human relationality rather than as objects that detract from or disrupt our humanity. In that context, digital media does not produce a set of sexual and gender identity categories that are 'alien' to extant cultural practices but prompts the production of both continuities and change.

So, what are the digital mechanisms that enable the production of new taxonomies of gender and sexuality? To think about this involves unpacking some of the different aspects and elements of digital media itself, for it is not and never has been just one practice, artefact, or experience. There are four that are important to consider: (1) the fact that digital media is a site for the conveyance of discourse that permits us to encounter new information, resources, categories, labels and ways of thinking that may have previously been unavailable in our lives; (2) the way in which interactivity involves opportunities not just for encountering and reading identity discourses but asks us to participate and engage with them as co-creative participants; (3) the uses of social networking for identity performativity that complexify subjecthood but ask us to think about our selfhood, including gender and sexuality, in ways which replicate 'conversational' and self-reflective engagement; and, lastly (4) the affordances of digital media in bringing together a range of different voices, including the voices of the marginalised and disenfranchised that, together, enable the challenging of norms and the sharing of new, alternative frameworks for discussing gender and sexual subjectivity. Digital media culture and digital technologies operate both as sites for *representing* identity (categories, selves) and sites for *performing* our identity (articulations, play, engagement, images and so on), and it is therefore important to delineate some of these different aspects rather than assume that all online engagement is the same, or that the Internet is a singular concept, activity and formation.

Firstly, we have the fact that digital media is a site for providing vast quantities of information – the discourses which make intelligible the cultural demands of gender and sexuality coherence. It is not simply that they are *there* and that there is a range to choose from, but that there is an interpellative effect in the 'encounter' with those discourses which can inaugurate us to commence a new kind of gender or sexual performativity, including perhaps one which we did not think possible. For example, the information on heteroflexibility as an identity label, or non-binary as a gender label, might be encountered in an online setting – indeed the most likely place to find these terms at present. In encountering, we may find enough of a 'fit' with how we perceive ourselves or might find that our questions about sexual or gender coherence in ourselves are answered by those labels. The outcome is, in the right circumstances and with the right conditions, that we go on to cite the label and the behavioural information that goes along with it, to re-configure or reconstitute our sense of selfhood and to stabilise and sustain such performances over time in both our online and offline engagement.

Key to making sense of this is the figuration of 'encounter'. Neither digital media, nor the technological use of it, nor the information, resources or discourses encountered on it *determine* who and what we are. Important here is that in thinking about the role of digital media we don't think of it in a 'media effects' capacity (McKee 2012, p. 505), which would be to understand the content of what we find online and the interactive activities of engaging with it as determining and causing our gender and sexual identities, and new configurations of it, in the act of reading or seeing it online. Such effects models, including those which, for example, assume gaming will cause violent behaviours, online pornography will cause sexual assault or right-wing propaganda will produce neo-Nazis, underestimate the complex practices of reading, interpreting, critiquing and self-reflecting that are a very significant part of the media audience process. Important, then, is recognising that while we might first *encounter* some of the new discourses, categories and labels in online settings, those same settings are also places and instances of identity *performance*. In her book *Bodies That Matter* (1993), Judith Butler went to considerable lengths to demonstrate that while identity might be a performance, it is never in itself a voluntary, conscious or deliberate individual act. Rather, it is "always a reiteration of a norm or set of norms" (p. 12). That is, a subject does not express or articulate an inner truth, but cites, repeats and mimes the norms, attributes and codes of coherent behaviour that *fabricate* the idea there is an inner essence (Butler 1990, p. 136).

We encounter the 'norms' of gender and sexuality in a range of settings – gender in particular from the very first days of life, with a number of disciplinary practices at play to ensure coherent gender performances as either masculine or feminine and some safeguards to ensure that there is limited confusion, mixing up, play or transition. Sexuality and sexual information has traditionally been made available a little later, typically less available to the very young. This implies that in the case of sexuality, there is always an encounter with the discourses that make the sexual meaningful. Such encounters may be through film and television content (Cover 2000), formal and informal sex education (Rasmussen 2006), news stories and even graffiti (Leap 1996). Today, it is very clear that digital media is providing sexual informational resources and entertainment most actively. The encounter with discourses of sexuality that provide the 'resource' of coherent performances through categories, names, classifications, expected behaviours, intelligibilities and coherences are meaningful and significant for the constitution of sexual subjecthood. It is in the moment of encounter with, say, the dominant discourse of sexuality as a binary-based, fixed and essential division into hetero/homo that a process of recognisable sexual subjectivity is inaugurated and a trajectory for a 'lesbian' or 'gay' or 'straight' subjectivity is initiated.

In digital media terms, then, we see a certain set of differences from the dominant kinds of 'encounter' I am describing here. The practices through which gender and sexual identity are performative involve encountering the discourses and, in so doing, *citing* the name, category or signifier of sexual and gender subjectivity. In performing an identity – which is never a conscious or voluntary act – one thus cites and repeats the category and the information given culturally that makes that category intelligible and recognisable to oneself and to others. Such performances are repetitive and come to stabilise over time, retroactively producing the *illusion* that the performances manifest from a fixed, inner identity core (Butler 1990, p. 143). This continues, no matter how gender and sexuality might be figured. What I am arguing here, however, is that the category, name, norm and signifier are not only without fixity and foundation (Butler 1990, p. 147), but that in the context of digital media environments, they have shifted unexpectedly and substantially. So, for many younger persons and older persons as well, there is a new competing framework or language or taxonomy of gender (beyond masculine/feminine norms) and sexuality (beyond hetero/homo, bisexual and LGBT norms) made available in online settings that might differ from the expectations of gender and sexual identity norms recognisable in everyday dominant liberal–humanist frameworks.

Secondly, we have the *fact* of digital interactivity. In a traditional media and communication setting, the discourses that provide us with the information to make sense of gender categories and sexual identity categories have typically been provided to us through linear pathways of sender–message–receiver. That is, expert senders, and ourselves as involuntary receivers of the information and resources that tell us what a coherent and intelligible and acceptable gender or sexual identity is. These include the resources that also allow us to participate in our own disciplining, normalisation and self-policing of our performances. Interactivity is an everyday part of online engagement, and it very often involves processes of *making identification* or *articulating the self*. Pull-down menus that ask a subject to choose, for example, between two terms in a dichotomy open the possibility of thinking about that which is outside of the list (outside the frame), including what other possible ways there might be for defining ourselves (Griffin 2016, p. 148). So, for example, when a gender choice list only provides 'male' and 'female', we are tacitly invited to consider what kinds of alternatives there might be to those two terms. Of course, that does not mean that we do so in practice; however, the interactive setting of digital media in which some of our time is spent writing and some of our time spent clicking and choosing does open up those sorts of questions in a way the traditional paper form does not. The limitations of a menu and interactive call to utilise that menu when, for example, setting up a social networking profile, are thus put quite literally in front of our faces, hailing us not only to answer according to that dichotomy but also to 'answer back' by considering such lists' limitations.

At the same time, quizzes and online surveys on, for example, sexuality appear regularly online, including those which, as Donna Drucker (2012) has pointed to, utilise the Kinsey 0–6 scale, attempting to peg users' sexual identity according to six categories (numeric) rather than two (hetero/homo) or three (hetero/homo/bi), again requiring click-based responses to narrow available choices to describe sexual experience, desire and self-perception. This is, of course, a bastardised version of Kinsey that oversimplifies the framework (and a long way off from the Kinsey research team in-depth interviews); it relies more on categorisation against one of the six specific positions on the scale than on conceptualising sexuality along Kinsey's continuum. It is a good example of some of the ways in which digital media helps facilitate processes of categorisation and classification, particularly in the context of 'weak' kinds of interactivity (clicking) versus the more engaged, critical and nuanced practices of interactivity (writing, editing, remixing), a difference which is often forgotten in the marketing of the term interactivity (Cover 2006).

When we start thinking, however, about how interactivity occurs as a practice of textual engagement, we have to consider the central factor of *co-creativity* that encourages users to play with, shift and change texts. This is a practice, then, which has disrupted the normative way in which the 'encounter' with discourse has previously operated along linear terms of author–text–readership. Media, expertise, education and other discourses once dominated the provision of information resources which were encountered and served as the discursive source for gender and identity. The discourse, then, has been that which is constitutive, as it has been accessed, encountered, read and interpreted in an unassuming way. Now, in an interactive digital setting, what changes is that the discourse is no longer simply *given* and *encountered* in a linear sender–message–receiver model. Rather, it is open to the long-standing cultural demand that we participate in the stories that make our lives sensible (Cover 2006). That is, the participatory nature of contemporary digital media was not a new 'invention' that drastically changed how we communicate but can be understood as the fruition of some deeply held desires, cultural demands and attachments to participating in and sharing processes of authorship and creativity.

If identity is a citation of the identity that precedes and exceeds our selves in discourse (Butler 1993, pp. 225–226), and if that discourse is made available today primarily through forms of mediation, then in an increasingly online world in which user–participants are also active co-creators, the citation of a category, signifier, name or intelligibility is not only *conditioned* by communication technologies but is one to which we contribute *actively* and *creatively*. So, we now have to account not only for audience interpretation or activation of meanings in reception of discourses of gender and sexuality but also – today – for the interactive environment in which participation in the creation of the text itself becomes normative. Here, identity is produced simultaneously with interactive and co-creative production of the very discourses that are cited. We can see this best perhaps, for example, in the proliferate online practices of remixed texts such as audio-visual fan music videos, slash video, mash-ups and digital stories utilising and combining both existing and new visual and audio material on sites such as YouTube. Remixed texts are a new and transformative form of user engagement with media that makes use of older texts as 'found material' in order to produce an ostensibly intertextual experience (Lessig 2008, pp. 11–12); remix delivers forms of collage, complexity and co-creativity directed towards a broader audience. YouTube, for example, as a digital form encourages remix and consumer co-creation (Burgess and Green 2009, pp. 4–5) in a way which can upset, adjust, co-create or re-create the discourses of sexuality, gender, relationships and normativity.

A user might, say, take a number of scenes from a television series communicating gender and sexual norms in one way, re-sequence them into a new order, juxtaposed and aligned, and place them against an audio track sourced from somewhere completely differently. While independently the two sources might be reiterating and reinforcing dominant gender norms, the new remix content actively and creatively might produce a different kind of resource describing a more complex way of thinking about gender identity. This has been an outcome in much older slash video production, which has been part of audio and video remixing since the use in the 1970s of video recorders among television fans to create new gender and sexual meanings (Penley 1997). This practice adjusts representations of straight television characters by re-sequencing scenes, taking out-of-context clips, adding them to a meaningful song, all in order to 'queer' the characters and make them appear to be in a romantic same-sex relationship (Cover 2010). It might, too, be a product that achieves this unwittingly but allows new meanings to emerge. Within the framework of the new taxonomy of labels, however, we could also interactively 'queer' the discourse by remixing and sharing a series of texts that reproduces such characters as asexual, as non-binary or as any among the dozens and dozens of new identity labels. We could unwittingly complexify a romantic relationship to appear a 'platonic attraction' per the new typology of attractions discussed in Chapter 3. And in the act of doing this, we could find ourselves unwittingly critiquing a set of gender or sexual norms and producing new configurations that do not fit easily within the prevailing logic. In other words, an encounter with the discourse in an interactive, co-creative sense means precisely that we are co-creating the very discourses that give intelligibility to gender and sexuality in ways usually without intent.

This is not, then, simply the *productive activation* of meaning in the act of reading and interpreting a text, but the *active production* of new textualities produced in everyday practices of 'playing' with content that were previously unavailable or difficult to achieve prior to contemporary digital affordances. The extent to which such a new text might come to have new meanings for identity, creating new, unexpected and unanticipated categories, significations and attributes in which the reader recognises (and thereby is actively reconstituted as a new kind of self), will vary. Re-constitutive transformations of identity are theorised within Butler's work on performativity from the perspective of the encounter with new discourses that may have been previously unavailable to the subject (Butler 1991). In the context of digital interactivity as an everyday practice – including, particularly, those practices of digital engagement that are less-ostensibly 'creative' or 'artistic' – new discourses are produced by the subject, allowing wholly new configurations of identity possibilities available for citation and re-configuration of selfhood.

Our third digital mechanism implicated in the affordances of digital media for the revised taxonomy of gender and sexuality involves the very contemporary role of social networking as a central site for the performance of identity. The relationship is a complex one (Cover 2012b), although we can make some sense of it by thinking through the interface between interactivity as a mode of engagement and performativity as that which constitutes our identities, subjectivities and senses of selfhood. Indeed, social networking is a site through which identities are both articulated purposefully and wilfully through our contribution of profile information, self-selected image uploads and participation in conversations. It is, however, also a site by which our identities are put in question, engaged with and tested for their coherence and intelligibility, particularly through persistent conversation, 'likes' (or failures to like) and replies, responses and taggings from friends, family and others. All of these complexify and alter how our identities are represented and articulated.

At the same time, and as with all identity performativity, this also leaves us open to seeing the inherent flaw – that repetition of the signifiers we cite and the extension of our identities over time are doomed to failure, showing up on critical examination precisely how constructed and unstable identity can be. Social networking is a master site for this breakdown of identity coherence over time, because our timelines and feeds not only present a story of ourselves but also present us in all our inconsistencies, demanding an impossible extent of labour to truly and effectively 'shore up' our identities as unified, unchanging, coherent and recognisable. This is one space in which the coherence of heterosexual and homosexual, masculine and feminine identity categories becomes available for critique in a digital media setting. What is fostered in this setting is not only an intensive self-reflective relationship with identity through the demands of both profile development and engagement with those who are engaging with that profile but also an opportunity for the 'flaws' in identity performativity to emerge. So, when a lesbian identity becomes 'broken' in an online setting because the coherence of that identity is not maintained across a Facebook timeline, for example (perhaps by evidence of desiring the 'wrong way', or failing to conform to an expected stereotype), then it is highlighted in a way which is also semi-public. What this has done, then, is draw attention to the public and private *need* for a better way of describing gender and sexual identity to prevent such slippages from emerging in the face of others on our Facebook newsfeeds. And the responsive strategies, of course, have included fostering the search for better categories (for example heteroflexible, demigirl, etc.) that help shore up identity coherence.

Fourthly and finally, the one most significant aspect of digital media that might have actively enabled the challenge to current and received identity norms is the fact that digital media has brought together voices of those who may not necessarily have found an easy 'fit' with dominant gender (masculine/feminine) and sexuality (hetero/homo) normativities. The Internet plays a significant and continuing role in connecting disaffected persons to each other in ways that give access to and produce new experiential knowledges (Byron 2015, p. 324). According to critic Lenore Bell, the fact that these new identity labels emerged first on Tumblr may be due to the fact that its unique format is more removed from the everyday real life social networks than sites such as Facebook. Tumblr's network of friends is typically less likely to be made up of those known in geographic, physical senses, and more through bringing together those who are "connected by interests, and are not bound by personal interactions in real life . . . tailored to the individual reader's interests" (Bell 2013, p. 33). However, I would argue (again) that we need to be very careful not to assume too great a disjuncture between online settings of networked communities and 'real' communities produced through concepts of geographic locality: the distinction is complex and the interconnections between the two are multiple.

Certainly, however, digital media has been responsible for forging communities of disaffected persons in ways which have allowed the production of new knowledges, languages and sensibilities, often thereby empowering those communities in the act of creatively discussing alternatives that make lives more liveable for those who find themselves unrepresented. At the same time, the networked environment also provides those individuals and communities with voices that can actively challenge the dominant, the expert-derived discourses and information that represent monolithic, narrow, binary-based identity regimes that exclude or fail to represent in a meaningful way and have often left possibly quite large numbers of people feeling that the available categories are too narrow, regimentary, constraining and unliveable. By making available spaces for disparate people who feel unrepresented by dominant discourses, digital networks afford the production of new identities and ways of experiencing selfhood and relationality.

A prominent example over the past decade of the role digital networked communities play involves the way in which the 'Furry' community developed. Furries are a subculture within science fiction and fantasy fandom, and practices involve dressing as non-human anime characters. While this is often theatrics and not necessarily about a bodily dysmorphia (Dobre 2012), the identification as a Furry – that is, as a person whose sense of selfhood is defined by the engagement in such play – is deeply felt, an attachment that is subjective and performative. Such play, of course, may involve more serious identification with animals themselves, as some choose to live lives in an everyday sense through the theatrics of being a wolf or a cat (Dobre 2012). The Furry community and the construction of identity did not simply emerge by itself, but came about through the gathering online of very dispersed voices of those interested in this particular activity, forging a language and a shared sense of community.

Bearing in mind that all communities, whether begun online or in geographical or affiliational settings, precede the identities they claim to gather and are thereby 'imagined' into existence (Anderson 1983, pp. 6–7), it is through the development and sharing of symbolic frameworks of identity (Cohen 1985, p. 76) that a shared language is constructed. In so doing, the discourse for a new identity is articulated. The Furry community example is a useful one because it demonstrates how digital networking and the formation of 'virtual' communities play a significant role in the impetus of a new identity label and the codes of practices that make that label intelligible, available for citation, and iterable. The conditions that make a Furry community and label possible are the same conditions that permit the new taxonomy of gender and sexuality terms to be constituted.

Sexual citizenship

While digital media, then, is a site which makes available the space for the critique of gender and sexual identity norms and for both the dissemination and co-creation of alternative discourses, it does not in itself cause these but rather enables a cultural response to existing needs, gaps, exclusions, unliveabilities and other shortcomings in the dominant, liberal frameworks of binary-based gender and sexual identity models. I would therefore like to turn attention across the remainder of this chapter to the five key factors which help us understand those shortcomings and which have sponsored the development of the new taxonomy, beginning with the rise of sexual citizenship as a recent framing for contemporary sexuality. Sexual citizenship is a cultural and discursive re-conceptualisation of sexuality in ways which appear to encourage the agency of self-definition in the terms of personal and collective identities built on individualised perspectives of sexual attributes in order to claim recognition, rights and respect (Weeks 1998, p. 36). Sexual citizenship is a concept usually used to make sense of the intersection between sexuality, gender and sexual experiences and the political, social and cultural milieu in which sexuality is practiced. It permits sexuality and identity to be understood in terms of a struggle for rights and protections (Evans 1993), and for the idea of sexuality therefore to operate at the interface between the private (the domestic setting) and the public (the rights and relationality setting).

By providing a way to perceive the contemporary cultural representations and lived experiences of sexuality (Johnson 2017), a citizenship framework re-figures how sexuality is done, bringing into concepts of sexuality the private aspects of lived experienced as well as simultaneously privatising and domesticating sexual issues and making them in some ways external to the institutional settings of public life. It is thus responsible for the establishment of same-sex marriage rights and the movement seeking marriage equality (Dreher 2017), and for what has sometimes been felt to be a normativisation of non-heterosexualities and non-traditional genders, such that both the exclusions from national, public or institutional life for sexual minorities and, simultaneously, the marginalisation of anti-establishment Gay Liberation and queer politics of the past occurs in favour of the inclusion of sexuality into ordinary, everyday belonging. In this context, then, the sexual minorities defined through the ordinary, dominant terminology of LGBT identities are encouraged "to define themselves both in terms of personal and collective identities by their sexual attributes, and to claim recognition, rights and respect as a consequence" (Weeks 1998, p. 36). This does not mean that sexuality is no longer permitted to transgress but rather that transgression becomes instead a "constant invention and reinvention of new senses of the self" that challenge dominant institutions and traditions but are *only* subversive in the sense that they generate demands for belonging rather than an undoing of norms (Weeks 1998, p. 36). That subversion is, arguably, an output of productive engagement with questions of subjectivity, identity and gender/sexuality within a contemporary neoliberal imperative to produce the self through individualised reflexivity, selectivity and promotion to produce the "best possible" contemporary self – which in social terms is usually a conformative self.

If it has been the case to provide the dominant LGBT regime with a normativity, or what has sometimes been referred to as a homonormativity, producing new exclusions for those who are unable to conform to the contemporary, de-politicised sexuality labels (Duggan 2002), then what relationship does sexual citizenship play in the production of new genders and sexualities? Why is it not enough that a liberal tolerance setting for LGBT sexualities and genders does not provide sufficient belonging for liveable lives? One aspect of this is the fact that sexual citizenship is a neoliberal framing of sexuality and gender, and neoliberalism operates by the subsumption of *everything* into market relationships, while generating a market logic as the way in which to determine and understand *everything*. In other words, sexual citizenship undoes what it achieved for LGBT authenticity because it effectively seeks new opportunities in the gaps and interstices for marketisation.

Consumption and consumerism are increasingly playing a role in the general shift in the construction of identity and the performance of identity categories, in contrast to a more strict, broadly felt perception of "inner authenticity" or belonging centred on kinship ties and geographic community. Consumption is understood as the means by which subjectivity is grounded, felt and articulated in late contemporary capitalist cultures (Jameson 1985). Through surveillance, marketing and representation, contemporary culture plays a central role in processes of normativisation and measurement that differ from the disciplinary function of categorised norms such as those which produce the more simplistic hetero/homo and normal/abnormal binaries. Rather, a neoliberal framing that mutually 'services' both the market and governance technologies of biopolitics (Foucault 2008) calls upon subjects to *plot* their sense of normativity as points on a broader distributional curve, allowing some flexibility to move away from the culturally given norm (Foucault 2007, p. 63). In that sense, subjects are produced in this framework not through normal (heterosexual) and abnormal (homosexual, bisexual) distinctiveness, nor through superior (masculine; public) and inferior (feminine; domestic) dichotomies. As long as subjects do not stray too far from the norm on a measurable distributional curve, the broader range of new taxonomic terms and labels more effectively allows governance to capture the information on which it depends for its own logical existence, and the market to capture, target and produce a broader range of identity positions.

The practices of individual subjective production, circulation and consumption serve to encourage, foster and promote neoliberalism's particular regime of truth such that it subsumes *ways of thinking in all other fields aside from the economic.* This framework includes ways of thinking about the self, subjectivity and identity, which "involves generalising it throughout the social body and including the whole of the social system not usually conducted through or sanctioned by monetary exchanges" (Foucault 2008, p. 243). Every social and identity activity falls under the framework of an economic rationality, including the governance of the self (Foucault 2008, p. 286). Within this framework, the *homo oeconomicus* or "economic man" is produced. This is not, for Foucault, the classical economic man who is understood to be a partner in exchange. Rather, this is a neoliberal re-modelling of the subject as that which manages itself within the bounds of the biopolitical and the economic as an *investment* – one is an entrepreneur of selfhood and invests in one's own production of subjectivity (Foucault 2008, p. 226)

Important here, then, is the fact that for *homo oeconomicus* to produce oneself as not only a subject but also a gendered and sexual subject requires engaging with a *marketplace* of sexual and gender categories. In this context, a broader range of gender and sexuality labels can be said to have become available as a felt response to the contemporary neoliberal call for *choice*: a subject seeks to produce oneself through finding and choosing the most *productive* way of describing/articulating sexual selfhood, where older models based on hetero/homo categorical exclusivity are unproductive in that they require intensive conversational explanatory frameworks. In other words, a logic of consumption operates, not as if choosing an outfit but as choosing how subjectivity will be perceived and articulated, pivoting between self-authenticity as a response to the call for coherence and agency as a response to the call for a deeper level of authenticity. That is, my gender and my sexuality are to be seen to *come from me*, even if the only way in which they can come from me is by giving the impression of participating in choosing. Labels such as 'sapiosexual' or 'agender demisexual' are not only part of the range of choice but are also productive in that they allow a potentially more efficient stereotype of sexual identity to be enunciated in a few words rather than a longer explanation of complex sexual specificity – an *economisation* of sexual "explanatory" discourse. And, importantly, the subject then has consumed those labels in an economic exchange in which the labour of subjectivity is exchanged for the purchase of that which coheres sexual identity (and, of course, leaves the subject free to go on to be an even better consumer).

This is a very pessimistic perspective, of course, on the cultural factors that constitute the new taxonomy. What matters here, however, is that sexual citizenship provides some very powerful and useful ways in which to encourage a more liveable society for those who – for whatever reason – are unable to identify with dominant norms. Yet at the same time, sexual citizenship is both a product of and in service to prevailing biopolitical governance technologies and to neoliberal marketisation. By producing a greater range of labels that helps in identification and liveability, it produces a greater range of *products* to consume in a society in which *homo oeconomicus* is the dominant logic. The older relationships between anti-capitalism and anti-heteronormativity are shattered (Altman 1979, p. 64), and a proliferation of labels, identities and ways of relating mirrors the demands for economic growth. In this context, perhaps the link between labels as identifiers of goods on shelves and our identity labels is an apt one.

Cults of authenticity and personhood

Although some aspects of neoliberal sexual citizenship disrupt or destabilise the older, dominant LGBT norms, they do not quite produce a fluidity – partly for the reasons described above, in that they are not measurable in governance terms and not identifiable within the application of a transactional market logic to sexuality and gender. However, another reason for this is perhaps best talked about as being the appeal of 'authenticity'. What I sometimes refer to as a 'cult of authenticity' continues to govern the contemporary production of the performative self, a self who responds to the cultural demand for coherence, intelligibility and recognisability in order to participate socially and to belong. Authenticity is a very important aspect of this requirement for coherence, for without authenticity, the subject is open to the accusation of incoherence, and therefore of being perceived as schizophrenic, abject, or inhuman. It is, of course, the case that the language that constructs the categories of sex, gender, bodies and sexuality is by no means stable, but changes, reacts to the "making available" of alternative languages – such as emergent sexuality labels – and undergoes sometimes disruptive shifts in the logic on which that discourse is founded. In that context, there is no possible genuine authenticity of identity. Rather, we are all always already from the beginning doomed to perform our identities against the failure of coherence and intelligibility, since no true repetition of ourselves over time is possible.

An important argument here, however, is that the older, dominant labels of sexuality and gender are more likely to produce problems of authenticity and coherence. This is for a few reasons. In the sexual setting of hetero and homo, the identity categories are old enough that there is enough evidence at both personal and social levels for us to know that the connection between the category on the one hand and the expected behaviours, attractions and desires on the other hand is not very secure at all. Indeed, everyday humour, suspicions, experiences and even acceptances of slippage occur. It is in the radical failure of the self-containedness of the two categories of heterosexual and homosexual that the new taxonomy of sexualities emerges, for the rather simple reason that it is very difficult for many people to perform a coherent and unified heterosexuality or homosexuality once the diffuse potentiality of complex sexual desire, erotic attachment, or romantic engagement is taken into account. Indeed, as Butler has noted, repetition is core to the project of articulating a coherent identity (Butler 1990, pp. 31–32); a repetition of stylised acts gives intelligibility over time (pp. 140–141), offering a retroactive sense of an inner identity core (p. 136). Repetition is, in a poststructuralist framework, always marked by its own internal potentiality of failure: an *exact* reiteration is impossible, and this can include the reiteration of a sex act, a desire or, most pertinently here, an identification. While Butler's early work proposed a kind of forgetting or "unthinkability" (Butler 1990, p. 77) of the failure to repeat the performance of subjecthood properly over time, it might be argued that, today, there is a greater awareness of the 'work' of identity as a laborious process (p. 70) in which there is a far greater realisation of being doomed to fail under categories that are too broad, too complex or, as with hetero- and homo-sexualities, in which there are too many known instances of the failure to repeat (a sex act, a desire, an identification) properly.

In this context, then, the imperative for authenticity in light of the failure of the hetero/homo distinction to operate seamlessly for all subjects results in a cultural demand for more complex categories through which subjects can perform an identity that, illusively, appears or feels *more authentic*. New sexualities, then, can be understood as identifications with labels through which one can account for the anomalies of attractions that run counter to the stereotyped logic of the labels heterosexual or homosexual, even though they continue to use the identity language and coming out practices of older sexualities. A wider range of categories answers the call for sexual identity authenticity. It provides a greater range of labels with *nuance*. The term 'greysexual' is an excellent example. It overcomes the possibility of a subject being identified on one side or another of a well-policed border in a new dichotomy of 'sexual' versus 'nonsexual', where a *border crossing* would decimate authenticity. That is, the avowed asexual who has, in the right circumstances, a sexual experience, cannot authentically be asexual. The greysexual person, where the term incorporates the occasional possibility of sexual expression, experience, desire or attraction, can be open to it and experience it without the accusation – that might come equally from oneself as from another – that one was not *truly asexual* to begin with.

Heteroflexible and homoflexible are other such identity terms that provide authenticity to sexual subjectivity. Where a slippage in heterosexuality or homosexuality casts suspicion (again, perhaps just as likely to come for the self as another), the authenticity of one's heterosexual identity has been known to become suspect in the latter half of the twentieth century. Eric Anderson (2008) has referred to the 'one-time rule' in which a single same-sex sexual encounter, or slip-up or articulated albeit unfulfilled desire will charge a heterosexual man, in some circumstances, with having always been gay, or having now changed to become gay. In gay male culture of the late-twentieth century, an avowedly gay man who has a sexual encounter with a woman has been at risk of being referred to as a 'traitor'. In both cases, the inference is that they are not *authentically* straight or gay. The terms heteroflexible and homoflexible, however, allow those who might have an occasional 'dalliance' outside of the strictures of heterosexual or homosexual expectations to be able to use an identity label that represents their experience more authentically rather than being (mis)recognised as a non-authentic heterosexual or homosexual. In other words, the new taxonomy provides opportunities for representing the self as an authentic self.

So, our second 'causal factor' is the fact that there is a deep cultural desire for authenticity and the broad set of micro-minoritised identity labels are more efficient and effective in providing authenticity for the reasons I have just described. Why, however, does authenticity matter? While I would prefer to opt for a sociality in which temporal coherence was not a key requirement for intelligible subjectivity, it remains that there is a deep desire to feel secure in one's subjectivity. Authenticity is central to generating that affect. Butler (1997) pointed to the fact there must at play be a *desire for subjection*, in the sense of the way in which Althusser's interpellation is a giving over to the rule of an ideology or discourse. She asked if it might be the case that there is a simple "love of the shackles" that constrain us into narrow, fixed, essentialist identity categories of gender and sexuality, and determined that the desire for subjection is a matter of the desire for existence (p. 27). That is, the regimes of power actively require subjection *to categories of identity themselves* in order to continue as a recognisably coherent and authentic social being. If we consider authenticity as a form of identity fixity over time, a disavowal of being one's identity's other, and an engagement in the 'hard labour' of policing one's actions, experiences, desires. attractions and wishes in order stay within the bounds of the identity category, then it remains important to recognise that this is done for the very sake of existence. Those who can disavow authenticity, however, need a grounding (as a broad-based critical label like queer), an alternative discourse (such as poststructuralist queer theory) and the skills in articulating that critical perspective in order to maintain, in Butler's term, survival and existence. Our need for existence as a subject is thus central to the need for a broader taxonomic range of identity and gender labels through which subjects can better avoid 'inauthentic' lives.

Labelling the gaps and responding to the abyss

With the above points in mind, it is worth thinking about what kinds of unliveabilities might have been experienced by those who, in the older, dominant discourse of hetero/homo and masculine/feminine categorical authenticity, were unable to present themselves in alignment with the available categories. In *Queer Youth Suicide, Culture and Identity: Unliveable Lives?* (2012a), I wrote about some of the ways in which we might understand queer youth suicide through alternative cultural studies approaches, primarily to respond to the question that if homophobia was a cause of sexuality-related suicide, why does the rate remain relatively the same over time when there has been a substantial implementation of social support and a very significant shift towards a liberal–tolerant society. A few of the other ways of thinking about the causes of suicidality included looking at relative disparities in happiness among those identifying as LGBT, where 'relative misery' among a community is a known suicide cause in some sociological scholarship; the way shame might be understood to persist despite liberal tolerance, where shame is a perceive suicide causal factor in some older scholarship; and the over-regimentation of sexual identities, where regimentation and regulation appear in Emile Durkheim's (1952) account of suicide causes and whereby some people feel like life is unliveable because they fall through the gaps and are unable to present themselves authentically within the given, narrow, regimented categories of heterosexual and homosexual.

The notable matter here is the question of 'gaps' – of what it means not to be represented and what the inability to be recognised as a subject does for liveability. Understanding the debilitating effects of the gaps between how one might 'feel' one's identity to be and the regimentary expectations of what is expected is significant for making sense of why there has been such substantial interest in a new taxonomy of identity labels that better represent those gaps and provide identity intelligibility for those who fall into the gaps. One question that is sometimes raised in relation to this point is this: if identity is performative, and it is given in discourse through a process of subjection, then how is it possible a person can feel that they are outside those discourses unless identity was always from the beginning determined biologically, genetically, at the level of the body? Such an argument would, of course, be to try and find an answer to essentialist/constructionist debates by coming to one side or the other. Although identity is constituted in discourse (in the available languages and cultural norms and practices), a wholly culturally determinist perspective on identity formation was certainly never the intention of Butler (1993), who pointed out that a radical constructionist perspective was just as dangerous as those discourses which argued for a wholesale biological or genetic essentialism to identity, particularly but not exclusively in relation to gender and sexuality. Both miss the point and the value of deconstruction (p. 8). Rather, the alternative is to understand that bodies, desire, genders and *felt* ways of being operate across different languages and registers each for us, even though we are required to disavow that complexity in favour of authenticity. Those who cannot disavow, then, are at risk – not necessarily of being accused of being incoherent or unintelligible, but of perceiving life to be unliveable if the affectively felt sense of self and the regimentary categories one is required to perform are at a mis-match.

For those who, for whatever reason, are unable to forge a deep sense of 'fit' with the available categories of gender and sexuality or are unable to perform coherently within those dominant categories over a protracted period of time, there is a consequential risk that imperils the ability to be recognised by others. As Butler (2005) notes,

> to question the norms of recognition that govern what I might be, to ask what they leave out, what they might be compelled to accommodate, is, in relation to the present regime, to risk unrecognisability as a subject or at least to become an occasion for posing the questions of who one is (or can be) and whether or not one is recognizable.
>
> *(p. 23)*

What this means, and what has concerned me from a health, mental health and wellbeing perspective, is that there is potentially a very significant difference between the one who finds the failure of recognition to be an occasion for questions about identity, and the one who is stranded in unrecognisability and incoherence. It is a matter of the uneven distribution of skills in critique, which is not to say that this uneven distribution aligns with other kinds of inequitable resource distribution, whether education, financial, racial or in terms of geography, mobility or age. Rather, what it means is that while some thrive in the face of a moment in non-recognition that, in interpellative terms, hails or calls upon us to rethink (to recognise) subjecthood by seeking out a new, alternative discourse or framing that provides intelligibility, others are positioned into an unliveability, because contemporary liberal–humanist culture persists in the underlying, base requirement for coherent, intelligible and recognisable identities. In other words, not being in a position to find an alternative grounding in order to perform and perceive oneself as a coherent and recognisable subject by questioning, critiquing or resisting the violence of social regulation or over-regulation is to risk *access to subjectivity*, social participation and belonging, to risk exclusion from intelligibility and selfhood. Naturally, where unintelligibility centres on questions of deeply held norms related to gender identity and the coherence of sexual orientation patterns played out over time, these risks tend to become exacerbated in ways that tend to be less prominent for other coordinates or categories of identity. And where unintelligibility and inability to be recognised *as a subject* (or to recognise oneself as a subject) in whatever terms are available become unliveable, suicide is one of the logics by which many continue to be respond to the unbearable, intolerable affect of unliveability (Shneidman 1985, p. 36; Kral 1994).

So what, then, might make possible a gap between how one 'feels' as a gendered or sexual subject and the available discourses? I would like to say a few words about how this might be understood, since it is not simply a matter of assuming the available discourse (whether the dominant binary discourses or the new taxonomy) will *exhaustively* constitute the subjects it purports to name. Rather, we need to understand the fact that there is a body at play – not a body that is genetically predisposed to desire one way or another or that is determinedly male or female, since such ideas are only legible and readable in *the terms of the available discourse*. Rather, the body of the subject is a body that can have aspects of performance, biology, attachment, parts, desires and ways of being that cannot be translated into the logic of the dominant discourse. For example, the body that feels itself androgynous or intersexed and cannot be shoe-horned into a category of masculinity or femininity. Or the body that affectively feels it desires in a way that does not conform to heterosexual, homosexual or bisexual regimentations.

We can think of this 'feltness' as a kind of bodily 'residue' of all that which is unassimilable to discourse in the process of an embodied subject materialising into a particular gender or sexual subjectivity. Such a concept of residue operates in a conceptually similar way to the Lacanian notion of *jouissance* – what Elizabeth Grosz (1989), following Irigaray, sees as a *remainder* "left unrepresented in a phallic libidinal economy" (p. 115). This is not necessary something we can assimilate to a mind/body dualism in which the mind has one identity and the body the other; rather, this is the unrepresentable in the context of the body that is materialised as a *product of culture* (Grosz 1994, p. 55). In our case, that is a product of gender and sexual discourses and the cultural demands for coherent, intelligible and recognisable genders and sexualities, whether in accord with dominant categories or alternative ones. The body as an animate organisation of flesh, muscle and tissue is, of course, always biologically "incomplete" to begin with (Grosz 1995, p. 104). Within that process of materialisation and subjection to discourse we can find the residue of that which is not made intelligible material. What I am thus arguing here is that there can be bodily aspects that feel like they rub against gender the wrong way or don't seem to work in a discursive gender framework, and there can be libidinal or erotic sensibilities or desires that remain unassimilable by the discourses that demand coherent orientations. In other words, at the site of the materialisation of the body into a coherent, culturally representable gendered and sexualised body, there are non-materialised residues that cannot be reconfigured or reconstituted *in accord* with the discourses of gender and sexuality. Obviously, this may change if different, new, alternative, emergent discourses are made available or, indeed, stumbled on, providing ways of recognising one's gender or sexual subjectivity and assimilating such a residue into a seemingly more coherent, intelligible and socially recognisable self. No subjectivity, of course, is totalised fully – what matters is that a coherent performativity depends upon the illusion of authenticity and totality – being totally masculine or totally feminine, for example, according to the older, dominant discourse in its most demanding and regimentary setting.

So, what use is this bodily 'residue' that upsets the possibility of performing *as if* a totalised subject within the contemporary cultural demands for subjects answerable as subjects? Is it external to language in a way which might provide a radical destabilisation of language itself? Possibly not. Butler is uncertain about the possibility of an exterior to language. She suggests that to "posit by way of language a materiality outside of language is still to posit that materiality, and the materiality so posited will retain that positing as its constitutive condition" (Butler 1993, p. 30). She goes on to point out that language is not opposed to materiality, as if in some dichotomy between the body and culture; at the same time, embodied materiality itself cannot simply be collapsed into languages of identity (p. 68). Nevertheless, for Butler, there is indeed a kind of 'outside' to what is constructed by discourse:

> this is not an absolute 'outside', [but] an ontological there-ness that exceeds or counters the boundaries of discourse; as a constitutive 'outside', it is that which can only be thought – when it can – in relation to that discourse, at and as its most tenuous borders.
>
> *(p. 68)*

Thus, any outside or exterior is always constituted in terms of the interior – it can only ever be known and imagined through the discourses available to us in the interior. This makes it difficult to bear witness to the 'residue' that is unassimilable to discourse and that, for some, may make an authentic performance of gender or sexual subjectivity untenable.

However, there are ways in which we can conceptually frame the idea of a 'space' in which a *particular* language or discourse has no entry, and thereby is unable to assimilate that which does not 'fit' in a cultural regime of gender and sexuality within the old dominant discourse prior to the new taxonomy. Jacques Derrida's theorisation of the *khora* (or 'chora') is helpful in this regard. For Derrida (1989), the chora as a receptacle or container can be thought; it is itself a concept that can be signified in language and discourse, but what it *contains* cannot. The chora signifies a place that "belongs neither to the sensible nor to the intelligible, neither to becoming, nor to non-being (the *khora* is never described as a void)" (p. 36) that can only ever be described a "bastard reasoning" (pp. 34–35). What the chora contains is that which cannot be reasoned or understood in the *available* discourse – it is the unsignifiable and the unknowable, and that can include both *felt* but *unintelligible* to an individual subject on the basis of the discourses available to that subject, implying it may well be intelligible in terms of other discourses that are presently *unavailable* to that particular subject. Thus, the chora is situated beyond the margins of an available discourse. Or, to be more clear, that which at a particular time for a particular person, society, culture or knowledge regime is unrepresentable, or for which identity classifications, names and signifiers do not (yet) exist.

To give an example, we could think about this in the case of, say, a subject whose gender identity might be read through the new taxonomy as 'nobi-sexual' (defined as having fluctuating or fluid gender feelings that are limited to genders either neutral and/or neither masculine or feminine – that is, movement around gender identification that does not at any stage fall into either masculine or feminine). That is fine for those us with access to a discourse that makes such gender complexity, malleability and movement intelligible, and either the new taxonomy or poststructuralist critiques of the power/knowledge framework of gender or discourses of androgyny can provide this stability, coherence, authenticity and grounding. However, what about for the subject who feels their gender is in some way moving about in this particular space, a little fluid, a little changeable but not quite either masculine or feminine? What if that subject has available to them *only* the dominant discourse that articulates gender as compulsorily masculine/feminine? Then that felt experience of being something other than the genders prescribed by the dominant, available discourse is relegated to the chora – felt, but unsayable; there is no language to make this gender understood.

Alternatively, in the context of sexuality and eros, a subject might have a felt experience of polymorphous diffusion of eros across the body that is unrelated to gender, to the genitals and to engaging with other bodies *as gendered bodies*. Indeed, such polymorphous perversity is, in much psychoanalytic discourse, perceived to be the universal human experience albeit repressed (Freud 1979, p. 178) and refocused in adulthood onto the genitals to relegate sexual expression to the domestic sphere and to ensure the body operates most effectively as an instrument of labour (Marcuse 1969). Such polymorphous perversity is very much sexual and erotic and may be felt at a point that denies repression; yet again it may be unassimilable to the dominant discourses of sexuality that prescribe a compulsory identification as coherent heterosexual, homosexual or bisexual and instead relegated to the chora. It is *experienced*, but as with much self-experience it is not accessed in a way that can be adequately described in the available languages (Belsey 1994, p. 10). Rather, it remains inaccessible to ourselves, although it may perhaps be readable and interpretable in some cases by those with access to alternative discourses. Indeed, for Derrida (1989), what occurs in the chora is an 'experience' that is "above all *not* an experience, if one understands by this word a certain presence, whether it is sensible or intelligible or even a relation to the presence of the present in general" (pp. 38–39). Thus, what might be experienced in that space in a particular subject is a particular felt experience of gender or of sexuality that is *beyond* thinkability within certain discourses available, even if this might have intelligibility in discourses not yet available to that subject.

If such experiences are to be located in the chora, which is not in itself a site of repression but a container for that which cannot be articulated in a discourse, then does it actually matter? For the subjects as I am describing them: yes. It matters because the disjuncture between cultural demand for coherent gender and sexuality, and the bodily residue of an alternative but deeply felt sense of gender or sexual selfhood (that may not necessarily yet be quite the same as subjectivity), can establish an inability *to be* in society, to articulate oneself in a recognisable way, even if one does not quite know why.

One way we can think of the problem as that which causes stresses, anxieties, suicidalities, unliveabilities and so on – at least in some subjects who may not have had the benefit of access to a broader range of gender/sexuality discourses – is through the geographic notion of a chasm. The bodily residue of the felt experience and the available or dominant discourses can be thought of as 'located' across a *chasm of non-translatability* between the two: a chasm of the impossibility of assimilation or recognition, preventing the subject from achieving the culturally demanded requirements of coherence, intelligibility and authenticity. The fact that this is located in the chora is what ensures there is no possibility of *translation* between the choral desire and the codes of gender or sexuality as they are known. What is in the chora 'speaks' a language, but one which cannot be understood; it is part of the languages of the "unsayable" (Budick and Iser 1989, p. XI). What it requires, then, is translation. Unfortunately in a poststructuralist perspective, translation itself is fundamentally impossible, as the act of translation demands a substitution or transformation of signifiers that are accessible (Derrida 1978, p. 210). Discourse cannot translate that which is in the chora, as it remains 'untouchable' to the signification in translation (Derrida 1985, p. 114). What we thus have in the chora is a set of felt experiences which are *monolingual*. While dominant discourses, as we know from Butler (1990), attempt to impose their categories and thereby re-configure the subject as a particular type of subject, their attempts to translate and capture these affectively felt bodily residues are simultaneously colonial in style and practice. Colonising the experience of otherness occurs in the act of language to reduce language to a singularity, or towards what Derrida (1996) refers to as the "hegemony of the homogeneous" (pp. 39–40). Since the logic of that which is within the chora is not intelligible to the colonising discourse, the experiences, desires and affects it contains remain unassimilable.

What then for the subject who has no available alternative discourse with which to make intelligible those deeply felt and sensed residues located in the chora into an expressible, speakable, performative subjectivity? The untranslatability of that which is contained in the chora (bodily desire, experience of desire; desires which cannot be understood in dominant terms) is what I refer to as the *chasm*. While it is plausible that a subjectivity can be performed in disavowal of the dominant (binary) codes of gender and sexuality, what is required is an alternative set of discursive codes which might bridge a translation across this chasm between the subject who is subjected to what is in the chora and the contemporary dominant hetero/homo discourse. This is necessary, because without the attempt to fulfil the social injunction *to be*, no subject is socially intelligible and must thereby be relegated to the margins. A discursive platform is necessary: a defence. In the case of a chora-located experience of gender and sexuality, we might find that Freudian polymorphous perversity is one *suitable* code that can bridge the chasm and translate the experience into that which is performable *as subject*, even if in opposition to the fixed, linear and categorical genital-focused sexuality and gender definitions of the dominant. A radical, albeit marginal, queer politics of fluidity might be another that provides a suitable grounding for that felt experience or sense of otherness, allowing a performance that meets the requirements of coherence, intelligibility and recognisability – even if the field of recognition is a marginal one located in alternative cultures. *This is to assume that such discourses can and will be available to a subject.*

Suicide, mental health concerns, breakdown, dislodged social participation and other ways of being positioned as 'unhealthy' are what otherwise occur without a sensible, suitable discourse through which to make these residues of the contained otherness intelligible. I have previously discussed (Cover 2012a) some of the ways in which identity regimentation – and its failure – can be understood to lead to suicidality in certain cases and under certain conditions, including those described above. To exaggerate the chasm metaphor into the trope of the abyss, we can note John Caputo's association of the abyss with suicide and the breakdown of coherent selfhood. For Caputo (1993), suicide occurs because the abyss is both an unknowability and a knowability in which the subject is "cut off from the comforts of a deep and reassuring ground" (p. 329), which in our case means to be cut off from an available discourse that presents an explanatory framework for a nuanced gender or sexuality to the world and, most particularly, to oneself.

With the context of this scenario in mind, I am arguing that the new taxonomy is – in part – an emergent response to the abject failure of the dominant, binary-based discourses of masculinity and femininity, to the heterosexual matrix and to both homophobic and liberal–tolerant discourses to provide a grounding for everyone, building ways to avoid the chasm and to ensure that which is relegated to the chora as the unintelligible sensibility of gender or sexuality is speakable and representable. It is a response that attempts to account for *diversity*, and particularly then for and on behalf of those who fall between the cracks, those whose felt sense of subjectivity leaves them unable to be a subject answerable as a subject, those who see themselves looking into the chasm or into the abyss of suicidality, because the inability to articulate one's gender or one's sexuality with coherence leaves life unliveable. Providing labels that address the possibility of a felt sense that does not conform to or is unassimilable by the dominant, masculine/feminine and hetero/homo frameworks presents the possibility of avoiding the abyss, of allowing that which is contained and untranslatable to speak in a way which has coherence and intelligibility in performativity and thus cross that chasm. And, finally, while other discourses might have done a similar job – including Freudian polymorphous perversity, the androgyny in popular culture of the 1970s, radical discourses of Gay Liberation, avant-garde anti-establishmentarian critiques, poststructuralist queer theory of the 1990s – the new taxonomy does a better and more efficient job, precisely because unlike the others it does not question coherence, intelligibility and identity themselves which risk leaving many feeling groundless. Rather, it, leaves the cultural imperative of authentic subjecthood intact while presenting a greater schema or range of categories, classifications and labels of genders and sexualities through which to be authentic and contained.

Disavowing fluidity: the underlying cultural demand of subjectivity

Our fourth explanatory framework for the emergence of the new taxonomy of classificatory terms relates somewhat more to the politics of some of the older debates in the 1990s between a more conservative, ethnic rights styled approach to LGBT rights that demanded a strategic use of coherent and consistent 'born that way' identities, and a queer politics that advocated an anti-establishment approach and an embrace of 'fluidity'. I described fluidity in Chapter 2 not in the everyday way that sometimes assumes genders and sexualities might be boundless, ever-changing, responsive to circumstance, like fluid moved into different vessels. For example, participants in Lisa Diamond's (2008) study of fluidity among women included participants who adopted the self-descriptor fluid because it was a better term than bisexuality for those who felt their attractions had nothing to do with desiring both genders *as genders* (p. 187). This is valuable; however, as a descriptor it recalls an individualism and an agency that is unhelpful in addressing cultural regimentations of categories.

Rather, fluidity in the poststructuralist sense I am using it in refers to the denaturalisation of the rigid categories as given in discourse, providing gender and sexuality with *contingency* and *historical temporality*. To invoke fluidity means to understand gender and sexuality as given in ways which are regimentary and constraining in discourse, and to acknowledge that the performances of identities may feel essential and natural but are effectively only illusions prescribed upon us so that we can meet the demands of intelligibility, authenticity and coherence in order to be subjects answerable as subjects. Fluidity also means to acknowledge relationality – the construction if identities according to categories and in ways which put subjectivity first are exclusionary. Relational approaches acknowledge that the I/You dichotomy (Game and Metcalfe 2011, p. 353) need not be oppositional, but that every identity forged is done so in the context of recognition and incorporation of the other rather than radically differentiating oneself from the other. A relational approach opens the possibility of a genuine mutuality that is more ethical in terms of engaging in a non-violent sociality. So, while fluidity has a complex set of meanings that take us down to the very kernel of subjectivity as culturally produced and regimented, much of the public assumption and negative critique of gender and sexual fluidity tends to focus on it in the more simplistic as boundless movement and change in an orgiastic frenzy of persistent instability.

The new micro-minority categorisations of gender and sexuality tend, in both their structure and much of their definitional content, not only to actively eschew the extant, older binary definitions but also to *reinforce* the force of categorisation and the public requirement for clear, coherent, intelligible and recognisable gender and sexual identities fixed over time. The demand for a more nuanced framework and taxonomy of labels is, arguably, in order to prevent any slippages that might undo the schemata of sexual labelling. That is, what they speak is that the older categorisations are not only unrepresentative, but precisely *because they are problematic* they are at risk of permitting slippages that do little for the underlying cultural requirements for *coherent* subjectivities – coherent within a category or bound. This reasoning, and the feelings underlying it, can most clearly be understood in thinking about the two identity categories of heteroflexible and homoflexible, which, themselves, have become two significant micro-minorities claiming rights for inclusion, often within an LGBT spectrum of sexual subjectivities. OkCupid describes the identity category homoflexible as "predominantly homosexual but open to an occasional heterosexual encounter". A crowdsourced comment from OkCupid user Katrina from Canada describes it in more personal terms: "Homoflexible means that while I am attracted to women generally, I am entirely capable of having sexy fun time with men" (www.okcupid.com/deep-end/identity/homoflexible). A heteroflexible orientation is unsurprisingly described in similar, but oppositional, terms: "Heteroflexibility is a form of a sexual orientation or situational sexual behaviour characterised by minimal homosexual activity in an otherwise primarily heterosexual sexual orientation that is considered to distinguish it from bisexuality" (www.okcupid.com/identity/heteroflexible). Notable in many such online descriptions, self-articulations and definitions of heteroflexibility and homoflexibility are the multiple affective terms such as *capable* (of experiencing same-sex sexual and erotic pleasure), *fantasies* (that may not necessarily be acted upon) and *infatuation* (that may not necessarily be of a "sexual" but "emotional" character). The terms homo- and heteroflexible distinguish a subject from bisexual, an orientation normatively described by OkCupid as "sexually attracted to both men and women" (www.okcupid.com/identity/homoflexible).

These labels, then, actively incorporate aspects of capability, nonsexual attachment and same gender or opposite gender fantasy *within* a category of sexual orientation, thereby overcoming the kinds of exclusions that have been produced by Anderson's (2008) 'one-time rule' (a cultural perception that a heterosexual man who has a sexual experience or fantasy about another man is thereby gay, even if that fact remained undisclosed to himself) and by same-sex masculine intimacy (in which masculine subjects can engage in same-sex kissing, hugging, or holding on condition these acts are stripped of all sexual connotation in public discourse). Heteroflexible and homoflexible sexual identity classifications address both of these ideas about masculine sexuality: they remove the 'one-time rule' from seeing a sexual encounter with the 'wrong' gender as *proving* a particular orientation or eradicating the previously claimed heterosexual identity on the one hand and, on the other, they restore sexuality and eroticism to same-sex relations.

An argument for the emergence of new practices of categorising sexualities such as the two 'flexible' labels is that they make existing dominant identity labels, such as heterosexual and homosexual, feel more secure. Rather than incorporating slippage or fluidity across categories, these new sexual identity labels actively reduce slippage by *assigning slippage itself* to particular subjects and to particular classifications, thereby reducing the possibility that either a heterosexual person or a homosexual person can 'slip', that is, that anyone is capable of finding themselves performing sexual or gendered selves, acts, attractions and desires different from those they thought they were classified within. In the twentieth-century regime of sexual identity distinctiveness, the hetero/homo binary operates as a "nodal point" which, as with many other binaries, actively prevents the *conceptual slippage* of the signified under the signifier (Mouffe 1995, p. 34), thus excluding alternatives to the hetero/homo regime as impossible articulations in cultural discourses. That is, in prior sexual regimes, homosexuality and heterosexuality were presumed to be mutually exclusive identities that were "totalised" against slippage. While Diana Fuss (1995) suggested that there is much evidence of the queer potential for multiple sexual identifications within the same subject which can compete with each other, "producing further conflicts to be managed" (p. 49), such conflict and nuance is responded to through the pretence that disavows complexity in favour of a sense of fixity, fixed orientation, and the 'totalisation' of that category across the entirety of a subject's being, stabilised across the entirety of that subject's life. As Foucault (1990) put it, there was a perception from the late nineteenth century that the "total composition" of a homosexual subject, for example, was marked by his homosexuality, "consubstantial with him, less as a habitual sin than as a single nature" (p. 43). That is, a subject – who is answerable in contemporary culture *as a subject*, is to be thought of not as a person who repeats, perhaps compulsively or unwittingly, a certain act, desire, attraction or feeling. Rather, he or she is framed as a personage, a full nature that does not permit change or movement, or to be also outside the categorical bound of a singular, unitary label.

The two key points here are that a regime of sexual categorisation has existed throughout the twentieth and twenty-first centuries as a way of managing conflict in subjectivity and regimenting the subject into a category, classification, name or signifier. Subjectivity *must* be performed with coherence, unity, intelligibility and recognisability across time. Multiplicity, confusion, curiosity and other more multifarious disruptions (or *fluidities*) are permissible only if they can be captured and re-subjectified. In that context, the proliferation of gender and sexual labels occurs as a *response* to the failure of the older, more narrow categories of heterosexual, homosexual and bisexual to account for and properly encapsulate sexual behaviour, gendered bodies, felt senses of selfhood and attraction and desire in totality.

Arguably, then, a broader set of categories or a grid of sexual identities operates to ensure that any slippage from heterosexual or homosexual is contained not as a "moment of weakness" or curiosity but as way of disavowing evidence of the unworkability of categories and labels of sexual identity. A more nuanced set of labels that will capture and subsume slippages is proffered, allowing flexibility without working outside the cultural demand for regimented, fixed and intelligible sexual subjectivities itself. The very force of the hetero/homo binary is overthrown as a nodal point in favour of ensuring sexual identity itself can remain essentialised against the "threat" of diversity and fluidity. When Butler (1990) called for a "radical proliferation of gender *to displace* the very gender norms that enable the repetition itself", she made clear that this was not merely a *propagation of categories* of gender that produce new identity norms in greater number, but a framework for moving beyond regimentary gendered ontologies since they "always operate within established political contexts as normative injunctions, determining what qualifies as intelligible sex, invoking and consolidating the reproductive constraints on sexuality" (p. 148). As Butler (1997) has put it, regulation impacts significantly on the liveability of the subject: "subjection is the paradoxical effect of a regime of power in which the very 'conditions of existence', the possibility of continuing as a recognisable social being, requires the formation and maintenance of the subject in subordination" (p. 27). Through processes of subjection and regulation, subjects are produced and required to perform, behave, and desire by maintaining and exploiting the cultural demand for "continuity, visibility, and place" (p. 29). That is, in the process of developing a sexual identity, young sexual subjects are culturally required to respond and "fit" within regulatory norms in order to fulfil the condition of existence through performing as a "recognizable social being" (Butler 1997, p. 27).

It is important not to prescribe these alternatives from within contemporary frameworks of sexuality and gender; in that respect, they may remain at least partly unknowable. As with the older regimentations of identity, the new taxonomy is marked by the fact that the subject answerable as subject remains *definitionally* built into each of the gender or sexual category labels, thereby articulating a classificatory system that is built not on relationality but individualism and exclusion. As Ken Plummer (1995) has remarked, there is a need to look for new stories that "take us beyond the limiting categories of the past" (p. 160). New stories that open the field of possibilities for inclusive sexualities must rely on a post-categorisational framing of sexuality through a concept of "fluidity", which is to hark back to one strand of Gay Liberation's proto-queer imperative for a liberation built on a "new diversity, an acceptance of the vast possibilities of human experience" (Altman 1971, p. 115). In the context of youth sexualities, Ritch Savin-Williams (2001) has produced a call for a framework for overcoming exclusions and producing new normativities by eschewing "sexual labels altogether and rely[ing] on descriptions of behaviours, desires or attractions" (p. 11). These arguments for fluidity are in stark contrast, then, from the activities of the taxonomy which operate to classify, regiment and curtail change, movement, slippage, criticism, anti-foundationalism and the de-subjectification of the subject.

Fluidity is thus problematic for those who do not have the conceptual framework for thinking about the disruption of subjectivity itself. So, we might say that fluidity is actively disavowed because of the unconscious but culturally important need to shore up the subject. This disavowal of fluidity that underpins the new taxonomy is not necessarily expressed in those terms; indeed, as subjectivity is so deeply entrenched and de-naturalised, it is not necessarily evoked in its own defence. Rather, fluidity is sometimes critiqued because it is seen to contradict social and scientific implications built on notions of essentialism and genetics (Diamond 2008, p. 236) and sometimes argued against because it disrupts the ethnic 'civil rights' model that has been responsible for the hard-won gains towards tolerance and legal protections of coherently categorised LGBT subjects (Epstein 1990). Concepts of fluidity – whether those of the more pedestrian free-flowing identity conceptualisation or those of the poststructuralist critique of subjectivity – are also very often related to a concept of instability. Instability, as Mari Ruti (2017) has recently noted, is being increasingly understood by contemporary queer theory as a cause of suffering (p. 41). Ruti relates instability to some broader global conditions such as compulsory mobility, forced migration and other kinds of disruptions that make life unliveable. Indeed, this is poignant in that if a struggle for new gender and sexuality labels is a struggle to provide grounding, letting grounding shake, moving those grounds, is directly contra to the purposes at hand. Or we could think of instability as the spilling over that, in Mary Douglas (1966) terms, is required to remain separated in order to fulfil the affective desire for purity. The upsetting of the strictures of categories that an everyday account of fluidity produces, like the upsetting of subjectivity that a queer theoretical assertion of fluidity generates, is deeply upsetting at a constitutional level to subjects themselves. The taxonomy does an excellent job of re-stabilising and providing a more easily liveable order.

The role of populism and anti-expertise

All of the fluidity-advocating approaches outlined above are, obviously, exceedingly disruptive from the perspective of subjectivity. If the aim of those seeking better, more inclusive and more ethical ways to do gender and sexuality is just that – to find better ways of doing gender and sexuality – that is not the same as calling for new ways to do subjectivity, identity and selfhood *per se*. So while, as with many queer theorists, I might strongly desire that destabilisation and, indeed, argue that the radical critique of subjectivity itself would actually produce *even better* ways of doing gender and sexuality, the fact remains that a poststructuralist, critical and queer theoretical perspective is not necessarily shared by everyone, not necessarily accessible to everyone and not necessarily able to divorce itself from a particular kind of elitism which marks much scholarship and academic theory. In that context, we need to think not so much about there being different, competing ways in which to upset the dominant discourses of gender and sexuality – or, worse, to make value judgements about which one is the 'right' one. Rather, what is needed is understanding some of the reasons why the fluidity-advocating approaches are excluded (or shored-up against) by the new taxonomy.

In addition to the reasons for its cultural development that I have given above, a perspective on this would involve locating the entirety of the taxonomy-generating enterprise within a broad cultural populism that has emerged over the past decade across a range of spheres. Populism, then, is the fifth and last 'cause' that I would like to discuss here. Populism in recent years is very much associated with the rise of Donald Trump in the United States, supported by a vocal minority called the alt-right who have been very much focused on the criticism of 'the establishment' which is – somewhat ironically – seen to be at fault for being too dominated by a liberal elite, that is, upper-middle-class subjects who are in positions comfortable enough to be able to articulate social justice claims. A populist coalition has formed on a global scale which denounces liberal politics of migrant inclusion, LGBT rights, gender equality and anti-racism; this is a coalition built to include those who feel disenfranchised economically, those who see a political divide between urban culture and rural and suburban life and those in power positions who feel that their status is at risk of slipping, such as hegemonic articulations of masculinity. Some of the disenchantment is, of course, well-justified. The new populism is actually not at all new. The current mode seen in many anglophone countries is merely a new generational articulation of the same kinds of populism well-utilised by leaders like Margaret Thatcher and Ronald Reagan, both of whom sustained their populist support in two ways: by creating wedges between different marginalised groups and by articulating right-wing programmes based on a false call for individual freedom and individual pleasure together in a way which figured the left as being simultaneously elite, anti-pleasure, anti-individual and as overly focused on an unappealing social conscience and justice framework (Fiske 1989, pp. 163–165). The kind of populism that leads to right-wing dictatorships has also been common for much longer in other parts of the world, including Africa and South America, albeit in somewhat different political and cultural settings.

Populism that takes the form of anti-expertise expresses itself on behalf of the new taxonomy of regimented categories in three specific ways. Firstly, the taxonomy might be said to be a direct backlash not merely to the dominant discourses of sexuality and gender, but to the ways in which they are presented as 'received wisdom' by the figure of the expert and the culture of the institution. There has been a widespread public realisation of what Foucault was first discussing in the 1970s – that medico-legal opinion fabricating itself as expertise and truth (Foucault 2004, p. 42), correlated with institutional controls, mechanisms of supervision and intervention (Foucault 1994, p. 51), has presented categorisations of gender and sexuality in ways which actively produce the figure of the 'abnormal', and that thereby result in injustice and exclusion. This critique of expertise has operated across the entire field of popular cultural politics, from feminism's disavowal of the early popular psychology view of women as automatically irrational and hysterical to the early lesbian/gay activists who sought to argue against the 'expert' idea of non-heterosexuality as an illness that can be cured. Certainly, this populist social justice perspective sponsors the much-needed reversion against decades of medical expertise which unethically and unjustly attempted to make the child who is intersex or the child with 'ambiguous genitalia' *fit* into one or the other of the masculine/feminine gender categories, having seen that which did not fit as an affront to taxonomic classification itself. Yet, there is a kind of populism at play that extends such arguments to question the expertise given by institutions such as sex education, medical and general practice, sexologists and others who articulate the dominant liberal ideas of gender and sexuality, even if those are comparatively benign in contrast to the late nineteenth- and early twentieth-century abnormalisations in gender and sexuality discourse.

Such a populist perspective – somewhat rightly – questions the wisdom of educators, doctors and LGBT rights politicians from a perspective that attempts to supplant expertise that describes how a contemporary man or woman, queer or straight should be, behave and act. This is not, in itself, surprising when the topics of gender and sexuality have been taken up with what Weeks (2017) identified as a "mass democracy" talking endlessly about gender and sexuality "through the globalized media, on television, in chat shows, confessional programmes, soap operas, reality shows, documentaries and advertisements; in cyberspace via social networks, dating and pickup sites and apps, blogs microblogs and vlogs", resulting in a diffusion of expertise (pp. 1–2). One response to this is that we see not only a diffusion of expertise on sex, sexuality and gender, but also a backlash against those who speak in such a way that appears to be an authoritarian or institutional expert speech. The reality television show or the confessional chat show has regularly looked to anomalies in gender and sexuality that operate as 'staged spectacle' in a way which comes to stand in for older realities and in which "sensations is preferable to truth" (Harper 2011, p. 2). While the older realities and truths of gender and sexuality are just as constructed as any new ones, there is a positioning that actively fragments the appeal of the older prompting a search for that which is more spectacular, albeit in ways which, as I have described above, do not go all the way to undoing the authenticity of subjecthood. It is a cautious fragmentation that an anti-expertise sensibility in a populist culture produces around gender and sexuality, doing both the 'good work' of upsetting the norms but at the same time motivated by something which has fundamentally shifted the rational approach to knowledge formation and critique and disavows the nuance and contingency that is sometimes more 'at home' in the discourses of certain elite and expert scholarly knowledge settings.

Secondly, a populist anti-expertise stance disavows the elitism of queer theory, poststructuralism and the fluidity accounts I have described above. This is at least partly because queer theory, which initially distanced itself from expert knowledge within the academy while locating itself academically in such a way as to produce critique (Tierney 1997), is for a newer generation associated with expertise and the liberal elitism of the humanities and social sciences, themselves under attack in many quarters globally. This is not to suggest that all of those who are in favour of the new taxonomy are familiar with queer theory – nor, of course, is it to suggest that queer theory has remained radically contained in the academy, for that is not the case either. Rather, where this older approach to critiquing the discourses of the dominant clashes in concept, in online discussions and in ways of framing futures, it is argued against to some extent as being that which always spoils, much like the feminism Sara Ahmed (2014) described that results in a populist eye-rolling when it says 'no' to that which others take up as natural (p. 154). Like the feminist, queer theory is the killjoy. Indeed, it can be argued that academic queer theory does itself its own disservice through forms of negativity that are at odds with the contemporary cultural discourse of positivism that marks certain North American expressions of identity and agency. Ruti (2017), for example, associates queer theory with a kind of negativity that, while usefully contrasting with the public valorisation of "success, achievement, performance, and self-actualization that characterises today's neoliberal society" (p. 2), simultaneously misses the point that there is a particular love (what Ruti calls "good feelings") that instantly make its argument less appealing among a broader population. In that sense, the anti-fluidity approach of the new taxonomy is more understandable because it has popular appeal and operates in the context of disavowing the nay-saying liberal elitism of academic discourses which undertake a further critique.

The reason for discussing populism is because of the way in which it produces a rhetoric that articulates an opposition to expertise, to liberalism and to the establishment or those who are perceived to have benefitted from the present cultural regime – particularly if they are liberals and experts and urban at the same time. Populism does not emerge as a result of a hatred towards or disappointment in liberal elites; rather, it has always been the product of crisis. As we know from Antonio Gramsci (1971), socio-political organic crises emerge in ways which demonstrate to the public that "uncurable structural contradictions have revealed themselves" (p. 400). The contradiction in this instance is two-fold. Firstly, as I have been arguing, the older regime of gender and sexuality has shown itself to have deep flaws related to inclusion and justice. At the same time, however, LGBT rights and feminism have been associated with a liberal elitism, making the received wisdom of contemporary dominant regimes of liberal gender and sexuality seem suspect. The suspicion is not from the left or from poststructuralist critique as in Marxist feminism or queer theory, but from a clustering of populist arguments that are, in the first instance, opposed to elitism and then secondarily to that which such elites stand for. As Dennis Altman and Jonathan Symons (2016) have pointed out, the landmark articulation in a 2011 speech by Hillary Clinton of the need to extend American-style LGBT rights to fight oppressive regimes around the world suddenly re-makes LGBT people, previously marginalised as the internal enemy, the liberal elite icons of western progressive modernity (p. 132). Simultaneously, of course, such a feminist argument has also been articulated over the past decade, usually in relation to justifying war in Iraq and Afghanistan, again casting some suspicion on versions of liberal feminism that otherwise seemed relatively secure in the west.

Between the critique of the dominant discourses of gender and sexuality (for failing to be inclusive) and the suspicion of these dominant discourses (for their service to a problematic establishment), they are popularly critiqued in the search for something other, a different taxonomy that comes from below. Stuart Hall argued that organic crises, of which this suspicion and criticism are undoubtedly a part, can be *formative*. He described such productive formation in response to crises this way:

> a new balance of forces, the emergence of new elements, . . . new political configurations and 'philosophies', a profound restructuring of . . . ideological discourses . . . pointing to a new result, a new sort of 'settlement' – 'within certain limits'.
>
> *(p. 15)*

Although intended to describe the operations of populist power blocs, this also quite nicely describes the way in which the new taxonomy of gender and sexuality operates as emergent. It has presented a new philosophy of gender and sexuality that is post-binary; it operates in an ideological fashion but also points to the new taxonomy as the 'real' in opposition to false consciousness of the older gender/sexual dichotomies, thereby presenting the new articulation as if a 'truth' (Foucault 1980, p. 118), and it has done so in a way which 'settles with limitations', which is a way of understanding the expanded representation of gender and sexuality labels without the undoing of underlying regimes that demand coherent subjectivity.

Conclusion: an ethics of groundings and release

Much of what I have been discussing in this chapter focuses on subjectivity rather than representation. The argument here is that the taxonomy is not so radical a change because it has not disrupted the cultural demand for coherent, intelligible and recognisable subjects. Indeed, it works more in favour of that cultural need than alternative and marginal discourses that have embraced fluidity. What the new taxonomy does, then, is actively combat the possibility of fluidity, denaturalisation and any other critique that would take away the grounding of intelligibility, fixity and coherence. This is not to say that such a production is inherently malicious or wrong, although as I have argued in Chapter 2, I tend to feel that it is unfortunate because the benefits of poststructuralist critique in forging everyday lives that are built on relationality and belonging rather than subjectivity, categorisation, normativisation and surveillance are potentially more ethical and open greater possibilities for responding to the vulnerable and precarious. Relational approaches are, by nature, anti-categorical because they acknowledge – in a deconstructionist sense – that oppositional or excluded categories of identity are very much part of the category through which one might make an identification (Game and Metcalfe 2011). That which is outside the frame or the border of an identity category is, by the very nature of framing, included within it – not as that which is different but because anything that is different is also a deferral of its incorporation. In that context, the new taxonomy is built on a framework of classificatory strictures that disavows the fluidity of relational, blurred frames. A relational approach, nevertheless, is more ethical because it demands a genuine mutuality that undoes the oppositional setting of the I/You dichotomy (Game and Metcalfe 2011, p. 353). In that sense, it thereby fosters at least the ethical potential of understanding of the other and understanding of otherness itself.

However, in saying this, if we were to disavow the new taxonomy altogether, we would be equally as unethical in the sense that it would be to fail to respond to the very *immediate* needs of those who benefit from the taxonomy the most, such as those whose lives would be unliveable without micro-minoritised categories that better represent felt experiences of gender and sexuality. Ethical responses can happen in more than one temporal framework, and while there is an immediacy at hand – including (I hope) as a grounding that can help prevent suicidality – there is a longer-term ethical response which is to argue that there is a continuing need to address the resource distribution that prevents many from accessing the more beneficial tools of critical theory, poststructuralism, queer theory and other nuanced theoretical and scholarly approaches to making sense of both the conditions and the future possibilities of gender and sexuality. These theoretical approaches are likely unknown to many who have not experienced the privilege of a university education and made particular subject choices to study in the humanities and social sciences (where they remain available), or the resources to make it possible to embrace a scholarly, nuanced, complex set of discourses that can help produce nuanced, responsive, relational and ethical subjectivities beyond the strictures of the demands for the coherent subject.

The new taxonomy is produced in the context of a generation born into digital media use which includes the widespread availability of information, languages, discourses and alternatives; the communicative form of interactive engagement that actively calls for collaboration in the creation of such approaches; the nuances and reflexivities of identities performed in online spaces; and the role of networking to bring together disparate voices of the marginalised. However, as I have been arguing, like all cultural emergences the new taxonomy does not come from nowhere, appearing online as if some alien language planted and appealing. Rather, it is constituted in its responsiveness to perceived cultural needs, and these include the five I have discussed here: the shift from a homophobic discourse to a sexual citizenship which presented the needs, albeit deeply problematic, of neoliberalism in its accompaniment to a rights-based discourse of tolerance; the needs for authenticity that persist despite the many arguments presented in scholarship against it; the needs of those whose genders and sexualities could not be expressed through the more narrow dominant discourses and thereby let too many 'fall through the cracks'; and the arguably populist needs for disavowing fluidity and anti-foundationalist discourses in order to shore up the needs of coherent subjectivity within the contemporary regime. Without trying to apply too much of a value judgement, this discussion is not intended to foreclose on the possibility that the emergent taxonomy of gender and sexuality labels has other uses, some of which may not yet have emerged as significant.

References

Ahmed, S., 2014. *Willful Subjects*. Durham, NC: Duke University Press.

Altman, D., 1971. *Homosexual Oppression and Liberation*. 2nd ed. New York: New York University Press.

Altman, D., 1979. *Coming out in the Seventies*. Sydney, NSW: Wild and Woolley.

Altman, D., and Symons, J., 2016. *Queer Wars*. Cambridge: Polity.

Anderson, B., 1983. *Imagined Communities: Reflections on the Origins and Spread of Nationalism*. 2nd ed. London: Verso.

Anderson, E., 2008. 'Being masculine is not about who you sleep with . . .': heterosexual athletes contesting masculinity and the one-time rule of homosexuality. *Sex Roles*, 58 (1), 104–115.

Bell, L., 2013. Trigger warnings: sex, lies and social justice utopia on Tumblr. *Networking Knowledge: Journal of the MeCCSA Postgraduate Network*, 6 (1), 31–47. Available from: http://ojs.meccsa.org.uk/index.php/netknow/article/view/296/136 [Accessed 18 January 2016].

Belsey, C., 1994. *Desire: Love Stories in Western Culture*. Oxford: Blackwell.

Budick, S., and Iser, W., eds., 1989. *Languages of the Unsayable: The Play of Negativity in Literature and Literary Theory*. New York: Columbia University Press.

Burgess, J., and Green, J., 2009. *YouTube: Online Video and Participatory Culture*. Cambridge: Polity.

Butler, J., 1990. *Gender Trouble: Feminism and the Subversion of Identity*. London: Routledge.

Butler, J., 1991. Imitation and gender insubordination. *In:* D. Fuss, ed. *Inside/out: Lesbian Theories, Gay Theories*. London: Routledge, 13–31.

Butler, J., 1993. *Bodies That Matter: On the Discursive Limits of 'Sex'*. London: Routledge.

Butler, J., 1997. *The Psychic Life of Power: Theories in Subjection*. Stanford, CA: Stanford University Press.

Butler, J., 2005. *Giving an Account of Oneself*. New York: Fordham University Press.

Byron, P., 2015. Troubling expertise: social media and young people's sexual health. *Communication Research and Practice*, 1 (4), 322–344.

Caputo, J.D., 1993. *Against Ethics: Contributions to a Poetics of Obligation with Constant Reference to Deconstruction*. Bloomington, IN: Indiana University Press.

Cohen, A.P., 1985. *The Symbolic Construction of Community*. London: Ellis Horwood and Tavistock Publications.

Cover, R., 2000. First contact: queer theory, sexual identity, and 'mainstream' film. *International Journal of Gender and Sexuality*, 5 (1), 71–89.

Cover, R., 2006. Audience inter/active: interactive media, narrative control & reconceiving audience history. *New Media & Society*, 8 (1), 213–232.

Cover, R., 2010. More than a watcher: 'Buffy' fans, amateur music videos, romantic slash and intermedia. *In:* P. Attinello, J.K. Halfyard and V. Knights, eds. *Music, Sound and Silence in Buffy the Vampire Slayer*. London: Ashgate, 131–148.

Cover, R., 2012a. *Queer Youth Suicide, Culture and Identity: Unliveable Lives?* London: Routledge.

Cover, R., 2012b. Performing and undoing identity online: social networking, identity theories and the incompatibility of online profiles and friendship regimes. *Convergence*, 18 (2), 177–193.

Cover, R., 2014. Becoming and belonging: performativity, subjectivity and the cultural purposes of social networking. *In:* A. Poletti and J. Rak, eds. *Identity Technologies*. Madison, WI: University of Wisconsin Press, 55–69.

Cover, R., 2016. *Digital Identities: Creating and Communicating the Online Self*. London: Elsevier.

Derrida, J., 1978. *Writing and Difference*, trans. A. Bass. Chicago: University of Chicago Press.

Derrida, J., 1985. *Ear of the Other: Otobiography, Transference, Translation*, trans. P. Kamuf. New York: Schocken Books.

Derrida, J., 1989. How to avoid speaking: denials, trans. K. Frieden. *In:* S. Budick and W. Iser, eds. *Languages of the Unsayable: The Play of Negativity in Literature and Literary Theory*. New York: Columbia University Press, 3–70.

Derrida, J., 1996. *Monolingualism of the Other, or the Prosthesis of Origin*, trans. P. Mensah. Stanford, CA: Stanford University Press.

Diamond, L.M., 2008. *Sexual Fluidity: Understanding Women's Love and Desire*. Cambridge, MA: Harvard University Press.

Dobre, C., 2012. *Furries: Enacting Animal Anthropomorphism*. Plymouth: University of Plymouth Press,

Douglas, M., 1966. *Purity and Danger*. London: Routledge.

Dreher, T., 2017. The 'uncanny doubles' of queer politics: sexual citizenship in the era of same-sex marriage victories. *Sexualities*, 20 (1–2), 176–195.

Drucker, D.J., 2012. Marking sexuality from 0–6: the Kinsey Scale in online culture. *Sexuality & Culture*, 16 (3), 241–262.

Duggan, L., 2002. The new homonormativity: the sexual politics of neoliberalism. *In:* R. Castronovo and D. Nelson, eds. *Materializing Democracy: Toward a Revitalized Cultural Politics*. Durham, NC: Duke University Press, 175–194.

Durkheim, E., 1952. *Suicide: A Study in Sociology*, trans. J.A. Spaulding and G. Simpson. London: Routledge and Kegan Paul.

Epstein, S., 1990. Gay politics, ethnic identity: the limits of social constructionism. *In:* E. Stein, ed. *Forms of Desire: Sexual Orientation and the Social Constructionist Controversy*. New York: Garland, 239–293.

Evans, D.T., 1993. *Sexual Citizenship: The Material Construction of Sexualities*. London: Routledge.

Fiske, J., 1989. *Understanding Popular Culture*. London: Unwin Hyman.

Foucault, M., 1980. *Power/Knowledge: Selected Interviews & Other Writings 1972–1977*, ed. C. Gordon and trans. C. Gordon et al. New York: Pantheon.

Foucault, M., 1990. *The History of Sexuality: An Introduction*, trans. R. Hurley. London: Penguin.

Foucault, M., 1994. *Ethics, Subjectivity and Truth*, ed. P. Rabinow and trans. R. Hurley et al. New York: New York Press.

Foucault, M., 2004. *Abnormal: Lectures at the Collège de France 1974–1975*, eds. V. Marchetti and A. Salmoni and trans. G. Burchell. New York: Picador.

Foucault, M., 2007. *Security, Territory, Population: Lectures at the Collège de France, 1977–78*, ed. M. Senellart and trans. G. Burchell. Hampshire: Palgrave Macmillan.

Foucault, M., 2008. *The Birth of Biopolitics: Lectures at the Collège de France, 1978–79*, ed. M. Senellart and trans. G. Burchell. Hampshire: Palgrave Macmillan.

Freud, S., 1979. A child is being beaten. *In: Penguin Freud Library, vol. 10*. London: Penguin, 161–193.

Fuss, D., 1995. *Identification Papers*. London: Routledge.

Game, A., and Metcalfe, A., 2011. Belonging: from identity logic to relational logic. *Continuum: Journal of Media & Cultural Studies*, 25 (3), 347–357.

Gramsci, A., 1971. *Selections from the Prison Notebooks of Antonio Gramsci*, ed. and trans. Q. Hoare and G.N. Smith. London: Lawrence and Wishart.

Griffin, F.H., 2016. *Feeling Normal: Sexuality and Media Criticism in the Digital Age*. Bloomington, IN: Indiana University Press.

Grosz, E., 1989. *Sexual Subversions: Three French Feminists*. Sydney, NSW: Allen and Unwin.

Grosz, E., 1994. *Volatile Bodies: Toward a Corporeal Feminism*. St. Leonards, NSW: Allen and Unwin.

Grosz, E., 1995. *Space, Time and Perversion: The Politics of Bodies*. London: Routledge.
Harper, T., 2011. *Democracy in the Age of New Media: The Politics of the Spectacle*. New York: Peter Lang.
Jameson, F., 1985. Postmodernism and consumer society. *In:* H. Foster, ed. *Postmodern Culture*. London: Pluto Press, 111–125.
Johnson, C., 2017. Sexual citizenship in a comparative perspective: dilemmas and insights. *Sexualities*, 20 (1–2), 159–175.
Kennedy, H., 2006. Beyond anonymity, or future directions for internet identity research. *New Media & Society*, 8 (6), 859–876.
Kral, M.J., 1994. Suicide as social logic. *Suicide & Life-Threatening Behavior*, 24 (3), 245–259.
Leap, W.L., 1996. *Word's out: Gay Men's English*. Minneapolis, MN: University of Minnesota Press.
Lessig, L., 2008. *Remix: Making Art and Commerce Thrive in the Hybrid Economy*. London: Bloomsbury Academic.
Marcuse, H., 1969. *Eros and Civilization: A Philosophical Inquiry into Freud*. New ed. London: Sphere.
McKee, A., 2012. The importance of entertainment for sexuality education. *Sex Education*, 12 (5), 499–509.
Miller, D., and Sinanan, J., 2014. *Webcam*. London: Polity.
Mouffe, C., 1995. Democratic politics and the question of identity. *In:* J. Rajchman, ed. *The Identity in Question*. London: Routledge, 33–45.
Penley, C., 1997. *Nasa/Trek: Popular Science and Sex in America*. London: Verso.
Plummer, K., 1995. *Telling Sexual Stories: Power, Change and Social Worlds*. London and New York: Routledge.
Rasmussen, M.L., 2006. *Becoming Subjects: Sexualities and Secondary Schooling*. London: Routledge.
Ruti, M., 2017. *The Ethics of Option out: Queer Theory's Defiant Subjects*. New York: Columbia University Press.
Savin-Williams, R.C., 2001. A critique of research on sexual-minority youths. *Journal of Adolescence*, 24 (1), 5–13.
Shneidman, E., 1985. *Definition of Suicide*. New York: John Wiley and Sons.
Tierney, W.G., 1997. *Academic Outlaws: Queer Theory and Cultural Studies in the Academy*. Thousand Oaks, CA: Sage.
Weeks, J., 1998. The sexual citizen. *Theory, Culture & Society*, 15 (3–4), 35–52.
Weeks, J., 2017. *Sexuality*. 4th ed. London: Routledge.

Made in the USA
Monee, IL
12 November 2026

3aa68a01-0045-4c2e-99e0-c13f023d23bcR01